# The Manyfacèd Glass

### Tennyson's Dramatic Monologues

# The
# Manyfacèd Glass

## Tennyson's Dramatic Monologues

by
Linda K. Hughes

Ohio University Press
Athens, Ohio   London

**Library of Congress Cataloging-in-Publication Data**

Hughes, Linda K.
  The manyfaced glass.

  Bibliography: p.
  Includes index.
  1. Tennyson, Alfred Tennyson, Baron, 1809–1892—
Criticism and interpretation.   2. Dramatic monologues—
History and criticism.   3. Monologue.   I. Title.
II.   Title: Manyfaced glass.
PR5592.D68H84      1987          821'.8          86–23599
ISBN 0–8214–0853–4

For
Carroll and Heather

# Contents

# Acknowledgments

The unpublished Tennyson manuscripts cited in this study are quoted by the kind permission of Lord Tennyson on behalf of the Tennyson Trustees, by permission of the Master and Fellows of Trinity College, Cambridge, and by permission of the Houghton Library, Harvard University. I also wish to thank staff members of the Trinity College and Houghton libraries for their courteous and prompt responses to my inquiries and requests.

The research and writing of this work were supported by two grants from the National Endowment for the Humanities. A 1980 Summer Seminar fellowship gave me the time and place to write the first chapter; a 1981 Summer Stipend enabled me to travel to the Houghton and Trinity College, Cambridge, libraries to examine Tennyson manuscripts. A 1982 grant from the University of Missouri Weldon Spring fund provided a leave from teaching duties that allowed me to complete the first draft of this study. A 1986 NEH Travel to Collections grant supported a second trip to the Houghton Library so that I could verify my earlier transcriptions from the manuscripts.

I wish to thank as well editors of the journals noted below for permission to reprint excerpts or principal portions of the following· essays I have published: "Tennyson's 'Columbus': 'Sense at War with Soul' Again," *Victorian Poetry* 15 (1977), 171–76; "Tennyson's Demeter: The Compassionate Poet," *Publications of the Missouri Philological Association* 2 (1977), 33–38; "The Reader as Mariner: Tennyson's 'The Lotos-Eaters,'" *English Language Notes* 16 (1979), 300–308; "From 'Tithon' to 'Tithonus': Tennyson as Mourner and Monologist," *Philological Quarterly* 58 (1979), 82–89; "Dramatis and Private Personae: 'Ulysses' Revisited," *Victorian Poetry* 17 (1979), 192–203; and "Text and Subtext in 'Merlin and the Gleam,'" *Victorian Poetry* 23 (1985), 161–68.

During the stages of writing this book, I derived benefit from several scholars who encouraged me and prodded me onward, questioned and challenged my assumptions or approaches, suggested alternative lines of inquiry or revisions, and performed innumerable acts of friendship and kindness. To thank each of them in the terms they deserve would try the patience of other readers and perhaps of these persons themselves. Let me say simply, to those who read the entire manuscript in draft form— Florence Boos, Carol T. Christ, John R. Reed, Larry Vonalt— and to those who read portions of it—Howard Fulweiler and Mary Lago—I give my warmest and deepest thanks.

Finally, I must thank Carroll and Heather. This thanks takes a different direction from the usual expressions of gratitude that often appear in acknowledgments. Carroll and Heather did not type or proofread a word, nor did they go to the library for or with me. But they always endured my absences with patience and wry humor. Even more, they were always there for me and have given me the kind of life without which scholarship alone would not be enough.

# 1. The Tennysonian Dramatic Monologue

*And all things that she saw, she multiplied,*
*A manyfaced glass;*
*And, being both the sower and the seed,*
*Remaining in herself became*
*All that she saw. . . .*

—*"The Palace of Art," 1832*

In 1892 Arthur Waugh pronounced that Tennyson "is most in-dividual, and—by a strange union of genius with originality—actually most dramatic, in the dramatic utterances which take the form of poems, and are not strictly drama at all. None of his predecessors has used the dramatic monologue with his energy and directness: and it is in this class of poetry that he is su-preme."[1] Waugh is well intentioned, certainly, but has he the right poet? Is not Browning the master of the dramatic mono-logue? And is not Tennyson's essentially a lyric voice? The answer to both questions is mostly yes. If, however, one is to make sense not only of Tennyson's characteristic voice but of his canon as a whole, one must take into account that almost a fifth of his poems, and some of his finest, are written in the dramatic monologue form.

Why did Tennyson write so many dramatic monologues? And if, as all agree, his dramatic monologues are so different from Browning's, how exactly are they different? Was Tennyson writing something other than dramatic monologues? The prob-lem is further complicated by the fact that Tennyson's poems written in (what at least appears to be) the dramatic monologue form are so diverse. It is hard to see what holds together, beyond

1

the use of a first-person speaker, poems as unlike as "Ulysses,"
"Northern Farmer, Old Style," "Rizpah," "Locksley Hall," and
"St. Simeon Stylites." But perhaps the very diversity of Tennyson's dramatic monologues is a clue to the genre itself. If, ultimately, we wish to know what Tennyson's dramatic monologues tell us about his poetic development as a whole, we must
begin by defining the form. To proceed otherwise would be like
casting a net without knowing which species is being taken.
This chapter, then, is devoted to exploring the taxonomy of the
dramatic monologue genre and to pinpointing what distinguishes the Tennysonian dramatic monologue, especially from
Browning's. As origins have much to do with identifying a species, let us first examine the various traditions out of which the
dramatic monologue evolved.

Two major schools of thought attempt to explain the rise of
the dramatic monologue in the Victorian age. One seeks to explain it in terms of the age itself, the other in terms of a solid
poetic tradition extending back to the Greeks. The most famous
proponent of the former view, and author of the seminal study
of the dramatic monologue, is Robert Langbaum.[2] Langbaum's
thesis is that the nineteenth century gave rise to the dramatic
monologue because it was a post-Enlightenment, relativistic
age. As the assurance of universal values receded, poets looked
within to the self rather than without for epistemological
validation—hence Langbaum's term, the "poetry of experience." The Romantic poet, says Langbaum, projects "himself
into the object, playing its role, knows himself in the object. He
therefore knows both himself and the object empirically,
through the reciprocal process of experience or self-objectifica-
tion.' . . . To know an object, the romanticist must *be* it" (25).
The Victorians developed the poetry of experience beyond the
lyric to the dramatic monologue for two reasons: the reaction of
Browning and Tennyson against Romantic confessional poetry,
especially after their exposure to hostile reviews (79); and the
dissolution of drama, particularly through the "psychologizing
and lyricizing reinterpretation of Shakespeare" (73).[3] Thus a
dramatic monologue differs from a traditional poem with a
first-person speaker other than the poet because the speaker of
the latter is only a "spokesman for an emotion." We cannot

sense the poet within the speaker, and there is no separation between the "utterance and the meaning of the poem" (72). Similarly, a dramatic monologue differs from a soliloquy within a traditional drama. The soliloquist focuses on self-analysis and internal debate whereas the speaker of the dramatic monologue directs his attention outward, reveals his character only incidentally, and so fosters a "disequilibrium" between "what the speaker reveals and understands" (146).

Langbaum explicitly rejects seeing the dramatic monologue as part of a long tradition of poems with first-person speakers, for that would turn virtually all such poems into dramatic monologues (75). Nevertheless, critics in recent years have adopted the approach Langbaum rejects. The first to stretch the origins of the dramatic monologue beyond post-Enlightenment literature was A. Dwight Culler in his influential essay "Monodrama and the Dramatic Monologue."[4] Culler sees the dramatic monologue as the descendent of two literary types, prosopopoeia and the monodrama. Developed by the Romans, prosopopoeia, Culler tells us, consists of depicting a historical or imaginary personage as if he were actually speaking, as in Ovid's *Heroides*. Exercises in prosopopoeia were popular in eighteenth-century British schools; through these exercises students could develop their elocutionary, oratorical, and expressive powers, particularly the last, since the student had to create through tone and diction an expression appropriate to the speaker (368). Prosopopoeia was thus a form readily at hand for nineteenth-century writers, and Culler discerns in Tennyson's early work several examples of prosopopoeia, including "Antony to Cleopatra" or "The High-Priest to Alexander" (368–69).

But the monodrama, according to Culler, is the more significant literary antecedent of the dramatic monologue. The monodrama originated on the Continent and was introduced into England in the late eighteenth century (369–76). The monodrama featured the "display of passions," not the intricacies of character, and the piece was usually backed up by musical accompaniment serving to underline each emotion as it was presented (370–71, 375). The shift from the monodrama to the dramatic monologue, then, was the shift from a focus on universalized, abstracted phases of emotion presented in sequence, to the concrete, particularized emotions or passions inherent in one individual's unique situation and character (382). Hence Tennyson's "Locksley Hall" and "Oenone," in which the dramatic characters are not highly particularized, betray the roots of dramatic monologue in monodrama, indeed exemplify the transition of one to the other (382).

Once Culler penetrated the eighteenth-century bounds of the dramatic monologue's origins, it was easy to press these origins back even further. Thus Alan Sinfield sees *prosopopoeia*, quite simply, as another name for the dramatic monologue until the Victorians developed the term we know. Prosopopoeia itself, Sinfield continues, embraces the complaint (traceable back to Theocritus and other bucolic poets), the epistle, and the humorous colloquial monologue.[5] Accordingly, Theocritus's complaint of Polyphemus, Joseph Warton's "Dying Indian," Ovid's *Heroides*, Drayton's *Heroicall Epistles* (1619), and Pope's *Eloisa to Abelard* are all pre-Victorian dramatic monologues (42–50). Within Sinfield's framework, Browning's "Soliloquy of the Spanish Cloister" and "Karshish" are derived from the tradition of the humorous colloquial monologue and the dramatic epistle whereas Tennyson's "Oenone" derives from Ovid (51).

Robert Pattison dispenses even with the term *prosopopoeia*. For him the dramatic monologue, as indeed all of Tennyson's poetry, descends directly from the idyll tradition first developed by the Greek Alexandrian poets. To Pattison the idyll is a form characterized by self-consciousness and eclecticism, its self-consciousness evident in deliberate erudition and the achieving of distance through frames and its eclecticism evident in a deliberate manipulation of forms traceable to the idyll's diverse origins in lyric, mime, and drama. The idyll's origins in lyric accounted for the frequent use of a first-person speaker, and the genre's origins in mime explained the use of realism and of dialect in some idylls. Most important for our purposes, perhaps, are the idyll's roots in drama, for the idylls demonstrated the same interest in psychological typology as did the great Athenian dramatists. Because of their interest in psychology, writers of idylls often employed the monologue form, which allowed them to isolate a mental state. However, unlike the lyric, the idyll-monologue never invited participation in the speaker's emotion. Nor was the idyll ever didactic. Instead the poet strove for a beautiful, objective rendering of emotional states. If this was not didactic, it was nonetheless, as Pattison remarks, "'useful' because it demonstrated the range of human feeling; one is not told what to think in the idyll form, but only shown, from a proper distance, what the shape of the psyche is." Thus, according to Pattison, although the dramatic monologue may seem to be an invention of the Victorian age, it is really an elaboration and development of the idyll, which had existed for at least two thousand years.[6]

Both Langbaum and those who see the dramatic monologue as part of an old, even ancient tradition, are right. Langbaum, by stressing the dramatic monologue as conceived within a subjective framework, then objectified by a first-person speaker, clarifies *why* the dramatic monologue was suddenly so popular a form in the Victorian age: it enabled the Victorians both to follow the Romantics in seeking truth within a subjective realm and to distance themselves from the subjective "I" through a more objective poetry. But Culler, Sinfield, and Pattison are surely also right in claiming that the form did not suddenly spring full-blown, like some Athena from a post-Enlightenment Zeus, in the Victorian age. A careful reading of Theocritus's "Spell" (given much attention by Pattison), even in translation, shows that the dramatic monologue has clear antecedents in the Classical age. "The Spell" is a monologue featuring a speaker, auditor, and dramatic situation, namely, a woman who casts a spell to bring back the lover who has abandoned her. There is even a revelation of character at the end of the idyll as the woman suddenly declares that she will use poison to murder the unfaithful Delphis should the spell fail to work.[7] Yet it is troubling that Pattison, who argues that the dramatic monologue is Tennyson's favorite form of the idyll (131), should also find that "The Palace of Art" and "Love and Duty" are, at least in spirit, dramatic monologues.[8] What then may be said to constitute a dramatic monologue?

Once again there are two major approaches to defining the dramatic monologue, the exclusive and the inclusive. Critics who approach the genre through the principle of exclusion try to distinguish the "true" dramatic monologue from the "false," the "elect" from those that fall by the wayside. Ina Beth Sessions represents the extreme exclusive view as she tots up the requirements of the genre: a speaker other than the poet, an auditor, a concrete setting, and so forth. Others have followed in her path, although in paths less narrow. What proponents of this view generally insist upon, however, is realism of character, concreteness of setting, and a clearly defined dramatic conflict.[9] Needless to say, this school of thought generally has little use for Tennyson's monologues. His finest monologues draw their speakers, not from history or the modern world, but from myth, and the exact setting and auditors implied for "Ulysses" have puzzled readers for some time. Nor can the speaker of "Locksley Hall" be called sharply delineated: we do not know who his companions are, what he thinks of them, or where he is going at the end of the poem; we do not get even so much as a peek inside the demesne of Locksley Hall. Somehow the exclusionists' dramatic monologue is always distinctly Browningesque.

Langbaum protests equally against the exclusive and inclusive approach. He desires neither a checklist nor a carte blanche for poems queueing to enter the inner circle of true dramatic monologues. His crux, familiar by now to all, is the monologue that results in tension between the reader's sympathy and judgment. Langbaum's dramatic monologue is autobiographical for both poet and reader. The poet projects himself, through an extension of sympathy, into the character in order to explore an aspect of self or being. The reader is able to detect the poet in the speaker through the telltale pole of sympathy and likewise projects himself or herself into the character to read the poem. Only by seeing the poem from the speaker's vantage point, through sympathy, can the reader understand the poem at all. So intent is the reader on sympathizing with the speaker that judgment, though not abandoned, must be temporarily suspended. Thus, in Langbaum's model, reprehensible characters or speakers with a skewed psychological or emotional state work best for the dramatic monologue: here the split or tension between sympathy and judgment is intensified, the relativism of truth is underscored, and the reader must likewise look within rather than to some external frame of reference.

Langbaum's other major criterion applies to the speaker. The speaker's utterance must have an essential gratuitousness, necessary both for the dramatic monologue's lyrical element and for the speaker's own pursuit of meaning: "The speaker does not use his utterance to expound a meaning but to pursue one, a meaning which comes to him with the shock of revelation. The speaker's pursuit of meaning accounts for the tone of improvisation in the best dramatic monologues, as well as for the speaker's rapt absorption in what he is saying and his strange lack of connection with the auditor" (189). Langbaum is unarguably right to focus on the relation between sympathy and judgment in the dramatic monologue. Morever, Langbaum's model admits many of Tennyson's monologues into the inner circle, including "Ulysses," "St. Simeon Stylites," "Rizpah," and "The Lotos-Eaters." Yet Langbaum may be more exclusive than he at first appears to be. One is never quite sure whether the poems Langbaum does not discuss are admissible.[10] Would "Locksley Hall" qualify? The speaker is highly wrought up by Amy's betrayal but hardly demonstrates "pathology of the emotions." What of "Lucretius," in which Tennyson, if he admirably captures the essence of Lucretius's philosophy and dramatizes "pathology of the emotions" (here due to a love philter), is also surely trying to convey a point of his own?

Several critics also cavil with Langbaum's tendency to absorb the dramatic monologue into an ironic framework. Culler argues that the dramatic monologue is marked by a "penchant *toward* judgment" (368; italics mine), through the poet's ability to manipulate tone.[11] Others have followed suit.[12] Michael Mason, for example, argues that Browning was less eager in his mature dramatic monologues to imitate character than to convey an attitude, to "speak out" obliquely behind the mask.[13] The point is that many poems often called dramatic monologues do not quite fit Langbaum's model.

This brings us to the inclusive approach to the dramatic monologue. Robert Pattison, with his emphasis on the idyll tradition, would certainly fall into this group. But the foremost spokesman for this approach is Alan Sinfield, whose *Dramatic Monologue* is the finest study of the genre to appear since Langbaum's. Sinfield's major criterion for the dramatic monologue is simple: any poem with a first-person speaker indicated as someone other than the author is a dramatic monologue. But his development of this assertion is far from simplistic. For example, his criterion of the first-person speaker allows Sinfield both to identify clearly a trait common to all dramatic monologues *and* to allow for the wide range of effects within the genre. Thus, he argues, the dramatic monologue can elicit responses that lie across the entire continuum between sympathy and judgment. "Many dramatic monologues," he argues, "swing decisively to the pole of sympathy and aim primarily to involve the reader in the sufferings of another," as in Browning's "Evelyn Hope" and "The Patriot" or Tennyson's "Tithonus" and "Rizpah" (11). At times the speaker can even serve as a "mouthpiece, more or less indirectly, for the poet's views," as in many of the statements made by Fra Lippo Lippi. Just as surely, the dramatic monologue can swing to the pole of irony and judgment, as in "My Last Duchess." Tennyson's paired poems, "Northern Farmer, Old Style" and "Northern Farmer, New Style," in themselves represent the form's ability to veer now toward sympathy, now toward irony and judgment (13). But the form is not typically didactic, even when sympathetic, because of the necessary distance imposed on the poet by the first-person device, which invites the reader to a larger view than that given by the speaker. Indeed, the subtlest way for the poet to convey his viewpoints, according to Sinfield, is to make "them arise incidentally in the words of a speaker who only partially understands them," as in "Karshish" or "Lucretius" (16–17).

Sinfield's inclusive model also allows for a range within which the poet can convey a sense of character. Sinfield chides those who take their cue for rendered character from the drama of Shakespeare or the realist idiom of Ibsen, reminding us that drama, too, can draw on the resources of myth and artificial heightening of language, as in *Oedipus at Colonus* (19–20). Thus he defends what many find disturbing in Tennyson's dramatic monologues and argues that "frankly poetic language," as in "Tithonus," "may suggest more fully [the speaker's] emotional state" than other means; and to him the rhetorical and lyrical effects of "Locksley Hall" qualify that poem simply as a *variety* of dramatic monologue, not some other species (20–21). Of course, the poet can establish the speaker's "otherness" through additional means as well, including distinctive language (for example, dialect), distinctive imagery (as in "Tithonus"), or, as is so often the case with Browning, writing "so uncompromisingly from the speaker's perspective that it is hard for the reader to perceive what is happening" (27–28). In fact, Sinfield elaborates a point first raised by Michael Mason, namely, that an accumulation of "realistic," concrete details, far from merely lulling readers into a sense of the speaker's reality, intensifies their awareness of the poet's presence behind the speaker. As Mason remarks, "the greater the colloquialism the more obtrusive the author's artistic, shaping activity is likely to be" (236). The point is clear if we think of Tennyson's "Northern Farmer, Old Style." In the first place, if we are used to Tennyson's distinctive voice of refined melancholy and haunting music in other poems, we are likely to find "Northern Farmer," as Henry James did the poet's person, distinctly "unTennysonian." In the second place, if we believe wholly in the earthy, crotchety, yet rather lovable farmer captured in the rough dialect of Lincolnshire, we also surely cannot help finding it odd that such a gruff, crusty man lets forth his final rumblings in rhymed couplets. In other words, Tennyson's "realism" intensifies our awareness of his artifice.

This point leads to Sinfield's most important contribution to our understanding of the dramatic monologue: its status as "feint." For if on one hand the titles of dramatic monologues and various hints that the speaker is other than the poet move the form into the realm of fiction, the use of the first-person speaker makes an "opposing claim for the real-life existence of the speaker on the reader's plane of actuality" through its use of the Romantic lyric "I." Thus the form lies, for "it sets up a fictional speaker whilst claiming for him, by the use of the first person, real-life existence."[14] As a result we sense the speaker as a distinct being in his own right and, simultaneously, sense the poet in the speaker. The genre's status as feint, moreover, enables a dramatic monologue to shift toward the poet's "I," in which case we have an orientation toward sympathy, or to shift toward the pole of fiction, in which case we more likely encounter irony and judgment. The more discrete markers we are given of the speaker (setting, colloquial language, auditor), the

9

closer we move toward fiction; the more amorphous the time and setting for the speaker, the more we move toward the poet's "I" (24–26).

Sinfield's is a clear and convincing way of explaining why we encounter irony more often in Browning than in Tennyson, and why irony more often occurs in poems that we consider atypically detailed and concrete for Tennyson—"St. Simeon Stylites" or the "Northern Farmer" poems. Sinfield's thesis also illuminates a characteristic reader-response to the form, the reader's awareness and experience of a "divided consciousness." Sinfield continues, "We are impressed, with the full strength of first-person presentation, by the speaker and feel drawn to his point of view, but at the same time are aware that he is a dramatic creation and that there are other possible, even preferable, perspectives" (32). This sense of doubleness not only is an inherent pleasure in itself but also reflects the complexity of life and truth, and so is an extremely rich resource for Victorian and modern poets alike (33–34). Sinfield's inclusive approach therefore has gone furthest in explaining why Tennyson and Browning can seem so different yet still be writing in the same form.

I wish to pursue further the dynamics of the dramatic monologue to see why the form allows the diversity Sinfield emphasizes. The literary event that is the dramatic monologue always involves three elements: the poet who composes, the speaker, and the reader who responds—all of whom meet and interact through the text, or the "spoken." It is helpful to map the potential trajectories of each element in any given monologue (see the accompanying figure). These diagrams demonstrate visually what so many have noted: the reader and poet always have a larger perspective than the speaker. The speaker can address or interact with only two possible beings, the auditor and, through his own utterance, himself (hence the recursive loop). But matters are vastly more complex with the poet and reader. The poet may channel most of his energies into imagining the speaker as a being in his or her own right, or the poet may use the auditor as a lightning rod for his own sensibilities and views (as is perhaps the case with Gigadibs in *Bishop Blougram's Apology*); the poet may create the speaker in order to direct his energies toward an exploration of himself; the poet may focus on what is spoken more

10

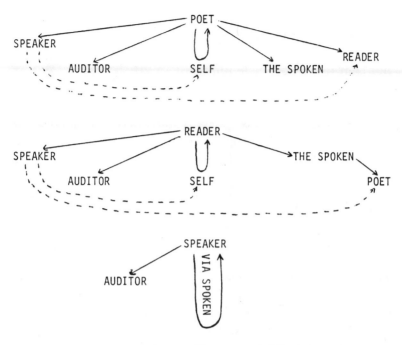

## DYNAMICS OF THE DRAMATIC MONOLOGUE

than on who says it; or the poet may above all have his eyes on the reader as he writes, hoping to affect the reader in some way. This last in itself can be a very complicated enterprise, as I hope my diagram concerning the reader illustrates. For the reader may be urged to contemplate the speaker for his or her own sake (as Pattison argues); may, through identifying with the speaker in an extension of sympathy, explore an aspect of self; may find in the auditor, whom W. David Shaw calls "the reader's friend,"[15] a center for the reader's own responses to the speaker; or, through what is spoken and the way it is uttered, arrive at some judgment of the speaker assumed to be analogous with the poet's view. Finally, through the speaker and what is spoken, the reader may, as so many critics have demonstrated, irresistibly try to arrive at some understanding of the poet himself.

Returning to the poet, we can say that most typically he directs himself not to one or another but to all the entities delineated in the diagram at once, but in different proportions in each monologue. This varying emphasis would then explain the di-

versity within the genre of the dramatic monologue. Viewing
the dramatic monologue through the diagrams also helps to explain our sense of some poems as failed dramatic monologues. It
is not that these poems do not belong to the genre but that the
poet has not drawn on the full resources of the form. Thus our
discomfort with "The May Queen," I think, comes from Tennyson's drawing on too few of the resources of characterization
and self-exploration in proportion to the attention lavished on
the sentiment of the poem and the literary shaping of the
spoken. In this poem, in other words, he is not using the full
range of the genre he employs. Indeed, the poet's complete or
partial exploitation of the full range of the dramatic monologue's
resources may clarify the Victorians' place in the genre's tradition. The Victorians did not invent the form but were the first to
discover its full range of dynamics.

The schematic I have given of the poet's involvement in the
dramatic monologue, then, explains why, in "Ulysses" or
"Locksley Hall" (and its pendant, "Locksley Hall Sixty Years After"), Tennyson seems to explore an aspect of himself, via the
form's recursive loop; why, in "Northern Farmer, Old Style," he
seems to present a speaker for his own sake; why, in "Northern
Farmer, New Style," he pivots and presents a satiric portrait
with a kind of moral point; or why, in "The Lotos-Eaters," he can
center the poem in the minds of his speakers yet also shape a
monologue that turns on the reader's response to gaps and ironies in the text. The dramatic monologue is, inherently, a loose
and baggy form, like the Victorian novel. Indeed, perhaps it was
because the Victorian age was the age of the novel that poets
embraced a form analogous to the novel in complexity.[16] To
grasp the full complexity of the form, one must imagine the separate diagrams I have given for poet, speaker, and reader super-
imposed and operating all at once. Thus, it is not that Tennyson
sometimes is and is not writing dramatic monologues; it is that
all the possibilities I have cited above are *built in* to the form.

But if viewing the dramatic monologue in these terms establishes that Tennyson, like Browning, wrote dramatic monologues, our sense of Tennyson's difference from Browning is
not abated; and it is time to articulate the distinctiveness of

Tennyson. This distinctiveness cannot be absolute. Any poet who can write both "Owd Roä" and "Demeter and Persephone" will elude compact generalization. Furthermore, if Tennyson could write dramatic monologues that strike us as Browning-esque, as in "St. Simeon Stylites," Browning could write dramatic monologues that are rather Tennysonian, as in "Childe Roland."[17] Still, if we focus on dramatic monologues considered most characteristic of each poet, we can at least advance partial generalizations.

The most obvious difference between Tennyson and Browning is of course that Tennyson's dramatic monologues typically (the Lincolnshire monologues apart) feature a more emphatically lyrical voice than do Browning's. The point is hardly new. In fact Tennyson himself was one of the first to note it. Both H. D. Rawnsley and Wilfred Ward record Tennyson as extolling Browning's dramatic genius and analysis of human character but complaining about the missing "music" or the "glory of [sweet] words" in his poems.[18] If we discount the element of rivalry with a brother poet, Tennyson is simply saying what others have said since about the distinctive textures of the two poets' works. For Browning, after all, had his own reasons for preferring a rougher texture and more colloquial language.

Browning's preference is related to his mode of characterization, and here we approach the central difference between Tennyson and Browning. It is a commonplace that Browning's characters are more discrete, more naturalistically rendered, than Tennyson's. We feel we should recognize Lippi or Blougram at a glance but would have trouble recognizing Tithonus in any old man, however ancient. We might recognize the village wife of Tennyson's poem of that name, but again, Tennyson's Lincolnshire monologues are a class unto themselves. Rather than decide that Tennyson's poems fail where Browning's succeed, however, we should instead ask why Browning's speakers should be more concrete, more emphatically *there*. Michael Mason gives us a leading thread when he remarks that Browning believed in the essential coherence of character. In fact, as Mason points out, Browning made this explicit in his comment on the character of Strafford.

*He was consistent to himself throughout* . . . those who carry their re-
searches into the moral nature of mankind, cannot do better than
impress on their minds, at the outset, that in the regions they
explore, they are to expect no monsters—no essentially discordant termination to any "mulier Formosa superne". Infinitely
and distinctly various as appear the shifting hues of our common
nature when subjected to the prism of CIRCUMSTANCE, each
ray into which it is broken is no less in itself a primitive colour,
susceptible, indeed, of vast modification, but incapable of further
division.[19]

The point, as Mason remarks, is that "a man's character will be
'consistent' if analysed in enough depth." And I think this is precisely the premise at work behind our experience of reading
Browning's dramatic monologues. Every chance remark or
aside, like those snatches of song Lippi keeps humming, every
sudden shift in argument, like Blougram's gambit of the cabin
metaphor, comes back to illuminate and revolve around a central core or crystal of character.

   The opposite seems true for Tennyson. We are struck, not by
the essential coherence, but by the essential fragmentation and
division of his speakers, by their divided mentality. The speaker's tortured vacillations in "Supposed Confessions," Tithonus's
simultaneous longing for death and evocation of the glorious,
sensuous desire he has known with Eos, or the hero's suspension between stark disillusionment and hope for the future in
"Locksley Hall" all come to mind. But if Browning has his reasons for colloquial language and rough diction, so too does Tennyson for the fragmentation and inconsistency of his speakers.

   For Tennyson renders the *consciousness* of his speakers (and for
one such as Tennyson, consciousness is inherently dialectic and
inconclusive) whereas Browning renders the *personality* of his.
"Personality" is variously defined as "the complex of characteristics that distinguishes a particular individual . . . in his *rela-
tionships with others*"; "the totality of an individual's emergent ten-
dencies to . . . interact with, perceive, react to, or otherwise
*meaningfully influence or experience his environment*"; and "the *organization* of the individual's distinguishing character traits, attitudes,
or habits."[20] "Personality," in other words, implies the orientation of the human agent to the world and others and the con-

crete *form* of his character—precisely the traits we observe in Browning's speakers. Naturally, therefore, Browning provides concrete settings and contexts in his dramatic monologues; he locates his monologues in the realm of personality, which is defined by its relation to the outer world.

But *consciousness* is defined as the "awareness or perception of an *inward* psychological or spiritual fact"; "*inward* awareness of an external object, state, or fact"; and "the state or activity that is characterized by sensation, emotion, volition, or thought: mind in the broadest possible sense"—again, precisely those characteristics of the human agent emphasized in Tennyson's speakers. No wonder that when we read Tennyson, we are struck by the vaguely defined settings and times of the monologues; Tennyson has located us in the inherently amorphous, oscillating, vibrating realm of consciousness. The difference between personality and consciousness is one of degree only: both personality and consciousness depend on an individual self and on the psychology of that self. But that self is perceived from different vantage points—one more interior, one more exterior—in the dramatic monologues of Tennyson and Browning. We see Tennyson's speakers as they are unto themselves and merely glimpse the outer world as it reacts upon them. We see Browning's speakers as they are in the world and are encouraged to fathom the depths within. Neither method is superior or inferior to the other; they are simply different.

Why should Tennyson and Browning have approached character in these diverse ways? Sinfield suggests that Browning was influenced by the eighteenth-century dramatic monologue, pushing its tendency toward naturalistic and dramatic presentation to extreme limits (55). Robert Pattison, in contrast, argues that Tennyson consciously worked out of the Classical tradition of the idyll throughout his career, a tradition that would have fostered his choice of mythic rather than realistic characters and his reliance on a frame.

But the most fruitful way to explain the difference is to look within the poets themselves. Growing up in the isolation of rural Lincolnshire would have encouraged Tennyson to look at human character similarly isolated from the outer world. The only crowd he regularly saw, after all, was the one assembled in the rectory dining room at Somersby. And the history of the large Tennyson family was also likely to have driven Tennyson's examination of character inward rather than outward. An adolescent boy witnessing his father's alcoholism, depression, and even violence is unlikely to be launched blithely into the outer world but to withdraw into the self. And the self for Tennyson seems always to have been characterized by inward divisions. If, presumably, he was torn between love and fear for his father as a youth, as an adult he veered between the impulse toward faith and an impulse toward doubt. Not surprisingly, therefore, it is a truism in Tennyson studies that Tennyson's thought was dialectic and that one of his major themes is the divided mentality. What better way to project all this than through the imagined consciousness of a first-person speaker? By such means Tennyson could avoid imposing a resolution on the oscillations of consciousness. For only death puts an end to consciousness, and perhaps that is why critics have noticed the obsessiveness of self-expression in Tennyson's speakers.[21]

Everything in Browning's background, however, conspired to make him see others in a worldly rather than an interiorized context. John Maynard's thorough account of the shaping influences on Browning's youthful character and poetic is our best source here.[22] Maynard notes, for example, Browning's probable exposure to the monopolylogues of Charles Mathews, a popular entertainer of the 1820s who dazzled audiences with a sequence of vivid, full impersonations, entailing complete changes in costume and makeup, of a series of characters (117–18). More to the point, Maynard gives an exhaustive account of the influences on Browning's conception of and approach to character. These influences include the caricatures and political cartoons of Robert Browning, Sr., Browning's own early readings in history and historical anecdote, his urban environment, and the essential cosmopolitanism of his family background. From all these Browning derived his awareness of the multiplicity of human characters, his interest in "the quirky traits that make up character" (85), and his habit of looking outward upon the world, free from any provincial narrowness. Thus, as a result of his own background, Browning not only places his speakers in the outer world (the realm of personality) but also evinces an interest in personalities for their own sakes. Tennyson, contrariwise, with his habit of looking within, has his speakers do the same, as he plumbs their consciousnesses. And if the consciousness of Tennyson's speakers so often seems distinctly Tennysonian, this is a potential property not only of the dramatic monologue but of the hazier boundaries of consciousness (as opposed to personality) as well. To sum up the difference between Browning's and Tennyson's approaches to the characters of their speakers, we might say that Browning pursued the *Ding an Sich*, an exploration of personality for its own sake; Tennyson pursued the *Ding an Mich*.

Tennyson and Browning's diverse approaches to character illuminate as well their monologues' distinctive textures—and the usual difference in the form of their monologues. Tennyson makes greater use of literary artifice—more obtrusive stanzaic and rhyme patterns—whereas Browning more fully exploits the convention of an auditor. These formal differences, I would argue, result from the poets' rendering of consciousness versus personality. Personality, as noted above, *implies* form; as an "organization of the individual's distinguishing character traits," it is itself a kind of datum, a penumbra within which the dartings of the mind are contained. Thus Browning's monologues follow, as it were, the curve delineated by the speaker's personality, by the characteristic swerves and swaths of his mind. J. Hillis Miller remarks that the form of Browning's monologues is "casual," "fortuitous": "The poem might have been written any number of different ways."[23] The form it takes is precisely the arc etched out by the speaker's personality: Karshish quite naturally turns from medicinal catalogues to the wonder of Lazarus's tale and back again. But consciousness is inherently amorphous and unstable; there is no readymade container into which it can be poured. It is rather like trying to bottle air. And just as air is encapsulated only by injecting it at high pressure into steel containers, so is Tennyson more likely to use insistent rhyme and stanza patterning in his dramatic monologues: these counterbalance his essentially diffuse and formless materials. Tennyson's containers, however, are not steely but crystalline, a haunting verbal music that serves as a transparent medium through which consciousness can be seen and viewed even as it

17

is being subjected to form. We get no transparency in Browning's sound; instead we encounter the roughness and texture of the *Ding an Sich* as his speakers sputter their clashing consonants into the ambient air.[24]

Because Browning portrays personality, furthermore, he naturally exploits the convention of an auditor more fully. In the world, we are largely defined by our relation to others. Thus the presence of the auditor in "Fra Lippo Lippi," "Andrea del Sarto," or *Bishop Blougram* helps bring to the surface the distinctiveness of the speaker, just as the imposition of infrared light on topography emphasizes features we might otherwise miss. The auditor's presence also underlines the fact that the speaker of Browning's monologues typically faces outward. Robert F. Garratt has usefully pointed out the presence of a "double mask" in many of Browning's poems: Browning dons the mask of the speaker, who in turn dons a mask with respect to the auditor.[25] The speaker's mask, that is, mediates between the speaker and the world. And just as we glimpse Browning the poet behind the mask of the speaker, we detect the lineaments of the speaker behind *his* mask: it is *because* the dying Bishop at St. Praxed's tries— and fails—to present himself as a holy man before his "nephews" that we know him for what he is.

In Tennyson the auditor is absent or part of the remote background, like the landscape in the *Mona Lisa*: it is there, but we have to look to notice it. Indeed, the list of poems with auditors is rather long—for example, "St. Simeon Stylites," "Ulysses," "Tiresias," "Rizpah," "Columbus," "Despair," and "Romney's Remorse." Auditors appear more consistently in the dramatic monologues composed after Tennyson's experiments with the drama in the 1870s and 1880s, a reflection of his greater awareness of the dramatic situation. Moreover, Tennyson could use the convention of the auditor to great effect. Part of the artistry of "St. Simeon Stylites," for example, is that the auditor is so amorphously defined: is Simeon talking to God or to himself? It is a question that cuts to the heart of the poem as a whole.

But auditors, those remnants from the outer world, can never quite be absorbed into the inner realm of consciousness, Tennyson's métier. Again, consciousness is "the *inward* awareness of an *external* object." Hence the evangelical lady who attends the dying mother in "Rizpah" is far more shadowy than Willy, the dead son whose voice moves in and out of the mother's consciousness at will.

A careful look at the distinctiveness of the Tennysonian versus the Browningesque dramatic monologue thus illuminates the differing approaches to character of the two Victorian poets and shows how formal distinctions necessarily follow from each author's approach. This examination also reinforces what has been said by Sinfield: both poets wrote dramatic monologues; they are different, not in kind, but in degree. And that said, we are free to respond to the work of each poet on its own merits.

But before we turn to Tennyson's dramatic monologues in detail, we should also consider why, aside from his approach to characterization, he found the form congenial. There are, of course, all those anecdotes of Tennyson's dramatic impulse—his comic imitation of the sun coming out of the clouds, his portrayal of Malvolio during his Cambridge days, his later superintendence of his own children's plays given on the lawn, and so forth.[26] He does seem to have had a genuine love of the theater, especially Shakespeare. Nor should we forget that his first ambitious composition was a drama, the incomplete but precocious *Devil and the Lady*, and that several of his later dramas were presented on the stage. Although it is more evident in Browning, we should not forget that Tennyson, too, had a dramatic impulse.

More to the point, perhaps, are certain ideas and habits of thought to which Tennyson would have been exposed among the Cambridge Apostles. This group is usually blamed more than praised for its effect on Tennyson, since its members urged a more public role upon Tennyson than he may have wished.[27] It would be pleasant to see in them a constructive influence. According to Peter Allen's history of the Cambridge Apostles, the most important principle of the group was its contention that opinions and beliefs were of only minor significance and that these were part of the superstructure of personality. The Apostles were less interested in debating ideas than in trying to penetrate, through an act of sympathy, to the human needs and motivations that underlay belief; in doing so they would uncover a truth that could be shared by all. Thus, when F. D. Maurice converted to orthodox Anglicanism, the Apostle James Spedding's response was, "I fancy that if I should ever perceive the *dramatic propriety* of his views—their foundation in *his* nature—it ought to satisfy me" (quoted by Allen, 5). So also wrote Arthur Hallam, Tennyson's most intimate friend, in his essay on Cicero: "The *inward* life of a great man, the sum total of his impressions, customs, sentiments, gradual *processes* of thought, rapid suggestions, and the like, contains a far greater truth, both in extent and magnitude, than all the fixed and positive forms of belief that occupy the front-row in his understanding."[28] It is not difficult, I think, to see a connection between the Apostles' views and Tennyson's habitual approach to human character and truth in his mature dramatic monologues. Indeed, the attributes of the "inward life" of a great man itemized by Hallam curiously resemble the features of consciousness given earlier. Moreover, the influence of the Apostles' principle of looking beneath opinions and beliefs (identified with personality, rather than consciousness) on Tennyson seems confirmed by his son, who tells us in the *Memoir* that his father "had a dramatic way of representing an opinion adverse to his own in a favourable light, in order that he might give it the most generous interpretation possible"[29]—precisely the method adopted by the Apostles in their discussion of opposed opinions.

An even more critical influence of the Apostles on Tennyson's development of the dramatic monologues may have come through Arthur Hallam's concept of sympathy. On 4 December 1830, Hallam presented to his fellow Apostles an essay entitled "On Sympathy." The principles of sympathy he sets forth bear a striking resemblance to the role of sympathy described by Langbaum in his own model of the dramatic monologue. Hallam begins by defining sympathy as "the simple affection of the soul, by which it is pleased with another's pleasure and pained with another's pain, immediately and for their own sakes."[30] After explaining how this capacity is developed in the infant through the process of association, he then connects the growth of sympathy to imitation.

> . . . the soul may desire another's gratification from the same impulse that leads a monkey to mimic the gestures of a man.
> Novelty is in itself an evident source of pleasure. To become

something new, to add a mode of being to those we have experienced, is a temptation alike to the lisping infant in the cradle and the old man on the verge of the grave. This may partly arise from that essential inherence of pleasure in every state to which I have alluded, partly from a pleasure of contrast and surprise felt by the soul on gaining a new position. . . . *To become this new thing*, to imitate, in a word, the discovered agent, *no less in the internal than the outward elements of action*, will naturally be the endeavor of faculties already accustomed in their own development to numberless courses of imitation. . . . It is then possible that through the desire to feel as another feels, we may come to feel so. (136; emphasis mine)

Here Hallam links imitation to the sympathetic identification with an other, in both the other's inward and outward aspects— very much what the poet must do when adopting a first-person speaker for the dramatic monologue. But Hallam comes even closer to the dynamic of sympathy in the dramatic monologue as he continues: "How, how can the soul imagine feeling which is not its own? I repeat, she realizes this conception only by *considering the other being as a separate part of self, a state of her own consciousness* existing apart from the present, just as imagined states exist in the future. Thus absorbing, if I may speak so, this other being into her universal nature, the soul transfers at once her own feelings and adopts those of the newcomer" (137; emphasis mine). As Hallam remarks later, "here the object is the same as the subject" (140), anticipating Langbaum's argument that "to know an object, the romanticist must *be* it" by more than a century.

Hallam even anticipates Langbaum's argument about the fusion of nineteenth-century sympathy and eighteenth-century critical awareness in the poet's donning of a role. He observes that in the process of identification cited above, "there is pleasure, in so far as it is a revelation of self; but there is pain, in so far that it is a divided self, a being at once our own and not our own, a portion cut away from what we feel, nevertheless, to be single and indivisible." He elaborates: "The soul, we have seen, contemplates a separate being as a separate state of itself, the only being it can conceive. But the two exist simultaneously. Therefore that impetuous desire arises. Therefore, in her anxiety to break down all obstacles, and to amalgamate two por-

21

tions of her divided substance, she will hasten to blend emotions and desires with those apparent in the kindred spirit"(138). As he later adds, "Now, although I have supposed it possible that the conception of a distinct conscious agent must pass through a process of imagination and feeling before it can be sufficiently realised to have any hold upon us, I must not be so misunderstood as to be thought to deny the intellectual conception itself. It is because the intellect apprehends another agent, that this process may take place, not because it is incapable of such apprehension"(141).

Hallam's central principle—through an extension of sympathy one imagines the other as a separate part of self, blending the two selves as far as possible so that the subjective and objective fuse—surely describes what we sense of Tennyson in relation to his first-person speakers in the dramatic monologue. In fact, according to Hallam's model the speaker would be precisely the *Ding an Mich*—which, as I argue, describes Tennyson's approach to character. How Hallam's thought may have influenced Tennyson cannot, of course, be known. Certainly it would be absurd to argue that Hallam's essay prompted Tennyson to write dramatic monologues; Tennyson began using first-person speakers in his poetry before he ever met Hallam.[31] Hallam simply may be describing what Tennyson himself was already doing. But I think we can assume that Hallam would have made Tennyson more conscious of the process of sympathetic identification and its poetic possibilities, for in 1832 Tennyson published lines in "The Palace of Art" that describe exactly the process of sympathy Hallam sets forth in "On Sympathy." Speaking of the Soul, the narrator says,

> *And all things that she saw, she multiplied,*
> *A manyfaced glass;*
> *And, being both the sower and the seed,*
> *Remaining in herself became*
> *All that she saw.*[32]

The lines echo Hallam's contention that the self, through sympathy, becomes an other by imagining the other as part of the self. More important, Tennyson here describes, for all practical purposes, one of the central dynamics of his own dramatic monologues: the fusing of subjective and objective through the poet's assuming the role of another while remaining aware of his own central core of self within ("the sower and the seed").

Thus I would argue that Tennyson's close contact with the Apostles and especially Hallam may have influenced his development of the dramatic monologue. The group did not help him to find or discover this form. But the group may have helped him realize a potential method for the dramatic monologue. It is significant that the first poem considered by critics as a "genuine" dramatic monologue, "Supposed Confessions," was published after he had come to know the Apostles.

The final reasons for Tennyson's finding the dramatic monologue so congenial are those hitherto most often cited: his deep sense of privacy, his sensitivity to criticism, and his own divided mentality. The dramatic monologue's inherent distancing of the poet from the spoken (no matter how close the identification with the speaker) could assuage Tennyson's defensiveness. The monologue also allowed him to escape the burden of the Romantic "I" whereby the poet was supposed to utter the deepest, most universal yet also most personal thoughts on every occasion. And what better way to center the unceasing dialectic of his own mind than in the dramatic monologue? He could unleash the oscillations of his own veering between, say, faith and doubt while controlling them through what William Cadbury calls the positive, whole form of the poem itself, as in "Supposed Confessions."[33] Or Tennyson could release one aspect of his divided mentality at a time, then juxtapose the results, as in his paired monologues (for example, "Ulysses" and "Tithon"). He could even participate in what he most desired yet feared (through the sympathetic identification used to flesh out first-person utterance) yet protect himself from his source of fear by conquering and encapsulating it through poetic form. We see this process in the early "Sea-Fairies," where Tennyson explores, yet distances himself from, the temptations of purely sensuous delights. That the dramatic monologue's possibilities of identification would have attracted Tennyson in and of itself is also possible. Kenneth Burke reminds us that "identification is affirmed with earnestness precisely because there is division. Identification is compensatory to division."[34] Tennyson may have turned to the dramatic monologue, that is, to objectify his inner divisions or, from the vantage point of one aspect of self, to identify with (yet gain distance from) another aspect of self. Thus, the dramatic monologue allowed Tennyson to express and explore personal concerns while eluding direct identification with his speakers, as even contemporary readers saw. In its February 1861 number the *Dublin Review* pronounced that Tennyson was a poet "whose eye turns with an introspective glance on his own subjectivity, [and] reproduces only, in place of distinct substantive creations, various phases of his own mind and peculiar states of his own idiosyncrasy" (515). His best monologues, however, are always more than exercises in autobiography; they are works in which Tennyson beautifully exploits and adapts the resources of the dramatic monologue form.

And without doubt the formal properties of the dramatic monologue also prompted Tennyson to turn to this genre so often. As we have seen, its dynamics offer the poet an extraordinary range and flexibility, and Tennyson thoroughly explored these in the course of his career. In fact, the extreme variety of his dramatic monologues makes approaching them a challenging process. If he could succeed masterfully in the form, as with "Ulysses" and "Tithonus," he could also fail abysmally, as with "In the Children's Hospital." If he turned to the form for apparently subjective ends, that is, to explore issues or emotions close to him (as in "The Ancient Sage"), he could also use the dramatic monologue simply as a vehicle for a technical experiment, as in "Boädicea." He also complicates matters by mixing forms—adding a narrative frame onto a monologue, interpolating lyric stanzas in the midst of a monologue ("The Brook"), arranging paired monologues together (the "Mermaid" poems), or achieving a startling new fusion of the lyric and dramatic (*Maud*).

Still, his dramatic monologues disclose, if not exactly a pattern (*pattern* implies too much consistency and neat categorization), at least a clear trajectory of development. Despite numerous exceptions, his earliest dramatic monologues—the juvenilia—are used most typically for subjective purposes, as the young Tennyson struggled to define himself, his art, and his world. After entering Cambridge and attaining an audience (however small) in the Apostles, Tennyson used his dramatic monologues to more objective ends. No matter how much we sense Tennyson in his speaker, his dramatic monologues of 1832 and 1842 faced outward more than the monologues he had hitherto written. This objectivity intensified as Tennyson matured and, beginning in 1874, tried his hand at the drama. The plays are related only tangentially to Tennyson's dramatic monologues, excepting "Sir John Oldcastle" and "Columbus." These two poems, like the plays, present a sympathetic but just treatment of historical figures and explore their relevance to the larger issues of the Victorian age. Yet Tennyson's interest in drama perhaps explains the sudden spate of dramatic monologues published in the 1870s and 1880s. Many of these monologues seem to be entirely public poems. Somewhere around 1885, however, the dramatic monologues seem used for increasingly subjective ends. Perhaps approaching death intensified Tennyson's dialectic sensibility, as the question of faith or doubt became more critical and therefore more tortured. At all events, both "The Ancient Sage" and "Locksley Hall Sixty Years After" seem to be Tennyson's attempt to still an ever more volatile inner dialectic.

The monologues also reveal a trajectory of development in formal terms. Tennyson's earliest works, naturally, are his weakest. Their most significant weakness is Tennyson's imperfect realization of the dramatic monologue's feint, its fusion of the poet's "I" with the pole of fiction; their most significant achievement is Tennyson's first attempt at rendering his speaker's consciousness. The 1830 *Poems, Chiefly Lyrical* show Tennyson gradually mastering the feint and the rendering of consciousness and also beginning to experiment with the adaptation of lyric elements to dramatic ends. The 1832 and 1842 dramatic monologues include some of his best works. Not only did Tennyson sustain his earlier technical development but he also began to broaden his range of fictive settings to include domestic life, classical myth, and contemporary society and its major issues. He also began to make increasingly subtle use of the dramatic monologue form itself—pitting, for example, the implied presentness of the dramatic form against the implied pastness of narrative in a single poem to help create the poem's meaning—and to refine his use of language until the very grammar of a dramatic monologue became a means of delineating the speaker's consciousness. At first glance the works of Tennyson's middle years suggest a slackening of his interest in the dramatic monologue. But a closer look reveals that in *The Princess* and *In Memoriam*, clearly not dramatic monologues, Tennyson nonetheless adapted techniques he had developed in the monologue form. We see this both in the seven fictive speakers, or tellers of the tale, in *The Princess*, and in the subtle rendering of the poet-speaker's consciousness in *In Memoriam*. Moreover, in *Maud* Tennyson reached his highest technical development of the monologue; not only is this poem his most sustained dramatic monologue, but in it we encounter entirely new ways by which Tennyson dramatized his hero's consciousness. The late poems, if not superseding *Maud* in technical development, and if overly prosy or preachy at times, still show Tennyson using the dramatic monologue in inventive and interesting ways: to flesh out or complete long narrative poems (for example, "The Holy Grail" in the *Idylls*); to render the personality rather than the consciousness of his speakers through the dialect of his Lincolnshire monologues; and to continue to exploit the formal properties of the dramatic monologue to create his poems' meaning.

We shall see something approximating these trajectories of development in the detailed examination of Tennyson's dramatic monologues that follows. I have divided the study into individual chapters, chronologically arranged, so that we can see the developments in Tennyson's dramatic monologues at any one time, as well as their range. Looking at his dramatic monologues in this way will enable us to see how varied, numerous, and, I think, successful were Tennyson's ventures in this form. Moreover, assuming that he had the dramatic monologue genre always at hand provides a key to understanding his poems written in other forms. To ask why, for example, "The Lady of Shalott" or "Mariana" are *not* dramatic monologues is to gain a fuller understanding of Tennyson's poetic craft and mastery; his reasons for using lyric and narrative forms for these poems are as concrete as his reasons for using the dramatic monologue for "Tithonus" or "Lucretius." Thus, in each chapter I juxtapose at least one lyric or narrative poem with contemporary dramatic monologues. This endeavor will, I hope, reveal why the dramatic monologue form is important to understanding Tennyson's poetry as a whole and why T. S. Eliot was correct to call Tennyson a great poet based on his "abundance, variety, and complete competence."[35]

# 2. Becoming the "Sower and the Seed": Dramatic Monologues from 1823-1830

> *Who shall know man, or freely explicate*
> *The many folds of character? or who*
> *Shall bear the lamp of subtle scrutiny*
> *Into the deep recesses of the heart?*
>
> —*The Devil and the Lady*

The "complete competence" for which Eliot praises Tennyson's poetry was, as with most poets, a gradual acquirement. Tennyson's earliest works are often flawed, even flat; yet they suggest how and why Tennyson began to write dramatic monologues. If as a mature monologist Tennyson typically functions as "sower and the seed"—assuming the role of another by imagining the other as an aspect of self—doing so presupposes several things. First, this technique presumes the poet's participation in his own poem (the recursive loop in the diagrams of chapter one) since the poet "remains" in himself while also "becoming" another. Second, successfully functioning as "sower and the seed" requires the poet to enter fully into imaginative sympathy, neither holding back nor giving only partial glimpses of the speaker's consciousness. And this process, in turn, assumes a certain psychological integration: in approaching the speaker as an aspect of self, the poet must be willing to face and admit the contents of his own consciousness if his resulting monologue is to ring true or to be rich, suggestive, complex. Third, to function as "sower and the seed," the poet must control the

29

dramatic monologue's "feint," must, that is, integrate the objective, or fictional, pole (setting, context, and so forth) with the subjective, or poet's "I."

Tennyson's earliest dramatic monologues typically display a fractured feint. Either the recursive loop is inactive, resulting in an objective, fictional, but wooden speaker; or the apparently subjective, participatory element in the poet's "I" is somehow dissonant with the poem's fictional pole; or both the poet's "I" and the fictional pole are invoked but inadequately realized, the speaker's consciousness being only partly rendered. These flaws derive in part from Tennyson's sheer youth and inexperience. But these omissions may also owe something to the peculiar circumstances of Tennyson's youth, the Somersby domestic troubles that, occurring amidst the seldom-easy years of adolescence, could have made particularly difficult the psychological integration necessary to assume the role of "sower and the seed." At the same time, domestic troubles may have impelled Tennyson toward the fictional first-person medium of the soliloquy and the dramatic monologue since it seems reasonable that family tensions needed expression as well as the distancing of fiction. *The Devil and the Lady*, an unfinished drama written in Tennyson's adolescence, suggests in its soliloquies one source of Tennyson's later interest in dramatic monologues; the work is a drama, and a comedy at that, but key soliloquies converge, as it were, toward the dramatic monologue form. The "Exile" monologues and "Remorse," on the other hand, reflect Tennyson's first—if unsuccessful—attempts at the dramatic monologue's feint and the rendering of consciousness.

With Tennyson's removal from Somersby to the relatively larger world of Cambridge, we see a change in his dramatic monologues, as evidenced in his 1830 *Poems, Chiefly Lyrical*. Cambridge brought not only release from the immediate effects of Somersby strife but also the friendship of Arthur Hallam and, in the Apostles, a new circle of readers for Tennyson's poetry. These factors, as well as the inevitable process of growing older, perhaps made the psychological integration necessary for the poet who would be "sower and the seed" more realizable. Certainly the 1830, versus the 1827, dramatic monologues show a marked improvement in Tennyson's control of the feint and the rendering of consciousness. The 1830 monologues also reveal Tennyson exploring new techniques and materials for the dramatic monologues: myth, lyric elements used for dramatic purposes, and paired poems. These advances, and the first successful rendering of consciousness in "Supposed Confessions," led naturally to the great dramatic monologues of the later 1830s and 1840s.

I

*The Devil and the Lady* and *Poems by Two Brothers* (1827)

The most frequently cited dramatic monologues of Tennyson's juvenilia are also his least typical. These are the group of historical and prophetic monologues published in 1827: "The Lamentations of the Peruvians," "Antony to Cleopatra," "The Druid's Prophecies," and more. One looks in vain for evidence of Tennyson's participation in these poems, but no poet's "I" seems to hover resonantly beneath his fictive speakers. These speakers are hollow mouthpieces cut adrift from the recursive loop that can dynamically link poet and speaker.

Only the soliloquies of *The Devil and the Lady*, the "Exile" poems, and "Remorse" point ahead to Tennyson's major dramatic monologues. These early works suggest Tennyson's first steps toward imagining an other as an aspect of self, especially "Remorse," but in all the technique of the feint is imperfectly sustained. A number of key soliloquies in *The Devil and the Lady*, for example, are discontinuous with the rest of the play in both content and technique. Rather than reveal the motivation or internal struggles of the play's characters, these soliloquies seem to express the anxieties of the adolescent Tennyson. And the soliloquies of two ostensibly contrasting characters, the devil of the title and Magus the magician, begin to merge in thought and image, as if they could be spoken by a single speaker. If Tennyson intended to write conventional soliloquies, these sustained first-person utterances often seem instead to convey personal exploration and expression. The imperfect fusion of these subjective soliloquies into the objective, fictionalized framework of the rest of the drama reflects Tennyson's lack of control over his materials and, perhaps, his inability to face and deliberately articulate personal anxieties.

Such troublesome anxieties would at least be understandable for an adolescent poet who was also the son of Dr. George Clayton Tennyson. Dr. Tennyson's losing battle with drink, melancholia, violence, and epilepsy has been told elsewhere, and need not be recounted here.[1] But we may recall that adolescent Alfred, "More than once . . . scared by his father's fits of despondency, went out through the black night, and threw himself on a grave in the churchyard, praying to be beneath the sod himself" (*Memoir*, I, 15). "Playfellow Winds," unpublished in Tennyson's lifetime but written in 1828 (shortly after his matriculation to Cambridge), also records Tennyson's despair. Speaking directly, without any intervening mask, he addresses his old friends of Somersby, "Playfellow winds and stars," whose eyes were

> *bright*
> *With sympathy, what time my spirit was cold*
> *And frozen at the fountain, my cheek white*
> *As my own hope's quenched ashes.*

> (lines 2–5)

In the midst of such scenes Tennyson wrote *The Devil and the Lady*, begun when he was fourteen, and revised (and abandoned) when he was no older than sixteen.[2] Its story tells of an aged magician, Magus, who must set forth on a journey and who summons a devil to guard the chastity of his young and beautiful wife, Amoret. Magus's precaution is warranted since a host of suitors descends on his cottage once he departs. Magus's journey is thwarted, however, and he returns home unexpectedly to find the devil with his hands full, at which point the manuscript breaks off. Between Magus's departure and return the devil has adopted the dress of Amoret and veiled his face in order to intercept Amoret's would-be lovers: with his "grim, fantastic nose" and "black and knotty teeth / That fence my jaws like hedge-stakes," he has, as he remarks, "lost / Much of original beauty since my fall" (act II, scene i, lines 67–70). The title of the play is thus two-edged: it refers not only to the contest between the devil and Amoret but also to the devil's duple (and duplicitous) identity as both himself and the veiled Amoret. Tennyson in this sense could have called the play "The Devil and the Devil."

If such wordplay sounds uncharacteristic of the mature Tennyson, so are other elements of the work: its boisterous humor, its action, and the vitality and energy of its verse—a far cry from the Tennyson who could identify so fully with lotos-eaters. Perhaps the play's least expected, and most boyish, element is the young poet's approach to characterizing the suitors. Here Tennyson imitates Elizabethan comedy of humors.[3] The suitors —Antonio the lawyer, Pharmaceutus the Apothecary, and so on —are frankly types. Their value to Tennyson is in allowing him scope to display his precocious learning and to play with language: each suitor's speech is peppered with jargon appropriate to his profession.[4]

Yet a closer look at the play reveals the characteristic Tennyson idiom. Charles Tennyson has remarked that even though those parts of the play composed earlier show an objective, external approach to character and theme (akin to the pole of fiction in dramatic monologues), later passages "mark the beginning of a more subjective attitude" (44–45). How is this "more subjective attitude" apparent? In the first place, it is interesting to consider the themes of the play: appearance versus reality (clearly hinted at in the title), youth versus age, and innocence and idealism versus experience and disillusionment. This last theme is especially interesting because in the play youth and innocence are only a yearning, an absence that Magus desires. There is not in fact one innocent character in the play. Magus is at times a doddering fool, and one who must ally himself with the devil to achieve his heart's desire; the devil of course lacks innocence, as a wry, cynical, Mephistophelian emissary from hell; Amoret hates her husband and encourages lovers; and the suitors could not be more quick to collude with Amoret in her desires. The play implies that youthful innocence is bound to be eclipsed.

But the best hint of Tennyson's subjective entrance into the play is that Tennyson did not seem able to write the work he wanted to. The play begins as a comedy of humors revolving around stock literary situations—a May/December alliance, a carping devil, and a hot-blooded suitor—all requiring the poet to remain aloof and distant, in control of the comedy, and his fiction. But time and again the subjective, reflective, and self-exploratory seem to intrude and always in the form of soliloquies spoken by the devil and Magus. This discontinuous alternation between subjective soliloquies and objective comedy of humors, between self-exploration and external rendering of character, suggests that if Tennyson was drawn to first-person utterances to express his personal concerns, he had not yet learned to integrate the poetic "I" into a fictional framework.

The play's soliloquies are nonetheless revealing, particularly those revolving around the play's central images of unsullied purity versus vile corruption. In act I, having summoned up the devil, Magus commits to the care of this "Spirit of Hell"

> My loving wife, to guard her chaste and pure
> As stainless snow, brushed by the windy wing
> Of Eagle on the stormy mountain top,
> Or like the virgin lily, whose rare sweets
> Combining with the ambient atmosphere,
> Do make a paradise of this fair earth,
> So delicate are its odours.

> (I, i, 77–83)

The passage acquires a certain lyric intensity as Magus expresses his longing for a world of edenic innocence untouched and untainted by sensuality of any kind. And the flower image ("the virgin lily") becomes a center; Magus cannot recur to the cause of his anxiety without likewise recurring to the image of the flower. The countermanding forces of disillusionment and experience are enunciated, appropriately, by the devil as he talks to Amoret.

> Oh! Amoret! there is no honour in thee;
> Thou art the painted vision of a dream,
> Whose colours fade to nothing, a fair rainbow
> Mocking the tantalized sight, an airy bubble,
> O'er whose bright surface fly the hues of light,
> As if to hide the nothingness within.
> Few will bear sounding; cast the plummet in

> *And it will draw up mud, vile, worthless mud.*
> *Gaze on the mirror of the silver lake*
> *In its clear picture deftly pencilling*
> *The soft inversion of the tremulous woods,*
> *But probe it not to the bottom: weeds, rank weeds,*
> *Darkness and swarming reptiles harbour there.*
>
> (I, v, 169–81)

This passage, too, acquires a certain intensity, the intensity not of hope but of fear and anxiety, and seems to express the young Tennyson's own fears about the fate of childhood innocence.[5] The play's subsequent soliloquies extend the pattern noted here: frequently the drama's comic elements disappear suddenly, giving way to sober contemplations of failed innocence presented in soliloquy form.

Act II, scene iii, opens with the devil's soliloquy, as he savors the treatment he will mete out to young Antonio. After the comic bantering of Antonio in the preceding scene, and even amidst the devil's own braggadocio, an anxious sadness concerning youth's disillusionment seems to invade the soliloquy and suggests Tennyson's own participation in the first-person utterance. In fact, the soliloquy recurs to the imagery contained in the devil's lines quoted above, which turn on the surface of a pool versus the vileness contained within.

> *Visions of happiness do float before thee,*
> *Gay-gilded figures and most eloquent shapes,*
> *Moulded by Fancy's gentle fingering*
> *To the appearance of reality,*
> *With youthful expectations and fond dreams,*
> *All rendered sunlike by the light of youth,*
> *Which glances on them, flit before thine eyes:*
> *But these shall be pinched out of thee—ere morn*
> *There shall be no sound place within thy person;*
> *Thou shalt be all the colours of the rainbow,*
> *With bruises, pinches, weals, ET CETERA;*
> *And various as the motley-coloured slime,*
> *Which floats upon the standing pool, wherein*
> *Do breed all kinds of reptiles—creeping things,*
> *Vile jellies and white spawn and loathsome newts.*
>
> (II, iii, 17–31)[6]

One might argue less here for Tennyson's participation in the soliloquy than for consistent characterization: naturally a devil would stress disillusionment and the overthrow of innocent appearance by dark and loathsome reality. But Magus's soliloquy after he returns to discover the devil thronged with suitors makes clear that the concern about innocence versus disillusioned experience extends beyond the devil's soliloquies—as if Tennyson were consistently drawn to explore personal anxieties in the first-person utterance of the soliloquy form. Thus, when Magus laments what the suitors would do to his dream of a stainless "virgin lily," he echoes the imagery of the standing pool provided by the devil, then explicitly relates this imagery to the contrast between boyhood and manhood.

> 'Tis even thus—
> And they would pluck 'from the casket the sole gem
> Of mine affections, taint its innocent lustre,
> And give it back dishonoured, they would canker
> My brightest flower, would muddy the clear source
> Whence flows my only stream of earthly bliss;
> Would let the foul consuming worm into
> The garner of my love. O Earthliness!
> Man clambers over the high battlements
> That part the principalities of good
> And ill—perchance a few hot tears, and then
> The seared heart yields to 't and Crime's signet stamps
> Her burning image there. The summer fly
> That skims the surface of the deep black pool
> Knows not the gulf beneath its slippery path.
> Man sees, but plunges madly into it.
> We follow through a night of crime and care
> The voice of soft Temptation, still it calls,
> And still we follow onwards, till we find
> She is a Phantom and—we follow still.
> When couched in Boyhood's passionless tranquillity,
> The natural mind of man is warm and yielding,
> Fit to receive the best impressions,
> But raise it to the atmosphere of Manhood
> And the rude breath of Dissipation
> Will harden it to stone. 'Tis like the seaplant
> Which in its parent and unshaken depths
> Is mouldable as clay, but when rude hands

*Have plucked it from its billowless Abyss*
*Unto the breathings of Heaven's airs, each gust*
*Which blows upon 't will fix it into hardness.*

(III, ii, 156–86)

It is a strange passage to appear in the midst of a comedy. Although dissonant in tone from the rest of the play, form and content fuse in one sense. For just as the "atmosphere of Manhood" and its "rude breath of Dissipation"[7] can freeze and harden the "natural mind" of "Boyhood," so the youthful zest of the play is suddenly frozen and displaced by this lengthy soliloquy. The imagery is very close to that of "Playfellow Winds," where Tennyson tells how his spirit became "cold / And frozen" during his Somersby boyhood. "Playfellow Winds," however, a lyric unmediated by a fictive mask, was not written until Tennyson was at Cambridge, when he could be said to have literal, physical distance from his father and his problems. The literary distance of fictive first-person utterance perhaps enabled Tennyson to explore in Magus's soliloquy what he may not have been able to face in a direct way. The soliloquy, that is, may have afforded Tennyson fuller expression of his anguish at his father's dissipation when he was only fourteen or fifteen and living in the midst of his father's household than when he was seventeen or eighteen and safely ensconced in Cambridge.

In revising the play, Tennyson pursued the darker undertones of the soliloquies already discussed. Some additions to the early draft are comic, especially the soliloquy in which the devil expresses dismay at having to guard a woman against her will; but the majority are notable for their melancholy. These include the frequently cited additions that ponder the intractability of linear time and Berkeleyan metaphysics (I, v, 229–44, and II, i, 25–57). The most important addition for my purpose, however, is the interpolation of a third scene in act I given over entirely to Magus's soliloquy. Here Tennyson recurs, through the mask of Magus, to the overthrow of innocence by the forces of age and anarchy. Magus begins by lamenting the anxiety that attends one who desires to hold on to something precious, and then, as he continues, arrives at the contrast of youth and age and the image of the short-lived flower.

37

*Distrust increases with increase of years,*
*She is the firstborn of Experience.*
. . . . . . . . . . . . . .
*                    from her counsel*
*We learn that many a gay flower, which disperses*
*Incense to every wandering air, fades off*
*And grows to a poisonous berry, which gives death*
*To all who taste it—that the broidered side*
*Of Life's fair tapestry, with its woven groups*
*Of gloomy imagery, and the inwrought splendour*
*Of flower and fruitage, showeth fair to the eyes*
*Of inexperienced immaturity,*
*But unto those whose rarity of locks*
*The hand of Time hath salted, she exhibits*
*The dark reverse of it,*
*The intertwinings and rough wanderings*
*Of random threads and wayward colourings—*
*A mêlée and confusion of all hues,*
*Disorder of a system which seemed Order.*

*(I, iii, 20-21, 29-44)*

Is this not similar to the devil's soliloquy of the first draft, where he contrasts the "Visions of happiness" and "Gay-gilded figures" of "youthful expectations and fond dreams" with the "various" hues of "the motley-coloured slime" inhabited by the brood of "all kinds of reptiles"? My point is this: most characteristically Tennyson explores in the play's soliloquies the issue of what the aging process brings. And this question could have been pressing for the adolescent Tennyson himself. Would he, like his father, have a fair start in life only to collapse in a mire of indulgence, disease, and disorder?[8] *The Devil and the Lady*, then, may suggest one reason for Tennyson's early interest in fictive first-person utterance: this medium may have provided him a means of voicing painful preoccupations he perhaps could not articulate in any other way. If he felt betrayed by his father, he also loved his father deeply—it was his father, after all, who educated the young Tennyson and encouraged him to become a poet—and it seems unlikely that the young Tennyson would have directly voiced resentment and horror at what seemed his father's betrayal, even to himself. The distance afforded by the play's soliloquies, that is, may have been necessary as much to distance the soliloquies' thoughts from himself as to distance himself from responsibility for the thoughts.

But Tennyson is not in control of this strategy. *The Devil and the Lady* was abandoned, quite likely, because Tennyson found himself writing in opposite directions all at once. On one hand we have the comic, externally conceived, objectively rendered suitors, and on the other hand the subjectively conceived characters of Magus and the devil as seen in their soliloquies. The Lady Amoret, oddly, appears almost nowhere at all, being allowed only a few lines before she is safely dispatched to bed—if the bed ever seemed safe to Tennyson.

Even with the two major characters, however, Tennyson is inconsistent. In dialogic situations the devil and Magus can be funny, the one wry and carping, the other paranoid in a fussy, silly way. But their characters expand in unforeseen ways when they begin to soliloquize. In fact they expand until their boundaries cross and they begin to merge. Thus, as noted above, Magus's melancholy perception of the surface and reverse side of "Life's fair tapestry" echoes the devil's observations on the fair visions of youth versus the vileness of experience to come. Similarly, once the devil articulates the image of the shining surface of the lake in contrast to the mud and weeds beneath, *both* the devil and Magus recur to this image, as though it were their shared province, as though they were a single speaker. Tennyson here seems to have gravitated toward a fictive speaker imagined as an aspect of self. But fusing the poet's "I" and a fictive speaker was impossible in the aborted drama. In the first place, Tennyson had committed himself to multiple characters, not one, and to characters interacting with others. In the second place, he practiced two discordant approaches to characterization, as seen in the suitors versus the devil and Magus. Accordingly, Tennyson veered between chameleon poet and, in the soliloquies, the egotistical sublime, between an objective surface and inner exploration. Only when Tennyson discovered the principle of imaginative sympathy, whereby an other is conceived as *part* of the self, and learned to control the dramatic monologue's feint, could he fuse the subjective and objective instead of trying one and then the other, and so arrive at the rendering of consciousness. For the play provides only hints of the characters'—or the poet's—consciousnesses. Perhaps Tennyson could not yet conceive another as part of the self because he feared his own self contained dark corners and vile realities he was not yet able to acknowledge.

The "Exile" poems in *Poems by Two Brothers* do not fully represent the oscillations of consciousness either, nor have they the redeeming liveliness of *The Devil and the Lady*. But these published monologues also suggest why Tennyson first turned to the dramatic monologue form and its feint. In the "Exile" poems Tennyson seems to exploit at once the dramatic monologue's inherent distance (or pole of fiction) and opportunity for personal expression (which merges a speaker's first-person utterance with the poet's "I"). As the exile of "Written by an Exile of Bassorah" stands on the boat and sees each familiar landmark fade into the distance, he bids farewell successively to the land, the city, the harp he hung on a palm tree, and the maiden "whose eyes [were] the load-star which guided / My course on this earth" (lines 27–28). The structure of the poem thus enacts the process of separation. And the terms of this separation are resonant: the speaker is severed from "the groves of my childhood," for "the deep waves have parted / The land of my birth from her desolate son" (lines 5, 17–18). Yet despite the suggestively personal element hinting at Tennyson's participation in this poem (versus the historical or prophetic monologues), the work fails. Why? The "Exile" poems are neither subjective nor objective enough. Tennyson has neither fully engaged his own feelings by conceiving of the exile as the *Ding an Mich* nor given life to a breathing, independent fictive personality. Instead the poems float, denied an anchor in the outer world or in the poet's self. Perhaps Tennyson still felt compelled to repress his troublesome self as much as possible. At any rate, it is interesting that in "The Exile's Harp" Tennyson is not content with the inherent distancing of the monologue itself; the speaker addresses his harp instead of himself, and relies on metonymy to avoid saying "I" any more than necessary.

> For where is the heart or the hand to awaken
> The sounds of thy soul-soothing sweetness again?

. . . . . . . . . . . . . . . . . . . . . . . . . .
*Those that see shall remember the hand that hath crowned thee.*

*(lines 7–8, 19, emphasis mine)*

The same dilemma of too little objectivity or subjectivity af-
flicts several other early monologues infused with hints of personal expression, including "I wander in darkness and sorrow"
and "The Outcast,"[9] much akin to the "Exile" poems. But "Remorse" is rather a different matter. This work merits notice not
merely because it anticipates "Supposed Confessions of a Second-Rate Sensitive Mind" but also because it is the first clear-
cut poem in which Tennyson attempts to render consciousness.
The poem's shape is determined by the movement of the speaker's mind, which turns now toward fear of impending punishment, now toward denial or acceptance of guilt. Like the later
"Supposed Confessions," "Remorse" also ends on a note of
vacillation and suspended action. Anticipating death, the speaker cries,

> *How shall I bear the withering look*
> *Of men and angels, who will turn*
> *Their dreadful gaze on me alone?*

*(lines 81–83)*

The text ends with an unanswered question, not a resolution.

As in "Supposed Confessions" also, one can discern clues to
Tennyson's personal involvement in "Remorse." But as in *The
Devil and the Lady,* this participatory element is not wholly integrated into the text; the feint is fractured. Having lamented that
remorse "Holds up the mirror to my view," the speaker
continues,

> *And I was cursèd from my birth,*
> *A reptile made to creep on earth,*
> *An hopeless outcast, born to die*
> *A living death eternally!*
> *With too much conscience to have rest,*
> *Too little to be ever blest.*

*(lines 18–24)*

The "And" that begins this passage is illogical; the passage in no
way follows directly from what precedes. Instead these lines

41

suggesting personal import—revolving, that is, around the issue of patrimony—suddenly erupt into the text. If Tennyson is invoking the recursive loop of the dramatic monologue, he has not yet learned to modulate his entry into the speaker's consciousness, as he does in "Supposed Confessions."

The poem's immaturity is also evident in the speaker's language. In Tennyson's best monologues the speaker's peculiar use of language works to delineate the speaker's consciousness. Tithonus's reference to his earlier self as a "he," not "me," reveals his sense of alienation from his former self and the entire round of mortal life; Ulysses's use of the subjunctive in the second verse paragraph of his monologue—"vile it were / For some three suns to store and hoard myself"—lets us know that Ulysses has not yet made up his mind to leave Ithaca but is rather engaging in an imaginative trial run. Thus, it may be an effective source of characterization that the speaker of "Remorse" so often uses language that distances himself from his sins and ascribes agency for these sins to external sources.[10]

> What shadowy forms of guilt advance,
> And fill me with a thousand fears!
>
> . . . . . . . . . . . . . . . . . . . .
> A reptile made to creep on earth,
>
> . . . . . . . . . . . . . . . . . . .
> Fiends! who have goaded me to ill!
> Distracting fiends, who goad me still!
>
> . . . . . . . . . . . . . . . . . .
> Yet is there that in me which says . .
>
> (lines 3–4, 20, 53–54, 61)

The middle lines are self-explanatory. But note that in the first two, the speaker does not claim or take responsibility for his guilt; *he* lies passive, while shades of guilt advance and invade. In the last quoted line, the speaker cannot even accept the responsibility of uttering a declarative sentence. All this may point to the speaker's cowardice and egotism (since he wishes always to protect his precious self), which keep him from either committing himself to his sins or seeking salvation.

But it is difficult to credit the poem with such subtlety. Instead the distancing effect of the speaker's language seems akin to the use of metonymy noted in "The Exile's Harp." With a volatile subject on his hands ("And I was cursèd from my birth"), Tennyson is not content with the given distancing of the dramatic monologue's fictional pole and doubly distances himself from the poem's matter through language that denies personal responsibility. Of course Tennyson at this stage was simply an inexperienced practitioner of the dramatic monologue; perhaps, too, he had not the confidence fully to imagine another as part of the self and then take responsibility for both speaker and self.

The most striking difference between "Remorse" and "Supposed Confessions," however, is that the former *has* nothing to confess; the cause of the speaker's guilt or the nature of his sin is never named. At least we know why the youth of "Supposed Confessions" feels guilty. In fact, it is the fullness with which the speaker's consciousness is imagined and rendered that makes "Supposed Confessions" so much more compelling. The two poems differ in content, but in structure and theme, even in approach to character, "Remorse" and "Supposed Confessions" are quite similar. The failing of "Remorse," however, is also a key to understanding it better as a product of Tennyson's muted, evasive self-exploration and self-expression. The poem is not about being guilty but about the fear of *becoming* guilty. The speaker scarcely looks backward; his eyes are riveted on the future. "Remorse" seems much more the poem of a young, and troubled, man than one might at first think.

Tennyson, then, wrote a variety of monologues in his earliest years of composition; "Antony to Cleopatra" rests side by side with the "Exile" poems, "Remorse," or the soliloquies from *The Devil and the Lady*. The latter works, however, illuminate the development of the mature dramatic monologues by revealing embryonic techniques perfected in the later works and by underscoring what Tennyson had yet to learn. The beginnings of Tennyson's rendering of consciousness (the *Ding an Mich*) and hence of the recursive loop are evident in the merging of presumably personal concerns with the soliloquies of the devil and Magus, or the speakers' monologues in the "Exile" poems and "Remorse." As I have suggested, these works' value to Tennyson may have been the chance they afforded him to articulate deeply rooted anxieties at a safe distance from any reader, and perhaps from the poet himself. But the integration of the poet's participation into fictional frameworks is clumsy at best. In fact, the subjectivity of many passages seems intensified precisely because such passages are at odds with the context of the surrounding work and hence are so easy to pick out. Two results follow. First, Tennyson cannot adequately render the consciousness of his speakers because his identification with them through the agency of sympathy is never sustained: he both approaches and avoids this identification. Second, he cannot sustain the feint of a dramatic monologue. He may work to create a viable fictive speaker, or to explore aspects of himself via the speaker, but Tennyson does not do both simultaneously. Hence we get a fractured feint, and fractured—even aborted—works as well.

But these earliest experiments still had their uses. Perhaps Tennyson noted how, in *The Devil and the Lady*, the soliloquies kept running away with him despite his ostensible (comic) intentions, and was thus impelled to explore fictive first-person utterance further. And "Remorse" seems to lead naturally to "Supposed Confessions." These works are flawed, then, but they seem the genuine beginning of a mode to which Tennyson recurred during the rest of his career.

## II
### Poems, Chiefly Lyrical (1830)

Tennyson's matriculation to Cambridge in 1827 marked a transition in his life and poetry alike. Away from Somersby and its difficulties, he met Arthur Hallam, surely the most important person in his life, and expanded his circle of friends to include the Apostles. The immediate results of this change in Tennyson's emotional life are apparent in two sonnets dedicated "To Poesy," both dating from Tennyson's Cambridge years. In the first ("O God, make this age great"), Tennyson states, "Methinks I see the world's renewèd youth / A long day's dawn, when Poesy shall bind / Falsehood beneath the altar of great Truth" (lines 6–8). In the second, written conjointly with Hallam, the speaker desires to gain acclaim

> Because I seek to bless my native earth,
> For this is the condition of our birth,

*That we unto ourselves are only great*
*Doing the silent work of charities.*

(lines 11–14)

In the first sonnet the imagery and tone of the "Exile" poems or the soliloquies of *The Devil and the Lady*, where the bright tapestry of youth and happiness is dragged in the mud or rent, give way to a vision of youth renewing itself. The second sonnet breathes a serene sense of community. Certainly not all of Tennyson's poetry from the Cambridge years loses its sad, melancholy strain in a burst of cheerful confidence. But Tennyson's contact with Hallam and the Apostles seems to have brought a rich influx of intellectual and emotional experience into his life, freeing him from his adolescent obsessions.

This change in his personal life coincided with a change in Tennyson's dramatic monologues. Just as in his personal life he no longer was forced to repress all his deepest emotions when he had Hallam as confidant, so in his best contemporaneous monologues Tennyson does not suppress, then release, subjective passages, as in *The Devil and the Lady*, but achieves a complex fusion of objective and subjective, of fiction and the personal, all at once. Perhaps less frightened of his inner emotions, and influenced by Hallam's essay "On Sympathy," he began to imagine an other as part of himself and to render consciousness in a way that typifies his best work in the monologue genre. A more experienced poet in 1830 than in 1827, Tennyson also began to evince the craftsmanship for which he became famous. Beyond heightening his powers of diction and image, Tennyson began both to explore and to exploit the formal properties of his medium to help create his poems' meaning. Thus, in "The Sea-Fairies" we get neither abrupt and dissonant personal effusions nor speakers who seem hollow mouthpieces, but instead speakers through whom Tennyson can at once explore the dangerous territory of sexuality and invoke the aesthetic distance of the dramatic monologue; the feint is intact instead of fractured. In the "Mermaid" poems he produces his first paired monologues, and in "Oriana" he begins to adapt emphatically lyric elements to the dramatic end of rendering consciousness. "Supposed Confessions" culminates the discussion of this chapter because it is the first dramatic monologue in which Tennyson wholly—and successfully—renders the consciousness of his speaker while also sustaining the dramatic monologue's feint. By the time of writing this poem, that is, he had truly become both "sower and the seed."

The 1830 monologues do look backward as well as forward. "The Idealist," "Hero to Leander," and "St. Lawrence" are little different in form and accomplishment from "Antony to Cleopatra" in the 1827 volume.[11] But "The Sea-Fairies" represents an advance, though it does not exactly render the consciousness of its speakers. In fact, "The Sea-Fairies" is important for showing that Tennyson could successfully use the dramatic monologue for other ends besides the exploration of a given consciousness. The poem instead seems to function as an exercise in controlled wish-fulfillment. Like Homer's Ulysses, who straps himself to the mast so that he can safely listen to the enchanting but destructive song of the sirens, Tennyson achieves control in the presence of temptation by clinging to the fictive form of the dramatic monologue. He may let the Fairies speak (as if the Lady Amoret were finally allowed to say what she had in mind for her suitors) and so allow himself to harken to forbidden sexual delights, but he does not enter the Fairies' consciousness. Tennyson, after all, could readily identify with those, like the lotos-eaters or Lucretius, who undergo temptation; but he rarely assumes the role of tempter. The Fairies do not explore their own depths but face outward, addressing the mariners who sail past their isle. Tennyson, accordingly, does not activate the recursive loop to merge his own, and his speakers', consciousnesses but gives attention to the shaping of the spoken and its potential effect on the auditors. Because the conduit of sympathy between poet and speaker(s) remains closed in this poem, the Fairies are at once a "we" and a "they," first-person speakers yet distanced from the poet.

The 1830 "Sea-Fairies" presents a vision of sensual delights enhanced by a backdrop of natural beauty. In the frame of the 1830 poem Tennyson first directs his mariners' eyes to "White limbs unrobèd in a chrystal air."[12] These Sea-Fairies are not nude but naked, which perhaps explains why the elder Tennyson removed this line altogether in 1853. The song of the 1830

Sea-Fairies sustains the overt sexuality introduced in the frame. Their first temptation directed to the mariners is to "come and play; / We will sing to you all the day." This "playing" seems an oblique reference to sensual pleasure. In the contemporaneous "Merman," the speaker, after singing all day, would at night "roam abroad and play / With the mermaids," that is, "kiss them often under the sea." The Fairies next offer the delights of a beautiful landscape, though one that, with its "gambolling waterfalls" and "revelling gales," is singularly attuned to their first offer of sexual bliss. At the end of the poem the Fairies return to insistently sexual enticements, when they ask the mariners to

> be our lords,
> For merry brides are we:
> We will kiss sweet kisses, and speak sweet words:
> O listen, listen, your eyes shall glisten
> With pleasure and love and revelry.
>
> (lines 32–36)

If the Fairies allude to the beauties of the landscape, this allusion is neatly sandwiched by the real emphasis in the poem, its appeal to refined sensual delights. Moreover, these delights are clearly presented as an escape from the ordinary, everyday world. The Fairies call on the mariners to "Leap ashore! / Know danger and trouble and toil no more"—lines deleted in the 1853 version, which thus loses the stark contrast between the imperatives and dangers of the mundane world and the sensual delights afforded by the realm of Faerie.

Yet there is a certain brittleness or fragility to the Fairies' monologue: the surface of the poem is all we have and defies any attempts to sound more interesting depths. Tennyson has not explored consciousness, though he has perhaps released one aspect of his own, that which could acknowledge the allure of sensuality. But he keeps this allure at bay by a peculiar use of the dramatic monologue that allows him to adopt an approach/ avoidance strategy for the temptations represented by the Fairies.[13] He can approach the temptation by giving voice to the Fairies; he can avoid it by his very role as poet, encapsulating the Fairies' invitation forever in form and thus turning it into a distanced thing.

Distance is also evident in "The Merman" and "The Mermaid," the only paired monologues of the 1830 volume. The objectivity of these poems is enhanced by the pairing itself: our attention is directed away from the poet and toward the interaction of the speakers (each the auditor of the other) and what they speak. This interplay between speakers and spoken, in turn, gives the poems thematic richness. On one hand the poems constitute a kind of humorous sexual debate between the speakers.[14] On the other hand, the poems explore different forms of artistry.[15]

This thematic richness is also augmented by another strategy that foreshadows Tennyson's best and most mature dramatic monologues—his drawing upon the resources of myth, as he had done in "The Sea-Fairies" as well. His exploitation of mermaid lore was a perfect way to fuse aesthetic and sexual issues. Mermaids have long been associated with the bewitching and destructive sexuality as well as the singing of classical sirens. Moreover, the mer-figure, half human and half fish, is a suggestive analogue for the artist, who through his humanity has one foot planted in the everyday world and who, through imagination, has access to alien and unknown worlds.

The pairing of different views of sexuality and art enabled Tennyson to explore another thematic layer in these poems: the issue of childishness. This theme is a clue to Tennyson's participation in these works, to the subjective pole of self-exploration that fuses with objective considerations to create rendered consciousness. The matter is clarified by one of Tennyson's sources for the poems, Sir Walter Scott's novel *The Pirate*.[16] In Scott's novel a mermaid masque (with a mermaid and merman singing alternating songs) takes place in a household that serves as a refuge from domestic troubles for the hero of the novel, a hero whose relationship with his father bears a striking resemblance to that which Tennyson experienced with his own father. If this connection was borne in mind by Tennyson as he composed, even if the connection was only an unconscious memory, the Scott source helps explain both Tennyson's subjective entry into the verse and the appearance of childhood as an issue in the poems. For both poems explore two forms of childishness: sexual immaturity and ethical and moral childishness.

In "The Merman," stanza II, the speaker demonstrates his sexual immaturity by imagining the feats and pranks of a bold boy.

> *I would be a merman bold,*
> *I would sit and sing the whole of the day;*
> *I would fill the sea-halls with a voice of power;*
> *But at night I would roam abroad and play*
> *With the mermaids in and out of the rocks,*
> *Dressing their hair with the white sea-flower;*
> *And holding them back by their flowing locks*
> *I would kiss them often under the sea,*
> *And kiss them again till they kissed me*
>    *Laughingly, laughingly;*
> *And then we would wander away, away*
> *To the pale-green sea-groves straight and high,*
>    *Chasing each other merrily.*

He then elaborates on this fantasy of nightlife, explaining how he and the mermaids would "call to each other and whoop and cry," and how he would once again stage a sexual ambuscade.

> *Then leaping out upon them unseen*
> *I would kiss them often under the sea,*
> *And kiss them again till they kissed me*
>    *Laughingly, laughingly.*

Certainly there is a hint of egotism and pride in the speaker's wish to force the mermaids into compliance. Yet his ultimate wish is a form of joyous communality. His final comment is "*We would live merrily, merrily.*"

With "The Mermaid" things are more complicated, and this is part of the point: as we move from "The Merman" to "The Mermaid," we move from the less complicated world of boyhood to the more complicated world of the feminine adult. The speaker of "The Mermaid" envisions mature, if malign, sexuality, for her grace and sexual wiles are fully developed. And whereas "The Merman" can discuss art (that is, singing) or sexuality but not both at once (all references to singing drop out of the poem when the speaker begins fantasizing about the mermaids), "The Mermaid," stanza II, fuses both concerns and explores them simultaneously.

## The Manyfaced Glass

*I would be a mermaid fair;*
*I would sing to myself the whole of the day;*
*With a comb of pearl I would comb my hair;*
*And still as I combed I would sing and say,*
*"Who is it loves me? who loves not me?"*
*I would comb my hair till my ringlets would fall*
  *Low adown, low adown,*
*From under my starry sea-bud crown*
  *Low adown and around,*
*And I should look like a fountain of gold*
  *Springing alone*
  *With a shrill inner sound,*
  *Over the throne*
  *In the midst of the hall.*

The "mermaid's" attractiveness is part of the power of her song and vice versa. Whereas the speaker of "The Merman" seeks centrifugal power—the bold voice and the bold kiss—the speaker of "The Mermaid" desires the centripetal power of passivity, the ability to attract and enthrall. This difference is part of the sexual debate between the two speakers but also part of an artistic debate: the female speaker finds her art satisfying and does not abandon the issue of singing as soon as she mentions it.

But although her answer to the "merman's" vaunted sexual boldness is sharp and pleasingly saucy—"I would not be kissed by all who would list, / Of the bold merry mermen under the sea" (lines 41–42)—she also reveals her ethical immaturity. She would use her powers of attraction only to subdue and destroy, not to create and unify: her song would arouse the slumbering sea snake who could only gaze passively at her. Worse, "all the mermen under the sea / Would feel their immortality / Die in their hearts for the love of me" (lines 28–30). Her childish egocentrism is apparent even in her diction. In "The Merman" there are five "me's" and three "we's"; in "The Mermaid" there are seventeen "me's" and only one "we." If, then, the female's mature sexuality highlights the boyishness of the male's sexuality, his desire for a form of community damns by implication her childish narcissism. Ironically, however, the "mermaid's" moral culpability creates the more sophisticated poem. "The Merman" seems less powerful, less resonant, than "The Mermaid." The reason is not far to seek. The male sings less to himself and more to others, which means he is oriented toward the realm of personality. But the female, singing more to herself than to another, anchors her song in the realm of consciousness. Consequently, her song allows more ingress to Tennyson's peculiar form of sympathetic imagination, and the poem is richer as a result.

Still, the pairing of these poems is important. With the more complicated interactions of the "Mermaid" poems Tennyson could explore *aspects* of himself—his desire for, yet distrust of, sensual indulgence, for example—without being forced to seek a resolution. He could also supersede the black-and-white contrasts of his earliest poems, where youth is a time of enchantment and adulthood a time of bleak disillusionment, and explore the gray areas in between—and as we know from "Tithonus," the gray or twilight areas of experience are Tennyson's forte. Further, by freeing himself from simplistic oppositions, Tennyson could become more objective and detached. He need no longer use the inherent distancing of the dramatic monologue as a defense, as he perhaps does in the "Exile" poems, but could exploit the form's distancing effect to chart new areas. These paired poems, then, show another instance of rendered consciousness and of Tennyson's ability to maintain the dramatic monologue's feint.

"The Ballad of Oriana," if not highly regarded now, enjoyed something of a vogue in Tennyson's time. FitzGerald has recorded his vivid impression of Tennyson's reciting the poem at Cambridge.[17] But the poem did not depend on the "hollow oes and aes" of Tennyson's recitations for its effect. When in 1849 Tennyson, at the request of Mrs. Gaskell, presented a copy of his poems to Samuel Bamford (a Lancashire weaver, author, and fervent admirer of Tennyson), Bamford wrote back to Tennyson to praise, among other poems, "Oriana": "Oh! your 'Oriana' has started the tears into my eyes, and into those of my dear wife, many a time. It is a deep thing" (*Memoir*, I, 286). "Oriana" is also one of the relatively few poems from the 1830 volume that Tennyson continued to reprint all his life.

Undoubtedly, as others have claimed,[18] the poem was begun as a technical experiment to see how far Tennyson could push the limits of a refrain, until the repeated phrase ("Oriana," of

51

course) ceased to be a mere echo and became something more. The poem is thus intensely lyric. Indeed, some may be surprised to see "Oriana" treated as a dramatic monologue at all. The poem does, however, feature a first-person speaker other than the poet. More important, Tennyson gives play to a subtle psychological development in the speaker as the poem progresses. Yet I do not wish to de-emphasize the lyric quality of the poem: I wish to stress it. For it is the fusion of the lyric and dramatic in "Oriana" that gives the poem its importance in this study. Tennyson had discovered in "Oriana" a technique he was to pursue on a much larger and more complex scale in *Maud*, whose triumph is precisely the fusion of the lyric and dramatic.

Tennyson even manipulates landscape in "Oriana" as he was to do in *Maud*. After the speaker begins by stating his heart's desolation and woe, he continues,

> *When the long dun wolds are ribbed with snow,*
> *And loud the Norland whirlwinds blow,*
>   *Oriana,*
> *Alone I wander to and fro,*
>   *Oriana.*

(lines 5–9)

Here we see Tennyson's familiar recourse to the pathetic fallacy. The speaker sees the same desolation in nature ("long dun wolds") that resides within; and the reference to the wolds "ribbed with snow" calls to mind the "red-ribbed ledges [that] drip with a silent horror of blood" in *Maud*. Both poems evoke, through the image of dessicated ribs, the ravages of death, only the speaker of "Oriana" sees all in terms of his frozen emotions (hence the repetition of Oriana's name—it is all he *can* express at this time) whereas the hero of *Maud* projects his heated psychological violence onto the landscape.

More important than landscape imagery, however, is, as in the later *Maud*, Tennyson's use of lyric elements—particularly the repetition of the word *Oriana*—to plumb and reveal the speaker's consciousness. At first, as in the lines quoted above, *Oriana* clearly functions as a mode of address, and Oriana appears to be an auditor. Only later do we discover that hers is a ghostly, and not entirely benign, presence. Our first hint of this comes when *Oriana* ceases to be a mode of address and becomes an appositive, as the speaker tries to evade his overwhelming sense of guilt and anguish by temporarily banishing Oriana to the realm of third-person reference, the world of the Other.

> *She stood upon the castle wall,*
>   *Oriana:*
> *She watched my crest among them all,*
>   *Oriana:*
> *She saw me fight, she heard me call. . . .*

> *(lines 28–32)*

The lines are no longer transitive but tautological, with the line's last word looping back to the first. The lines go nowhere because the speaker cannot face the next phase of his narrative. Only when a figure appears on whom the speaker can displace his guilt—"forth there stept a foeman tall . . . Atween me and the castle wall"—does the speaker again address Oriana as a "thou." But the "thou" returns with a slight difference. The emotional gradient of the poem rises as Oriana becomes the speaker's confessor: "The damnèd arrow glanced aside, / And pierced thy heart . . . my life, my love, my bride, / Oriana!" (lines 41–43).

From here Oriana is subtly and gradually transformed from confessor into haunting ghost in the speaker's mind, for to his inner vision Oriana "smilest, but . . . dost not speak." When he cries "What wantest thou? whom dost thou seek,/Oriana?" the only reply is the hollow echo of his own voice.

> *I cry aloud: none hear my cries,*
>   *Oriana.*
> *Thou comest atween me and the skies,*
>   *Oriana.*

> *(lines 73–76)*

It is a chilling commentary that the presence of Oriana now steps between the speaker and the heavens as the foeman did between the speaker and Oriana. She has become victimizer as well as victim in the speaker's mind, foe as well as beloved. Her haunting presence and the speaker's emotional (and verbal) paralysis combine to drive the speaker to the verge of madness, a frightening realm of undifferentiated, meaningless echoes:

> *I dare not die and come to thee,*
>   *Oriana.*
> *I hear the roaring of the sea,*
>   *Oriana.*

(*lines 96–99*)

The assonance and internal rhyme of "roaring" and "Oriana" in these closing lines are not accidental; finally "roaring" and "Oriana" mean the same thing, as if the speaker were condemned to hold his ear to an empty shell forever.[19] Tennyson has adapted the lyric (and balladic) device of the refrain to dramatize his speaker's descent into madness.

The verbal and psychological subtlety of "Oriana" suggests another 1830 poem, "Mariana."[20] If not so fine as "Mariana," neither is "Oriana" so bad a poem as some think. The comparison of the two, however, is valuable not so much as an exercise in judgment as in clarifying one other form of technical advance in *Poems, Chiefly Lyrical*, Tennyson's skill in choosing a dramatic versus a narrative or lyric format for a poem. Both the speaker of "Oriana" and Mariana suffer from a form of emotional and psychological imprisonment, an imprisonment refracted through the obsessive refrains of the poems. Moreover, although Mariana does not narrate her own poem, the landscape, as readers since John Stuart Mill have noted, is perceived through the medium of her consciousness. Mill praised Tennyson for his "power of *creating* scenery, in keeping with some state of human feeling; so fitted to it as to be the embodied symbol of it, and to summon up the state of feeling itself, with a force not to be surpassed by anything but reality."[21] This mode of creating landscape reached its culmination in *Maud*. Why, then, is "Mariana" not also a dramatic monologue? To ask this question is to see Tennyson's stroke of genius in making "Mariana" a third-person narrative. In keeping with Mariana's utter desolation, passivity, and entrapment, she is not even given direct access to her own perceptions.[22] Instead, the narrator's language encrusts the burden of her refrain as surely as the black moss encrusts the flower-plots.

With "Oriana" the case is entirely different. The speaker of "Oriana" is constrained, not by what is without—by a lover who fails to appear—but by what is within, the memory of a dead face that can transform itself into a haunting and even threatening spirit. Accordingly, just as the poet approaches Mariana from without, in the guise of third-person narration, so he approaches the speaker of "Oriana" from within, via the dramatic monologue. Thus "Oriana" not only looks ahead to *Maud*, where Tennyson further developed the means for rendering consciousness first used in the 1830 ballad, but also suggests Tennyson's more mature grasp of the technical advantages of the dramatic monologue versus the lyric or narrative form.

Another notable quality of "Oriana" is that one cannot easily detect Tennyson's participation in the poem. If the diagrams of chapter one were applied to this poem, the lines radiating toward the speaker and the spoken would be darkest, and the recursive loop that denotes the poet's participation would be only faintly suggested. Presumably Tennyson participates in the poem; otherwise he could not render the consciousness of his speaker from the inside, as the *Ding an Mich*. But the very haziness of this personal participation signals the growing maturity of Tennyson's dramatic monologues. First, Tennyson in "Oriana" activates all at once the elements of the speaker, the shaping of the spoken, the auditor, the poet's personal participation, and, one hopes, the reader's response. Second, "Oriana" shares with the mature dramatic monologues the poet's turning away from seemingly self-absorbed and obsessive exploration, as in Tennyson's earliest monologues, to a more outward-facing and objective art.

It is above all in "Supposed Confessions," however, that Tennyson is "the sower and the seed," able to remain in himself yet become an other, to fuse objective fiction and subjective participation. For this reason the poem is often cited as a failed dramatic monologue: many critics contend that the voice of the speaker is not adequately distanced from Tennyson's own, that the "Supposed" in the title is a mere ruse. The charge arises

because in this poem Tennyson has achieved his most characteristic strategy with the dramatic monologue, the rendering of
consciousness, clearly evident from the vacillations that provide
the poem's structure as well as its closing lines. Moreover, Tennyson's entry into the speaker depends on the kind of imaginative sympathy Hallam had described in his essay, whereby an
other is explored as an aspect of self. No wonder so many readers have difficulty distinguishing the speaker from Tennyson:
beyond the fact that Tennyson explores an aspect of self in
order to explore the speaker, he centers the poem in that amorphous, hazy world of consciousness, whose boundaries are so
much less discrete than those of personality. Yet to argue that
the work is actually a lyric effusion parading under the title of a
dramatic piece is to miss the genuine distancing, the fiction, of
the poem. If the poem explores modes of religious doubt Tennyson himself experienced—or so *In Memoriam* suggests[23]—the
presence of an additional theme gives Tennyson a larger perspective than the speaker can possibly have.

This theme is one shared by the "Mermaid" poems, the trials
and challenges encountered by one moving from the realm of
childhood to adulthood. While at Cambridge Tennyson wrote to
his Aunt Elizabeth Russell, "What a pity it is that the golden
days of Faerie are over! What a misery not to be able to consoli-
date our gossamer dreams into reality!" (*Memoir*, I, 34). In this
letter he both admits the appeal of childhood imagination and
shows his reluctant awareness of a larger and more complicated
reality. The speaker of "Supposed Confessions" is caught between the realms of "Faerie" and "reality": proud of his ability to
surpass the narrow, enclosed world of the child, he is frightened
and disoriented by the complexities and uncertainties of adult
perception. Perhaps this poising between two realms reflects
the divisions of Tennyson's own childhood loyalties, his simultaneous kinship with the intellectual but gloomy, morbid, and
undisciplined world of his father and the simple, unthinking,
emotional faith held by his mother. That he would have been
able to portray this conflict would certainly suggest he had
moved beyond it and so could achieve dramatic distance in the
poem.

"Supposed Confessions," then, deals with issues of religious doubt only insofar as these doubts are linked to the speaker's painful transition from childhood to adulthood.[24] The poem's central lines in this respect are those describing the world of the child.

> *He hath no care of life or death;*
> *Scarce outward signs of joy arise,*
> *Because the Spirit of happiness*
> *And perfect rest so inward is;*
> *And loveth so his innocent heart,*
> *Her temple and her place of birth,*
> *Where she would ever wish to dwell,*
> *Life of the fountain there, beneath*
> *Its salient springs, and far apart,*
> *Hating to wander out on earth,*
> *Or breathe into the hollow air,*
> *Whose chillness would make visible*
> *Her subtil, warm, and golden breath,*
> *Which mixing with the infant's blood,*
> *Fulfils him with beatitude.*
>
> (lines 48–62)

The insistent enclosure of the child's world in these lines suggests limitation as well as protection, and this redounds on poems like "The Merman" and "The Mermaid," in which we also encounter an escape from the world of everyday reality to a self-enclosed world under the sea and where a fountain is associated with one who sees the self as the center of the universe.

More important, the speaker's troubled relation to his mother and his uneasy stance between the worlds of adult and child cause the issue of identity to be central to the poem. This issue is most apparent when the speaker cries amidst his feeling that he has betrayed his dead mother, "Myself? Is it thus? Myself?" (line 87).[25] This unease about his identity so infuses the speaker's consciousness that it infiltrates even his language. When in the opening passage he tries to remind himself of what Christianity means to mankind, he says that it includes "Goodwill to me as well as all— / I one of them: my brothers they: / Brothers in Christ" (lines 27–29). Were Tennyson not writing a dramatic monologue, one would be tempted to say he had lost control of his language. The idea of Christian fellowship is clear enough in "Goodwill to me as well as all" without needing to be elaborated by three successive phrases. The elaboration, however, is precisely what enables Tennyson to render his speaker's consciousness. Note that each of the three elaborating phrases—"I one of them: my brothers they: Brothers in Christ"—is an appositive. In other words, the speaker is attempting to name, to identify, himself and his relation to believers. That he has so much trouble naming this relation points to his underlying religious doubts; that he has trouble naming himself points to his doubts about his own identity.

The issue of identity is also made clear through Tennyson's skillful use of allusion. Rejecting his mother's charge (or the one he imagines her making) that he suffers from spiritual pride, the speaker rejoins, "I think that pride hath now no place / Nor sojourn in me. I am void, / Dark, formless, utterly destroyed" (lines 120–22). Surely the lines are a deliberate echo of Genesis 1:2, "The earth was without form, and void, and darkness was upon the face of the deep." The allusion is a way, then, of suggesting that the speaker, unbeknownst to himself, is in the process of *creating* an identity for himself. He is not there yet, hence his pain, but he has far transcended his simple childhood self. Indeed, only because the childhood self has been destroyed can he begin to create his adult identity.

Of course, the allusion also underscores the fact that the speaker cannot entirely turn his back on his mother's faith. Even while he withholds complete assent to Christianity, he (unknowingly, one guesses) cites its sacred text. But the Genesis allusion itself is counteracted by another account of creation. When the speaker describes his first deliberate step away from his enclosed childhood world, his quest for religious truth in the face of doubt, he uses a metaphor to describe Truth that captures the very source of conflict that makes the adult world so painful to the speaker, the scientific account of creation that throws Genesis into doubt.

> "It is man's privilege to doubt,
> If so be that from doubt at length,
> Truth may stand forth unmoved of change,
> An image with profulgent brows,
> And perfect limbs, as from the storm

> *Of running fires and fluid range*
> *Of lawless airs, at last stood out*
> *This excellence and solid form*
> *Of constant beauty."*

(lines 142–50)

These examples show how fully Tennyson has mastered his own chosen medium: the speaker's every utterance redounds upon his dilemma, his suspension between doubt and faith, adulthood and childhood, allegiance to himself and allegiance to his mother. This recursiveness is almost a joke: the speaker thoroughly explores his consciousness without being aware that he has done so. Perhaps it is in this respect that his is a "second-rate mind."

Tennyson, however, is very much aware of the speaker's essential state, and this awareness provides the poem's aesthetic distance. One need only think back to "Remorse" to see how far Tennyson had come in 1830. The difference between the two poems constitutes a poetic rite of passage in itself, as Tennyson travels from the undifferentiated outpourings of the earlier poem to the concrete, wholly realized utterance of a given consciousness in "Supposed Confessions." This transition was made possible in part, it seems, by Tennyson's own psychological growth. As Sir Charles Tennyson notes, although the poem seems highly personal, the mere fact of publication implies that Tennyson "regarded the mood as something which he had definitely put behind him" (90–91). He had learned, in other words, to be highly personal and highly objective at the same time. He had learned the dynamics, that is, of the Tennysonian dramatic monologue.

More important, "Supposed Confessions" reflects Tennyson's mastery of techniques underlying his most characteristic dramatic monologues. He dramatizes the speaker's consciousness, letting the poem take its shape from the oscillations of the speaker's mind and skillfully controlling language to delineate further the speaker's mind state. In so doing, Tennyson gives attention at once to the elements of the speaker and the spoken as they appear in the diagrams of chapter one. The poem is also shaped to invite the active participation of the reader since we must sympathize with the speaker if we are to discern not only the poem's religious issues but also the psychological dilemma that underlies the speaker's religious crisis. Finally, through the sympathetic imagination Tennyson conceives the speaker as an aspect of self, activating the recursive loop to explore and merge simultaneously his own and the speaker's consciousness. The poet's "I" and the poem's fiction are thus equally compelling, and the feint is sustained. Having learned to overcome the fractured feint of his earliest dramatic poems, Tennyson in 1830 had mastered and expanded the medium of the dramatic monologue. Having become the "sower and the seed," he was ready for wider fields.

# 3. Beautiful Other Worlds: The Dramatic Monologues of 1832 and 1842

*Distinct in individualities,*
*A various world! which he compelled once more*
*Through his own nature, with well mingled hues,*
*Into another shape, born of the first,*
*As beautiful, but yet another world.*

—*"The Ante-Chamber" (1834)*

By 1834, "The Ante-Chamber" suggests, Tennyson had become highly conscious of the poetic process involved in creating his speaking portraits: the painter Eustace (to whom the lines of my epigraph refer) fuses self and other in creating his portraits on canvas just as Tennyson did in his dramatic monologues. The 1832 and 1842 dramatic monologues thus sustained the achievement of the 1830 volume. With minor exceptions, the new dramatic monologues reveal Tennyson in complete control of the form's feint, the fusion of the pole of fiction and the poet's "I." Even in a poem like "Ulysses," which Tennyson himself avowed was deeply personal, the independent fictiveness of his speaker is fully maintained. And the rendering of consciousness remains Tennyson's most characteristic approach to dramatizing his speakers, particularly in the best monologues of this period.

But Tennyson also extended his use of the monologue form in several ways. First, simply because he had mastered the dramatic monologue's feint, he was free to extend the poems' range. That is, having learned to integrate smoothly the pole of fiction and the poet's "I," Tennyson could now open up and expand his fictive worlds to achieve new breadth and flexibility. In the new volumes, accordingly, we encounter the first of Tennyson's classical monologues, in which Tennyson adapts the materials of classical myth to the dramatic monologue. At first, in "Oenone," this integration was clumsy, but Tennyson quickly assimilated these materials and, in so doing, tapped one of the richest veins of his poetic inspiration. The classical monologues have the advantage of conferring upon the speaker an inherent fictiveness through the independent tradition of myth. Tennyson could establish the speaker in his or her own right with a few broad strokes, then focus on rendering the speaker's consciousness and on activating the recursive loop to create poems at once objective and suffused with the intensity of Tennyson's own participation. Tennyson also looked to his own age for the materials of his monologues and could address broad issues of his own day—the crisis of faith, the role of art, the ills of a mercenary society—yet avoid didacticism or breast-beating by remaining at once fictive and sincere. Thus we encounter such poems as "St. Simeon Stylites," "Will Waterproof," and "Locksley Hall."

The 1832 and 1842 dramatic monologues also reveal Tennyson's growing awareness of and interest in the role of the reader in the dramatic monologue. This development, like the enlargement of his fictive frames of reference, may have been due as much to Tennyson's increasing confidence and audience as to conscious refinement of technique. Still, this attention to the reader's role created a proliferation of new poetic strategies and forms within the dramatic monologue genre. On one hand, for example, this period saw the emergence of Tennyson's domestic monologues (for example, "The Miller's Daughter"), notable less for their rendering of consciousness or fusion of subjective and objective than for their deliberate shaping to engage the reader's sympathies and emotions, to move the reader. In works like "The Lotos-Eaters" and "Ulysses," on the other hand, Tennyson shaped poems that invite the reader's active participation in the process of the poem; separate and seemingly contrary strands of consciousness are deliberately juxtaposed, and the reader is left to find coherence or connection among them.

Tennyson also created poems with a distinct satiric thrust, as with "St. Simeon Stylites" or "Amphion," in which the recursive loop for both poet and reader is suspended at least in part and in which the spoken is shaped to invite the reader's judgment more than the reader's emotional response or participation.

Finally, the monologues of 1832 and 1842 reflect Tennyson's continuing and refined awareness of the formal properties of the dramatic monologue (versus the lyric or narrative) and their implications for meaning. For example, the implied pastness of the narrative form versus the ongoing present of the dramatic monologue is exploited in poems as diverse as "The Gardener's Daughter" and "The Hesperides" to create part of the poems' very meaning: the medium is truly part of the message. This new development in Tennyson's dramatic monologues is especially apparent in the contrast between two of Tennyson's best poems of the period, the dramatic monologue "Ulysses" and the narrative "Morte d'Arthur." Toward the end of this period he also began to create multiple perspectives in a single poem, as if expanding upon the dramatic monologue's inherent dual perspective (through the feint) to see how far this element could be taken. This last development not only gave rise to such poems as "Edwin Morris" but also prepared for Tennyson's next poetic enterprise, the long poems of the 1840s and 1850s.

In sustaining the achievement of the 1830 dramatic monologues while introducing an enlarged fictive world, increased attention to the reader, and heightened sensitivity to form itself, the dramatic monologues of 1832 and 1842 give proof of Tennyson's "variety, abundance, and complete competence" perceived by Eliot. To appreciate this advance, we must look at the poems in detail. These works can best be approached by dividing them into groups into which they naturally fall: dramatic monologues related to Tennyson's female portraits and domestic poems, the classical monologues, and those that feature a contemporary setting and examine major social issues of the day.

## II

The first group of poems—"Fatima," "The Sisters," "The May Queen," "The Miller's Daughter," and "The Gardener's Daughter"—all grew out of the female portraits that Tennyson began to publish in 1830. Despite their common source, however, the new poems differ in strategy. "Fatima" and "The Sisters" are notable for Tennyson's rendering of the speakers' consciousnesses whereas "The May Queen" and its successors shift away from the pole of the speaker to the pole of the spoken and the emotional effect of that utterance on the reader. "The Miller's Daughter" and "The Gardener's Daughter" share the affective function of Tennyson's domestic monologues, but they are also important for the skill with which Tennyson uses the formal properties of the dramatic monologue versus those of the narrative and lyric.

The 1830 female portraits (for example, "Lilian," "Claribel," "Isabel") are not dramatic monologues; typically a male speaker who cannot be distinguished from the poet addresses and characterizes the sundry women of the titles. Nor, despite the attention lavished on them, do these women seem palpable. As Tennyson himself said, "All these ladies were evolved, like the camel, from my own consciousness."[1] Yet in this comment perhaps lies a hint of why Arthur Hallam admired these poems, and why he observed, shrewdly, that they were "a graft of the lyric on the dramatic" (197). In the portraits Tennyson attempts to harmonize mood, image, and character, though the general insipidity of the females suggests that these first portraits were little more than poetic exercises. But a change occurred in 1832, when Tennyson allowed his females to speak for themselves and so to enter the arena of the dramatic monologue.

"Fatima" bursts into the gallery of Tennyson's other demure maidens with much the same effect as a belly dancer in full regalia might have had who invaded a tea given by Queen Victoria. Alone among all Tennyson's women, Fatima seethes with sexual passion and is allowed to express that passion without being undercut by the text. More to the point, Tennyson makes effective use of the dramatic monologue to convey this passion. Fatima's is as yet unfulfilled passion, and the intensity of her desire coupled with her frustration has almost unhinged her mind, a point aptly rendered through the odd twists and turnings of her consciousness. Blinding heat and light dominate her monologue, suggesting both the presumably Arabian setting and the urgency of her desire. She herself is unable to distinguish between setting and self,[2] as we see in the first stanza.

> *O Love, Love, Love! O withering might!*
> *O sun, that from thy noonday height*
> *Shudderest when I strain my sight,*
> *Throbbing through all thy heat and light,*
>     *Lo, falling from my constant mind,*
>     *Lo, parched and withered, deaf and blind,*
>     *I whirl like leaves in roaring wind.*

Her love, conceivably, is given to shuddering, but if she means also the literal sun, the statement is not quite logical—and aptly so. She has indeed fallen away from a "constant mind," whirled away by the intensity of her sexual obsession.

The poem's final stanza underscores the confusion of a mind dissolved before physical desires. Throughout most of the poem Fatima speaks as one who is scorched, withered, whirled by the fire of love. Suddenly, however, she *is* also that fire, that sun poised in the sky, subject and object all at once.

> *My whole soul waiting silently,*
> *All naked in a sultry sky,*
> *Droops blinded with his shining eye:*
> *I will possess him or will die.*

The dislocations in perspective are a rendering from within of the dislocations of her own consciousness.[3]

Fatima is a Mariana in reverse: both are becoming deranged by the absence of their lovers, but Mariana's is the madness of unending isolation and the caged self, Fatima's of unending anticipation and unleashed desire that must crush the very flowers (line 12) in its frenzy. Fatima is thus presented through the medium of the dramatic monologue, which, like Fatima herself, is poised on the boundary between isolation (the solitary speaking voice) and the larger world (the world of the reader and, potentially, the auditor)—unlike Mariana, who, encased within narrative form, can never have direct, unmediated expression.

"The Sisters," also published in 1832, fuses the deranged sexuality of "Fatima" with the formal and psychological properties of the balladic form Tennyson had earlier worked out in "The Ballad of Oriana." The speaker's consciousness is rendered less through Fatima's dislocations of perspective than through details of the story and modulations of the refrain. The speaker's sister was seduced and abandoned by "the Earl" and died not long after. To avenge her sister, the speaker has in turn seduced the Earl and killed him—but not before responding to his physical allure. Her story is thus a perverse mixture of jealousy ("She was the fairest in the face"—line 2) and grief for her sister ("She died: she went to burning flame"—line 7); of hatred and desire for the Earl ("I hated him with the hate of hell, / But I loved his beauty passing well"—lines 22–23). So much, in fact, did Tennyson want to underscore the sexuality of the poem that he uncustomarily revised a draft to make the finished version more, not less, sexually charged. In the seduction scene an early draft merely had the speaker say, "Upon my heart he laid his head"[4]—intimate, yes, but quite conventional. In the published version the speaker says, "Upon my lap he laid his head." The Earl is clearly voyaging into forbidden territory, and this detail helps intensify and prepare for the speaker's ultimate response to the Earl, one of fused violence and desire.

> *As half-asleep his breath he drew,*
> *Three times I stabbed him through and through.*
> *O the Earl was fair to see!*
>
> *I curled and combed his comely head,*
> *He looked so grand when he was dead.*

> *(lines 28–32)*

This ultimate response is at once maternal, oddly phallic (through the juxtaposition of stabbing and loving), impassive, and impassioned. Clearly she is mad, and it is no surprise that at least one critic has argued that the poem influenced Browning's "Porphyria's Lover."[5]

Her madness is made clearer because, as in "Oriana," Tennyson merges the pathetic fallacy and the lyric device of the refrain. For the most part the speaker relates her story in the past tense, locking the action into the world of what is past and done.

In each stanza, however, she comments on the wind in the present tense, and this refrain is the true barometer of her mind in the lasting present world of the dramatic monologue. At first the wind is merely "blowing in turret and tree"; it is "howling" as she relates her sister's death, "roaring" as she brings the Earl home, "raging" as she approaches the murder, and finally "raving" as she actually kills him. In the final stanza the wind is once more simply "blowing," but by now we know what is really "blowing" through "turret and tree," the speaker's own blighted consciousness, cut loose and set adrift under the pressure of powerful conflicting emotions.

Compared to "Fatima" and "The Sisters," "The May Queen" is quite tame, and most readers would probably welcome some perversity in the poem to relieve what now seems its excess sentimentality. But "The May Queen" represents a different poetic strategy, for this and similar poems mark the beginning of Tennyson's domestic poetry, a vein that has received increasing attention of late.[6] These poems in general attempt not so much to trace the oscillations of consciousness but to appeal to and enlarge the sympathies of the reader. The dramatic monologues written in this vein, that is, gravitate toward the pole of fiction, or objectivity, with Tennyson keeping his eyes on the reader more than on himself, and away from the pole of subjectivity, or the poet's "I."[7]

Tennyson evokes subtle pathos as he moves from the poem's first section (set in May) to the second (set in December, on New Year's Eve). Many have noted Alice's pride in the first, so absorbed in her village triumph as May Queen that she is indifferent to the languishings of her would-be lover Robin. She is not really evil, simply proud of the life and beauty that blossom in her and that answer to the May without, beauties to which Alice is far from indifferent: "All the valley, mother, 'ill be fresh and green and still, / And the cowslip and the crowfoot are over all the hill, / And the rivulet in the flowery dale 'ill merrily glance and play" (I, 37–39).[8] This same love for nature creates the pathos of the following section, entitled "New-Year's Eve." Here Alice is no longer peremptory ("You must wake and call me early, call me early, mother dear"—I, 1) but precatory ("If you're

67

waking call me early . . . mother dear"—II, 1), chastened by an approaching death that makes her realize just what she must relinquish.

> *When the flowers come again, mother, beneath the waning light*
> *You'll never see me more in the long gray fields at night;*
> *When from the dry dark wold the summer airs blow cool*
> *On the oat-grass and the sword-grass, and the bulrush in the pool.*
>
> (II, 25–28)

The reader seems invited by such passages, not to judge or extoll Alice, but to be moved by her plight and perhaps to think of the reader's own mortality that binds him or her to the speaker.

Tennyson's recourse to this kind of poetry has been much commented upon, and the usual reasons given, the pressure exerted by the reviewers, the Apostles, and the age as a whole on Tennyson to come out of his palace of art and address his peers, seem quite right. Tennyson may once again have been particularly influenced by Arthur Hallam. In his essay on sympathy Hallam could be said to discuss the pathos on which "The May Queen" turns and to suggest how this creation of pathos could find some links with both the poet's and the reader's consciousnesses.

> The perception of suffering in another interferes with our satisfaction in contemplating him, and . . . this contrast produces pain. Besides, as the image of his enjoyment recalled images, and thereby awoke realities of pleasure in ourselves, so the perception of suffering makes us recollect our own suffering, and causes us to suffer. Thus by a second chain of associated feelings, the soul arrives at the same result, at union of joys and sorrows, in other words, at sympathy. (135)

Moreover, in another "Essay on the Philosophical Writings of Cicero" (written in 1831), Hallam further connects this exercise of feeling both with proper perception of psychology ("the man who is deficient in susceptibility of emotion will make a sorry survey of mental phenomena"—163) and morality: "In spite of . . . grievous errors . . . there was this merit in the Epicurean theory, that it laid the basis of morality in the right quarter. Sentiment, not thought, was declared the motive power: the agent acted from feeling, and *was* by feeling: thoughts were but

the ligatures that held together the delicate materials of emotion" (167). It is logical that, faced with the demand that he address morality and the age in his poetry, Tennyson would have
taken the path of sentiment toward this function, an avenue
suggested not only generally by the legacy of the Romantic poets but explicitly by Hallam.

The function of "The May Queen" as an appeal to the reader's
emotions is made clearer by its contrasts with a probable source,
George Darley's *Sylvia; or, The May Queen*, published in 1827.[9]
Although *Sylvia* never enjoyed wide popularity, it was esteemed
among many literati, including Coleridge and Elizabeth Bar-
rett.[10] Tennyson clearly knew Darley's work, of which he speaks
respectfully in a letter to Richard Monckton Milnes (himself a
friend of both Darley and Tennyson) in January 1837.[11] There is
even an account, never verified, that Tennyson, "whose own
early lyrics were yet young, was so struck by Darley's power,
that he volunteered to defray the cost of publishing his verse."[12]

Darley's *Sylvia* would naturally have attracted Tennyson.
Notable for his lyricism and metrical virtuosity, Darley experi-
mented with irregular meters that recall Tennyson's similar
practice in a poem like "The Sea-Fairies." In a way that anticipates Tennyson's own mixing of forms from the 1832 volume
onward, Darley also mixed forms with abandon; *Sylvia* combines
prose, blank verse, lyrics, songs, dialogue, soliloquies—and
more. Similarities in plot exist between Darley's and Tennyson's May Queen poems as well. Sylvia lives alone with her
mother, whom she loves and frequently addresses, as does
Alice. *Sylvia; or, The May Queen* even features a symbolic death
and rebirth of the May Queen, and her lover Romanzo is at one
point led to think he has been abandoned and betrayed by her.
Finally, the imagery and rhythm of one of Darley's intercalated
songs, sung by the village peasants to Sylvia when she is
crowned Queen of the May, bear a loose resemblance to those of
Tennyson's poem, as the excerpt below demonstrates:

> *There's a bank with rich cowslips, and cuckoo-buds strewn,*
>   *To exalt your bright looks, gentle Queen of the May;*
> *Here's a cushion of moss for your delicate shoon,*
>   *And a woodbine to weave you a canopy gay!*

. . . . . . . . . . . . . . . . . . . . . . . . . . . . .

*Then around you we'll dance, and around you we'll sing!*
*To soft pipe, and sweet tabor we'll foot it away!*
*And the hills, and the vales, and the forests shall ring*
*While we hail you our lovely young Queen of the May!*

(111)

But a striking difference separates Darley's and Tennyson's works: Darley's setting for his dramatic poem is artificial and emphatically literary, complete with fairy machinery obviously indebted to Shakespeare's *Midsummer Night's Dream*. Only one contemporary note is struck in the entire poem, when Darley has Andrea, servant to Romanzo and a buffoon modeled on Bottom,[13] mention political reform in reference to the personal reform that will come with his marriage ("reform!—it is the order of the day, and shall be radical in my constitution"—198). Darley's poem, then, appeals to the reader's refined aesthetic sensibility, not emotional sensitivity. Perhaps Tennyson's "May Queen" came into being because Tennyson wanted to work his own reform on Darley, making a kind of verse and subject matter he admired in *Sylvia* more accessible to the age by giving it an emphatically contemporary setting and appeal (the literary "Sylvia" is domesticated into plain countryside "Alice").[14] If so, Tennyson succeeded, moving John Stuart Mill to declare, "This poem is fitted for a more extensive popularity than any other in the two volumes. Simple, genuine pathos, arising out of the situations and feelings common to mankind generally, is of all kinds of poetic beauty that which can be most universally appreciated. . . . In this poem there is not only the truest pathos, but . . . perfect harmony and keeping."[15]

But of course Mill was speaking of the 1832, not the 1842, version. Tennyson ruined the delicate pathos of the 1832 version when he attached the bathetic Conclusion with its heavy-handed sententiousness: "But still I think it can't be long before I find release; / And that good man, the clergyman, has told me words of peace" (lines 11–12). James Kincaid is right to claim that "in the Conclusion Tennyson almost risks humor by having little Alice still around" (223) after the more fitting close of the "New-Year's Eve" section. Tennyson's erring judgment in adding the Conclusion certainly proves that, if even Homer nods,

Tennyson could sometimes sleep—and snore. But one can fathom private reasons for the addition. By 1842, with Hallam dead at the age of twenty-three, perhaps Tennyson found his earlier portrait of a blossoming life suddenly cut down too painful and added a kind of benediction: "To lie within the light of God, as I lie upon your breast— / And the wicked cease from troubling, and the weary are at rest" (lines 59–60). The problem is that the benediction is dissonant with the rest of the poem in content and technique. The 1832 sections of "The May Queen" are essentially pagan: they are about the waxing and waning of the life force and the pain of an individual consciousness experiencing the contrast. The stock phrases of a Christian tract in the 1842 Conclusion are both cloying in themselves and fundamentally at odds with the preceding sections. More relevant to this study, the dramatic techniques of the Conclusion and the 1832 sections seem at odds. If Tennyson shifted the 1832 poem toward the pole of fiction, he could not add a section redolent of the poet's "I" without simply imposing this new section on extant verses. Tennyson's participation in his dramatic monologues usually enhanced the evocativeness and immediacy of these poems. But in "The May Queen," what seems a personal entry into the poem betrays him into the fractured feint of his earliest works. When Alice shifts from pathos to preaching, the fiction of her fragility—and beauty—is exploded.

We encounter another Alice in "The Miller's Daughter." Here, however, Alice's husband is the speaker, who looks back over the years during which the couple wooed, wedded, and have so long lived together. Some have objected to the sentimentality of "The Miller's Daughter," but the poem is far less sentimental than its source, Mary Russell Mitford's "Queen of the Meadow," a tale of courtship and love seen in its first blossoming.[16] Tennyson's speaker tells the story from the vantage point of age, when both husband and wife face death. In fact, Tennyson has carefully shaped the poem (especially the 1842 version) to mingle the simultaneous joys and sorrows associated with sympathy as defined by Hallam; and once more the whole point of the poem seems to be to encourage the reader's sympathetic participation in that mingling.[17] Not coincidentally, with such an aim, the poem has an underlying democratic ethos (as did Tennyson's source) since the poem demonstrates that there is no bar to sympathy and love between the son of a squire and a miller's daughter.

The poem reflects not only Tennyson's growing objectivity and interest in his audience and the age but also, in its final form, his sensitivity to the implications of the dramatic monologue and other forms. His reworking of the 1832 version shows a firm sense of direction as he strengthened the poem's fictive world to reinforce the poem's theme, the passage of time and consequent loss versus the warmth and sweetness of love early and late. In 1832, for example, the speaker when young was "son and heir unto the squire"; in 1842 the youth's father has lately died, so that his dawning love for Alice is a recovery that compensates the other loss. In 1832 no obstacles faced the young lovers; in 1842 the mother thought "I might have looked a little higher," but overcomes disappointment because of her love for her son and all he loves. Similarly, Tennyson added in 1842 the loss of a child to offset the otherwise unalloyed marital bliss of the 1832 version ("Although the loss had brought us pain, / That loss but made us love the more") and substituted for a rather innocuous intercalated song on the forget-me-not one that directly faces the threat to love posed by the passage of time.

> *Love that hath us in the net,*
> *Can we pass, and we forget?*
> *Many suns arise and set.*
> *Many a chance the years beget.*
> *Love the gift is Love the debt.*
> > *Even so.*
> *Love is hurt with jar and fret.*
> *Love is made a vague regret.*
> *Eyes with idle tears are wet.*
> *Idle habit links us yet.*
> *What is love? for we forget:*
> > *Ah, no! no!*[18]

As the above song indicates, "The Miller's Daughter" freely mixes forms: the dramatic monologue, narrative (in the story the speaker repeats to Alice), and lyric or song.[19] This mixing reflects Tennyson's heightened awareness of the properties and possibilities of each form. Narrative is a perfect structural counterpart to the flow of linear time since a narrative itself unfolds in time and conventionally (as here) relays a sequence of events that unfold chronologically. Moreover, narrative typically is locked into the past; it is the telling over what has already gone by once—but no more—upon a time. But the dramatic monologue always unfolds in an unending present; forever, as we read a dramatic monologue, the persona speaks *now*, at this moment.[20] How apt, accordingly, that Tennyson mixes the two forms here, where he explores how much is lost to the flow of time yet how much can be preserved in an endless present. His revisions in 1842 deliberately add to the interplay of past and present, narrative and dramatic monologue. The 1832 version began with narrative: "I met in all the close green ways . . . The wealthy miller's mealy face." The 1842 poem begins squarely in the present ("I see the wealthy miller yet"), creating a vantage point from which the past can be surveyed and a picture of the miller so healthy, happy, and imbued with life that, though he is now lost and recoverable only through memory, this memory is almost (not quite) enough to cancel the loss: "His memory scarce can make me sad." The challenge faced by the speaker at this point in time is of course just what *can* survive time: "somewhat flows to us in life, / But more is taken quite away" (lines 21–22).

In 1832 the speaker wishes he and Alice will die the same day to escape further awareness of loss, and then the speaker directly begins narrating the story of their shared past. In 1842 Tennyson holds off the narration for one more stanza, letting time hover in the present as the speaker reaches out for that in the present which, again, *almost* compensates for time's flow.

> *I'd almost live my life again.*
> *So sweet it seems with thee to walk,*
> *And once again to woo thee mine—*
> *It seems in after-dinner talk*
> *Across the walnuts and the wine—*

> (lines 28–32)

Another significant revision occurs after Alice, at the request of the speaker, sings the first of two songs. Even the 1832 version had the husband responding to the song in time present, but in

1842 Tennyson expanded the circle of present or timeless time in lines that make explicit the whole rationale behind the mingling of the tenses.[21]

> *And now those vivid hours are gone,*
>   *Like mine own life to me thou art,*
> *Where Past and Present, wound in one,*
>   *Do make a garland for the heart.*

(lines 195–98)

Without blinking or evading the past, the speaker comes to understand that, through love, love itself can be rescued from time, and the poem ends with a beautiful and unsentimental acceptance of both love and time, loss and recovery. For he invites Alice to walk over the same landscape where their courtship occurred, a landscape now virtually dead and dry, like their own physical selves. Their walking, or going, is an unobtrusive way of signaling the loss as well as the preservation of that landscape.

> *Arise, and let us wander forth,*
>   *To yon old mill across the wolds;*
> *For look, the sunset, south and north,*
>   *Winds all the vale in rosy folds,*
> *And fires your narrow casement glass,*
>   *Touching the sullen pool below:*
> *On the chalk-hill the bearded grass*
>   *Is dry and dewless. Let us go.*

(lines 239–46)

Tennyson, in effect, has so handled form that the poem in its exploration of time takes the very shape of the mill stream that figures so prominently in the poem. Like the stream, the poem is mostly given over to flow, the flow of narrative and linear time. But, just as the mill stream has also formed a glistening "higher pool" (line 64) that, embraced by banks, escapes the flow, so also the poem is a dramatic monologue rooted in the present and within whose bounds the speaker discovers in speaking that love can be rescued from time and held forever in the present.

"The Gardener's Daughter" is yet another domestic monologue that seems crafted, with its theme of love, to engage the reader's emotions. Like "The Miller's Daughter," the poem also mixes forms and, in so doing, again reveals Tennyson's sensitivity to the implications of form. Although largely a narrative, "The Gardener's Daughter" also exhibits markers of the dramatic monologue, and the mixed forms occur for the same reasons they do in "The Miller's Daughter": both works explore the ability to recover some element from the past and preserve it forever, through love, in the present.[22] But "The Gardener's Daughter" is about more than time and love; it is also explicitly about art, including art in relation to time and love. The point is suggested by the poem's very title. "Garden" evokes the notion of the *hortus conclusus* (the garden of love), the cycles and seasons of time and nature and re-created life in the form of growth and fruits, whereas "daughter" suggests the product of marital love, a sign of a new generation (hence the passage of time), and a form of newly created life. Because the poem is about art, love, and time, the poem is situated both inside and outside time, in the present and ongoing process of the dramatic monologue and in the finished past of narrative, an interplay that perfectly answers to the aim of art to rescue life's experiences from the running tide of time and to preserve it forever. Tennyson signals as much to the reader in the very first lines of the poem: "This morning is the morning of the day, / When I and Eustace from the city went." The doubling of the morning through repetition mirrors in the art of Tennyson's poem the fact that events can have a double existence inside and outside time if they are transmuted into the material of art. And so, although the poem is also designed to evoke sympathetic contemplation and participation in the story of love, it can be read on several levels.

But the poem is of special interest because, in early drafts, it was more decidedly a dramatic monologue than is the finished work, where the narrative ethos prevails. "The Gardener's Daughter" is thus a prime exhibit of why and why not Tennyson chose to exploit the peculiar resources of the dramatic monologue.

That the poem was at one point designed emphatically as a dramatic monologue is made clear by the following draft in Trinity Notebook 17, a passage that here serves as the poem's opening lines.

> Dear Walter, if your ear be dispossest,
> And if your time lie fallow to your hands,
> As may be to a young unmarried man
> That living from the moment does not own
> A settled business—and twere well you did—
> My present purpose chimes with that request
> Which you have often made me to ~~relate~~ recount
> Some little of the story of my love
> But if in speaking I ~~should lapse into~~
> ~~An overfullness, or~~ too much translate
> My colours into language bear with me.
> ~~One Art includes the elements of all,~~
> ~~But he doth well that but develops one.~~
>     These little paintings in their costly frames
> That stud the chamber like so many lights
> Are treasures to me dearer than my eyes.
> That city-house with leaning balconies—
> Those steeples darkening thro' a silver steam—
> This cedar in the garden & the rest—
> Which I will never part with while I live
> Are fragments of the tale I am to tell.[23]

The passage is notable in two ways. First, it shows that Tennyson could easily create a clear auditor or dramatic situation if he wanted one. Second, the lines suggest Tennyson's personal participation: the unmarried Walter, with too much time on his hands and in need of a settled profession and domestic life, is more than a little like Tennyson himself, who, in early 1833, would have seen his own best friend Hallam engaged to Emily Tennyson and settling down to read law preparatory to his marriage.[24] In fact, numerous passages appearing in drafts but abandoned later combine a more distinctly dramatic format with sentiments that seem quite personal. For example, the two verse paragraphs below open a lengthy passage that tells how Eustace and the speaker, here cousins, lose their last remaining common relative and how the speaker cannot mourn.

> Love at first sight, my Walter, Love first-born
> To whom belonged the birthright of the heart
> Made this night thus: but with the morrow came
> My cousin to my chamber, bringing me
> A letter edged and sealed with funeral-signs:
> For yestermorn, we walking in our joy,
> The third last brother of my father's house

> *Left each an orphan of all kindred blood*
> *But that which branches in the other's veins.*
>     *Chiefmourner Eustace went: but as for me*
> *Localities, as dear as childhood, held*
> *The will to follow: neither could I go,*
> *Nor could assimilate peculiar grief:*
> *Like nature quick to hide the grave with life,*
> *Grieved that I grieved so little, I lay mused*
> *In some more spacious sadness lightly worn,*
> *For all things changed themselves to jubilee.*[25]

The lines on the speaker's lack of grief occur only within a passage explicitly structured as a dramatic monologue (note the reference to the auditor "Walter"), and they seem personal, especially since they really have so little to do with the rest of the poem as published.[26] Ricks speculates that the lines relate to Tennyson's ambivalence about his father's death, but they could also bespeak Tennyson's guilt over the joys of being in love with Rosa Baring after Hallam's death. The lines could even refer to Tennyson's response to his grandfather's death, either imagined or real,[27] especially since a double-canceled draft of "The Ante-Chamber" describes the cousins as "Orphans we . . . poor purses, wealthy hearts: / Our sole dependence on an aged man / The third last brother of my father's house."[28]

Tennyson's deletion of such passages can be explained in several ways. First, they may have been deleted simply because they *were* personal. Tennyson's revisions would then underscore his striving for greater impersonality and objectivity in his poetry at this time, as well as his notorious sense of privacy. The existence of these unadopted passages reminds us, however, that if Tennyson tried to cover his tracks of entry into a dramatic poem, he still made use of the dramatic monologue's recursive loop. Indeed, since Tennyson was often slow to write down the lines he composed in his head, many of the dramatic poems of the period with few discernible traces of Tennyson's personal participation (in drafts or finished form) may nonetheless have begun with a process of sympathetic identification, another imagined as an aspect of self.

Second, these passages may also have been deleted to further the function of the poem as a domestic monologue. If Tennyson were indeed shifting his emphasis to the reader, he may have felt that in this poem passages emphasizing the poet's "I" conflicted with his larger aim. But a third reason Tennyson deleted the lines may be his growing craftsmanship in wielding the dramatic monologue versus other poetic forms. Although "The Gardener's Daughter" suggests that art can give permanence to experience—a point aptly conveyed through the timeless present of the dramatic monologue—the poem's emphasis is on *framing*, since the speaker is a painter.[29] Thus, Tennyson not only gives over most lines to a narrative, one that inherently "frames" past experience, but also calls attention to the process of making art, to enclosing experience within the bounds of a picture or poem: "Fancy, led by Love, / Would play with flying forms and images" (lines 58–59). At the end of the story, prior to the unveiling of the speaker's portrait of Rose ("Behold her there . . . the most blessèd memory of mine age"), the narrative is called "This prelude" (line 267), a neat backward-glancing framing of the framing narrative. The finished poem, then, hovers on the inside and the outside of time, like the speaker's description of the garden, one in which the sounds of passing time are clearly audible but where the garden goes on blooming forever.

> *Not wholly in the busy world, nor quite*
> *Beyond it, blooms the garden that I love.*
> *News from the humming city comes to it*
> *In sound of funeral or of marriage bells;*
> *And, sitting muffled in dark leaves, you hear*
> *The windy clanging of the minster clock.*

*(lines 33–38)*

Robert Pattison's judgment is apt: "The poem is a description of perfection through art, and it is itself artistically perfect" (71). Part of Tennyson's artistry is evident in his revisions, which undermine without entirely undoing the poem's status as a dramatic monologue, so that the poem hovers between the present (and presence) of the dramatic monologue and the pastness (and past tense) of narrative.

Tennyson's 1830 female portraits thus led to two very different kinds of dramatic monologues in 1832 and 1842. On one hand "Fatima" and "The Sisters" render the consciousness of women speakers unhinged by passion. On the other hand, "The May Queen," "The Miller's Daughter," and "The Gardener's Daughter" situate their readers less in the speakers' consciousnesses than in a domestic world that evokes the reader's response to and sympathy with domestic affections. But all these poems make skillful use of the dramatic monologue form itself, whether to present a given consciousness or to suggest (through Tennyson's mixing of forms in a single poem) part of the poem's meaning.

II

The classical monologues do not merely engage the reader's feelings. These dramatic monologues are often cited as Tennyson's best because they make such full use of the form's resources. Tennyson gives independent life to his fictive speakers yet infuses the poems with personal reverberations, imagining the speaker's consciousness as an aspect of his own. At the same time, Tennyson often makes use of the auditor convention, and he carefully shapes the spoken to create poems that demand a reader's active participation. "Oenone" is notable for its interrelation of narrative and dramatic and for Tennyson's first—and flawed—attempt to integrate classical materials into the pole of fiction. "The Hesperides" and "The Lotos-Eaters" are more interesting for their attention to the reader. "Ulysses," perhaps Tennyson's single most famous monologue, is notable for activating almost every possible element of the dramatic monologue at once. And all these poems derive their meaning in part from the dramatic form itself—a point made clearer when the dramatic monologue "Ulysses" is compared to the narrative "Morte d'Arthur."

"Oenone" appears to be the outgrowth of Tennyson's desire to create another female portrait. Oenone herself is actually a cross between Mariana and Fatima.[30] If at first she laments that she is "all aweary of my life" (line 32), by the end of her monologue she has the will, passion, and energy of a Fatima as she declares her desire to wreak revenge upon Paris and Helen and sets out to find Cassandra. As do "Mariana" and "The Gardener's Daughter," "Oenone" has a strong narrative component: Oenone relates the story of how Paris came to her, "white-breasted like a star," bringing with him the Hesperian apple; how Paris came to judge of gods; and how, his choice being Aphrodite and her gift of "the fairest and most loving wife in Greece," Oenone came to be alone. The narrative element is appropriate to her turning to the past for consolation ("while I speak of it, a little while / My heart may wander from its deeper woe"—lines 42–43); but simply because the past *is* past, a closed experience out of which, in her case, Oenone can draw nothing that will connect with her present self, the narrative element is abruptly broken around line 215, and the poem ends squarely in the present of the dramatic monologue.

> *Cassandra . . . says*
> *A fire dances before her, and a sound*
> *Rings ever in her ears of arm'ed men.*
> *What this may be I know not, but I know*
> *That, wheresoe'er I am by night and day,*
> *All earth and air seem only burning fire.*

The dramatic monologue format is especially apt for this poem in other ways. First, as we are told in the poem's frame, Oenone "Sang to the stillness." She speaks, but no auditor is there; her wished-for auditor is instead on his way to Helen. Oenone has only the comfort of her own voice, a subtle means by which Tennyson can underscore her isolation. Second, the dramatic monologue buttresses the poem's theme of creation and destruction—of love, of art, of civilization. The theme is announced in the following lines:

> *I will speak, and build up all*
> *My sorrow with my song, as yonder walls*
> *Rose slowly to a music slowly breathed,*
> *A cloud that gathered shape.*

(lines 38–41)

Troy was created by art, by music, and now hovers on the brink of destruction. Oenone's music can create only the sorrow that follows from the destruction of Paris's love for her. If we are to focus on Oenone's creation of song and the shape it takes, it will hardly do for us to encounter a narrator's rather than Oenone's own words. Finally, although the movement is somewhat obscured by the descriptive details that cluster as thickly as the "bunch and berry and flower" attending the goddesses' entrance in the poem, the dramatic monologue is also ideal for revealing the oscillations of consciousness as Oenone shifts from her "Mariana" to her destructive "Fatima" phase.

Tennyson's personal participation in this poem via the recursive loop is not easy to fathom. We are aware of him only insofar as he resembles Oenone (and vice versa) as artist. Like her, he is busily building a song, and the heavy artifice of the rhetoric and decorative detail confirm his industriousness; like Oenone's his own perspective on the goddesses is as one who may "behold them unbeheld." It is easier to detect the emphasis given to the shaping of the poem, especially as Tennyson moved from the 1832 to the 1842 version. The manipulation of perspective, for example, is especially fine. Oenone's quotation of Paris (lines 68ff.) is more than a means of furthering the story; it is a dramatic way of stating her enthrallment to Paris, the power his erotic attractions and art have over her. Thus, when he speaks, Oenone is rendered passive: "while I looked / And listened, the full-flowing river of speech / Came down upon my heart." "My heart"—Oenone is no longer present as a fully rounded human being with her own separate consciousness. One thinks of "The Lady of Shalott," where Lancelot's art ("'Tirra lirra' . . . sang Sir Lancelot") invades the lady's mirror and eclipses her presence so that she momentarily disappears from the poem. The enthrallment of Oenone is worse since as the speaker of her own poem she *lets* Paris's words supplant her own.[31] His words in the 1842 version, furthermore, illuminate the theme of creation and destruction regarding art. Paris can sing prettily: "'For the most fair,' would seem to award it thine, . . . loveliest in all grace / Of movement, and the charm of married brows" (lines 71, 73–74). Unfortunately, his song is a lie, a fraud, created only to destroy Oenone's heart. Tennyson's management of perspective regarding Pallas is also effective. She may well be the nominal moral center of the poem, but when Paris judges in Aphrodite's favor, Pallas completely disappears from the poem, and only Hera's departure is mentioned.

Even Tennyson's handling of the frame was beautifully modulated as the poet moved from the 1832 to the 1842 poem. In the 1832 version the frame was merely picturesque and focused more on Troy than Oenone.[32] In the 1842 version, every line is functional, adumbrating through an emblematic landscape the entire shape of the monologue to come. The "swimming vapour slopes athwart the glen, / Puts forth an arm," and "loiters, slowly drawn," just as Oenone, round whose neck "floated her hair or seemed to float in rest," wanders forlorn and "loiters," lingering at noon slowly to draw out her song (lines 3-4, 5, 18). Our attention in the frame is then drawn to the richness of lawns and flowers, a landscape corresponding to the richness of the bower where the goddesses appear. But below all "roars / The long brook falling through the cloven ravine / In cataract after cataract to the sea" (lines 7-9), with Troy in the far distance—an apt emblem for Oenone's passion, kept beneath the surface through most of the monologue but violently spewing forth at the end as she, too, looks to Troy in the distance.

Tennyson's shaping of the poem also resulted in superior management of characterization as he moved from the 1832 to the 1842 version. The 1832 Paris himself moralized on the significance of the apple—"in aftertime [it] may breed / Deep evilwilledness of heaven and sere / Heartburning toward hallowèd Ilion"—this sounding more like Pallas than the Aphrodite he chooses. Oenone, in 1832, told how much more beautiful than the goddesses was Paris, something a deserted woman moving towards revenge is unlikely to tell over in retrospect. Both passages were accordingly dropped.[33] Conversely, a felicitous addition was made of Oenone's outburst against Eris, "the goddess of strife,"[34] a passage that, coming between two verse paragraphs given over to lament, not only shows the rhythms of Oenone's consciousness and prepares for her final outburst at the poem's conclusion but also tells us of Oenone from within. Oenone need not wish to meet Eris and express her hatred; Eris is within. And the landscape Oenone chooses for meeting the goddess—"ruined folds, / Among the fragments tumbled from the glens, / Or the dry thickets" (lines 217-19)—is an internal landscape of the mind destroyed by experience. Thus, Tennyson's revision enables us to see a given consciousness reacting to and molded by experience.

Yet for all this careful shaping of the poem, the poem does not quite cohere, and perhaps Tennyson was telling us as well as

James Spedding something when he singled out "Oenone" as one of the poems made "less *imperfect*" through revision.[35] The flaw is the "self-reverence, self-knowledge, self-control" passage spoken by Pallas. As many have noted, the problem with the passage is not merely that its didacticism has the delicacy of a sledge hammer but that the passage is out of keeping with the rest of the poem in tone and structure—even Oenone follows Aphrodite's example of passion, not Pallas's example of self-control.[36] Pallas stands "apart" figuratively and structurally as well as literally. The problem is in fact twofold. One is a matter of poetic bad faith. Tennyson may have thought he identified with Pallas, but like Paris, he really responds to and participates in the sensuousness associated with Aphrodite; the riot of "Violet, amaracus, and asphodel, / Lotos and lilies" (lines 95–96) versus the bare ruined quire of a text on "wisdom in the scorn of consequence" (line 148) tells us as much. But, ironically, the problem can also be ascribed to Tennyson's attempt at good faith as a poet dealing with classical matter. The classical bark, if an objective vehicle into which Tennyson can easily slip, also comes laden with a good deal of freight, in this instance the story of Troy's downfall and the notion of an entire civilization's decay. "Oenone" was Tennyson's first classical monologue, and we can see his inexperience in dealing with this type of dramatic monologue as he tries to telescope a subject requiring twelve books in *Idylls of the King* into the bounds of a poem not quite three hundred lines long.[37] The landscape, the oscillations of consciousness, the reflexivity of many lines in a poem partly about art—all these are fine. But the analysis of culture and ethics eludes Tennyson's control, and he did not attempt to link a classical monologue with the fate of an entire realm in his published verse until "Lucretius," published in 1868.

Instead he wisely learned to limit the allusiveness of his setting, though some might think that in "The Hesperides" he limited allusiveness to the point of unintelligibility. "The Hesperides" has been interpreted as an allegory, variously, of art or of religious myth-making. And no wonder: the poem seems to offer a field day for hunt-the-allegory, with its numerology, dragon, garden, apples, and epigraph from Milton—the last not only poet but Christian poet and myth-maker *par excellence*. If one

83

focuses on "The Hesperides" *as* a dramatic monologue with a prefatory frame, however, seeing how Tennyson uses the form and its resulting structures, some interesting new perspectives on the poem emerge. The poem does seem to be about art, but not so much the artist as the creation of art, the actual process itself.[38]

First, the frame: in "Oenone" the frame functions, as with all frames, to create aesthetic distance, but more important, to create a perspective from which the poem should be viewed, guiding the reader to see that Oenone's lament will be about mists that gather shape, flowery bowers, and the cataract of passion that must have its release. The frame of "The Hesperides" is equally functional: it introduces the auditor Hanno, the reader's counterpart and ally, and representative of the "real" world. For Hanno's is the world of linear time and space. He is most emphatically a voyager, caught in the stream of time (the frame is rendered in the past tense of narrative) and the currents of the ocean on which he sails. And he can hear the song of the Hesperides only as long as he floats out of the current (he is in "calmèd bays" when he hears the song), and then only obliquely: "[There] Came voices, like the voices in a dream, / Continuous, till he reached the outer sea" (lines 12–13). When he returns to that current, the "outer sea," the music stops. The world of Hanno and the world of the Hesperides can meet, but only tangentially.

Ultimately Hanno is not the primary but the secondary auditor; the Sisters really sing to themselves: "If ye sing not, if ye make false measure, / We shall lose eternal pleasure" (lines 23–24). The Sisters are both "ye" and "we," singers and sung-to. The structuring of the frame in relation to the "Song" is, then, an embodiment of the relation of the real world and poetry. Hanno may front the poem, causing by his arrival the beginning of the hearing of the song, but once there he is secondary and essentially disappears. Just so, the "real" world may spark poetry, but once the poem begins and the creative process takes over, the real world is no longer the point of contact but a secondary shadow. As Tennyson wrote in "The Ante-Chamber," art is "born of the first"—the "various world"—and is "as beautiful, but yet another world."

In this respect, the change in tense and mode from the frame (past-tense narrative) to the Song (the ever-present tense of the dramatic monologue) is essential and illuminates the theme of art-making Tennyson explores. One of the markers of the dramatic monologue identified by Loy D. Martin is also essential. As Martin notes, dramatic monologues of the nineteenth century are typified by the use of nonstative verbs. The difference between a stative and nonstative verb is defined thus: "With a state, unless something happens to change that state, then the state will continue: this applies equally to standing and to knowing. With a dynamic situation, on the other hand, the situation will only continue if it is continually subject to a new input of energy."[39] The definition is a key not only to the dramatic monologue—the monologue will stop and disintegrate unless the speaker keeps speaking—but to the process of writing and creating art. Only with the poet's continued influx of energy and imagination does the poem get written; if his energy stops, so does the art. All this is opposed to the "real" world, which, like Hanno's voyage in linear time and space, will continue unless something is done to stop it. Loy D. Martin's observation illuminates why the Sisters must keep singing: their "eternal pleasure" of making art can last only as long as the art is in fact being made. And if the Song is then about the making of art, the poet's singing to himself in order to create at all, the poem's extreme self-referentiality becomes more explicable. Not only do the Sisters sing to themselves on an enclosed island; it seems likely that the numbers they allude to refer to the "numbers," the metrics, of the song they sing.

> In a corner wisdom whispers. Five and three
> (Let it not be preached abroad) make an awful mystery.
> For the blossom unto threefold music bloweth;
> Evermore it is born anew;
> And the sap to threefold music floweth,
> From the root
> Drawn in the dark,
> Up to the fruit.
>
> (lines 28–35)

"Five and three," they sing, followed by a line that has precisely eight beats; "threefold music," they chant, followed by a line

The Manyfaced Glass

with three beats ("Evermóre it is bórn anéw"); "threefold music," they again intone, and three lines perfectly matched in a
cadence of two beats each immediately appear.

When one sees this, however, the poem almost explodes.
Either the poem is full of mystery, rife with floating symbols
that never seem to settle,[40] or it becomes baldly literal: eight is
eight and three is three. Either the reader listens, haunted and
intrigued by the music, or begins counting the number of beats
per line. No wonder the Sisters keep singing, participating in the
process of art, and fear the one from the East who will try to
possess and parse the apples—it is another, though much more
oblique, version of "We murder to dissect."

The focus on the creative process also helps illuminate the
structure of the poem, loose at best. True, the numbered stanzas all develop some opposition. Stanza I opposes singing and
silence, the West (itself a twilight world between the glare of
prosaic day and the utter darkness of night) and the East. Stanza
II contrasts the timeless, ongoing world of Father Hesper
("twinkle not thy stedfast sight") and the dragon with the world
subject to linear time, change, and destruction ("Kingdoms
lapse, and climates change, and races die")—and so on. But the
Song is also highly repetitive, the ending highly arbitrary. There
is no reason for the song to end, and indeed, the poem presupposes that it does not; it is simply that Hanno, and we, move
back into the world of linear time and out of that of art.

"The Hesperides" could not be the poem it is without the
dramatic monologue form; Tennyson has here exploited the resources of the dramatic monologue versus the narrative (the
frame) to perfection. But if this is so, why was the poem dropped
after 1832? I do not think the difficulty is the poem's theme; that
is, I do not think Tennyson would have had cause to reject the
stance he takes on art in "The Hesperides." Yes, as G. Robert
Stange has argued, the poem presents an enclosed world of art;
and yes, as James D. Merriman has argued, the poem attributes
negative qualities to the Sisters, especially their sublime indifference to the lapsing of kingdoms and their hope that the "old
wound of the world" will not be healed.[41] Both Stange and
Merriman are right: it may not be good that *in the process of actual
creation* art is so indifferent to the travails of social life; on the

86

other hand, that is simply how things are. "The Palace of Art" might seem a tract written in opposition to "The Hesperides," but "The Palace of Art" is about the possession, the hugging close to oneself, of art, not the process of creation. I rather suspect Tennyson's second doubts about and withdrawal of "The Hesperides" derived from the very reasons the poem is such a favorite these days: it is a peculiarly modern poem in its self-referentiality, its hovering between infinite open-endedness and nothingness. Tennyson, increasingly sensitive to the reader and his or her response in this period—especially since he now had a real audience—may have deleted the poem simply because his audience wasn't quite ready for it. For he himself never rejected it and "regretted that he had done away with it from among his 'Juvenilia' " (*Memoir*, I, 61).

"The Lotos-Eaters" is neither as allusively broad as "Oenone" nor as self-enclosed as "The Hesperides." Tennyson takes a well-known story for the poem, something "The Hesperides" lacks, but does not try to deal with his mariners' immediate situation *and* the whole cause for the fall of Troy, as in "Oenone." "The Lotos-Eaters" can also be situated between "Oenone" and "The Hesperides" in its use of a frame. As with that of "The Hesperides," the frame of "The Lotos-Eaters" creates an isthmus between two worlds, here the world of action and the world of isolation and withdrawal, and carries the reader to that juncture. "'Courage!' he said, and pointed toward the land"— and we are there. But, as in "Oenone," the frame of "The Lotos-Eaters" adumbrates the monologue that it frames. Its slow rhythm and drowsy movement—"the slender stream / Along the cliff to fall and pause and fall did seem"—give us immediate contact with the ambience of lotos land that is shortly to be celebrated by the mariners.[42] In effect, the frame also adumbrates the song by giving us two perspectives at once—in the frame, Ulysses' and the lotos-eaters' perspectives; in the song, the mariners' and the reader's (as I shall shortly discuss). The frame even provides two perspectives, and blurs and mixes them, by having the mariners' speech quoted *in* the narrative frame—one of only two instances of this among Tennyson's dramatic monologues ("Lucretius" is the other). These dual perspectives are entirely appropriate as an introduction to the mariners, for their own dilemma is being caught between two worlds. Like Hanno, they are voyagers, denizens of linear time and space, which is how they arrive at the island in the first place; but having stumbled upon the isle of lotos, they want to exchange their former world for one like that of the Hesperidean Sisters. And, just as readers in "The Hesperides" must give themselves over entirely to the Sisters and participate in their world or else destroy the poem's mystery through analysis, in this poem the reader is invited both to participate in and to become separate from the mariners' world.

Indeed, if "The Hesperides" is about the making of art, "The Lotos-Eaters" could be about the reading of art since the reader's participation in the poem is an inherent part of the text. Partly this is a matter of "gaps" in the text. As the mariners' mingled consciousnesses shift from affirmation to plaint in the odd versus the even-numbered stanzas, it is up to the reader to see, or try to see,[43] how these oscillating movements fit together. Additional gaps occur with the questions posed in the even-numbered stanzas. Instead of being carried smoothly and peacefully to rest by every line, which happens in the odd-numbered stanzas, we are left strangely suspended by the questions the mariners raise: "Why should we only toil, the roof and crown of things?" "Is there any peace / In ever climbing up the climbing wave?" (lines 69, 94–95). As the mariners themselves do not answer these questions, the reader is left to jump into these moments of *aporia*, exploring matters that may or may not coincide with issues the text itself raises.

Not that Tennyson was a sluggard in shaping the spoken. In this respect he is much more a Ulysses than a lotos-eater. For the beauty of "The Lotos-Eaters" is Tennyson's shaping of the text to give full rein to his speakers' consciousnesses,[44] himself, and the reader all at once. He inserts no overt, thematic passages (like the lines Pallas speaks in "Oenone") to guide our response to the mariners' song. Nor, though there are ironies in the poem, is irony alone really the point: our response is not a simple matter of accepting or rejecting the speakers' statements. Even if we reject the mariners, they have achieved a kind of "thereness," remaining unto themselves like the Epicurean gods they envy. But in this poem the reader takes over the role of voyager the mariners renounce, using sympathy for a sail and judgment for a rudder. And if, as many have argued, the poem is "about" the conflict between isolation and communality, this meaning emerges in the process of reading.

Upon beginning the Choric Song, the reader immediately encounters a plethora of delicious, seductive images: rose petals softly falling to the ground, "cool mosses," and dew-drenched blossoms. We can readily participate with mariners who praise sweet music that "gentlier on the spirit lies, / Than tired eyelids upon tired eyes" (lines 50–51), for the statement seems innocuous, even agreeable, enough.

Things do not remain so simple, however. "Why are we weighed upon with heaviness," the mariners ask in the next stanza, "And utterly consumed with sharp distress, / While all things else have rest from weariness?" (lines 57–59). Who is this "we"? Does it apply to all humanity or, as we begin to suspect, to the mariners alone? The effect of this plaint is not to invite the reader's participation but to remind readers of their separate existence of life. We also, as readers, may experience the toil and restlessness of life, but we do not, we cannot, remove to an isle of narcotic bliss—or only at great expense. Suddenly the mariners' protestations sound less like genuine indignation at the intrinsic injustice of life and more like self-pity.

Our sympathy is reengaged, though, when the mariners next appeal to a universal impulse in humanity, the desire to be at one with the natural process of time and change. The mariners' description of the "full-juiced apple, waxing over-mellow, [which] / Drops in a silent autumn night" (lines 78–79) seems to be another version of Keats's "To Autumn," an affirmation and acceptance of process that leads to serenity and harmony. Yet "Hateful" to them is the "dark-blue sky, / Vaulted o'er the dark-blue sea" (lines 84–85), another emblem of wholeness and complementarity. And they acknowledge the inevitability of death, not so that they can participate in the full life cycle, but only to rationalize evading the cycle altogether. "Let us alone," they intone,

> Let us alone. What is it that will last?
> All things are taken from us, and become
> Portions and parcels of the dreadful Past.

*Let us alone. What pleasure can we have*
*To war with evil? Is there any peace*
*In ever climbing up the climbing wave?*
*All things have rest, and ripen toward the grave*
*In silence; ripen, fall and cease:*
*Give us long rest or death, dark death, or dreamful ease.*

                                        *(lines 90–98)*

They embrace death but reject the action and conflict (which readers experience in making their way through the poem) that lead to growth, the necessary complement of death.

The tensions I have thus far traced between the pull on the reader's sympathy and judgment are found even in the 1832 version of the poem.[45] However, at this point the tension in the original poem breaks, and the text ends by exploring only the delights of the lotos. In both versions of the poem the rhythm shifts as the poem nears its close. But in the 1832 version the shift is to a compressed rhythmic beat that approximates the cadences of Anglo-Saxon verse of the sort Tennyson later used in "Merlin and the Gleam" to enunciate his commitment to an energetic pursuit of art.

> *We will eat the Lotos, sweet*
>
> . . . . . . . . . . . . . . . . . . . . . . . .
> *And no more roam,*
> *On the loud hoar foam,*
> *To the melancholy home*
> *At the limit of the brine,*
> *The little isle of Ithaca, beneath the day's decline.*
>
> . . . . . . . . . . . . . . . . . . . . . . . . . .
> *Hark! how sweet the horned ewes bleat*
> *On the solitary steeps,*
> *And the merry lizard leaps,*
> *And the foamwhite waters pour;*
> *And the dark pine weeps,*
> *And the lithe vine creeps,*
> *And the heavy melon sleeps*
> *On the level of the shore:*
>
> . . . . . . . . . . . . . . . . . . . . . . . . .
> *Oh! islanders of Ithaca, we will return no more.*[46]

The ironies of the poem dissolve into the affirmation of a rhythm that quickens and gathers strength as the mariners approach their goal of utter withdrawal and stasis. Perhaps in 1832 Tennyson found the mariners' temptation to abandon the voyager's role too attractive (and why not, since as artist he was also Hesperidean), and so poet, mariners, and reader are plunged into a swift stream of rhythm that leaves all beached on the isle of lotos.

In 1842, of course, Tennyson substituted the ending we now know. He also inserted a new stanza (stanza VI) to achieve a poetic structure that maintains the tensions of the earlier stanzas. In stanza V, having appealed to natural process as a rationale for abandoning their voyage, the mariners appeal to another form of wholeness, that achieved through memory. How sweet, they argue, "To muse and brood and live again in memory, / With those old faces of our infancy / Heaped over with a mound of grass" (lines 110–12). Here lotos-eating can achieve continuity and wholeness in the face of loss, an especially resonant appeal for Tennyson after Hallam's death in 1833, and one difficult to reject by any reader. In 1832 this stanza led directly to another positive aspect of lotos-eating, the aesthetic delights it imparts to perception (stanza VII).

But in the 1842 poem the appeal to transcendent wholeness is followed by the interpolated stanza, which again acts to distance us from the mariners. In opposition to the now-dead faces they knew in youth and can reach only through memory, the mariners turn to the still-living faces of their wives and sons, directly accessible in time and space. But the mariners recoil from these living faces precisely because they are so linked with voyaging. They are right to guess that change has been wrought in their absence, but they forget, as the speakers of "The Miller's Daughter" and "The Gardener's Daughter" do not, that love can transcend change: "surely now our household hearths are cold: / Our sons inherit us: our looks are strange: / And we should come like ghosts to trouble joy" (lines 117–19). Although they themselves applaud the return of the "ghosts" of those they had known in youth—through memory—they insist that their own return as "ghosts" would cause dismay and disruption. Indeed, the mariners end the stanza not only refusing to embrace wholeness and continuity in all forms but actually embracing its antithesis—disorder: "Let what is broken so remain. / The Gods are hard to reconcile: / 'Tis hard to settle order once again" (lines 125–27). The stanza emerges as a rather shocking assault on the reader, who, like the rejected wives and sons, lives in the world of time and change. Hence the mariners' subsequent appeal to the sensuous delights of perception inspired by the lotos is much less appealing, for the image of living, waiting faces lingers behind the sumptuous images of "emerald-coloured water" and the "woven acanthus-wreath divine" (lines 141, 142).

As the poem moves to its close in stanza VIII, there is thus an accumulated force of ambivalence that prepares us to view the mariners' celebration of the Epicurean gods as a penultimate stroke. They again reject a life of action and determine to "live and lie" in the "hollow Lotos-land" like the gods who are "careless of mankind" (lines 154–55). But the rhythm shifts, as they turn their gaze upon the toils from which the gods are exempt,[47] to an energetic rhythm that evokes, not affirmation and joy, but conflict and doubt. Instead of the short, compressed lines of the 1832 version, the lines are long, sinewy, and complex.

> they smile in secret, looking over wasted lands,
> Blight and famine, plague and earthquake, roaring deeps and fiery sands,
> Clanging fights, and flaming towns, and sinking ships, and praying hands.
> But they smile, they find a music centred in a doleful song
> Steaming up, a lamentation and an ancient tale of wrong,
> Like a tale of little meaning though the words are strong;
> Chanted from an ill-used race of men that cleave the soil,
> Sow the seed, and reap the harvest with enduring toil.

> (lines 159–66)

In the 1832 ending the reader participates in pictures of merry lizards, winding vines, and bleating ewes; here the reader is confronted with a compendium of all the earthly ills upon which the mariners, preferring to identify with the gods who do not sympathize with man's hard plight, deliberately turn their backs. The mariners' preference for the ghosts of dead familiar faces to living, even dearer faces was an indirect assault on the reader; this is direct. For in rejecting humanity, the mariners turn their backs on *us* as well and, in so doing, break the conduit of our sympathy. At the poem's end they have cut themselves off in a rather frightening absoluteness of isolation.

Tennyson's beautiful handling of the poem's metrics reinforces the poem's structure as a vehicle for the reader's participation.[48] Whereas the slow, delicate, languid verse of most of the Choric Song allows the reader to participate in the delights of torpor and sensuous beauty along with the mariners, the final stanza breaks the pattern and precipitates the reader back into the human world of struggle and toil. The poem in fact shows Tennyson exploiting every element of the dramatic monologue: he can himself participate in both the world of the lotos and the voyager, let the mariners have their say uninterrupted, and allow—and guide, through his very shaping of the poem—the reader's participation. The poem is at once intensely personal and utterly objective.

So far most of the poems I have discussed were begun before and published in the 1832 volume of poems. The remaining poems examined in this chapter were all begun about the time of Hallam's death or after, and all reveal the imprint of that most central experience of Tennyson's poetic career. The first responses to that death were lyrics that do not shrink from assuming the Romantic lyric "I": "Hark! the dogs howl!" (the germ of *In Memoriam*), "Whispers," and "On a Mourner." What does this tell us? In the first place, it tells us that Tennyson was not afraid to own the pain of grief. In grieving for Hallam, Tennyson faced pain, but it is unlikely that he simultaneously experienced guilt, fear, or ambivalence—perhaps the case when Tennyson wrote *The Devil and the Lady* and its soliloquies. In the lyrics, at any rate, Tennyson felt no need to distance himself from his own emotions through the dramatic monologue as distancing defense.   Perhaps the shift to the lyric indicates Tennyson's growing confidence in his poetic voice, though characteristically, as Ricks notes, when Tennyson came to publish "On a Mourner" in 1865, he substituted "thy" for "my" and deleted the poem's most directly identifiable personal passage.[49] Tennyson's use of the lyric for his personal expression in the wake of Hallam's death also tells us what I hope has become clear by now, that in the 1830s and 1840s Tennyson had grown to use the dramatic monologue for (relatively) more objective ends, the lyric for (relatively) more subjective ends.

It is interesting that at the end of "On a Mourner" "virtue" is compared to a "household god," followed by a concluding stanza alluding to Troy and Aeneas. Perhaps this simile suggested the subject of Ulysses, but when Tennyson came to write the famous poem of that name, he ended up with something akin to and yet utterly different from "On a Mourner." The kinship between "Ulysses" and the lyric lies in Tennyson's personal participation in both forms. As Tennyson reported to James Knowles, "There is more about myself in 'Ulysses', which was written under the sense of loss and that all had gone by, but that still life must be fought out to the end. It was more written with the feeling of his loss upon me than many poems in 'In Memoriam'."[50] I have examined elsewhere in detail the possible correlations between Tennyson's own life and "Ulysses."[51] These include Tennyson's and the Apostles' sense that Hallam's was a "heroic" intellect and that to be associated with him was to live (in nineteenth-century terms) on a heroic plane; Hallam's and Tennyson's wanderings and adventures together on the Continent; Tennyson's own worry about becoming a mere "name" after his 1832 volume was published, and in the absence of his closest literary advisor and supporter; and the factors that would have disposed Tennyson to be ambivalent toward his own family in the aftermath of Hallam's death. Tennyson's friends, too, help us to see Tennyson's personal involvement in the poem. Some critics consider Tennyson's adoption of the "mask of age" in "Ulysses" a mere ruse, a way of hiding behind a mask so that he can say what he really wants to say, or an oblique means of expressing a death wish. Yet Robert Monteith's letter to Tennyson in December 1833 suggests that the poem's mask of age is a perfect and accurate rendering of the feelings of those bereaved by Hallam's death.

> One feeling that remains with me is a longing to preserve all those friends whom I know Hallam loved and whom I learnt to love through him. He was so much a centre round which we moved that now there seems a possibility of many connections being all but dissolved. Since Hallam's death I almost feel like an old man looking back on many friendships as something bygone. I beseech you, do not let us permit this, you may even dislike the interference of common friendship for a time, but you will be

glad at length to gather together all the different means by which you may feel not entirely in a different world from that in which you knew and loved Hallam. (*Letters*, I, 103–4)

Monteith's letter can almost serve as a gloss on the personal elements of "Ulysses."

But if Tennyson fully exploited the dramatic monologue's recursive loop in "Ulysses," he simultaneously created an objective poem through his shaping of the poem, one that both invites the reader's participation and gives his speaker Ulysses ample rein, a separate life of his own. Scholarship devoted to "Ulysses" proves both the degree of the reader's participation in the poem and the poem's objectivity. No one has trouble agreeing what "Hark! the dogs howl!" or "On a Mourner" is all about. But many readers have taken "Ulysses" to mean quite other than what Tennyson said it meant, arguing that it is not about heroic endurance but a portrait of a Satanic egoist, a suicidal speaker, an antihero in every way. The poem in fact has been carefully shaped to leave gaps in the text, the same kind of entrances for the reader Tennyson managed so beautifully in "The Lotos-Eaters," as the poem traces the oscillations of Ulysses' consciousness in the four verse paragraphs.

In the first paragraph we see a Ulysses frustrated beyond all measure by what he feels is a kind of imprisonment, and he vents this frustration by projecting scorn on all about him—the "still hearth," the "barren crags," the "agèd wife," and the "savage race" who, he feels, force him to break up his capacity for unlimited action into discrete little parcels of acts: "I mete and dole."[52] The second paragraph shows a shift in Ulysses' consciousness. As an alternative to his enforced idleness, he lives over again in memory his great deeds and unlimited "roaming" and imagines undertaking a new quest:

> vile it were
> For some three suns to store and hoard myself,
> And this gray spirit yearning in desire
> To follow knowledge like a sinking star.
>
> (lines 28–31)

Significantly, he does not yet say he *will* go; all is spoken in hypothetical terms: "Life piled on life / *Were* all too little"; "vile it *were*."

His kaleidoscopic consciousness shifts once more, and he returns to the domestic sphere of the hearth, but with a difference. His frustration largely dissipated through his imaginative journeys of the second verse paragraph, he can return to his immediate surroundings in the third with an enlarged and gentler perspective. Focusing on Telemachus, he invokes to himself all that Telemachus can achieve through his patience and "slow prudence": the very impressive achievement of uplifting a people, whom he now terms "rugged" (which implies the capacity for will and endurance—Ulysses' own traits) instead of "savage."[53] He finds that he can sympathize with both his son and his people,[54] but in doing so is only reminded of the residual differences between himself and them. He is thus led to an epiphany from within—he is indeed different: "He works his work, I mine." He now makes his decision to move.

As opposed to the generalized statements and hypothetical voyage of the second paragraph, the last paragraph offers a concrete proposal born of Ulysses' imaginative testing. He looks directly to the port and, confident of the rightness of his quest, exhorts his mariners to "push off." And so the poem ends with its stirring lines, the emphatic vigor and stateliness of which serve to reinforce Ulysses' decision. And, I think, the reader is invited to second that decision (though many must send their regrets); for as we see the softening and enlarging of Ulysses' character as he contemplates his quest, a recognition we can come to through the gaps between paragraphs and the oscillations of his consciousness, we can see that it is right and just for him to depart.

Ulysses thus lives as a character in his own right, one with whom we can sympathize and one we can judge. Tennyson's objectivity in the poem is due partly to his having chosen just the right speaker, one through whom Tennyson could explore and filter his own feelings, yet one who has, through tradition, a story and life all his own. The result is a poem we can view, as it were, through a stereoscopic viewer. If we close one eye, we see Tennyson plain. If we close the other, we see only Ulysses. When we open both eyes we see a poem rich in resonance and depth because of the vibrations and subtle overlapping of the two intersecting images.

There is an additional reason for Tennyson to have used the dramatic monologue for "Ulysses" beyond the interplay he could achieve among poet, speaker, and reader (and text). The form of the dramatic monologue itself leads us to the very heart of the poem and its theme. Loy D. Martin has remarked that three linguistic categories—"adverbial phrases signifying temporal proximity," "present participles of non-stative verbs used as adverbs," and "verbs of progressive aspect"—act to make the nineteenth-century dramatic monologue a poetic structure "viewed from inside the time sequence in which it occurs": "The dramatic monologue, in one of its principal functions, creates a poetic moment of a certain duration which is viewed internally and which is contiguous with an implied extra-textural past and future of indefinite extent. The 'present' of the dramatic monologue is thus implicitly one open-ended fragment in a succession of fragments which do not, even projectively, add up to a bounded whole" (62, 61, 65). The dramatic monologue, again, is on the inside of time. All this matters intensely for "Ulysses" because the dramatic monologue is a means of achieving exactly what Ulysses most desires: a resistance to closure, to endings. One might say that "Ulysses" is Tennyson's "Do not go gentle into that good night"—only he is not addressing the dying or dead Hallam but that part of himself that was as one with Hallam ("I am a part of all that I have met"), crying out that this part of himself shall not be enclosed and extinguished but must go on into the future.

In the poem itself all this is translated into the linguistic forms Tennyson so masterfully chooses to render Ulysses' consciousness. The opening lines betray Ulysses' fear that he is becoming divided from a part of himself. He first refers to himself in the third person—"It little profits that an *idle king*"—and the one "I" of the first verse paragraph is hemmed in, buried in the third line after a succession of modifying phrases, and surrounded by things: hearth, crags, wife, and race. Moreover, the tense is both the simple present ("I mete and dole") and the habitual, the finite and the infinite, bespeaking Ulysses' anxiety that he is caught in a trap of eternal enclosure. Thus the last line of the first paragraph has three nonfinite verbs—the savage race "hoard, and sleep, and feed" unendingly—and then a finite verb that acts like the clicking of a trap: "know not me." His people are thus part of a larger process, but a process that leads only to enclosure—of Ulysses.

Accordingly, Ulysses desires precisely that "untravelled world" of ongoing present time "whose margin fades / For ever and for ever when I move." Significantly, his desire *not* to "make an end" is contrasted with diction ("hoard") that recurs to the closed lives of his people as he sees them. But he most fears closure from within, the possibility that he will "hoard myself" rather than connect with an ongoing present activity that is itself linked back with his past and forward with his future. Curiously, "To follow knowledge like a sinking star, / Beyond the utmost bound of human thought" was originally part of "Tiresias," where the latter wishes "I were as in the days of old."[55] For Tennyson, therefore, the lines would have connoted both the future and the past.

In the third paragraph Ulysses shuts rather than opens doors on time—"I *leave* the sceptre and the isle," "When I am *gone*"—but Ulysses is accepting the only kind of closure he can accept, a closure on the closure represented by his isolation in Ithaca: "He works his work, I mine." He is then ready for the end of the poem that, in its very language, with its present-tense "are" and the succession of incomplete infinitives, opens out onto an eternal present, onto infinity: "To strive, to seek, to find, and not to yield."[56] Each infinitive is thrown down like a gauntlet against the threat of imprisoning stasis and death, which "closes all," and, though some remark on the slowness of this last line with all its pauses, I find the sound reminds me of the successive smacks of the oars smiting "the sounding furrows" as Ulysses and his mariners set off on their voyage into a dynamic, open-ended time. Yes, Ulysses fails to say where they are going, what they are seeking or will find. But this is, in the poem's own terms, irrelevant. All that matters is to resist closure and to keep moving, no matter that eventually they will be swallowed by the ultimate closure of death, which can never be escaped. The poem is in fact startlingly amoral. So desperate is Ulysses (and, perhaps, Tennyson) to keep himself and all he has experienced on the inside of time that all other considerations are virtually meaningless. And to convey all this, Tennyson has chosen exactly the right form, the open-ended dramatic monologue itself situated squarely inside time.

A discussion of "Tithonus," the poem customarily linked with "Ulysses," must await a later chapter since that poem was published in 1860 and reflects the Tennyson of a later stage. But "Tithon," the poem written in 1833 (and later reworked into "Tithonus") does need to be examined, for it truly is a pendant to "Ulysses," a kind of commentary and answer to the poem written on 20 October 1833. "Tithon" suggests that merely moving forward in time does not ensure the connection between past, present, and future that Ulysses so ardently desires. There is a kind of twilight space between nonclosure and connection, and one can get lost in between. That is why Tithon says, in lines not incorporated in the 1860 poem, he wants "to shoot the sunny interval of day, / And lap me deep within the lonely west" (lines 26-27). He wishes to shoot the gap in which he has become lost in one swift leap and get outside time forever. In fact, in the Trinity manuscripts Tithon goes as far as to threaten Eos with Death, so insistent is he on making his escape.

> *Release me lest I rise, go forth & call*
> *From under yon dark fields that dream below*
> *The shape I seek—he thus implored invade*
> *The Incorruptible & thou some time*
> *Returning on thy silver wheels behold*
> *Even on these cool & gleaming thresholds Him*
> *Thou knowest not [,] the uncertain shadow feared*
> *Of Gods & men.*[57]

He is willing to destroy time and the whole universe, if necessary.

That his endless residence in time has brought no connection is made clear in his relationship with Eos. Because he is now impotent, the physical side of their relationship is a permanent part of the past; yet she is eternally present beside him. Hence he cannot have the unalloyed pleasure of memory *or* physical rapture. Again, he has only the twilight world between these two. As a result, Eos is both the beloved and his imprisoner, an ambivalence not quite worked out in 1833—and most likely the reason Tennyson did not publish this poem along with "Ulysses" in 1842. Perhaps the difficulty arose because, as someone loved by Tithon and a part of his past, Eos could so easily become identified with Hallam (and Tennyson with Tithon). This identification, however, jars against the role of Eos as a representative of cruel, endless time.

Yet if Tennyson did not have command of one strand of the poem in 1833, his mastery of the dramatic monologue form is in full evidence here. It is a stroke of genius to use the dramatic monologue for a poem on Tithon, the form itself deeply ironic since it is situated inside time—exactly what Tithon wants to escape. He longs to be a part of a third-person past-tense narrative, where he never comes to full consciousness and is locked safely away into the past. Instead, he is, as we have him, centered in his consciousness, entirely apt for one whose body has withered away, and the entrapment is so painful he begs for mere oblivion.

"Tiresias" was begun at the same time as "Tithon," and it, too, belongs to a later period; it was reworked and published in 1885. One wonders if the poem would have more power if Tennyson had selected as speaker Menoeceus, the one upon whom Tiresias prevails to kill himself for the good of Thebes, rather than Tiresias. At the moment, however, it seems necessary to say only that the poem was perhaps a form of wish-fulfillment, an attempt to create a poem about an untimely death that was not futile but carried out for the good of all.[58]

The most fruitful comparison, then, may not be between "Ulysses" and the classical monologues begun simultaneously though published later, but between "Ulysses" and "Morte d'Arthur,"[59] apparently written a short time after "Ulysses" in 1833 or 1834. These two poems can be seen as pendants not only in theme but also in form. Both poems draw on myth and enable Tennyson to explore his response to the death of Arthur. In both a lost fellowship is mourned (Ulysses his mariners, Arthur his "goodliest fellowship of famous knights"); Ulysses misses the pain and joy he experienced "with those / That loved me" whereas Arthur mourns the sleep of his knights—"the men I loved." And both poems explore ways in which the past may be related to the present; Bedivere's fear of empty isolation, given in soliloquy form, is very close to the fears expressed in Ulysses' monologue.

" . . . *whither shall I go?*

. . . . . . . . . . . . . . . . . . . . . . . .

*For now I see the true old times are dead,*

. . . . . . . . . . . . . . . . . . . . . . . .

*And I, the last, go forth companionless,*
*And the days darken round me, and the years,*
*Among new men, strange faces, other minds."*

*(lines 227, 229, 236–38)*

Yet Bedivere, unlike Ulysses, undertakes no voyage into the future. He is left on shore, a lonely figure watching his past recede from him as the barge carrying Arthur disappears into the distance.

*Distance* is in fact the key word here. If "Ulysses" suggests a Tennyson in the denial stage of grief, insisting that the dead are not really dead and that he can take all with him into the future, "Morte d'Arthur," as the very title suggests, shows Tennyson accepting the death of Arthur. (Curiously, beneath the draft of "Morte d'Arthur" in Trinity Notebook 17 is one of Tennyson's many sketches, this of a man with a large, domed head, eyes closed in sleep—the sleep of death, one suspects.) Thus, after lamenting his lost knights, Arthur says what Ulysses could never say, "But let what will be, be" (line 24). The focus of conflict in the poem, however, is not Arthur but Bedivere, whose dilemma is how to preserve what Arthur stood for. His first impulse is to preserve part of the physical trappings of Arthur, just as the persona of *In Memoriam* at first longs for the physical hand of the dead Arthur: "What record, or what relic of my lord / Should be to aftertime, but empty breath / And rumours of a doubt?" (lines 98-100). Bedivere must learn that to keep, he must let go, letting pass the physical Arthur—who, in the course of the poem, himself becomes emphatically a *thing*, a framed picture (lines 169-70) or "shattered column"—in order to hold on to the spiritual meaning of Arthur that can survive in the mind and imagination. Thus our last look at Bedivere is not of a man voyaging, but one "revolving many memories" (line 270). Memories are all he has left, and to acknowledge this is also to acknowledge the permanent absence of Arthur as a person. The sentiments of the poem, insofar as they are personal, are in fact very close to those of section LXXXV of *In Memoriam*,

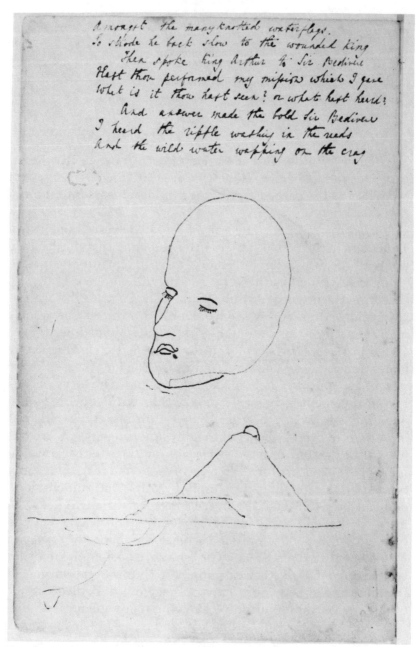

Draft of "Morte d'Arthur," Trinity Notebook 17 (0.15.17),
folio 10v.

written at about the same time as "Morte d'Arthur" and appearing with it in draft form in Trinity Notebook 17: "'Tis better to have loved and lost, / Than never to have loved at all"; "My old affection of the tomb, / And my prime passion in the grave." Both poems, that is, breathe a sense of acceptance, if sad and troubled, of the indisputable fact of Arthur's death.

All this illuminates why "Morte d'Arthur," though also drawn from myth and resonant with personal sentiment, should, unlike "Ulysses," be cast as a past-tense narrative. Just as Arthur is enclosed in a frame, looking "as in a picture," so also the form of the poem locks Arthur—and Bedivere's last meeting with him—into the past, out of time and not recoverable as a physical presence. The style of the poem, with its stately, often archaic diction, reinforces the distance from which Arthur is viewed and the pastness of his passing. As well, the narrative form enables Tennyson to use the setting of the poem, an icy, rough, but sublime winter landscape, not as a key to a persona's perception, but as a kind of absolute value indicator and point of reference. Death surrounds Bedivere completely; only his memories survive.

Curiously, however, Tennyson did not let "Morte d'Arthur" stand alone when he published it in 1842 but enclosed it within another frame, the first-person narrative entitled "The Epic" (written *c.* 1837–38). Many in Tennyson's time and in our own have decried the encasing frame as a defect, a transparent defensive device meant to cloak the poet's insecurities and his sense of identification with the "Morte d'Arthur." But others, notably Walter Nash, have demonstrated how "The Epic" provides a thematic and stylistic complement to the "Morte d'Arthur," underscoring its emphasis on faith and fealty in contrast to the modern doubts voiced in the attached frame.[60] I am particularly struck by the way "The Epic" initiates a play between past and present, narrative and dramatic, giving the two poems together a resonance they lack singly.

"The Epic" explicitly questions how dead the past is and whether there is any way to resuscitate it, preparing for this same theme in the "Morte d'Arthur" but adding to it the theme of art, an issue that further distances the "Morte d'Arthur" as an *artwork*,[61] yet brings it closer to Tennyson as poet: "For nature brings not back the Mastodon, / Nor we those times; and why should any man / Remodel models?" Even the handling of the speaker initiates this simultaneous bringing close and distancing of the narrative framework, as if Tennyson were playing with a zoom lens as he wrote, putting "The Epic" in the mouth of a first-person speaker, yet having him utter a past-tense narrative throughout.[62] Moreover, he splits the poet from the narrator. As Walter Nash remarks:

> Tennyson allots the explicit role of poet to an *alter ego*, a character named Everard Hall, and relegates himself, as "I", to the position of a privileged observer, half-drowsing, half-attentive, recording an event and being caught up willy-nilly in its implicatory power. It is the familiar literary device of using a narrative figure to suggest on the one hand a detachment from events—a truthful irresponsibility—and on the other a deep sympathetic involvement in whatever significances and consequences the events may produce. (330)

But it is above all the poem itself, the "Morte d'Arthur," that is given a new wavering between distance and immediacy by "The Epic." The "Morte d'Arthur" is not only presented as a relic of the past in the sense of an imitator of a bygone epic tradition. Like the body of King Arthur within the poem (and of Arthur Hallam without), it is emphatically a *thing*, a fragment rescued from the fire in which other books were burnt: "'But I,' / Said Francis, 'picked the eleventh from this hearth / And have it: keep a thing, its use will come.'" In all these respects "The Epic" causes the "Morte d'Arthur" to recede in the distance, a literary fossil embedded in its own and the frame's narrative. But by a brilliant stroke, Tennyson uses the frame to signify that the "Morte d'Arthur" is *read* by the poet Everard Hall, suddenly shooting the lines back into the time frame of the present, as the deictic phrase that concludes "The Epic"—"to this [not *that*] result"—indicates. This device, however, does not bring Arthur and Bedivere alive as dramatic characters; no person but only a *voice* is given presence through the addition of the frame. Structurally, therefore, the two poems interact to embody the very lesson that Bedivere must learn: the dead body of the past *is* past; but it can be recovered as an imaginative voice. The closing of "The Epic" is simply another way of stating what the interacting poems have already signified. The narrator of "The Epic" *can* voyage with Arthur, unlike Bedivere, but only within the context of a dream vision that is both disembodied and truly present. Tennyson, through the interplay of narrative and dramatic, has likewise created a work that is true to the myth on which it is based, true to the personal feelings that inspired the "Morte d'Arthur," but also one that can inhabit the present of the reader's world.

To compare "Ulysses" and "Morte d'Arthur," then, is to see how brilliantly Tennyson could select the appropriate form for a given poem. The dramatic monologue situated inside time is a perfect medium for "Ulysses," the past-tense narrative an ideal vehicle for "Morte d'Arthur." "The Epic," neither one form nor the other, acts to situate the "Morte d'Arthur" between the past and the present, just as Bedivere desires Arthur to be.

"Ulysses" underscores as well Tennyson's achievement with all the classical monologues of 1832 and 1842. These works show how Tennyson successfully assimilated classical materials and so opened up another fictive—and beautiful—world for his dramatic monologues. He also shaped poems that demanded the reader's increasingly active participation and, by means of the sympathetic imagination, rendered the consciousness of his speakers not only through oscillating movements of mind that left significant gaps in the text but also through increasingly subtle language that itself served as a gauge of the speaker's mind state. All these achievements, as well as Tennyson's shrewd adaptation of dramatic versus narrative formal properties, make it easy to see why the classical monologues are justly admired as some of Tennyson's finest poetry.

## III

The Victorian reader's world is explicitly addressed in the last group of monologues I wish to discuss in this chapter; in these Tennyson retains the contemporary setting of the domestic monologues but addresses the intellect and aesthetic sensibility of his readers (as he did in the classical monologues) as well as their emotions. It seems clear that he also addresses himself as he confronts many problems of the age. But if the recursive loop is in full operation in these poems, so is his command over an objectified and distanced art, and it is difficult to say just where the subjective and objective begin and end.

These works, however, like the Victorian world they depict, are diverse, diverse in strategy and approach. Although most dramatize the speaker's consciousness, "St. Simeon Stylites" shifts to the realm of personality. We are also introduced to Tennyson's use of humor and satire in these poems. In "Will Waterproof's Lyrical Monologue" humor enhances Tennyson's distance from his speaker, a distance necessary for a speaker who is, like Tennyson, a poet questioning the role of art in the Victorian age. Humor is made subordinate to the purpose of satire in "St. Simeon Stylites" and "Amphion," in which case the reader is invited to judge the speakers more than to participate in their consciousnesses. And "The Two Voices," as well as the poems that conclude this chapter's discussion, show Tennyson beginning to experiment not only with mixed forms but with multiple perspectives as well.

"The Two Voices" is problematical in content—the overly sweet picture of domestic harmony at the end seems out of place after the intense doubt and conflict of the beginning—and also in form. The poem is dramatic since a voice indicated to be other than the poet's speaks in the present tense, yet there is more than one voice, and a past-tense narrative element as well: the poem begins, "A still small voice spake unto me." Yet in the first three hundred or so lines (composed in 1833),[63] one can see a clear rationale for the form Tennyson used.

One might say that in "Thoughts of a Suicide," the name under which the 1833 lines were composed, Tennyson created a dramatic monopolylogue: there is one speaker but many voices.[64] The original title indicated that these voices were centered in a single consciousness, just as several conflicting emotions operate within the speaker of "Supposed Confessions." Both "Supposed Confessions" and "Thoughts of a Suicide" concern a divided mind, but in the latter Tennyson makes the division explicit formally, splitting the strands of the mind into separate voices. Moreover, the formal device has psychological implications. The centering in the mind has become radical: we get no hints of names, times, places. The outer world has disappeared completely. Instead the mind has become a world unto itself, peopled with different voices rather than persons and places, until the emphatic enclosure within the mind becomes a nightmare world.[65] One of the speaker's greatest fears is that consciousness is all there is, a fear enunciated by the dark voice: "For every worm beneath the moon / Draws different threads, and late and soon / Spins, toiling out his own cocoon" (lines 178–80). Tennyson, of course, was to use the splintering of one mind into several voices to great effect in *Maud*, which in this connection might be entitled "Thoughts of a Lover, Duelist, and Manic-Depressive." Only whereas the very length of *Maud* and its shift in voices emphasize that poem's radical centering in consciousness, Tennyson achieves this end in "The Two Voices" by having a narrative overlay enclose the voices, functioning as a container (as in "Mariana") that bounds and locks them within the braincase. Both the dark voice and the narrator's "I" may allude to that beyond pure consciousness—the dark voice to physiology,[66] the "I" to sympathetic emotions and intuitions of a larger existence—but as long as they address their thoughts to each other, nothing else exists but the enclosed mind.

Presenting a mind in dialogue with and unto itself gave Tennyson the opportunity to exercise both the subjective and the objective, the personal and the fictive, poles of the dramatic form. He could explore, as so many have noted, his skepticism and his hope without endorsing either, and subsume and distance both sides into a portrait of a torn and self-tortured mind in the grip of radical isolation. He could also present for his readers' contemplation the grounds of faith and doubt. Indeed, Tennyson was careful to delete lines that threatened to become too personal, including those undoubtedly referring to Hallam.

> *When thy best friend draws sobbing breath,*
> *Plight thou a compact ere his death*
> *And comprehend the words he saith.*
>
> *Urge him to swear, distinct and plain,*
> *That out of bliss or out of pain*
> *He will draw nigh thee once again.*
>
> *Is that his footstep on the floor?*
> *Is this his whisper at the door?*
> *Surely he comes. He comes no more.*[67]

So far, so good: Tennyson is at once subjective and objective, successful in rendering his speaker's consciousness, true to himself and the age, and very much in control of dramatic versus narrative form. But the ending he composed in 1837 or 1838 is at once appropriate and out of keeping with the rest. The "I," that is, is entirely right to see that the answer to radical skepticism is to break out of the self:[68] it is "more life, and fuller, that I want." Thus, around line 400 elements of the larger world suddenly erupt into the poem. We learn that it is Sunday morning and that the "I" has been locked up in his room when he releases the casement and literally lets in the larger world. And now for the first time, instead of merely talking about fusing heart and head, the speaker practices it, blessing the family on its way to church, revelling in the beauties of nature—and hearing at last the voice, not of certainty ("I may not speak of what I know"), but of affirmation: "Rejoice! Rejoice!" It all ought to work, but it does not. Beyond the difficulty of the too-good-to-be-true husband, wife, and child, there are formal difficulties. The dialogue of voices that dominates the first part of the poem may disappear, but so also does the immediacy generated by the dramatic monologue. The last part of the poem is rendered almost entirely in past-tense narrative, and this inevitably seems distant, pale, robbed of any immediate presence after the dramatic format of the preceding internal debate. At the same time, the appearance of the affirmative voice means that, though to a much lesser degree, the narrator's mind is in fact still communing with itself rather than with the larger world—an implication that undermines the entrance of the outside world with the speaker's opening of the casement. The poem is almost a brilliant accomplishment, but not quite.

"St. Simeon Stylites" was begun, it appears, around the same time as "The Two Voices." Nothing like "St. Simeon" had ever been published by Tennyson before—graphic and even rough in its diction, full of grim humor, yet reflecting sympathy for the man obsessed with grotesque penances.[69] The appearance of "St. Simeon Stylites," however, seems quite explicable when it is seen as a pendant to "The Two Voices," which it immediately follows in Ricks's edition. If the dilemma in "The Two Voices" is being locked into the isolation of pure consciousness, St. Simeon appears to be one who, terrified of confronting the self and the emptiness of spirit he might find there, has moved the lines of battle outward, to the body. Simeon professes disgust for the flesh, "which I despise and hate" (line 57). Yet ironically the body has become his anchor, his emblem of spirituality, and his refuge from the pains and fears of self-examination. Simeon, in other words, has come to confuse reification with deification—the same problem Arthur faces with his knights in "The Holy Grail."

Tennyson has beautifully shaped the spoken to reveal Simeon's reification of spirituality. At times Simeon spouts a torrent of nouns, of *things:*[70] "Patient on this tall pillar I have borne / Rain, wind, frost, heat, hail, damp, and sleet, and snow" (lines 15–16). Although in some early drafts Simeon begins his monologue by using adjectives to describe himself—"polluted, blurred, / Blained, rank, corrupt"[71]—in the published version Tennyson has him refer to himself as, emphatically, a thing: "Although I be the basest of mankind, / From scalp to sole one slough and crust of sin." Indeed, he reifies his very self, speaking of himself as "a *sign* betwixt the meadow and the cloud" (line 14) at the beginning of his monologue and as an "example" (lines 185, 220) at the poem's end.

To Simeon, "hymns" and "psalms" are important for their physical sound, not their sense: "I drowned the whoopings of the owl with sound / Of pious hymns and psalms"—and, ironically, through the assonance of "owl" and "sound" Tennyson lets us hear the owl rather than the hymns. Simeon is also obsessed with quantities rather than qualities. He carefully tots up the heights of his successive pillars (lines 85–90); has counted to make sure he "bow[s] down one thousand and two hundred times, / To Christ, the Virgin Mother, and the saints" while others, including the heavenly hosts, sit at ease (lines 103–10); and prophesies his own death, not to the nearest hour, but to the nearest minute: "I prophesy that I shall die tonight, / A quarter before twelve" (lines 217–18). The ludicrousness of it all is too much for Tennyson to resist, as the humor of Simeon's alluding to his former chattering teeth, "which now are dropt away" (line

29), and to himself as one "whose brain the sunshine bakes" (line 161) clearly show. We see, not a saint, but a half-baked, toothless old man.

Yet the seriousness of Simeon's reification is not neglected either. For all his expressed hatred of his body, he has come to see it as a source of power. He thus mentions those "that came / To touch my body and be healed, and live" (lines 77–78) and relishes the thought of the honor done to his body when he is dead.

> *I say, that time is at the doors*
> *When you may worship me without reproach;*
> *For I will leave my relics in your land,*
> *And you may carve a shrine about my dust,*
> *And burn a fragrant lamp before my bones,*
> *When I am gathered to the glorious saints.*
>
> *(lines 189–94)*

One is reminded of the Bishop of St. Praxed's and his lust for just the right tomb to encase his mouldering bones.

The analogy to Browning's work is entirely apt. Tennyson did not generally fail to write "Browningesque" dramatic monologues because he could not. Indeed, "St. Simeon" was written before the dramatic monologues for which Browning is most famous had even appeared.[72] This monologue reminds us of Browning because we are nearer than in most of Tennyson's monologues to the realm of personality and the orientation of the self to the world—entirely apt for one whose problem is a faith so uncertain he must cling to all the external assurances of salvation achieved through a life of penance performed before the world as before a theater. Indeed, Simeon's utterance is explicitly shaped for an audience:[73] these catalogues of mortifications, hymns, and aves are recited not as reminders—Simeon is almost unnaturally aware of his records—but for the sake of those he hopes are listening, his admirers below and, he hopes, God above.

And yet, just as in Browning we glimpse the soul or consciousness underlying the veneer of personality, so do we with Tennyson's Simeon. For the tragedy, as opposed to the satiric comedy, of Simeon is that he cannot entirely escape his con-

sciousness, a fact neatly underlined by Tennyson's very use of
the dramatic monologue format. Simeon has his defenses—one
suspects the very length of his monologue is his way of evading
silence and a confrontation with his inner self (versus his outer
self as "sign"). In the past he could escape the court of consciousness by clinging to his body, but now that is done for,
rotted away at last after a life that would have killed most in
thirty days. Thus his reliance on penances for salvation and
sainthood is punctuated by doubt so painful that he immediately
scampers back to more and greater penances.

> And I had hoped that ere this period closed
> Thou wouldst have caught me up into thy rest,
> Denying not these weather-beaten limbs
> The meed of saints, the white robe and the palm.
>
> O take the meaning, Lord: I do not breathe,
> Not whisper, any murmur of complaint.
> Pain heaped ten-hundred-fold to this, were still
> Less burthen, by ten-hundred-fold, to bear,
> Than were those lead-like tons of sin that crushed
> My spirit flat before thee.
>
> (lines 17–26)

But the concreteness of his penance is never enough, and he has
at times, like Tennyson's other doubters, become paralyzed
with doubt.

> then they prate
> Of penances I cannot have gone through,
> Perplexing me with lies; and oft I fall,
> Maybe for months, in such blind lethargies
> That Heaven, and Earth, and Time are choked.
>
> (lines 98–102)

Significantly, time and space (or "Earth") are above linked with
heaven. After a life of reifying the spirit, he cannot doubt the
physical without doubting heaven, too—and yet presumably his
recourse to the physical began because he feared his doubts,
hence his insistence on the enormity of his sin. His decayed body
is an emblem for a decayed faith, but Simeon cannot allow himself to see this.[74] He really is pitiful as well as absurd.

"St. Simeon," then, is a masterful portrait of a speaker's complex psychology. It is also a poem designed, like "The Lotos-Eaters," for a reader's active response, as the many gaps in the text show, whether in the form of Simeon's questions—for example, "Am I to blame for this, / That here come those that worship me?"—or the ambiguity of phrases like "Thou, O God, / Knowest alone whether this [the healing of the lame and sick] was or no" (lines 122–23, 81–82). The reader is clearly invited to see things other than as Simeon sees them yet also to see why—and sympathize that—Simeon's perspective is what it is.[75] And Tennyson? Where does he figure in the poem? Unquestionably Tennyson has created an unTennysonian speaker, one so different from his usual personae that, though we lose sight of Tennyson the man, we are very aware of Tennyson the artist who can create such a poem.[76] But if we think of "St. Simeon" in relation to "The Two Voices," it is also possible to see how Tennyson could also be exploiting the monologue's recursive loop in the poem. For if "The Two Voices" is about the pain of doubt, "St. Simeon" shows that reaching for certainties can be even worse. It is far better to doubt and have two voices in one's head than to torture the body and find oneself still not quite free from doubt after all.[77] "St. Simeon," in other words, may be a poem in which Tennyson obliquely explores the validity of doubt.[78]

Tennyson's ability to fuse the humorous and the serious in "St. Simeon Stylites" surfaced again in two rather different poems not written until about 1837, "Will Waterproof's Lyrical Monologue" and "Amphion." Both explore the role—and dilemma—of the artist against the backdrop of a prosaic Victorian world. Yet the poems function as contrasts. "Will Waterproof" is warmly humorous, and the reader is invited to participate in the consciousness that Tennyson sympathetically renders. "Amphion," however, is satiric, and the recursive loop remains closed to both poet and reader.

"Will Waterproof's Lyrical Monologue" fuses not only the themes of art and time but also the themes of most of the poems published in 1842: myth (since the inebriated Will invents on the spot a myth about the tavern and head waiter he patronizes); the loss of a loved friend (a thousand hours, Will says, have "fallen into the dusty crypt / Of darkened forms and faces"—

lines 183–84); politics ("But for some true result of good / All parties work together"—lines 55–56); and the progress that means, as King Arthur says, the old order must yield to the new ("I hold it good, good things should pass"—line 205). The poem is thus a kind of summation and assessment of what Tennyson had achieved thus far and suggests Tennyson's active participation in the monologue.

The question of poetic achievement was also a subject Tennyson explored in two drafts of a lyric, never published, beginning, "Wherefore, in these dark ages of the press, / . . . should I, / Should any man desire to print his rhyme?"[79] In this fragment Tennyson worries about becoming a mere "popular property," hearing "his name / Shot like a racketball from mouth to mouth / And bandied in the barren lips of fools." In the second draft of the poem, elaborating upon his fears in a way that echoes "Will Waterproof" ("now I take my glass, / Walk in and out and laugh or sulk at ease"), he finally states a creed of poetic independence: "What this Art-Conscience preaches I to that / Lend credit, not to him or him and least / The general throat." All this is very well—certainly very clear—and no doubt afforded Tennyson the comfort of self-expression. But as verse it is not only too glaringly personal but also too pompous and smug. What Tennyson needed, and what he earlier found in "Will Waterproof," was a means of fully venting his personal anxieties and yet distancing himself and the audience from a theme that could so easily lend itself to poetic hubris. Moreover, Tennyson needed a strategy to keep the monologue's feint intact. Otherwise Tennyson would too easily be identified with his own speaker. The answer was humor, which poked fun at Tennyson's problems and his persona even as he explored them. Out, accordingly, went the "haunting verbal music" into which it would be so easy to pour strains of melancholy lament. In came a rollicking balladic meter that keeps the tone light and aptly captures the rhythms of a mind slightly inebriated.

Even Will's name hints that the poem's subject is both serious and comic, and the setting implies the theme of the artist. Will, fast approaching middle age and rampant obscurity, arrives at The Cock for his daily pint of port; he is undoubtedly, as has been suggested,[80] a parody of Will Shakespeare at The Mermaid. But if he is impervious to—*proof* against—the fertility and life associated with water, then he faces the problem of failing artistic powers.[81] Yet Will's name also suggests the endurance of will and fortitude. "Proof" suggests a form of test, perhaps even the page proofs of Will's "random rhymes," but also the proof of alcohol Will drinks, alcohol that could be a means of poetic inspiration or an escape from failure. Indeed, one of the delightful things about the poem is that we never quite know whether Will is serious or merely boozy, genuinely inspired by the special port he drinks or merely drunk. The very ambiguity is a means of structurally underpinning the crux of the poem: can he continue to create poetry?

One of the enemies of Will's poetry is time. At the outset he asks the head waiter, "How goes the time?" (line 3). It is a larger question than we might at first expect. For time is a robber—of Will's verses ("make me write my random rhymes, / Ere they be half-forgotten"—lines 13–14); of his youth ("I had hope . . . To prove myself a poet: / But, while I plan and plan, my hair / Is gray before I know it"—lines 165, 166–68); of his youthful aspiration ("when the Poet's words and looks / Had yet their native glow"—lines 193–94); and of those he loved (the "dusty crypt / Of darkened forms and faces"—lines 183–84). The dramatic monologue, situated on the inside of time, is thus set in opposition to the impetus of linear time that drains away all Will once had and locks it into the past. Only the dramatic monologue, furthermore, can capture the immediacy and transience of Will's foray into instant myth-making. For his drinking deliberately invokes the Muse. The pint of port must be "no vain libation to the Muse" (line 9), who, he hopes, will lift him above the flow of time where he can regain contact with his vanished past, transcend the petty frets of life (the "critic-pen, / Or that eternal want of pence"—lines 41–42), and spin out his songs.

The Muse seems to grant Will's wish, arriving in a way that parodies the religious act of communion.

> *I pledge her, and she comes and dips*
> *Her laurel in the wine,*
> *And lays it thrice upon my lips,*
> *These favoured lips of mine.*

*(lines 17–20)*

And so at the end of the poem's first section Will claims to have achieved that larger view he seeks.

> *This whole wide earth of light and shade*
> *Comes out a perfect round.*
> *High over roaring Temple-bar,*
> *And set in Heaven's third story,*
> *I look at all things as they are,*
> *But through a kind of glory.*

*(lines 67–72)*

In the second section Will is now convinced the Muse has visited him, a visit once more described in an irreverent parody of communion: "She . . . Used all her fiery will, and smote / Her life into the liquor" (lines 109, 111–112). Suddenly Will's prosaic surroundings take on grandeur. The very waiter bears a halo, not round his head but about his hands (which brought the wine), and Will is suddenly inspired to invent his myth. "The Cock was of a larger egg / Than modern poultry drop" (lines 121–22), who, spying the plump waiter as "A something-pottle-bodied boy" (line 131), clutched him and

> *Flew over roof and casement:*
> *His brothers of the weather stood*
> *Stock-still for sheer amazement.*
>
> *But he, by farmstead, thorpe and spire,*
> *And followed with acclaims,*
> *A sign to many a staring shire*
> *Came crowing over Thames.*
> *Right down by smoky Paul's they bore,*
> *Till, where the street grows straiter,*
> *One fixed for ever at the door,*
> *And one became head-waiter.*

*(lines 134–44)*

The myth is charming in its whimsy and genial ridicule, but is hardly the stuff of epic or lasting art. The whole thing evaporates in the third section, accordingly, and Will is left wondering how he thought to create "legend . . . Among the chops and steaks" (lines 147–148), a question not far removed from Everard Hall's in "The Epic." And now he faces the very things— "that half-crown, / Which I shall have to pay" (lines 155–56); the fear that "of the fulness of my life / I leave an empty flask"(lines 163–64)—he sought to evade at the outset. It could be that the Muse has left as suddenly as she arrived or that she was never there at all: Will's disenchantment could be simply the after-effect of boozy euphoria.

The poem's ending is a playful tease rather than a clear-cut resolution of Will's difficulties as an artist. Will simply lets go of his own problems and focuses on the waiter instead, for whom he wishes a long life and, when the waiter dies, "carved cross-pipes" and a "pint-pot" instead of "carved cross-bones." Apparently the myth of The Cock and the head waiter does not last. And yet it does, in a way. Will, letting go of it, finds that he can keep the myth as a pleasant memory ("I hold thee dear / For this good pint of port"—lines 211–12). More important, his earlier flight of fancy has had this effect at least, that it makes him forget himself, look more closely at the waiter, and appreciate him. Ultimately the reader must judge the monologue by the same standards: we know that it is not one of Tennyson's great-est poems; the question is whether we like Will better after hear-ing him talk. I do, and find myself admiring Tennyson's ability to take a wry look at himself, his poetry, his sorrows, even religion, through humor that distances and imparts to the monologue the same warmth and mellowness that the port gives to Will's perception. The distance afforded by humor was something Tennyson was to draw on again in his Lincolnshire monologues many years later and again with very pleasant effects.

But just as Tennyson wrote the mellow "Northern Farmer, Old Style" and then appended the satiric "Northern Farmer, New Style" in the 1860s, so he wrote the satiric "Amphion" at about the same time as "Will Waterproof." "Amphion" is the antiphonal voice of "Will Waterproof." In both Tennyson exam-ines the problems of art versus the age, but he mocks rather than sympathizes with the speaker of "Amphion," blocking the recursive loop in order to shape the poem into an ironic revela-tion of the speaker that enables us to see another view beyond his own.

The speaker is *not* Amphion; he only wishes he lived in the "days of old Amphion" when "song was great" (lines 10, 9), but he concludes that instead he lives "in such a brassy age / I could not move a thistle" (lines 65–66) with, not a lyre, but his fiddle. The problem, however, seems to be the speaker himself. He has no real respect for myth, which he gets wrong. It was Orpheus who moved the trees and stones as he played, not Amphion— who built the city of Thebes to music, as Camelot was built in the *Idylls*.[82] Nor does the speaker venerate the order and harmony generally associated with myth and art; his mythic vision is one of jingling dissonance and disorder. He imagines that when Amphion / Orpheus sang, "The gouty oak began to move, / And flounder into hornpipes"; "The linden broke her ranks and rent / The woodbine wreaths"; "The country-side descended";[83] and the yews, "a dismal coterie; / Each plucked his one foot from the grave, / Poussetting with a sloe-tree" (lines 42–44). Will Waterproof resorts to humor *because* he gives death its due; the speaker of "Amphion" makes a mockery of death, like the hardened sinner in "The Vision of Sin."

The speaker also shows scant respect for modern poetry, as seen in his outrageous parody of Wordsworth—"Better to me the meanest weed / That blows upon its mountain" (lines 93–94). Nor does the speaker value the sympathy that Wordsworth urged and that Will Waterproof practices toward the head waiter. The speaker of "Amphion" simply dislikes and dismisses those among whom he lives.

> But what is that I hear? a sound
>   Like sleepy counsel pleading;
> O Lord!—'tis in my neighbour's ground,
>   The modern Muses reading.
> They read Botanic Treatises,
>   And Works on Gardening through there,
> And Methods of transplanting trees
>   To look as if they grew there.
>
> The withered Misses!
>
> (lines 73–81)

The allegorical implications in these lines—the efficacy of the Muses in transplanting the art of one age into the new poetry of another, the hints of the Garden of Eden and Adam's curse of work—are Tennyson's none-too-subtle means of pointing up a moral. This moral was recorded by Emily Sellwood Tennyson

117

years later as "Genius must not deem itself exempt from work."[84] One in fact is disappointed to see that the moral can be so clearly and concisely put. The poem is better when Tennyson is more indirect. The slack poet who claims that hard work at poetry is useless even before he begins gets only one response to his "art": the sparrows

> *Scarce answer to my whistle;*
> *Or at the most, when three-parts-sick*
> *With strumming and with scraping,*
> *A jackass heehaws from the rick.*

*(lines 68–71)*

The joke is that when the speaker fiddles, another myth, to which the speaker is oblivious, is at work: the myth of Echo.

"Amphion" is not very successful. Satire demands an entirely objective viewpoint, but Tennyson most excelled when he could imagine another as part of himself, no matter how much poetic distance he achieved. Shorn of Tennyson's sympathetic participation, the poem easily descends into didacticism, lacking the ambiguity and play of "Will Waterproof." Accordingly, the doggerel twanging of the verse, though apt for the speaker, lacks not only the rationale of inebriation in "Will Waterproof" but the latter's charm as well.[85]

"Lady Clara Vere de Vere" seems to have been inspired by personal experience, Tennyson's ill treatment at the hands of Rosa Baring.[86] The poem's speaker is an embittered young man in the country who has been flirted with, then abandoned by, the socially "superior" Lady Clara. His declaration that "I could not stoop to such a mind" (line 20) as hers is reminiscent of Tennyson's unpublished sonnet, "How thought you that this thing could captivate?" where Tennyson derides the woman's "conventional" speech "so void of weight"—comments generally taken to refer to Rosa. And the "lion" on Lady Vere de Vere's "old stone gates . . . not more cold to you than I" (lines 23–24) was to reappear on the garden gate in *Maud*: "A lion ramps at the top" (I, 495).

The poem's subject, then, allowed ample opportunity for Tennyson to activate the dramatic monologue's recursive loop. But Tennyson does not render his speaker's consciousness

through the sympathetic imagination that approaches another
as an aspect of self. All the poem's energies are instead directed
toward the Lady, the auditor. She is berated for her hard-
heartedness, her pride, and her part in the suicide of Lawrence,
another hapless youth of lower social caste than she.

> Lady Clara Vere de Vere,
>   When thus he met his mother's view,
> She had the passions of her kind,
>   She spake some certain truths of you.
> Indeed I heard one bitter word
>   That scarce is fit for you to hear;
> Her manners had not that repose
>   Which stamps the caste of Vere de Vere.

*(lines 33–40)*

Lawrence's mother had recourse to self-expression, but the auditor Lady Clara, a captive audience ensnared within the bounds
of the poem and forced to listen without the chance to reply,
does not. Here the dramatic monologue subserves the function
of revenge: the very form imprisons the auditor while the
speaker can hurl any form of abuse at her he wishes. Thus in
"Lady Clara Vere de Vere" the dramatic monologue has only a
negative function; it is not a way of achieving distance and objectivity but only a way, perhaps, of achieving catharsis. As in
some of Tennyson's earliest poems that centered on painful
emotions, the dramatic format here seems used to distance
Tennyson from emotions he himself is reluctant to face.[87] At all
events, if, as seems likely, the poem was prompted by Tennyson's unhappy love affair with Rosa, he may have written too
soon.

"Locksley Hall," probably written at least two years after
"Lady Clara Vere de Vere," is like the former poem in two ways:
it deals with a young man spurned in love because of social caste
and, as generally accepted in the wake of Ralph Rader's work,
grows out of Tennyson's relationship with Rosa. But "Locksley
Hall" is a vastly superior poem. The poem may have the same
outbursts, the same passion, the same desire for revenge
against a woman that we see in "Lady Clara," but the later poem
is squarely centered in the speaker's consciousness, not directed
toward an auditor. The revenge element is distanced because

this strand of consciousness exists side by side with many other strands of consciousness, giving us perspective on the revenge and, more important, a full and rich portrayal of the speaker's inward sensibility.

One of the curiosities of "Locksley Hall" is the amount of time devoted by the speaker to narrating past events. The opening lines of the poem situate the speaker and his monologue firmly in the present—"Comrades, leave me here a little, while as yet 'tis early morn"—but the hero paces no more than a few steps before he is lost in the past: "Here about the beach I wandered, nourishing a youth sublime" (line 11). The mixing of past and present is not the result of Tennyson's desire to frame experience, as in "The Gardener's Daughter." Rather, the interplay of past and present cuts to the heart of the speaker's psyche. One could say that the entire monologue turns on the issue of time, a focus natural for a poem that features a young speaker: as Tennyson said, "The whole poem represents young life, its good side, its deficiencies, and its yearnings" (*Memoir*, I, 195). Youth is a borderline time, on the threshold of the future, yet just emerging from the past of childhood and wanting to make the present all its own. But more than his youth, the speaker's disillusionment with Amy forces him into a troubled relationship with time. Interestingly enough, in the lyric "Come not, when I am dead," addressed to another woman who has spurned the speaker and who is about to wed—a likely reference to Rosa's approaching marriage—Tennyson says, "I am sick of Time." The speaker of "Locksley Hall" has the same malady. Amy's jilting has killed the future he had imagined for them, made a mockery of the past with all its memories of exchanged tendernesses and vows, and rendered his present miserable. In the poem the speaker must accordingly work out his relation to time in the wake of disillusionment. Just as in the golden hour of mutual love with Amy he was suspended between a storm and a dawning—"And she turned—her bosom shaken with a sudden storm of sighs— / All the spirit deeply dawning in the dark of hazel eyes—" (lines 27–28), so here he moves from the dawn to the storm; the poem begins at "early morn" and closes with a loud storm approaching Locksley Hall.

The twistings and turnings of the speaker's consciousness in the course of the monologue have been admirably mapped by several readers.[88] Basically, though, one might say we witness the speaker trying to do all he can to escape the present, either attempting to regress into an idyllic past or to catapult himself immediately into the future, as Tithon wished to do, until he recognizes the folly of both. Thus at the beginning he harks back to an ideal boyhood when time itself was a harmony, not a jangled discord: "When the centuries behind me like a fruitful land reposed; / When I clung to all the present for the promise that it closed: / When I dipt into the future far as human eye could see" (lines 13–15). But note that all this is expressed in the past tense; this time is over, for Amy, too, was a part of that past; and in eclipsing herself from the speaker, she has also cast darkness on his memories of early youth.

And so he turns to the future, imagining the revenge that time will bring against Amy: "He will hold thee, when his passion shall have spent its novel force, / Something better than his dog, a little dearer than his horse" (lines 49–50). Revenge, however, is not much of a future for an idealistic youth. Worse, revenge lies only *in* the future, of little comfort to the speaker's lacerated ego, and so he is thrown back into the present, where he cannot rest comfortably either: "Cursèd be the social wants that sin against the strength of youth! / Cursèd be the social lies that warp us from the living truth!" (lines 59–60). Finding the past, present, and future all problematical, the speaker is quite justified in asking, "What is that which I should turn to, lighting upon days like these?" (line 99). And so he repeats the whole process, regressing to the past,[89] imagining possible futures, landing in and recoiling from the present, his tumbling passions keeping him from pursuing any strategy for long. The poem is a perfect rendering of the oscillations of consciousness.

The poem also, of course, embodies several strands of the Victorian age: its love of progress and sturdy faith in itself as a leader in the annals of time, yet also its social blights and its uncertainties about the changes in society and technology wrought by progress. Tennyson beautifully fuses the subjective and the objective, the private and the public, while being faithful to each. Dwelling on contemporary problems follows naturally from Amy's jilting of the hero for a mercenary marriage.[90] Moreover, the speaker's youthful idealism is so bound up with his love for Amy that disillusionment in one quarter inevitably leads him to doubt in the other. Likewise, the question for Victorian society, as for the hero, was how to relate its own past, present, and future. "Locksley Hall" thus demonstrates how far Tennyson had come to understand and exploit the range of the dramatic monologue, which could be directed toward external and internal situations and issues all at once. It was a lesson T. S. Eliot did not miss either, whose "Love Song of J. Alfred Prufrock" is at once intensely poetical (rather than naturalistic), intensely psychological, and also a portrait of an empty and benumbing social order.

But the ending of "Locksley Hall" is not so clearly successful. If we are to believe that the speaker has resolved his relation to time, why must he allude to the destruction of Locksley Hall instead of accepting it as part of the past that will always be just that—a part of the past that can be transcended? Perhaps this allusion is simply the speaker's way of renouncing the viselike grip of the past on him. Even granting this, however, there is the difficulty posed by the grand sweep of the last lines that lead to a rhetorical climax, versus the diffuseness of what they assert: "For the mighty wind arises, roaring seaward, and I go." As Ricks asks, "Go? Where, and to what?"[91] In "Ulysses" this strategy works because for Ulysses the only thing that matters is to keep going. But in "Locksley Hall" the closing lines are presented as a kind of resolution ("For . . . I go"), and they ring false. The problem, I think, is integrally linked to the achievement of the poem. Tennyson has rooted the poem so inveterately in the realm of consciousness that he runs full force into the dilemma of consciousness: consciousness ends only with death, and any other termination is temporary, arbitrary, imposed. Yet the poem must end. The same difficulty was to arise in *Maud*. It seems perfectly plausible that the later poem, like consciousness, should go on so long. The problem is in bringing it to a close.

After "Lady Clara Vere de Vere" and "Locksley Hall," Tennyson used yet another strategy for approaching the theme of jilted love in "Edwin Morris," a strategy that harks back to "The Gardener's Daughter" and forward to *The Princess*.[92] Like "The

Gardener's Daughter," "Edwin Morris" seeks to frame an ear-lier experience, unlike "Locksley Hall," which captures its speaker in the very process of responding to disappointed love. The speaker of "Edwin Morris" is once again a painter, or at least a sometime painter, and as does "The Gardener's Daughter," "Edwin Morris" clearly opens in a dramatic context with the un-named speaker gesturing to his work: "I was a sketcher then: / See here, my doing" (lines 4–5). But the meaning of the expe-rience that the speaker is about to retell has not endured into the present. As we learn at the poem's end, Letty is not a pres-ence in her own right in the speaker's memory but only one of many glancing lights of the landscape of the past. Just so, we get a glancing use of the present-tense dramatic form at the poem's outset, and then the entire story of the poem, like the speaker's dead love for Letty, is absorbed into the unbroken past tense of narrative, framed and held there forever.

In that narrative, however, Tennyson anticipates a strategy he was to use in *The Princess*, splintering the narrative into three different perspectives: the speaker's own and those of Edwin Morris and Edward Bull. We do not know the speaker's name, but it ought to be Edmund to chime with the similar names of the other two. For clearly Edwin and Edward, the one overly idealistic about love, the other overly reductive, represent the two extremes between which the speaker steers in remember-ing his de-idealizing and yet not altogether meaningless love af-fair with Letty.[93] Indeed, the words of Edwin and Edward (nar-rated by the speaker) triply frame the central episode of the speaker's being shooed away from Letty by her mercenary rela-tives: Edwin and Edward's words precede the central episode, their viewpoints bracket the speaker's own, and encased by the narrator's past tense and voice, their own words are literally framed.

Thus the central episode is distanced from us and the speaker through the splintering of perspectives and the predominance of past-tense narrative over the dramatic—a perfect formal means of saying what the speaker himself says when he reverts to present-tense utterance in the poem's final lines. His love for Letty is cut off, gone, over; it can recur only as gossamer frag-ments of memory.

*So [I] left the place, left Edwin, nor have seen*
*Him since, nor heard of her, nor cared to hear.*

    *Nor cared to hear? perhaps: yet long ago*
*I have pardoned little Letty; not indeed,*
*It may be, for her own dear sake but this,*
*She seems a part of those fresh days to me;*
*For in the dust and drouth of London life*
*She moves among my visions of the lake,*
*While the prime swallow dips his wing, or then*
*While the gold-lily blows, and overhead*
*The light cloud smoulders on the summer crag.*

                  *(lines 137–47)*

There is no need for a storm to engulf and destroy the lake or Letty's "Tudor-chimnied bulk"; time has done it all, as we see in the mellow acceptance of the pastness of the past by this speaker, a lesson the hero of "Locksley Hall" has yet to learn.[94]

    The mixed forms and multiple perspectives of "Edwin Morris" recur in "The Golden Year" and "The Vision of Sin" and make the appearance of *The Princess* a few years later seem almost an inevitability. In "The Golden Year" a speaker begins in the present and then narrates the words of the poet Leonard and the Carlylean James on the status of the Golden Age; hence Tennyson can explore multiple perspectives without explicitly choosing among them. As well, the narrative element of "The Golden Year" adds a layer of the past that balances Leonard's pushing the Golden Age into the future and James's ensconcing it in the present.

    Of greater interest than "The Golden Year," however, is "The Vision of Sin." Here, in a brilliant handling of mixed forms and perspectives, Tennyson creates a poem that touches all at once on the role of art, faith versus doubt, politics, love versus lust, or to condense, on idealism versus cynicism, and the role of experience and perception in shaping each. The poem as a whole is not a dramatic monologue but rather the narrative of dream vision, with the poet's "I" relaying all. The narrative strategy is in fact crucial, necessary to allow the successive displacement of perspectives that occur as in a dream and that enable Tennyson to represent different orders of experience and seeing—impossible if he were to center all in the single speaker of a dramatic monologue. We begin by sharing the dreaming poet's vision of another poet, the youth who "rode a horse with wings, that would have flown, / But that his heavy rider kept him down" (lines 3-4). The youth enters the palace with a "child of sin," and the next section, with a shift as of a kaleidoscope, lets us see what happens inside the palace, the frenzied dance of sensuality that is beautiful and attractive, but maniacal and destructive: "Twisted hard in fierce embraces, / Like to Furies, like to Graces, / Dashed together in blinding dew" (lines 40-42). The kaleidoscope shifts again, and the dancers are entirely displaced, giving way to an order of experience that the dancers have forgotten yet which dwarfs them.

> And then I looked up toward a mountain-tract,
> That girt the region with high cliff and lawn:
> I saw that every morning, far withdrawn
> Beyond the darkness and the cataract,
> God made Himself an awful rose of dawn,
> Unheeded.
>
> *(lines 46-51)*

We are not told how to relate these different orders of being and experience, only that they exist side by side. And as a way of achieving yet another perspective, we are enabled to view the dreams not only from without but also, in the fourth section, a dramatic monologue, from within. Here the very poet's "I" is momentarily displaced as the debauched sinner, presumably the youth of the opening section now grown old, is allowed to speak for himself.

In the debauched speaker's monologue, Tennyson could explore the darkest corners of his own doubts and sensibilities and yet, as it were, hold these in check through their juxtaposition with the other perspectives of the poem. One could never say that the speaker of the fourth section represents Tennyson, but that there are personal elements in the monologue seems clear from the references to disappointed love (" 'Tell me tales of thy first love—/ April hopes, the fools of chance'"—lines 163-64) and to a political philosophy that Tennyson espoused directly in other poems.

# The Manyfacèd Glass

"He that roars for liberty
    Faster binds a tyrant's power;
And the tyrant's cruel glee
    Forces on the freer hour."

(lines 127–30)

Most intriguing, however, is the fact that the debauched sinner
is in many ways a parody, or rather a reduction through time
and trouble, of Will Waterproof. Like Will, this speaker also arrives at an inn and hails the waiter, but in less mellow terms.

"Wrinkled ostler, grim and thin!
    Here is custom come your way;
Take my brute, and lead him in,
    Stuff his ribs with mouldy hay.
. . . . . . . . . . . . . .
"Slip-shod waiter, lank and sour,
    At the Dragon on the heath!
Let us have a quiet hour,
    Let us hob-and-nob with Death.

"I am old, but let me drink;
    Bring me spices, bring me wine;
I remember, when I think,
    That my youth was half divine.

"Wine is good for shrivelled lips,
    When a blanket wraps the day,
When the rotten woodland drips,
    And the leaf is stamped in clay."

(lines 63–66, 71–82)

No longer does a Muse dip her laurel in the wine and lay it on the
favored lips of her invoker; this speaker's very lips, like his heart
and joy, are shriveled, compressed and clotted by the weight of
experience. The speaker then runs through his black litany of
that which does not suffice—works, name, fame, friendship,
virtue, political idealism, love. But the speaker is somehow not
unattractive. Like Will he does not hesitate to laugh at himself,
and the grim unwaveringness of his gaze shows he is willing to
abide by the way he sees things. It is just that he sees only death.

The poem's last section, then, recurs to the "mystic mountain-
range" set above a plain of decay and death, the world of the old

libertine. But the only answer provided by the world of spirit is cryptic at best: "To which an answer pealed from that high land, / But in a tongue no man could understand" (lines 221–22). This is hardly comforting if one wants to answer the debauched sinner, yet the poem itself tells us that it is easier to understand failure, disillusionment, and sin than idealism and hope: the libertine's monologue is the longest section of the poem, well over a hundred lines, but the antiphonal voice is given only four lines in the last section, and then the voice is indecipherable.[95]

It is ultimately a very mysterious poem. We are simply given the parts of the dream, and it is up to us to assemble any significance, just as the reader at the end of *The Princess* is left to make sense of the prince's weird seizures and to decide whether the narrator moving in his "strange diagonal" has or has not pleased himself. Tennyson, in other words, has used the peculiar resources of the narrative and dramatic forms in "The Vision of Sin" to produce utterly objectified art.

"The Vision of Sin" not only is diverse in form itself but also reminds us of the larger diversity of the monologues with contemporary settings published in 1842. Freed by his control of the dramatic monologue medium, Tennyson could explore poetic strategies as varied as the age he drew upon for his fictive settings. He could render the consciousness of his speakers or the personality of Simeon; he could activate or close the recursive loop of personal participation; he could successfully mix forms within a single poem; he could invite the reader's active participation or judgment—and all while exploring the issues of faith, the function of art, and social injustice that absorbed the thinkers of his time.

To look back on the poems of 1832 and 1842, then, is to see the growing assurance and skill with which Tennyson handled the dramatic monologue, whether he used it in "pure" form or mixed it with other forms to create richly diverse poems, "beautiful other worlds." These new worlds included the realms of domestic life, classical myth, and contemporary society, and the expansion of the pole of fiction to include these worlds is one of the achievements of Tennyson's monologues during this time. As I have noted throughout this chapter, Tennyson's other advances included an enhanced attention to the reader as respondent to and participant in the dramatic monologues, increasingly subtle language used to indicate speakers' mind states, and a new sophistication in drawing upon formal properties of the monologue to help create a poem's meaning. Now Tennyson was ready, not to abandon the dramatic monologue, but to draw upon all he had learned in mastering the form as he approached the long poems of his middle years.

# 4. A Sharper Sense:
# The Dramatic in the Poetry of
# 1847–1855

*Strange, that the mind, when fraught*
*With a passion so intense*
*One would think that it well*
*Might drown all life in the eye,—*
*That it should, by being so overwrought,*
*Suddenly strike on a sharper sense.*

*—Maud, II, 106–11*

Tennyson was not afraid to reverse his early contention that "if I meant to make any mark at all, it must be by shortness" (*Memoir*, I, 166). *The Princess* (1847), *In Memoriam* (1850), and *Maud* (1855) were accordingly written, though Tennyson did not entirely abandon shorter works in these middle years. "The Brook" is a dramatic monologue resembling "The Miller's Daughter"; other short poems include "Ode on the Death of the Duke of Wellington" and "To the Rev. F. D. Maurice," important for showing the emergence of Tennyson's public voice in his role as poet laureate. Of the three long poems, only *Maud* is wholly dramatic: *The Princess* is a narrative; and *In Memoriam*, Tennyson's most famous work, consists of connected lyrics. Tennyson's recourse to the dramatic mode, it seems, diminished in his middle years. *Maud* excepted, this is true. Yet all three long poems reflect the lessons Tennyson had learned from writing dramatic monologues. *The Princess* depends on individual characters from the Prologue assuming a dramatic persona; *In Memo-*

*riam* renders the consciousness of the poet's persona; and *Maud* is both a culmination of and extension beyond all of Tennyson's earlier dramatic monologues.

## I
### The Princess

"The most significant thing about *The Princess*," Sir Charles Tennyson maintains, "is its persistent use of a dramatic method, which gives it a liveliness and power not present in anything that he had previously written" (222). Sir Charles is right to focus attention on the dramatic elements in *The Princess*. Two aesthetic strategies, one explicitly dramatic, are basic to the poem's design and theme. The first, though not itself a dramatic device, is shared by many of Tennyson's dramatic monologues: a frame. True, Tennyson had also used frames for narrative poems, including "Godiva," "Morte d'Arthur," and "The Day-Dream." But as previously noted, "The Epic" transforms the "Morte d'Arthur" into a quasi-dramatic poem, and "The Day-Dream" itself mixes dramatic and narrative elements. Most typically, then, Tennyson had before 1847 used the frame for dramatic poems; and as in "The Hesperides," "The Lotos-Eaters," and "Oenone," Tennyson uses the opening frame, or Prologue, in *The Princess* to establish both the artist's and the reader's perspectives. In part, as many have noted, the Prologue works simply to establish *The Princess* as a medley. The mingling of age groups, classes, and sexes on the lawn of Sir Walter Vivian's estate (where he hosts a Mechanics' Institute), the fusion of the playful and the serious ("sport / Went hand in hand with Science"—lines 79–80), and especially the items heaped inside Sir Walter's house prepare for the theme, form, and tone of the story shortly to be related.

> on the pavement lay
> Carved stones of the Abbey-ruin in the park,
> Huge Ammonites, and the first bones of Time;
> And on the tables every clime and age
> Jumbled together; celts and calumets,
> Claymore and snowshoe, toys in lava, fans
> Of sandal, amber, ancient rosaries,
> Laborious orient ivory sphere in sphere,

*The cursed Malayan crease, and battle-clubs*
*From the isles of palm: and higher on the walls,*
*Betwixt the monstrous horns of elk and deer,*
*His own forefathers' arms and armour hung.*

*(lines 13–24)*

Here, that is, are heaped the shards of various times, just as *The Princess* is set both in the present (in the Prologue) and a never-never-land past (in the narrative proper); tools of the north (the Prince's realm) and the south (Ida's realm); the products of art and war (both prominent in the "summer's tale"); the playthings of men (celts and calumets) and women (fans), and of children (toys) and adults.

More important, the frame acts to establish Tennyson's artistic perspective. The story of the Prince and Ida is related within the close of a Gothic ruin, whose walls "through one wide chasm of time and frost . . . gave / The park, the crowd, the house; but all within / The sward was trim as any garden lawn" (lines 93–95). The lines, surely, are Tennyson's way of announcing that although he remains within the realm of art, his story is one that opens out onto—is relevant to—the present age, even as the tellers of the story stay within the ordered sward but look out through a chasm onto the present throng gathered at Sir Walter's.[1] Fittingly, therefore, *The Princess* contains references to nineteenth-century social issues and scientific theories despite the narrative's fairy-tale setting. The references are at once anachronistic and crucial to the artist's perspective, and the reader is clearly invited to see why this is so: Tennyson is willing to abandon neither the realm of art nor that of Victoria.

The frame also introduces the tellers of the succeeding tale, just as the frames of Tennyson's dramatic monologues introduce those poems' speakers. Seven young men are gathered at Sir Walter's for the festivities, and all participate in relating the narrative, "Seven and yet one, like shadows in a dream" (line 222). This line, added only in 1851, is an important key for the reader. Like the earlier description of the place where the tale is told, this line alerts readers that what follows is unreal—dreamlike—yet "real," grounded on seven young Victorian men who merge, more or less, into a single whole. The added line of

131

1851 is of course also related to the contemporaneous addition of the Prince's weird seizures, and the added line in the Prologue helps us to see why the weird seizures were incorporated at all. The Prince's weird seizures cause the real and unreal to coalesce, so that "the Princess Ida seemed a hollow show . . . And I myself the shadow of a dream, / For all things were and were not" (III, 169, 172–73). That is, the addition of the "seven and yet one, like shadows in a dream" in the Prologue, and the weird seizures in the narrated tale, hint to the reader that the whole poem is a kind of "weird seizure," utterly unreal, and yet —insofar as it is relevant to Victorian social issues—intensely real. We may, as readers, consider *The Princess* only a fairy tale, but Tennyson lets us know that this is our choice.

*The Princess* is more directly related to the dramatic monologues than by its frame, however. Each of the seven tellers of the tale becomes in effect a monologist, assuming the character of the Prince: a dramatic element is built into *The Princess*. Moreover, the particular handling of the tellers-as-monologists reflects all that Tennyson himself had learned from writing dramatic monologues and suggests that his use of this device was highly conscious. In the first place, the use of seven different speakers reflects what he had discovered in poems like "The Two Voices," "Edwin Morris," and "The Vision of Sin,"[2] the efficacy of the dramatic for juxtaposing multiple perspectives within the bounds of a single poem. Taken singly, the various perspectives are "shadows," partial glimpses or facets of the whole, but taken together they have the force of a single vision that should be heeded. Tennyson's allowing each speaker from the Prologue suddenly to "become" the Prince also suggests that Tennyson was conscious of what Sinfield terms the dramatic monologue's feint. Because each of the seven sections of *The Princess* is related by an individual speaker, each section effectively claims the authenticity of an "I," yet as readers we are also made aware (via the Prologue) that this "I" is a pure fiction. Hence the "I" of each section, like the entire poem if viewed as one long "weird seizure" told within an enclosed garden of art that opens onto the Victorian world, is both false and true, real and unreal. This is, after all, something Tennyson knew from fusing the subjective and objective in his dramatic monologues:

in writing them he was disclosing a part of himself, speaking "truly," yet creating an objectified fiction, speaking "falsely," and so giving us two perspectives at once. *The Princess* subsumes not just two but manifold perspectives; in the closing frame, or Epilogue, we discover that the poet of the group has written down after the "fact" what was orally related within the sward, having tried to retain elements of all the speakers (the men), the singers of the connecting lyrics (the women), and what each group desired to see incorporated into the tale.

Examining the affinities between the dramatic monologues and *The Princess*—the seven monologists (or tellers) whose voices merge, and the feint embedded in each of the poem's seven sections—in fact carries us to the heart of the poem's themes and Tennyson's rationale for choosing the form. Tennyson's handling of multiple voices and perspectives did not merely allow him to mix, for example, the tragic and the burlesque, but was crucial to his examination of the position of women in society. Tennyson recognized that the difficulty women faced was their subjection to a single stereotyped role that defined and prescribed their natures. Thus he has the Prince point out to his father, who rattles off the traits of the prevailing stereotype as if he spoke a litany, the error of his view: "you clash them all in one, / That have as many differences as we" (V, 172–73). The medley form resulting from seven different speakers is Tennyson's (formal) way of doing justice to women; were he to provide only one perspective in the poem, he would be practicing artistically the same thought process that results in the stereotyping of, and hence injustice to, women. Instead he steers a "strange diagonal" between the reality and unreality of each speaker or "I" and among the many speakers who participate in relating the tale.

The medley form relates directly to another of Tennyson's themes, the inherent link between men and women; for the medley is not wholly unified or free from dissonance, just as men and women are not entirely congruent and face, in and out of the poem, the possibility of a "war" of the sexes; but neither is the medley form a disunity, consisting of self-contained and isolated parts. The medley form's thematic implications hence further clarify both Tennyson's use of seven speakers—they

133

impart multiple perspectives and coalesce imperfectly into one voice—and the question of why he dropped the introductions of each speaker that existed in a draft, even though these introductory characterizations underscored the dramatic nature, the "fictiveness," of each section.[3] To have retained the introductions that further individuated each speaker would have tipped the balance away from a loose unity ("seven and yet *one*") and toward a more emphatic pluralism ("*seven* and yet one")—this last at odds with Tennyson's desire to underscore the linking of his poem's parts and, by implication, of the sexes.

Tennyson's explicit references to art in the poem therefore reflect, not disingenuous self-consciousness, but the poem's larger design and meaning, its fusion of form and theme. The connection between art and the relation of men and women is overtly embodied in the narrative. The poem is called *The Princess* but is related from the Prince's point of view. Male speakers relate the narrative, but women sing the linking songs, as if Tennyson were playing with the notions of the aggressive and perceiving male, here responsible for the onward drive of narrative, and the emotional and beautiful woman, responsible for singing the poem's pure lyrics. But if the poem is to succeed, the lyric and narrative must cohere in some fashion, just as, according to the Prince, men and women are "not like to like, but like in difference. / Yet . . . liker must they grow" (VII, 262–63).

Even many of the names Tennyson chose for his personae emphasize the link between men and women. Many have noted that the Prince contains within himself feminine as well as masculine traits, as does Ida. Few have remarked, though, that if Ida as a feminine name comes from Old Norse *idh*, meaning "labor" (compare Ida's laboring on behalf of women and a mother's labor in giving birth), the "Old English *Ida*, a man's name, was from the same root."[4] The male and female are inextricably linked in Ida's very name. Similarly the Prince's friend Florian, whose name derives from Latin meaning "flowery" or "blooming," is attracted to Blanche's daughter Melissa, whose name is derived from Greek for "bee"—as if to say that the bee and flower, though different, are part of one symbiotic relationship.[5] Thus the art *of* the poem and references to art *in* the poem reinforce Tennyson's attention to women and their relationship to men.

The poem's closing frame, or Epilogue, returns to the theme of art and recapitulates the significance of the medley form for the poem as a whole. The men and women who have participated in the telling discuss how the tale should be written down, until there "rose a little feud betwixt the two" sexes—a reminder of the dissonances between male and female that can become a war of the sexes and of the dissonances of the medley form. Yet all fall into a general concord, agreeing that the poet of the group should write down the tale and reminding us of the potential for harmony between men and women and of the loose concord of the poem's parts. Finally, just as the tale was told in an enclosure that looked out on the social gathering on Sir Walter's lawn, so the Epilogue begins by focusing on the enclosed world of art and then moves outward to focus on Sir Walter, those gathered on his estate, and with a glance toward France across the water, the social and political issues of the day.

Tennyson later was to say of *The Princess* that it was, "after all, only a medley" (*Memoir*, II, 71). But this "only" is not, I think, "little" in terms of artistic achievement. And this achievement is in part the offshoot of the dramatic monologues. From writing the dramatic monologues, Tennyson had learned to use frames with skill, to juxtapose multiple perspectives, to use a fictive, dramatic "I," and to see exactly what doing so signified. The result in *The Princess* is a handling of the medley's mixed voices and perspectives that leads us to the heart of the poem's meaning.

## II
### *In Memoriam*

Even before embarking on *The Princess*, Tennyson had composed much of his most famous work, *In Memoriam*, begun in 1833 at the time of Arthur Hallam's death. *In Memoriam* clearly is not a dramatic monologue: we are given no indication that anyone other than the poet speaks. Perhaps one reason Tennyson is rarely thought of as a dramatic poet is that the work most closely associated with his name is not explicitly dramatic. In contrast, Browning's most ambitious and famous long poem, *The Ring and the Book*, is unambiguously dramatic. But even more than with *The Princess*, Tennyson's earlier practice with the dramatic monologue affected the final shape and texture of *In Memoriam*. Tennyson, of course, had additional models when he set about structuring his long poem, including Shakespeare's *Sonnets* and the psalms. Yet if Tennyson had not already written poems like "Supposed Confessions," "The Lotos-Eaters," "Locksley Hall," and "Ulysses," *In Memoriam* would not have become the poem it did when Tennyson decided to incorporate lyrics written apparently at random into one larger work.[6] *In Memoriam* may not be a dramatic monologue, but it is structured, or shaped, as Tennyson's dramatic monologues had been, as the rendering of the speaker's—here the poet's—consciousness.

Shaping the poem as if it were a dramatic monologue would have solved one of Tennyson's greatest dilemmas in publishing the poems devoted to Hallam: revealing overwhelmingly intimate emotions and exploiting Hallam's memory for public verse. All Tennyson scholars have had to work around Tennyson's obsession with privacy. His letters from Hallam and the correspondence between Tennyson and Emily Sellwood were dutifully destroyed by Hallam Tennyson at his father's request. And even while the lyrics of *In Memoriam* were being written, Tennyson was touchy about having anyone besides close acquaintances read the poems. In 1844, responding to one of the manuscript's several misplacings, Tennyson wrote to George Venables, "I suppose I must myself have slipt it behind your books to keep it out of people's way, for I scarcely liked everyone who came in to overhaul those poems" (*Letters*, I, 226). Obviously, a poet with such feelings would lapse into hypocrisy or sacrilege if he made these poems public. What Tennyson must have realized he could *not* do was publish the poems in the order in which they were composed. In that case he would indeed have published a diary, with complete fidelity to his mental history and his inward responses to Hallam's death.

But if he dissolved the original order of composition and rearranged the poems, he would, though allowing innumerable traces of the personal to remain, create something far more impersonal and fictive.[7] Tennyson in effect adapted the dramatic monologue's feint and turned it inside out. The contents, the actual statements, of a dramatic monologue are true relative to the speaker, who is a fiction; but the contents or statements of *In Memoriam* are false, or fictive, relative to Tennyson-as-speaker, whose authenticity is left unchallenged. Thus we see Tennyson moving a poem written in 1833 to a place late in the poem, where it became section LXXXV, whereas the 1833 poem was preceded by, for example, section I—written after 1837—and section VIII, which appears to have been written in 1850.[8] Or we see him deleting lines that reflect his feelings at the time of a section's composition in favor of what must be called the section's dramatic propriety in the overall sequence of *In Memoriam*. Section XVIII, for example, was written in 1834, shortly after Hallam's burial. In its published form, the section moves from the consolation that Hallam's body rests in England to the infinite absence of Hallam ("The words that are not heard again"). But as originally written, the poem moved in the opposite direction, starting with the inescapable death and then moving toward the consolation of having Hallam back in his native land. Changing the order of the poem not only let the emphasis fall on alienation rather than consolation—entirely apt for the section's placement among the early lyrics—but effectively disguised Tennyson's immediate feelings and, possibly, his motivation in writing the poem shortly after Hallam was interred.

As well, the very act of sequencing the poems turned "truth" into fiction[9] and so created aesthetic distance. The first line of section XXVIII, for example ("The time draws near the birth of Christ"), takes on different meanings depending on whether it is read by itself as an 1833 composition or as part of a larger structure. By itself, the section's first line means merely that Christmas approaches. But read in context, the line resonates with new meaning. Section XXVIII is placed after an entire unit of sections (sections XXII through XXVII) revolving around the path of life, the journey of life through time. The reference to the "time [that] draws near" in section XXVIII hence implicitly connects the approaching Christmas with the path the poet formerly trod with Hallam and now plods in isolation. This linking of times suggests the resolution the persona will come to in the future, when he sees that the links between himself and

Hallam are not broken; and in so foreshadowing the poet's resolution of grief, the line also links the past, present, and future of
the poem, just as the path motif merges the past, present, and
future of an individual lifetime. By being placed in sequence,
then, the line evokes a self-referentiality that could never occur
in an isolated lyric written from the perspective of a particular
point in time. For the "time" that "draws near the birth of
Christ" is also the "time"—the very sequencing—of the poem
itself.

Thus, for Tennyson, one solution to the dilemma of making
public the sacredly private was to falsify the literal truth of the
lyrics in order to present another kind of truth. Certainly his
attitude toward sequencing the lyrics became markedly impersonal by the time the poem neared its final form. As Tennyson
said to James Knowles, "If there were a blank space I would put
in a poem."[10]

Dissolving the separate lyrics' original state and forging a sequence also created an effect that Tennyson had exploited in
"The Lotos-Eaters" and "Ulysses": significant gaps in the text.
Minimally, the space between each printed section becomes a
notation for the passing of time. Sometimes the passage of time
between sections appears to be brief, as in the "Fair ship" sequence, where the poet's mind returns to the ship in section
after section as the ship makes its way from "the Italian shore"
to England. At other times the passage of time seems longer, as
in the movement from section LXXI to section LXXII. The
former concludes a unit of sections exploring the relationship
between sleep and death and the possibility of union with Hallam in dreams; section LXXI thus ends with a dream that recap-
tures Hallam's presence by making a "night-long Present of the
Past." But section LXXII opens on the first anniversary of Hallam's death: "Risest thou thus, dim dawn, again . . . ?" To
make sense of this transition from section LXXI to section
LXXII, we not only must posit a passage of time long enough for
the speaker's mood to change utterly but must also inject ourselves into the textual gap to explore how the speaker was impelled from a serene to a violent mood. The gaps of the text
produced by the sequencing thus do not merely denote the passage of time but, maximally, create a poem that demands an ac-

tive reader response. Tennyson himself seemed to desire placing demands on the reader; he considered writing a less hopeful
poem than *In Memoriam*, "showing that all the arguments are
about as good on one side as the other, and thus throw[ing] man
[and the reader] back more on the primitive impulses and feelings."[11] The poem's gaps were doubtless crucial in the poem's
popularity in the Victorian age. For inevitably there is something of *us* in the poem as we read through, as Queen Victoria's
famous annotations of the poem so well attest.[12]

The gaps in the text are also responsible for simultaneously
attracting readers who stress the poem's faith or those who
stress its doubt. Parts of the poem, that is, emphasize design,
wherein all is "toil cöoperant to an end" (CXXVIII), "all" including the poem, nature, and the divine cosmos. Other parts of the
poem stress open-endedness rather than design, averring that
the lyrics are only "short swallow-flights of song" (XLVIII), here
for a moment and then gone, and defending the validity of
doubt.[13] Although Tennyson has given the rhetorically powerful end position to the side of faith and design, the poem itself
does not really negate its own open-endedness. Instead design
and open-endedness lie side by side, with the reader free to emphasize whichever is most attractive and personally meaning-
ful. Victorian readers liked the comforts of faith, hence Tennyson's rumblings about writing a contrary, less hopeful poem;
but T. S. Eliot's praise for the poem's doubt and censure of its
faith is to be expected every bit as much (*pace* Eliot) as Queen
Victoria's response: the poem—structurally—allows for both.
The gaps that posit the passage of time and allow one to stress
either a progressive pattern carried on the crest of linear time's
wave or disjunct lyrics that allow neither the poem nor the universe to cohere entirely also help to explain Tennyson's use of
two different titles for the poem: "The Way of the Soul" and
"Fragments of an Elegy." Both titles are right depending on
how one looks at the poem. One emphasizes the sequencing,
one the discrete lyrics; one the linear flow of time, one the song
that goes nowhere but sings forever in its place. The beauty of it
all is that the poem ends up hovering between the two, and this
hovering reflects Tennyson's ultimate relation to Hallam: he
hopes to be carried to Hallam by the flow of time, but if not (or

meanwhile), there is the contingent connection with Hallam through memorializing him in the utterance of individual lyrics. One begins to see more and more why Tennyson claimed that the poem was "very impersonal . . . as well as personal" (Knowles, 182). The poem's structure is at once a detached, objectified artistic creation and a reflection of Tennyson's most personal connection with Hallam.[14]

That the structure of *In Memoriam* is both personal and impersonal, true and fictive, leads to the final, and most critical, connection between *In Memoriam* and the dramatic monologues. For ultimately the long work is shaped to reveal the oscillations of the poet-mourner's consciousness. Tennyson knew very much what he was saying when he claimed that "the different moods of sorrow as in a drama are dramatically given" (*Memoir*, I, 304); in arranging the poem he drew directly from what he had learned in writing his dramatic monologues. In fact, consciousness is rendered at four different levels.

The first level is self-evident. As in "Supposed Confessions" and "Locksley Hall," in which the speaker's mind moves back and forth around a central issue, darts forward to an imagined future or back to a remembered past, so we observe the flux and reflux of the poet's mind as we move from section to section in *In Memoriam*, or from stanza to stanza in an individual section. This mode of representing consciousness has received the most critical attention. Alan Sinfield, for example, observes that

> *In Memoriam*, markedly more than most previous poetry, aspires to express directly the mind of the poet. External objects are pertinent mainly in so far as they throw light upon his thoughts and feelings, syntax inclines towards the immediate recording of sense data unsifted by the patterns of logic, and images are made to carry a rich significance without the assistance of explicit linking devices. The poet does not pause to explain his meaning; we have to follow the workings of his mind and interpret the relevance for him of the images upon which he bestows so much attention.[15]

The reader response Sinfield describes is in fact exactly that required by the dramatic poems. And if we have learned to read those earlier poems, we automatically know how to approach the poet's shifting attitudes toward grief in the first eight sections of *In Memoriam* or to note the significance of the structure of section LXXXV, where the poet reaches out to a second friend in the wake of Hallam's death. The poet declares to this living friend that "I woo your love: I count it crime / To mourn for any overmuch" (lines 61–62) but has barely uttered this when he tears himself away to contemplate Hallam for another thirty-five lines. That is, we need only observe the mind's swath to see what the poet says directly, that

> *If not so fresh, with love as true,*
> *I, clasping brother-hands, aver*
> *I could not, if I would, transfer*
> *The whole I felt for him to you.*
>
> *(lines 101–4)*

The poem's most elemental mode of rendering consciousness, then, results from both the individual lyrics Tennyson composed at various times and above all from his sequencing of the lyrics. True, Wordsworth's *Prelude* or *Intimations Ode* also exhibits the flux and reflux of the mind, so that in part *In Memoriam* simply extends the Romantic tradition. The difference between Tennyson's and Wordsworth's 1850 poems is Tennyson's insistence on the fictive element of his poem, as his invocation of "drama" suggests. Only by seeing *In Memoriam's* sequence as a dramatization of consciousness could Tennyson become aware of "blank spots" or gaps so large they failed to show how the mind moved from one point or phase to another. Tied up as it is with the very sequencing of the completed poem, this first level of rendered consciousness embodies "The Way of the Soul" acknowledged by Tennyson in one of his private titles.

The "Way" of the poet-mourner's soul, or consciousness, is also dramatized by a second structural device. In relation to the poem's inner chronology of three years, Tennyson has structured the poem according to what I call the "curve of catharsis." That is, although Tennyson divided the poem into three "years," the first year accounts for half the poem's sections; the remaining two years are squeezed into the second half.[16] We must assume that this delegation of so many sections to the first year is deliberate; if Tennyson simply filled in "blank spaces" as the poem evolved, he could surely have expanded the second two

141

years to make them as long as the first. That granted, we must also see that this structuring has psychological implications. There is, of course, the idea of catharsis: after speaking so much of his grief, his fears, and his love of Hallam in the first year, the poet needs to say less in the remaining two.[17]

More interesting are the implications of this structuring for the speaker's inner state, implications that Tennyson had also explored in "Tithon." Causing the first year to "last" twice as long as the next two is a way of indicating structurally how slowly time passes for the poet, as for Tithon, in that first year. Not coincidentally, two echoes of "Tithon" occur in the sections making up the first year. One, cited by Ricks, appears in section XXII, in which Tennyson borrowed an unadopted passage from "Tithon" to form line 12, "There sat the Shadow feared of man." The second, more significant echo occurs in section XLI. Here the poet, fearful, like Tithon regarding Eos, that he and Hallam are henceforth to be separated by different forms of existence and time, longs "to leap the grades of life and light, / And flash at once, my friend, to thee" (lines 11-12)—just as Tithon longs "to shoot the sunny interval of day, / And lap me deep within the lonely west" (lines 26-27). As with Tithon, then, time for the poet in the first year is a wasteland that seems to stretch out forever; under the pressure of intense grief time passes slowly because each day is so difficult to get through. Additionally, with Hallam dead, both the past and the future the poet hoped to share with Hallam have been obliterated; all the poet has left *is* the present: "Let Love clasp Grief lest both be drowned," he cries, rather "than that the victor Hours should scorn / The long result of love" (I, 9, 13-14). In these circumstances, to telescope or compress time in the first year would be a threat to the only thing left to the poet.[18]

But this threat exists only as long as the poet perceives time in strictly linear terms. When in the poem's second two years he begins to see that time can be viewed cyclically and that within this perspective linear time is simply a stream carrying him to Hallam (at which point both will reside in the cycle of immortality), time becomes compressed, as if the poet were hurrying toward the end that will unite him with Hallam. So changed is his outlook that in the final year, he packs three anniversaries into as many sections: Christmas (CV), New Year's Eve (CVI), and Hallam's birthday (CVII), a far cry from the careful separation of anniversaries by long expanses in the first year. But by this time the anniversaries signify not so much the forward impetus of linear time as a reassurance of cyclical time: the year rounds annually to an important day whose significance endures. And, not coincidentally, the three anniversaries he juxtaposes are all days of birth, not death: of Christ, the New Year, and Hallam.

The third and equally broad level at which Tennyson renders the consciousness of his poet-persona should be familiar to anyone who has closely observed the handling of the verse paragraphs in "Ulysses." Just as Ulysses alternates between a sense of enclosure and expansion in the verse paragraphs of the dramatic monologue, so *In Memoriam* is arranged to reflect a systolic-diastolic pulsing between separation from and union with Hallam, until the closing sections enunciate only a sense of fusion with Hallam. This level of rendered consciousness underlies and stabilizes the mind's movement from section to section and enables us to see the larger shifts of mind as the poet moves through time. The opening sections of the poem (sections I through VIII) of course emphasize the poet's sense of utter separation from the dead Hallam; but this strain is counterposed by the "Fair ship" and burial sections that follow (IX–XXI), when the physical remains of Hallam are brought back to England, giving the poet the minimal comfort of union in place.

Another four cycles of separation-union occur. In the second the poet's sense of being left alone on the path of life (XXII–XXVII) is countered by the remembrance of how the tradition of Christmas keeps links alive, and from here the poet considers the issue of immortality and to what degree the poet and Hallam can be linked when each is situated on a different side of immortality (XXVIII–XLIX).

But if there is no immortality, there is no link between Hallam and the poet at all. Hence the next phase of the poet's sense of separation from Hallam begins in section L, where the separation is posited by the poet's very beseeching, "Be near me when my light is low." This phase of separation, the start of the third cycle, continues in the poem's expression of most intense doubt (L–LVIII), only to be countered by the poet's calling on Sorrow to be his bride in section LIX—a muted union and perhaps a grim echo of Marlowe's "Passionate Shepherd to His Love." The mention of one form of union leads to another, slightly more hopeful exploration of how the poet and Hallam are linked on the far sides of immortality, here considered through the relation of death to sleep and the possibility of recapturing Hallam in dreams. This phase culminates in the full presence of Hallam—but only in a dream—a whole night long (LIX–LXXI).

The first anniversary of Hallam's death ushers in thoughts of separation once again (marking the start of the fourth separation-union cycle), but these are less painful thoughts than those with which the poem began. Once the pain of the anniversary itself is survived, the poet probes the effects of a Hallam separated from the world and deprived of fame (LXXII–LXXVII). He also ponders his severance from Hallam's and his mutual past, as when the poet revisits Cambridge, or the life they would have shared had Hallam lived, married Emily, and begotten children. Significantly, these musings are punctuated by the return of and invocations to spring, a sign that the poet is becoming aware of life continuing underneath and beyond his sense of separation from Hallam. Hence this phase of separation (LXXVIII–LXXXIX) culminates in a serene, mellow, accepting memory of Hallam and the poet enjoying a lovely spring day at Somersby. Hallam is no longer there, but the memory is so full and lovely that death intrudes only as a muted reference to the "grave" into which Venus had fallen and then virtually disappears amidst the beauties of the day.

> *And brushing ankle-deep in flowers,*
> *We heard behind the woodbine veil*
> *The milk that bubbled in the pail,*
> *And buzzings of the honied hours.*

> (LXXXIX, 49–52)

Section LXXXIX leads into, more than it is countered by, the next and crucial sections devoted to the possibility of union with Hallam (XC–XCVII). Here the poet invokes Hallam to revisit and receives a kind of answer in the trance experience of section XCV. And so the poet is able to conclude this section by affirming that despite their physical separation they are joined by love, no matter how mysterious: " 'I cannot understand: I love' " (XCVII, 36).

At the start of the fifth cycle the poet must face one last form of separation: the rift with the locus of memory occasioned by the move from Somersby (XCVIII–CIII). Yet even as the poet prepares to leave, he is shown how to transcend this last separation and achieve union with Hallam. The dream recounted in section CIII is a reminder that his very poetry can forge a link between them despite movement through time and space— these two both imaged in the river the poet travels in his dream. From this point on the poet considers only forms of union, whether through time that leads him to Hallam (CV), social ties (CVIII–CXIV), or above all a love that embraces Hallam, mankind, nature, and God (CXV–CXXXI).[19]

This systolic-diastolic rhythm of separation and union that forms a larger structural element of the poem and the poet's consciousness might be likened to "Fragments of an Elegy," another working title for *In Memoriam*. For each of the five pulsations at once carries along the larger sequence but also embodies the shape of the poem as a whole. It is as if we have five different elegies, each successively more affirmative and hopeful, until we reach the end. The first three modes of rendered consciousness, then, embrace both "The Way of the Soul" and "Fragments of an Elegy."[20] And whereas the first mode retains much that must have been a reflection of Tennyson's personal feelings at the time of composition, the second and third modes reflect an impersonal shaping to achieve deliberately sought effects.

Tennyson renders the poet's consciousness in *In Memoriam* by means of a fourth technique, however. This last level of rendering at once incorporates the "Way of the Soul" and "Fragments of an Elegy," and is, while the most subtle artistically, perhaps also the most intensely personal imprint Tennyson left on the poem. Alan Sinfield has done much to direct attention to this level by showing how frequently Tennyson's use of syntax, pronouns, and imagery redounds on the poet's perception of himself in relation to Hallam. Sinfield notes, for example, the significance of the pronoun *thou* in the "Fair ship" sequence: "This adaptation of 'thou' to the ship is deeply poignant: we think that the pronoun should refer to Hallam, but he is only a corpse and no more responsive to direct address than the boat in which he forms a part of the cargo" (*Language,* 82). In fact, throughout the poem the poet's perception of himself and his art (and all else, for that matter) is directly linked to the way he perceives Hallam. One cannot discern the link in every single section, but the correlations are pervasive enough to be a significant part of the poet's consciousness. When Hallam is perceived as one whose spirit is sundered from the body, so also does the poet portray himself as a fragmented being. When Hallam is perceived to have grown larger through death, so also does the poet think of himself as having grown and expanded.

At the poem's outset Hallam's death is pre-eminent. The fact of his death is so overwhelming that not once is he named in the first five sections (Sinfield, *Language,* 81). He is utterly eclipsed as far as the poet is concerned and so cannot appear in the poem. And just as Hallam is eclipsed, so the poet tries to eclipse himself; he casts himself in a passive, fragmented role as he flees from responsibility for his own language. Thus, in section II, a stationary tree, the "Old Yew," is given the power of action, not the poet—the yew grasps at the tombstones, nets empty skulls, coils around bones—while "the stones," not the poet, "*name* the under-lying dead" (lines 1, 2). The most the poet can try to do is escape utterly from himself: "I seem to fail from out my blood / And grow incorporate into thee" (lines 15–16). In section III, similarly, the poet surrenders his power over language to Sorrow, who is given the power of direct speech,[21] and in section IV he surrenders his very will: "To Sleep I give my powers away; / My will is bondsman to the dark" (lines 1–2). When the poet asserts in section V that "words, like Nature, half reveal / And half conceal the Soul within" (lines 3–4), he is not merely uttering a universal problem of language but, in a dramatic context, making explicit what has been occurring implicitly in the previous sections. Unable to see himself whole and powerful when Hallam is neither, he relegates power to an autonomous language, in using which he speaks only with the passive voice: "But that large grief which these [words] enfold / Is given in outline and no more" (lines 11–12).

In the "Fair ship" sequence, as Arthur comes nearer and, in a sense, is to be joined with the poet in one place, the poet can summon the energy and power to do his own naming, and so it is "my lost Arthur's loved remains" that approach (IX, 3). Moreover, as Arthur journeys, so also does the poet: "I hear the noise about thy keel; / I hear the bell struck in the night," he proclaims in section X (lines 1-2). And in section XII, he undertakes an imaginative journey: "Like her [the dove] I go; I cannot stay" (line 5). But it is a journey of a peculiar kind. In this series of lyrics the poet can see Arthur Hallam only as a physical presence, a body sundered from soul: "And dead calm in that noble breast / Which heaves but with the heaving deep" (XI, 19-20). And so the poet sees himself in the same fragmented terms: "I leave this mortal ark behind, / A weight of nerves without a mind" (XII, 6-7). Similarly, when Hallam's physical remains are safe, as we find in the reference to burial (XVIII), the poet can begin to think of a form of endurance, too, though of a sort almost apart from his inner self: "The life that almost dies in me; / That dies not, but endures with pain, / And slowly forms the firmer mind" (lines 16-18). And, able to see Hallam in more integrated terms, he is also able to come closer to owning his own discourse in the beautiful Severn-Wye section: "My deeper anguish also falls, / And I can speak a little then" (XIX, 15-16).

By the time of the first Christmas sections (XXVIII-XXX), the family has come to think of Hallam as a ghost ("an awful sense / Of one mute Shadow watching all" [XXX, 7-8]) and thus can sing of the ghostly, or spiritual, self that transcends death: " 'They do not die / Nor lose their mortal sympathy' " (lines 22-23). This avowal, along with the remembrance of Christ occasioned by the Christmas holiday, leads naturally to the consideration of immortality in the next subdivision (XXXI-XXXVII). At this stage Hallam is thought of as immortal, but the poet can posit no direct link between them; hence the poet emphasizes the mystery of those, like Lazarus and Christ, who have experienced death, and the disjunction between heavenly (Hallam's sphere) and earthly (the poet's sphere) verse. The latter occurs in the Urania-Melpomene debate in section XXXVII, and it is doubtless significant that the debate is put into the mouths of the personified Muses; the poet, perceiving Hallam as disjunct and other, though alive, cannot yet own and so integrate the voices of the two spheres in himself.

When, conversely, the poet slips into an abyss of doubt, Hallam momentarily disappears from the poem. The poet calls to Hallam in section L but uses the grammatical form of the suppressed "thou"; he invokes Hallam precisely because the latter is absent: "Be near me when my light is low" (line 1). In section LII the sense of Hallam's presence recurs, and so the poet can address him ("I cannot love thee as I ought"—line 1) and claim his own discourse, in however qualified a manner ("My words are only words"—line 3). But again, as the doubt returns, Hallam disappears entirely from the poem in the next four sections, and the poet is left with "no language but a cry" (LIV, 20).

Hallam returns as a presence with the poet's recovery from most intense doubt; yet Hallam still seems distant from the poet. Perhaps this sense of nearness yet distance accounts for the sudden outbreaking of analogies in sections LIX through LXVI, as if to reflect the poet's sense that he and Hallam are forced to move in parallel lines instead of being able to converge. But as the poet beats on the parallels again and again, a convergence does begin to take place. The parallel or analogy used in section LXII, for example, would have been especially resonant to Tennyson. Here he thinks of Hallam, in relation to himself,

> *as one that once declined,*
> *When he was little more than boy,*
> *On some unworthy heart with joy,*
> *But lives to wed an equal mind;*
>
> *And breathes a novel world, the while*
> *His other passion wholly dies,*
> *Or in the light of deeper eyes*
> *Is matter for a flying smile.*

*(lines 5–12)*

The lines surely allude to Hallam's early passion for Anna Wintour, a passion superseded and quenched when Hallam looked into the "deeper eyes" of Emily Tennyson.[22] The poet's sister was a link between the two men when Hallam lived, and the buried allusion to this link signals an approaching nearness in the present. Hence the poet works through the parallels and a sense of Hallam's distance to a closer apprehension of Hallam and to more direct statement.

148

*Till out of painful phases wrought*
*There flutters up a happy thought, . . .*

*Since we deserved the name of friends,*
*And thine effect so lives in me,*
*A part of mine may live in thee*
*And move thee on to noble ends.*

*(LXV, 6–7, 9–12)*

The correlation between the poet's perception of Hallam and his depiction of himself continues in a group of sections (LXXII–LXXVII) initiated by the anniversary of Hallam's death. Here the poet considers the earthly fame Hallam lost through his early death. Now, just as Hallam was unable to say all he might have to his fellow men because of death, the poet withholds words likewise: "I see thee what thou art. . . . But there is more than I can see, / And what I see I leave unsaid, / Nor speak it" (LXXIV, 6, 9–11). And, just as Hallam's earthly fame is quenched but countered by the applause accorded his soul elsewhere (LXXV), so the poet denigrates the fame of his own verse (LXXV–LXXVII) but celebrates that in them which links him with Hallam's soul: "To breathe my loss is more than fame, / To utter love more sweet than praise" (LXXVII, 15–16).

This brings us to the famous trance experience of section XCV, where the union of Hallam and the poet implicit in the correlations I have been tracing becomes active and conscious. This section has been much and ably discussed by scholars who have explored the significance of the section for the poem as a whole, its relation to the Romantic visionary experience, and its language. I find particularly significant the section's mode of presentation. Section XCV is part of a connected group of sections invoking union with Hallam (XC–XCVII), but whereas all other sections in this grouping are couched in the present tense, section XCV is relayed in the past tense. Again, I think the reason for this shift lies in the correspondence between the way Hallam is viewed and the way the poet's imagination works. As the opening stanzas of the section show, the trance experience is one that cannot be shared with anyone but Hallam. It is only "when those others, one by one, / Withdrew themselves from me and night" (lines 17–18), when the poet is "all alone" (line

149

20), that the mystical union occurs, achieved through the "silent-speaking words" (line 26) of Hallam's letters that answer to the poet's own words. Nor could the trance last long: "At length my trance / Was cancelled, stricken through with doubt" (lines 43–44) as the immediate union subsided. The past-tense narrative for this section is entirely appropriate to relate a trance that could not remain a lasting present experience and to keep faith, as it were, with Hallam and the intimacy of their experience: the past tense and the frames that surround the central experience both function to distance readers from it. Yet, if the trance itself is canceled, the closeness of Hallam and the narrator prevails, as we see in sections XCVI and XCVII. Defending honest doubt in section XCVI, the poet holds up Hallam as an example of one who, "perplext in faith, but pure in deeds, / At last he beat his music out" (lines 9–10). But of course in the poem the poet is also beating *his* music out, working through from doubt to faith. The line, in essence, fuses Hallam and the poet without the poet's having to say so directly. The effects of section XCV are, in other words, still active. And thus the poet announces in section XCVII, "My love . . . sees himself in all he sees" (lines 1, 4). Although this section begins with analogical thinking, the poet comparing the relation of his and Hallam's spirits to wedded partners, the analogical apparatus is dropped as the section progresses, and the poet moves to the direct identifications of metaphor. Hallam may remain mysterious, but the two are unquestionably fused through the power of love: " 'I cannot understand: I love' " (line 36).

The grouping of sections devoted to the trance experience is followed by another describing the move from Somersby (XCIX–CIII). The shock of leaving a place so intimately and lovingly associated with Hallam—the trance of section XCV occurred here, after all—is enough to make Hallam recede again and to become a "he" once more in, for example, section C. And the repetitions of section CI—"Unwatched," "Unloved," "Unloved," "Unloved," "Uncared"—deftly capture, through a prefix that means the negation of ties, what the poet most fears: the physical move may unloose the ties so strong in the group of sections immediately preceding. But the fruits of the trance experience are not negated. In the dream of section CIII the poet sees, as he well should by now, that his poetry forms a link with Hallam that transcends time. And, just as Hallam is "thrice as large as man" in the dream (line 42), so also the poet, as he advances toward Hallam, "waxed in every limb" (line 30). Truly conjoined, they sail forever together in eternity despite what linear time may bring.

In the conclusion of the poem, therefore, the links between Hallam—who is now perceived as vital, living, pervasive, near—and the poet's imagination are rife. The poet joyously invokes the bells of the New Year because the dead Hallam is dead, and the newer, living Hallam is alive and present (CVI). The poet fixes on social ties and issues (CVIII–CXIII) because he is so sure of the tie between Hallam and himself. Or he celebrates Wisdom (CXIV) because that is what he perceives Hallam to embody and has himself learned to pursue. He returns to the house of section VII but no longer fixes on the tomblike "Dark house," but on the "Doors," avenues to entry, since he is now assured of access to Hallam's spirit. Indeed, he sees Hallam everywhere now, and so asserts, but only now, that despite contrary appearances love and hope have always infused his verse (CXXV). The point is not whether the assertion is true or false but that he can make the assertion *only* now, having directly invoked Hallam to infuse his poetry in section CXXII. Finally, assured of inner harmony because he sees himself in harmony with Hallam, the poet sees harmony in everything: "all, as in some piece of art, / Is toil cöoperant to an end" (CXXVIII, 23–24); and because he now sees Hallam as vaster, larger, so, too, his love is "vaster passion now; / Though mixed with God and Nature thou, / I seem to love thee more and more" (CXXX, 10–12). Given the inner harmony and energy occasioned by the thought of a Hallam such as this, the poet has the power to announce and own directly what he has heretofore implied only indirectly: "Far off thou art, but ever nigh; / I have thee still, and I rejoice" (CXXX, 13–14). At one with Hallam, he is at one with his own voice and need not disavow or seek to escape the responsibility of his own poetry.

Tennyson's final and subtlest mode of rendering consciousness, then, is to construct the poem so that the poet's vision of himself, his poetry, and the world is correlated in some way with what he perceives Hallam to be. That is, underneath the poem's surface Tennyson is throughout dramatizing an unbreakable link between the poet's consciousness and Hallam, even when the poet may seem to doubt this link. This kind of dramatization can be glimpsed in some of the earlier dramatic monologues. In "Ulysses," too, the attachment to something, in his case to moving, journeying, open-endedness, underlies and informs his every word. But never before had Tennyson achieved what he did with the rendering of consciousness in *In Memoriam*. It is not merely that Tennyson sustains the rendition at such great length but that the rendering takes place at several levels simultaneously, as if to imply the many levels of response to a major crisis in life: the mundane, day-to-day response (the first level of rendering); the larger patterns or pulsations—biorhythms we would call them today—into which the mundane responses fall (the curve of catharsis and pulsations of separation and union); and the rocklike foundation of the mind, which is usually unconscious but can, after psychological health is regained, become fully conscious and realized (the fourth level of rendering).

This last level of rendered consciousness is also significant in terms of the poem itself. As noted above, this technique at once incorporates the patterns of "The Way of the Soul" and "Fragments of an Elegy." On one hand, the poet's perception of Hallam *evolves*, as Hallam shifts from being blotted out to becoming merely a physical presence, a memory, a spirit far off, and then gradually a spirit who grows and comes closer and closer to the poet until they are fused forever. No doubt one reason the poet so comes to prize and rely on process is Hallam's subjection to process. Both Hallam and the poet, that is, experience the "Way of the Soul."[23] But at any given moment in the poem, the poet is also, as it were, fused with Hallam through the correspondence between the perception of Hallam and the working of the poet's imagination. Consequently, whether we look at an individual lyric—a "Fragment"—or at the whole poem—the "Way"—we get the same answer: Hallam and the poet are ineradicably joined. This pattern imparts a certain relativity to the poem's philosophical and religious stances. Tennyson grumbled, "They are always speaking of me . . . as if I were a writer of philosophical treatises."[24] The dramatic component of *In Memoriam* certainly suggests that its truths are *not* philosophical: the poet sees all as part of a divine plan at the end, not because it is verifiably true, but because his own existence has coherence now that he is sure of Hallam's existence and proximity. The lines do not cancel the earlier passages of doubt; the different passages are simply seen from different perspectives. And certainly it is implied that if Hallam's immediacy were in question, no shred of religious faith would compensate the poet. Always the poet begins with the personal, not the cosmic.

Indeed, this fourth level of rendered consciousness is an astonishingly personal gesture toward the Hallam loved by Tennyson. Tennyson's very structuring of the poem is a testament of love and answers at a larger level to the quotations or echoes of Hallam in the details of the poem.[25] Yet this intensely personal tribute is not immediately apparent when we read; rather, it is deeply embedded in the text and emerges only when one looks closely at both the larger poem or "Way" and the individual lyrics or "Fragments." Perhaps the poet's assertion that words "half reveal and half conceal" has relevance for the entire poem as well as for the part in which it occurs.

At all events, the event of *In Memoriam* has to end, and here again Tennyson faced the difficulty of ending a poem grounded on the premise of process, the lasting process of consciousness ended only by death. Not surprisingly, Tennyson relied on the resource of a frame to close the poem, the Epilogue, which acts with the Prologue to impose limits within which the lyrics proper can endlessly vibrate and sing. But though some readers feel the Epilogue too much imposes an ending on the poem, it is entirely appropriate in at least one way. Tennyson does not so much concretize and reify what he has learned from the poem (as the Prologue unquestionably does) as he simply recapitulates its entire movement through diction and syntax, especially in regard to the issue of time. The first one hundred lines of the Epilogue, that is, are given over to the flow of linear time that dominates the early sections of *In Memoriam* proper. The discourse is broken up into many separate sentences, and the sequence of the wedding is told in strict chronological order. But beginning with line 101, shortly after the departure of the bride and groom, the rest of the Epilogue is one long sentence, as if to assert that despite the flow of time it is all one; the poet's vista suddenly opens out onto the near and distant future as well as the immediate present and the past; and the whole poem culminates, emphatically, in the present-tense verb *moves*—eternally dynamic and open-ended, as are the closing words of "Ulysses." Instead of locking the poem into a definitive ending statement, he simply recapitulates the process of the lyrics, suggesting that process gives way to more process, unendingly.

*In Memoriam*, then, is not only Tennyson's masterpiece but also one made possible in part through Tennyson's earlier dramatic monologues. If Shakespeare's *Sonnets* and other works are models for the poem, Tennyson drew as well upon his earlier dramatic poems in casting the discrete lyrics into one long poem. Having learned the effects of textual gaps and means of rendering consciousness in his monologues, he used both techniques to create the poem most closely associated with his name.

III

Interlude: "The Brook" and Tennyson's Emergent Public Voice

Between the publication of *In Memoriam* in 1850 and *Maud* in 1855, Tennyson also worked at some shorter poems. Probably the most important of these for Tennyson was "To the Vicar of Shiplake," written on the day of his wedding to Emily Sellwood. But for our purposes the most significant short poems written between *In Memoriam* and *Maud* are "The Brook" and those that marked the emergence of a new voice in Tennyson's poetry. "The Brook," another dramatic monologue, typifies the interchange between dramatic and nondramatic modes in Tennyson's middle years whereas Tennyson's emergent public voice meant that his choice among various poetic modes could be even more conscious and deliberate.

In "The Brook" Lawrence Aylmer, returned to England after twenty years' absence in India, muses by the brook his brother Edmund loved. Edmund, yet another avatar of Arthur Hallam, is long dead, his life nipped short while he was abroad in Florence before life ever flourished in him (lines 9–15). But Edmund left behind his verses on the brook, which Lawrence recites to himself, all now mixed in his memory with the "good turn" he did for his first love Katie Willows many years ago: enduring the endless gush of talk from her father Phillip (by whose farm the brook flows) so that Katie could mend her lover's quarrel with her cousin James. At the end of the poem Lawrence discovers that the now-widowed Katie has returned from Australia, for he encounters Katie's daughter, who at first seems to be the ghost of her mother when a young girl. The poem then ends by implying that Lawrence is to be rewarded for his earlier "good turn" done for Katie so long ago.

"The Brook," as Donald Hair observes, is essentially a later version of "The Miller's Daughter."[26] Both poems use mixed forms (dramatic, narrative, and intercalary lyrics); both rely on the use of a millstream or brook to serve as a symbol of time's flow; and both revolve around themes of loss versus continuity and reconciliation. This last is evident in the opening and closing lines of the poem. Lawrence begins, "Here, by this brook, we parted"; but the poem closes with the young Katie saying to Aylmer, "You will be welcome—O, come in!" Aylmer is urged, that is, to come out of the cold of loss and loneliness and into the warmth of love and human relations. The brook, though, is used far more deliberately as a symbol of time's passage than is the millstream in "The Miller's Daughter." Like the millstream's "higher pool" that escapes the stream's flow, the brook not only "chatter[s] over stony ways" but also "bubble[s] into eddying bays" (lines 39, 41). But the use of flowing water to image both the losses to and continuities that transcend time is multi-layered in "The Brook." The brook is a reminder of the death of Edmund, since Edmund so loved the brook, but also the locus of his ever-present spiritual voice, since the intercalary songs written by Edmund endure.[27] And if the brook flows inveterately, as does linear time, it also is a link with eternity and its cycles, as emphasized by the intercalary songs. Each interpolated lyric ends with the brook's "flow / To join the brimming river, / For men may come and men may go, / But I go on for ever." As Hair remarks, "The 'brimming river' is a version of the 'great deep,' the mysterious source and end of all life. In this context, the brook is a metaphor for human life, which, through children and the generations they represent, goes on forever" (69).

In all these respects "The Brook" is simply an extension of

"The Miller's Daughter" but mixed, as it were, with the spirit and "plot" of *In Memoriam*; it begins by focusing on the death of a young man but ends by hinting of an impending marriage. Yet the interpolated lyrics do not merely provide the poem's major symbol; they also are integrally linked with and advance the poem's larger narrative. The second lyric, for example, mentions the brook's chatter, which leads naturally to the mention of Phillip's own incessant chatter, and prepares for the central incident soon to be related. The interpolated lyrics of "The Brook," then, are even more directly functional than those in "The Miller's Daughter." This is hardly surprising, for "The Brook" was written after *The Princess*, in which Tennyson made the lyrics a major link among the seven parts of his narrative. That a technique developed in a narrative poem should come back and appear in a dramatic poem underscores, again, the frequent and rich interaction of dramatic and nondramatic in the poems of Tennyson's middle years.

The purely nondramatic intrudes upon "The Brook," too. For the second way it differs from "The Miller's Daughter" is that Tennyson entirely breaks off from the dramatic mode at the poem's end, identifying for the first time the speaker of the preceding monologue ("So Lawrence Aylmer, seated on a stile. . . . Mused, and was mute"). It is one of the few times Tennyson abandoned the dramatic in a monologue to relate a central incident—here, the return of Katie and her children after Lawrence had assumed Katie was gone forever. But the broken dramatic line is appropriate. On the one hand, Lawrence Aylmer has been too dense. He has recited but not really listened to Edmund's verses on the brook. Missing the import of the brook's relation to eternity, he ends his own utterance with "All are gone." In a sense, Aylmer does not deserve to close the poem and to announce the continuing cycles of life embodied in the young Katie or his own chance for renewed love. On the other hand, the break with Lawrence's monologue is his reward as well as punishment. Katie is given the final words not only because she displaces Lawrence's focus on permanent loss and is a direct manifestation of the ongoing cycles of life but also because she gives to Aylmer, locked out first from Katie's love, then from England, then from the past, and then from the poem, the chance to *come in.* The technique is a structural way of saying that something outside Lawrence and his sense of age and loss exists and will disclose something wonderful if given a chance to speak.

The ambience of this poem, as of most of the poetry discussed in this chapter, certainly bears out James Kincaid's assertion that the comic vision dominated Tennyson's work in the middle years. *Comedy* as Kincaid uses the term also implies social relations, and thus one of the other interesting developments of the 1850s is the emergence of Tennyson's public voice in such poems as "Ode on the Death of the Duke of Wellington" and "To the Rev. F. D. Maurice." The relevance of these poems for a study of the dramatic monologues is their illustration of how far Tennyson had evolved from his earliest poetry. Once so cloistered within himself that he resorted either to the conventionality of the works in *Poems by Two Brothers* or else to the protective use of the dramatic in *The Devil and the Lady,* Tennyson was able in the 1850s to develop a poetic voice that was consciously, comfortably, and confidently public. No doubt this new voice was the result of Tennyson's increasing integration into the social order through his marriage and his receipt of the laureateship. Thus in the Wellington ode, he draws attention away from himself and to the Duke as he calls on the entire nation to join with him in doing honor to the fallen leader. The verse epistle addressed to Maurice is itself a social invitation to "come . . . to the Isle of Wight" and so flee the persecutions of dogmatic theologians.[28] The relaxed, generous urbanity of Tennyson's voice is itself an implicit counterargument to the dissensions of religious dispute, and as a further social gesture he publishes the poem and allows the reading public, as it were, to overhear his conversation.

The point, ultimately, is that Tennyson by this time had gained enough confidence in his verse not merely to use the lyric openly to express his personal emotions, as in the preceding decade, but to speak *in propria persona* as public poet to Victorian society. This being the case, his recourse to the dramatic monologue, it can be inferred, will be even more deliberate and conscious. To one of Tennyson's most famous dramatic poems let us now accordingly turn.

IV

*Maud*

*Maud*, the third long poem of Tennyson's middle years, is in some ways the antithesis of *In Memoriam*. After seventeen years of writing lyrics bounded by a strict rhyme scheme and meter, Tennyson rebounded into a poem of almost infinite variety in meter, rhyme, and expression. Yet *Maud*, though clearly related to such earlier dramatic monologues as "Oriana," is also an outgrowth of the elegy that preceded it.

*Maud* began with a germinal lyric—"Oh! that 'twere possible"— and was, as Tennyson remarked, then written *"backwards."* In *Memoriam* was not precisely written backwards, but it was certainly not written "forward" either. From the experience of writing *In Memoriam* Tennyson had learned what one could do with individual lyrics arranged, rearranged, and sequenced to body forth an emerging, oscillating consciousness over time. His discovery in the elegy that gaps between numbered sections could become notations for time's passage was especially important for *Maud*, in which the sequencing of sections is tied not only to unfolding linear time but also to a plot: the hero's initial bitterness and alienation, his gradual falling in love with Maud despite the harm done to his father by hers, Maud's return of love for the speaker, the death of Maud's brother in a duel with the speaker, the speaker's madness, and finally his recovery, however ambiguous, and decision to go to war. *In Memoriam* has been compared to a diary; in *Maud* it is as if Tennyson assumed the point of view of a modern videotape crew, recording the subject only at significant times—except that the recording is done from within rather than from without.[29] Although completely different in texture from *In Memoriam*, however, *Maud* employs the same underlying technique. A persona's consciousness is rendered through the sequencing of lyrics, with the gaps between lyrics serving as notations of time and as entrees for the reader.

Others have noted resemblances between *In Memoriam* and *Maud*,[30] but generally the implications of these similarities for the role of the dramatic in Tennyson's middle years have gone unremarked. That Tennyson would adapt the technique of *In Memoriam* to *Maud* indicates, I think, not only Tennyson's awareness of how far a dramatic model pervades the structure of *In Memoriam* but also how important the dramatic mode had become to his poetry as a whole, so that he could use some or all of the techniques he had developed in his earlier dramatic monologues in all three long poems beginning with *The Princess.*

In adapting dramatic techniques for *In Memoriam*, he even discovered new modes of rendering consciousness, which he could then introduce back into a clearly dramatic poem like *Maud.* For *Maud*, like *In Memoriam*, also renders multiple levels of consciousness simultaneously. Like *In Memoriam, Maud* of course depicts the oscillations of consciousness over time through its very sequencing, as the hero, like the poet, moves from prostration to affirmation. And in both poems we also witness the turnings and twistings of an individual mind within a given section. Thus, in part I, section X, of *Maud*, we see the hero working through his jealousy spawned by seeing Maud with a rival, nouveau riche lord. He fulminates against the lord and his father for their ill-gotten wealth and the lord's banality, then recognizes his own inner pangs of jealousy: "A wounded thing with a rancorous cry, / At war with myself and a wretched race, / Sick, sick to the heart of life, am I" (I, 363–65). Although from here he may seem to launch into different topics, he is still processing his jealousy. He begins the third stanza of section X by ranting against "this broad-brimmed hawker of holy things," the Quaker who has come to preach peace; but talking about the Quaker is really a pretext for talking about himself, as his answer to the Quaker's homily indicates.

> *Put down the passions that make earth Hell!*
> *Down with ambition, avarice, pride,*
> *Jealousy, down! cut off from the mind*
> *The bitter springs of anger and fear.*

(I, 375–78)

The avarice, undoubtedly, is the lord's; the jealousy is entirely the speaker's own. He next turns to wishing he could hear Maud sing her battle song again, not to inspire him to action, but so that he can trust her not to love the lord. And his call at the end for a great leader to arise is clearly self-exhortation; he is rousing himself to be a leader, a noble man of action in contrast to the lord, "a captain . . . A bought commission." And lest readers miss the point, Tennyson added in 1856 the lines that explicate the hero's wish for a great leader: "And ah for a man to arise in me, / That the man I am may cease to be!"

Coexisting with the oscillations of consciousness evident in the poem's sequenced sections are larger movements or patterns of consciousness. In *In Memoriam* the poet's mind, above and beyond individual sections, oscillates between a sense of separateness from and linkage with Hallam. *Maud*, too, has this systolic-diastolic rhythm of the mind, but the hero of *Maud* may be said to oscillate between feelings of wildness and calm, or madness and sanity. At the poem's outset he is clearly in the throes of a wild mood not far removed from madness. His first words are "I hate,"[31] and he proceeds to fulminate against everything in his purview, including himself (part I, sections I–IV). Maud's battle song, which he hears for the first time in section V, has the power to calm him; the line lengths at once shorten, and the hero's own speech ineluctably takes on the steady rhythms of the ballad she sings: "A passionate ballad gallant and gay, / A martial song like a trumpet's call!" (I, 165–66). He is relatively calm and steady until he sees his rival in section X and then is off on an erratic binge of consciousness again. So it continues through part I. In a moment of quiet meditation he discovers that he does not want to die before fully realizing love with Maud (XI), then breaks out fuming at the scorn shown him by Maud's brother (XIII). He exults in having led Maud home, tries to come to terms with the brother, halts at the very idea ("the deathbed desire / Spurned by this heir of the liar"), yet prevails (XVIII–XIX). He ends up, at the end of part I, singing a song that is wild and disordered only in its passion, for "Come into the garden, Maud" is absolutely regular in meter, catching the rhythms of the dance the hero hears while he waits outside in Maud's garden.

The whole pattern begins again in part II: the hero is wildly disordered after the duel and his flight to the Breton coast but finds he can be calmed by looking on a shell. This calmness cannot be maintained, and he surrenders to the wildness of insanity, when he can call out to Maud's father as to a gray wolf that must howl over the dead cub, his son: "He has gathered the

bones for his o'ergrown whelp to crack; / Crack them now for
yourself, and howl, and die" (II, 293–94). At the end the hero
emerges from his madness into a state of relative calm, aware of
himself and of that through which he has passed, but ready to go
to war, itself a phenomenon at once of wildest insanity and absolute order and discipline.

As with *In Memoriam* also, the systolic-diastolic rhythms of a
consciousness are conjoined to a larger temporal pattern that
takes the curve of catharsis.[32] The foreshortening of time in
*Maud* takes place not through sections assigned to individual
years, as in *In Memoriam*, but through line lengths and lengths of
the parts of experience through which the hero must pass. Hence
the longest of all sections is section I of part I, which has nineteen
stanzas and (along with sections II through IV) the longest metrical lines (six feet). Having vented so much mental poison in the
opening section, it is as if the hero need never give way to such
ranting again; part of the catharsis is already complete. And,
even though it takes the hero twenty-two sections to work
through hate to exultant love in part I, he needs only five sections in part II to work through grief, guilt, and madness. Part
III, at which point the hero's catharsis is almost complete, has
only one section. Thus the very divisions of the poem also work
to reveal the speaker's consciousness, letting us see how the act
of expression helps drain away the festering mental pressures
that have accumulated over the unhappy years of the hero's life.

Tennyson renders consciousness at yet another level. As with
the poet of *In Memoriam*, the hero's perception of reality affects
the very way he speaks—or can speak. When he is most immersed
in his own morbid consciousness, all humanity is only a thing,
other and alien. But the more he begins to surface, the more he
begins to see humanity, or parts of it, as significant others.
Hence his recourse to self-analysis, when he has most distance
on himself, is often linked with the appearance of *thous* and *wes* in
the text.

In the opening section, when the hero is most self-engrossed,
not a single *thou* appears. He obliquely announces his problem in
the eighth line of the poem: "There yet lies the rock," the rock
that fell with his father at his death, and "crushed, and dinted
[him] into the ground" (I, 7). His father's death under the pres-

sure of debt and despair is an ever-present fact, yet so frightening that the speaker cannot approach it openly. Only by speaking as one fragmented, divided into bodily parts that pursue their autonomous functioning, can the hero describe the death.

> *the roots of my hair were stirred*
> *By a shuffled step, by a dead weight trailed, by a whispered fright,*
> *And my pulses closed their gates with a shock on my heart as I heard*
> *The shrill-edged shriek of a mother divide the shuddering night.*

(I, 13–16)

Unable to feel whole and active himself, it is hardly surprising that he sees men as things also controlled by outside forces. "Only the ledger lives," while the poor of each sex become mere "swine" (I, 35, 34); "Sleep must lie down armed," like a man, but a man on whom the sound grates is only a "wakeful *ear*."

By section VI of part I, however, the hero is beginning to be roused from self-absorption by the influence of Maud. Having met Maud the night before, when she sweetly smiled and greeted him, he is for the first time able to distinguish between inner and outer reality: "Morning arises stormy and pale, / No sun, but a wannish glare . . . I had fancied it would be fair" (I, 190–91, 195). The presence of Maud's brother is enough to prompt him back to reification of the human, as the brother becomes merely "that jewelled mass of millinery" (I, 232). But the hero goes on to analyze himself and his utter loneliness (I, 252–67), and words and things are suddenly transformed. Words are a problem, not because they are full of lies, but because the hero is trying so hard to express truth: "the new strong wine of love . . . made my tongue so stammer and trip" (I, 271–72); and the human is reified only in the sense that it is deified: "I saw the treasured splendour, her hand, / Come sliding out of her sacred glove" (I, 273–74). By the time we reach section XII it is the hero who faces the threat of reification from others, not vice versa.

> *Who shall call me ungentle, unfair,*
> *I longed so heartily then and there*
> *To give him the grasp of fellowship;*
> *But while I past he was humming an air,*
> *. . . . . . . . . . . . . . . . . . . . . .*

*And curving a contumelious lip,*
*Gorgonised me from head to foot*
*With a stony British stare.*

*(I, 457–60, 463–65)*

For the hero has learned to say "thou"—to Maud—as we see in section XVIII: "Make answer, Maud my bliss, / Maud made my Maud by that long loving kiss, / Life of my life, wilt thou not answer this?" (I, 655–57). The last section of part I is thus a song addressed entirely to another, to Maud, to come into the garden. It is a song that, unlike the opening lines of the poem, awaits an answer, for it can only be completed by the appearance of Maud.

Or so the hero thinks. Instead, of course, the song, like the echo mentioned in the poem's first stanza, is answered by death. The murder of the brother immediately removes all possibility of a full relationship with Maud. In shooting the brother, the hero also shoots Maud into the distance, and she herself, like the dead brother in the hollow, becomes only a thing: "Then glided out of the joyous wood / The ghastly Wraith of one that I know" (II, 31–32). And, of course, the other result of the duel is to push the hero deeper into himself once more. True, glimmers of the lessons of love remain, so that when he reifies all of humanity, he includes himself: "Strike dead the whole weak race of venomous worms, / That sting each other here in the dust; / We are not worthy to live" (II, 46–48). But alienation and self-immersion dominate and culminate in madness, when he is buried so deeply in himself he seems to reside in a separate world ("And my bones are shaken with pain, / For into a shallow grave they are thrust, / Only a yard beneath the street"—II, 243–45) and when all human discourse is reduced to "idiot gabble" (II, 279), mere counters that preclude genuine communication.

We know the hero has emerged from madness, conversely, when in part III he is able to dream that Maud speaks to him as a "thou" (" 'let trouble have rest, / Knowing I tarry for thee' " [III, 12–13]) and when he regains his ability to make distinctions and to engage in self-analysis: "And it was but a dream, yet it lightened my despair" (III, 18). Thus the hero can participate at last with others—"I stood on a giant deck and mixed my breath / With a loyal people" (III, 34–35)—and even identify with them:

"We have proved we have hearts in a cause, we are noble still"
(III, 55). Ultimately the poem's first verbal phrase ("I hate") is
counteracted by its last ("I embrace"). Hence beneath the surface flow of the speaker's mind, we can always discern a relation
between the way he feels about himself and the way he is able to
perceive and speak of others.

In another way, too, Tennyson simultaneously renders different levels of consciousness, through a technique that goes
beyond *In Memoriam*. In the elegy, the poet merely announces at
one point that beneath all, "Sorrow deepens down." In part II of
*Maud* we actually *see* this happening. Under the influence of grief
and guilt the hero speaks, inevitably, in irregular and jagged
lines.

> *Is it gone? my pulses beat—*
> *What was it? a lying trick of the brain?*
> *Yet I thought I saw her stand,*
> *A shadow there at my feet,*
> *High over the shadowy land.*
> *It is gone; and the heavens fall in a gentle rain,*
> *When they should burst and drown with deluging storms.*
>
> (II, 36–42)

Suddenly, in the next section, the hero's mind is riveted by a
shell.

> *See what a lovely shell,*
> *Small and pure as a pearl,*
> *Lying close to my foot,*
> *Frail, but a work divine,*
> *Made so fairily well*
> *With delicate spire and whorl,*
> *How exquisitely minute,*
> *A miracle of design!*
>
> (II, 49–56)

As these absolutely regular lines of three feet each follow forty-
eight lines of irregular and unstrung lines, we sense, reading
them in sequence, what we are only later told (II, 106–11): the
lines introducing the shell are situated at the level of sense perception, at the very surface of consciousness, while beneath, the
stream of troubled consciousness floods on. It is a remarkable

achievement, as if Tennyson had learned not to discuss but to dramatize the uses of a "sad mechanic exercise" he mentions in *In Memoriam.*

Still, Hallam Tennyson was quite right to link *In Memoriam* and *Maud* when he opened his chapter on the 1855 poem. Tennyson himself implicitly linked the two poems when he called one "The Way of the Soul" and the other a "Drama of the Soul" (*Memoir*, I, 393). But why is *In Memoriam* a "Way" and *Maud* a "Drama"? Part of the answer lies in differing subject matter since the hero's inner conflicts are both more sustainedly intense and more sustainedly violent than the poet's in *In Memoriam.* And of course *Maud* is clearly dramatic. The hero is indicated to be other than the poet; there are no Arthur Henry Hallams wandering about in the poem, nor any Rosa Barings or Emily Sellwoods, for that matter. Moreover, Tennyson foregoes a frame this time and plunges us directly, as in "Ulysses," into the medium of the speaker's consciousness.[33] Finally, because in *Maud* Tennyson was freed from the formal constraints of *In Memoriam*, he could use an even wider range of means dramatically to represent the consciousness of his speaker.

For *Maud* also depends for its existence on Tennyson's earlier dramatic monologues. A. Dwight Culler has provided a valuable history of the monodrama tradition in England,[34] but I cannot agree with him that *Maud* is of a different genre than Tennyson's dramatic monologues, a monodrama *versus* a dramatic monologue. Tennyson did not add the subtitle *A Monodrama* to *Maud* until 1875, twenty years after its publication. Nor, for that matter, did he use the term *dramatic monologue* until 1881 when the term was appended to "Despair" as a subtitle. Clearly, however, he had written dramatic monologues before 1881. Rather than place *Maud* in a separate category, then, I prefer to see it, as does Alan Sinfield, simply as an expanded monologue.[35]

*Maud* is a culmination of the earlier dramatic monologues because it adopts their techniques while pushing the techniques even further. Thus, as in "The Lotos-Eaters," gaps play a critical part in the text of *Maud*: these gaps enable readers to take an alternate perspective from that espoused by the speaker[36] and enable Tennyson to render a given consciousness over an expanse of time, so that we get a larger arc etched out by the self or soul rather than the brief glimpse afforded by catching the speaker at only one critical moment. As in "The Sea-Fairies," the "Mermaid" monologues, and especially "The Hesperides," Tennyson pursued in *Maud* his earlier penchant for metrical variation; but by the time of writing *Maud* he had discovered that this variety could be used to psychological ends. The same is true of alliteration and rhyme, which Tennyson had earlier used in "Oriana" to psychological effect; in *Maud* the technique is simply expanded, but so far that it generates new effects, as we shall shortly see. Finally, as in "Tithon," Tennyson employed image patterns in *Maud* to carry much of the poem's meaning. If *Maud* seems different from "Tithon" in this respect, it is simply that there is more poem in *Maud*, so that the image patterns are fuller and more complex.

The image patterns of *Maud* and the overall psychology of the speaker have already received attention by fine critics and need no further discussion here.[37] But the new uses to which Tennyson put lyric devices in a dramatic poem deserve further exploration. John Killham argues that "it is truer on the whole to say that the drama is subordinate to the lyrics, rather than the reverse" (224). But I hold with Dr. Mann, whose essay on *Maud* Tennyson reviewed before publication and certainly approved. As Mann says, "The syllables and lines of the several stanzas actually trip and halt with abrupt fervour, tremble with passion, swell with emotion, and dance with joy, as each separate phase of mental experience comes on the scene. The power of language to symbolize in sound mental states and perceptions, has never before been so magically proved."[38]

The broader strokes by which Tennyson uses meter to render consciousness have already been noted: the "curve of catharsis" achieved by having the hero begin with the longest metrical lines to which, once partly relieved of his bitterness, he never recurs; and the steadying effects, as reflected in meter, of Maud's military ballad or the shell on the hero's sensibility. Indeed, this latter effect is repeated in many of the exulting lyric sections, often called "arias"—versus the "recitatives" in which the hero falls back upon the inner divisions that wrack him. The lyrics indeed have an arialike effect, but they are used for psychological purposes, showing how the conscious awareness of love steadies the hero. For almost always the lyrics (for example, part I, sections XI, XII, XVII, XXII) are notable for the regularity of their rhythm, their steady pulses, which make the hero's return to his inner divisions more emphatic. This is especially true as we move from the steady rhythm of "Come into the garden, Maud," when the hero is so in harmony with the universe that the whole world seems animated with his love, to the jangled, irregular meter of part II, after the duel.

Throughout the poem Tennyson ties the metrical line to the speaker's psyche, so that it follows the gradient of his emotions as they rise or fall.[39] Thus in part I, section VIII, when the speaker sees Maud in church, the opening lines are three metrical feet long. The moment Maud lifts her eyes, the lines suddenly expand to four feet, reflecting the quickened emotions of the speaker. Similarly, in section XIX, when the speaker recounts his conversation with Maud about his mother, most of the lines are three feet long, but they expand to four whenever he touches on painful elements of his past.

> *I trúst that I díd not tálk*
> *To géntle Máud in our wálk*
> *(For óften in lónely wánderings*
> *I have cúrsed him éven to lifeless things)*
>
> . . . . . . . . . . . . . . . . . .
>
> *I am súre I did but spéak*
> *Of my móther's fáded chéek*
> *When it slówly gréw so thin,*
> *That I félt she was slówly dýing*
> *Véxt with láwyers and hárassed with débt:*
> *For how óften I caúght her with éyes all wét.*
>
> (I, 695–98, 701–6)

Beyond the very words Tennyson chooses for his speaker, he indicates the inner pressures operating on the hero's mind by the very line lengths as well. Hence the metrics of part III reinforce what Tennyson himself said of the hero at the poem's end, that he is "sane, but shattered."[40] The relative sanity is indicated in the regularity of the rhythm—five beats throughout—but the shattered state is indicated by Tennyson's pitching the lines in pentameter verse, just one notch below the hexameters that open the poem. Never before had Tennyson used his metrical

variations in quite this way, either in the earlier dramatic monologues or in *In Memoriam*, where the form prohibited effects like
those he achieved in *Maud*.

Still more fascinating is the way Tennyson uses rhyme and
alliteration in the poem as reflectors of the speaker's consciousness. Here Tennyson's penchant for reading *Maud* aloud may be
a clue. Tennyson's obsession with reading *Maud* was so marked
that Virginia Woolf (through her aunt, Julia Margaret Cameron, Tennyson's neighbor on the Isle of Wight) remembered it
long after Tennyson's death and made it his leading trait in her
private theatrical, *Freshwater*. There, speaking to Mrs. Cameron
(due to leave for India at two thirty), Tennyson says, "And how
am I going to read *Maud* to you when you're in India? Still—
what's the time? Twelve fifteen? I've read it in less. Let's
begin."[41]

Besides offering merriment for Virginia Woolf, though, Tennyson's eccentricity may suggest that only by hearing *Maud* do
we understand it fully. And what is likely to emerge from hearing instead of reading *Maud* is a sharper awareness not only of
varying meters but also of words linked by rhyme and alliteraation.
tion. I first noticed this myself in trying to read aloud the following line from part I: "Not he: his honest fame should at least by
me be maintained" (I, 18). The "me-be" rhyme is rather difficult
to glide through; and in trying to enunciate correctly, one also
hears as a lingering echo the "he" that begins the line. The three
rhyming words, that is, inevitably become linked through sound
when they are said aloud: "he . . . me be." They also seem to
form a message, which "translated" is that "he is I." The line
refers to the hero's father, and in fact what the speaker fears is
precisely that he is becoming like his father: "What! am I raging
alone as my father raged in his mood?" (I, 53). A listener, however, might have detected the point much earlier simply by listening carefully.

I am suggesting that the words linked by rhyme and/or alliteration form a kind of subtext to the speaker's utterance, with
the speaker unconsciously linking words to express feelings
that he will not or cannot consciously articulate.[42] The subtext
does not seem to operate in every stanza, but when present, it

often produces powerful and startling resonances. In part I alliteration is most often used to link words meaningfully; in part II rhyme seems most important; and in part III alliteration and rhyme are brought equally into play.

In part I, when the hero sees workmen refurbishing the Hall to which Maud and her brother will shortly return, he not only utters "Maud" four times in lines 69 to 72, so that the name functions almost like an incantation, but also links Maud alliteratively with all that he finds fair: "Maud-my-mother-moon" (line 72). Thus, when he says in the next line that "My dreams are bad," we may rightly regard him as an unreliable speaker. A similar phenomenon occurs in section IV. Speaking of Maud, the hero says, "But sorrow seize me if ever that light be my leading star"; yet the alliteration emphatically links "light" and "leading," which we may hear above the particulars of his statement.[43] Alliteration, however, also acts to underscore the bitterness that resides in the depths of his mind and his paranoia about Maud's brother. In section X, when the speaker fears that Maud's brother is pushing the rival lord forward as a suitor (I, 352–65), the alliteration links "bound-bride-blithe-brother-be," as if to say beneath the surface, if Maud becomes a bound bride, her brother will be blithe. Rhyme functions similarly in part I. In section XIX the hero tries to accept Maud's praise of her brother (I, 750–59), but the rhyme links "blind-mind-kind," suggesting that only a blind mind can be kind to the brother. Again, in section XX, despite the generous words spoken of the brother on the surface, the rhyme links "name" and "blame" (I, 790–91), as if, for the speaker, to name the brother is to blame him.

The subtext wrought by sound effects becomes even more interesting in part II, where the linkages effected through rhyme are dominant. In section II, stanza V, the speaker muses on his exile in Brittany and the phantom that haunts him, and the rhyme illuminates his inner state with the following pairings: "here-fear" (here is fear); "below-know" (the speaker knows in the depths of his mind the cause of his malady and fear); "Maud-overawed" (the speaker is overawed by the presence of Maud's phantom). In section IV, stanza vii, the speaker tells of a dream he had of Maud that dissolved into the cold phantom as dawn arose, and the rhymes are again peculiarly resonant: "rolled [the] old, behold [all was] cold"; "head [is] dead, [I] fled [my] bed"; "eye [I] cry" (II, 184–95). In the succeeding stanza of section IV both rhyme and alliteration come into play as the speaker adjures the ghost to leave him alone: "again [there is] pain [in the] brain"; [there is] doubt-about [and] without"; "doubt [is] deathlike," "pass-pain-pass"; "will [I am] without."

But above all the subtext becomes important in section V, when the surface coherence of the speaker's mind is broken up by madness. His pain and his emotional progress are both implicitly recounted through patterns wrought by rhyme: "dead-dead-head"; "pain [in the] brain"; "bad-sad-mad" (II, 239–59). "Dead-head" is in fact the most frequent rhyme in section V, as if the hero unconsciously recognizes his madness. Moreover, the speaker seems unconsciously to recognize his pattern of experience, passing as he has from the sin of the duel ("bad") to grief ("sad") to insanity ("mad"). And as the mad scenes close, the subtext of rhyme also says that it is time for madness to pass: "enough-rough"; "sleeper-deeper"; "dumb-come" (II, 334–42).

With the speaker giving listeners, in effect, a readout of the depths of his mind through the words he highlights into significance through rhyme and alliteration, it is especially interesting to see how the pattern works out in part III, the source of so much controversy. Some argue that part III gives us a fully redeemed hero; others contend that he is clearly suicidal. The subtext suggests that the darker reading is more appropriate. The alliteration in the first stanza of part III reinforces the speaker's assertion that Maud has appeared at last in beneficent guise to him: "fear-fell, face-fair" (III, 1–14). But the rhyme suggests that the speaker is more than a little in love with easeful death: "west-blest; rest-breast." The same contrast is evident in the third stanza (III, 29–37), where the hero acclaims the purity of his new-found cause in war, his participation with his countrymen, and the disappearance of the "dreary phantom." The alliteration reinforces this surface meaning: "morbid-mock-disease-die." But the rhyme suggests that a death wish resides beneath the surface: "I-eye-die"; "cry-fly"; "breath-death." Even the alliteration swings over to the side of death in the fourth section (and originally the end of the poem in 1855). The speaker on the surface may intone the greatness of glory, but alliteration links the following: "darken-darkness," "desire-deemed-done," "deep-deathful." The most chilling of all, though, is the rhyme of the poem's last stanza. The "mind" of the speaker may feel it "kind" that he is "assigned" to his doom (and "God" and "doom" may be linked through alliteration), but the rhyme also says that he is "still-ill." If on one hand the hero announces that he is sane, he also tells us, from within, that he is nonetheless shattered.

This concept of the subtext, if correct (and I think it is), helps explain Tennyson's passion for reading the poem in other than psychological terms. If we recall again that Tennyson not only saw but may also have made suggestions for Dr. Mann's essay before it was published, we can see why the essay includes the assertion that "in the successful employment of this kind of word-music [that is, using "sound" to symbolize "mental states and perceptions"], the author of *Maud* stands entirely unrivalled" (199).

The subtext also suggests that Tennyson had considerable distance on the hero's glorification of war as a noble collective enterprise and emblem of his recovery from madness.[44] If he is not fully recovered, however, just what effect has Maud and her love had on him? and how is Maud to be related to the many references to war? The issue of the poem's title is relevant here. Culler finds it odd that Tennyson should "call the poem after the lady rather than the protagonist. . . . But then it is odd to add a subtitle ["or the Madness," the original subtitle in Tennyson's MSS] which stands as if in apposition to Maud but obviously is in opposition to her" (*Poetry*, 207). The title and original subtitle, however, are not really so odd. If we recall how carefully Tennyson selected characters' names in *The Princess*, we can expect him to have done so in 1855 as well.

Tennyson in fact could have found no better name than Maud, and it is a clue to what his poem is all about. For *Maud*, as E. G. Withycombe informs us in the *Oxford Dictionary of English Christian Names*, is derived from the same source as *Matilda*, the Old German *Mahthildis*, a compound of *mahti*, meaning "might" or "strength," and *hildi*, "battle" or "strife."[45] Maud's name, that is, at once suggests the power of Maud and her love for the hero, the hero's inward and outward strife as he tries to move from morbidity to affirmation through the power of love, and the battle that at first seems to rage only in civilian life but later becomes the literal battle to which the hero commits himself at the end. In these respects "Maud, or the Madness" could mean any of the following: (1) Might vs. Madness, (2) Strife and Madness, or (3) Battle as Madness. No wonder James Bennett remarks that the hero views Maud in "two distinctly different ways. . . . he sees her as both loving and war-like."[46] The dual perspective on Maud is inherent in her very name. Tennyson's choice of a title is also apt because, like the poet and Hallam in *In Memoriam*, the hero is attuned to the meaning of Maud no matter what he does—whether he is embroiled in inner strife at the poem's outset, responds to the power of Maud's love, or commits himself to battle and to a death that, he thinks, will reunite him with Maud. The title, finally, implies that in Tennyson's mind all three parts of the poem were fully unified, despite the problems part III has posed for readers.

Why would Tennyson have written a poem in which love, war, and strife are so integrally related? Ralph Rader has offered the best answer. Documenting the sources of the poem's plot in Tennyson's unhappy love affair with Rosa Baring and Tennyson's thwarted engagement to Emily Sellwood, Rader asserts that Tennyson's creation of *Maud* "was also an act of cathartic recapitulation by which he defined and judged his early life and attempted to put it behind him."[47] Recently Robert B. Martin has added ancillary biographical evidence for the poem's violent emotions and preoccupations with recovery from madness. Martin sees a connection between the weird seizures added to *The Princess*, the trance experiences of *In Memoriam*, the "insane ravings" of *Maud*, and Tennyson's own mental and emotional breakdown in the years 1844–45 under the pressure of his losses in the wood-carving scheme, his sense that the possibility of marriage was further away than ever, and his fear that he would follow the same disastrous path of his father (278). Martin's linking of the three long poems to Tennyson's feelings and fears is significant. In chapter three we saw that, as opposed to his earliest poetry, Tennyson began to use the dramatic mode for increasingly objective ends in the 1830s and 1840s. It is hence revealing that, as Tennyson moved further and further away from his troubles, and presumably gained more distance on them, he wrote increasingly dramatic poems to depict them. It seems likely, then, that *Maud* is the most emotionally violent of the three long poems of Tennyson's middle years because only by the mid-1850s had he achieved enough emotional security—thanks to his marriage and the laureateship—to face squarely the devils that had so plagued him.[48] And perhaps the hero must go to his death at the end because Tennyson felt it was time to kill off that part of himself that identified with the hero.

In *Maud*, then, we encounter a culmination of all Tennyson's preceding dramatic monologues, and a kind of pinnacle as well. The poem is an objectified, controlled dramatic fiction, yet a poem suffused with hints of personal participation and made compelling by the merging of the speaker's and poet's "I." In the 1832 and 1842 monologues, Tennyson began to refine language until grammar became an index to a speaker's psyche, as in "Ulysses." Language is not only used thus in *Maud* but is successfully deployed throughout a poem over one thousand lines in length. Finally, the speaker's consciousness is rendered, not solely in ways we have seen before (the mind's oscillations or gaps between sections), but in startlingly new and inventive ways. Tennyson's earlier adaptation of lyric elements to dramatic ends in "Oriana" has been taken so far that lyricism itself—metrics, rhyme, alliteration—became a dramatic technique.

*Maud*, as well as that much lighter poem entitled "The Brook," attest to Tennyson's continuing interest in the dramatic mode during his middle years. Equally important, however, is the evidence that the dramatic techniques he developed through 1842 and beyond informed and helped give shape to his other major, and nondramatic, poems: *The Princess* and *In Memoriam*. The use of monologists and the dramatic feint in *The Princess* and the subtle rendering of consciousness in *In Memoriam* revealed the imprint of the dramatic monologues and also prepared for Tennyson's most sustained dramatic monologue, *Maud*. If, in writing all three long poems of his middle years, Tennyson was reexperiencing old passions and feeling new ones so that his passions "so intense" caused him "suddenly [to] strike on a sharper sense" of his life and his art, this "sharper sense" leading to some of his finest poetry had a distinctly dramatic bent.

# 5. Merlin's Manyfacèd Glass: The Dramatic Monologues from 1859–1892

*And so to the land's*
*Last limit I came—*
*And can no longer,*
*But die rejoicing,*
*For through the Magic*
*Of Him the Mighty,*
*Who taught me in childhood,*
*There on the border*
*Of boundless Ocean,*
*And all but in Heaven*
*Hovers The Gleam.*

—*"Merlin and the Gleam"*

With *Maud* Tennyson came to the "land's last limit" of the dramatic monologue. Either he could "no longer" or was afraid, in the face of adverse reviews, to go beyond the technical achievements of *Maud*; and it was left to later poets to take up where Tennyson stopped. In the later poetry, Tennyson rather adapted the techniques of the dramatic monologue he had already wrought to wider uses: to round off or continue long poems, to present historical personages and speakers of dialect, and to embody the moral and spiritual themes that so obsessed him in his last years.

Admittedly, some of the late verse represents a falling off, poetry of the sort that prompted attacks from the next generation for its "rhetorical moral fervour," sentimentality, and ruminative discursiveness.[1] We encounter vatic visions in "The

175

Higher Pantheism" and, at worst, simplistic, even hysterical "moral fervour" in poems like "In the Children's Hospital" and "Happy." One might call it the onslaught of prose in Tennyson's poetry; significantly, Tennyson now began to use preliminary prose drafts for his poems. Why Tennyson grew discursive and oracular, as if he wanted to be Merlin in earnest, is uncertain. FitzGerald attributed the change to diverse causes. Tennyson erred, he thought, in having left "his old County, and gone up to be suffocated by London Adulation. He has lost that which caused the long roll of the Lincolnshire Wave to reverberate in the measure of Locksley Hall. . . . Nor do I mean that his Decay is all owing to London, &c. He is growing old: and I don't believe much in the *Fine Arts* thriving on an old Tree. . . . [Emily Tennyson] & other aesthetic and hysterical Ladies have hurt A.T., who, *quoad Artist*, wd have done better to remain single in Lincolnshire, or married a jolly Woman who would have laughed & cried without any reason why."[2]

The dramatic monologues of 1859–92 do not explain the new strain of sententiousness, but they exhibit the symptomatology. Of the approximately thirty-six dramatic monologues Tennyson wrote in this period, all but four have clearly indicated auditors, a structural hint of Tennyson's own surer sense of a listening audience and his orientation outward. More significant, of the thirty-six monologues, only a handful can be said to render consciousness, the inward awareness of external life, and Tennyson's richest vein. Thus, in his late phase Tennyson turned away from his forte,[3] with clear, and sometimes unfortunate, results.

However, if we must admit that the aged Merlin's "manyfacèd glass" was sometimes clouded, he did not entirely lose the Gleam, and there is also cause for "rejoicing" in the late dramatic monologues. Tennyson's Lincolnshire monologues, for example, not only are delightful in themselves but also suggest Tennyson's internal adjustment toward homeostasis. In response, as it were, to the mandarin style of the *Idylls* or the description of Enoch Arden's fish basket, Tennyson created dialect poems pitched in the rough, gnarled idiom of crusty characters whose earthiness is inseparable from the earth of Lincolnshire. Moreover, the dramatic monologues frequently served as an impetus to the writing of Tennyson's best late poems. Writing the mediocre monologue "The Grandmother," for example, seems to have sparked the revising and publishing of the superb "Tithonus." Both poems deal with the desirability of death; and, as Ricks remarks, a 10 April 1859 letter from Jowett (who suggested the subject of "The Grandmother") recorded Jowett's response to visiting Arthur Hallam's grave.[4] Perhaps it is only a slight exaggeration to say that without the dramatic monologue the *Idylls* might never have been completed either. Tennyson could go no further than the first four idylls, published in 1859, until he determined how to handle the legend of the San Graal. When the solution came, it came in the form of a dramatic monologue, written immediately after two preceding dramatic monologues, "Lucretius" and "The Golden Supper" (itself the conclusion to *The Lover's Tale*).[5] Finally, there is cause to rejoice in the late dramatic monologues because some of them are among Tennyson's finest poems, early or late, including "Tithonus," "Lucretius," "Rizpah"—all of which are centered squarely in the realm of consciousness—and "Demeter and Persephone."

To map fully what Tennyson did and did not accomplish in his late poems, let us examine them according to groupings into which they naturally fall: the continuations of the domestic monologues, the use of the dramatic monologue to complete long poems, the dramatic monologues sparked by Tennyson's verse dramas, the dialect poems, the "prophetic" or sententious monologues, and the final classical monologues.

I
## Domestic Monologues

The late domestic monologues include "The Grandmother," "Rizpah," "The First Quarrel," "In the Children's Hospital," "The Sisters," "Tomorrow," "The Flight," "The Wreck," "Happy," "Charity," and "The Bandit's Death." As in the 1832 and 1842 domestic monologues, these poems seem designed to engage the reader's emotional participation in domestic affections. James Kissane terms these "pathetic monologues,"[6] and unfortunately most of these poems justify his adjective in both its senses. One example will suffice. "The Wreck" opens with a

woman frantically confessing her sins to a nun in whose con-
vent she has taken refuge. The woman had abandoned her child
when she escaped a wretched marriage and fled with another.
Although fever is allowed some part, the child's ensuing death is
more clearly linked to the mother's abandonment; and the same
day the child dies, a tidal wave wrecks the boat on which the
mother sails. As the mere summary indicates, the poem is melo-
dramatic and sentimental, and the dramatic monologue actually
intensifies both qualities: the speaker's monologue constitutes a
form of penitence as she "tells against" herself in her sorrow and
regret. Tennyson may have a clear rationale for the monologue
form, but he omits any serious engagement with the substance
of the poem. He has not imagined his speaker as an aspect of
himself, nor, as in the dialect poems, has he created a character
interesting in her own right. With both the recursive loop and a
realized speaker eliminated, the monologue, like too many others in this same vein, is left to float or sink according to its story
(the spoken) and its palpable designs on the reader. And so there
is more than one "Wreck" among the late domestic monologues.

The exception is "Rizpah," which demonstrates the enduring
vitality of Tennyson's poetry that lay in reserve beneath a sometimes sickly surface. "Rizpah" dispels any notion that Tennyson's late poetry failed because of a narrative ethos; this poem,
like "The Wreck," clearly relates a story: a mother driven mad by
grief and then beaten for her very madness has rescued the
bones of her son hanged for robbing the mail coach, his corpse
having been left on the gallows as a warning to others. The
poem also refutes the charge that Tennyson inevitably writes
worse when he has a clear moral or religious theme since "Rizpah" reflects his horror at the doctrine of eternal punishment.
The dying mother disdains the Evangelical doctrines of her auditor who, ostensibly on a charitable mission, sits at her bedside.

> *Election, Election and Reprobation—it's all very well.*
> *But I go tonight to my boy, and I shall not find him in Hell.*
> *For I cared so much for my boy that the Lord has looked into my care,*
>
> . . . . . . . . . . . . . . . . . . . . . . . . . . . . . . . .
> *And if he be lost—but to save my soul that is all your desire:*
> *Do you think that I care for my soul if my boy be gone to the fire?*
>
> (lines 73–75, 77–78)

Everlasting punishment seems ignoble and narrow compared to the passionate love of the mother; if God is the father, he can hardly retain his divinity and be less loving than she. The lines also exemplify Tennyson's insistence that love can survive death and his hope that those bound by love in life are rejoined after death—themes common not only to *In Memoriam* but also to the pathetic "Happy" and "The Sisters."

What, then, makes "Rizpah" different from these last two poems? Part of the answer is yet another theme: the insufficiency of the merely conventional.[7] Public or codified manners, morality, religion, and law are seen as no match for the irrational, passionate law of maternal love that knows no bounds. The strict law of the lawyers and a vengeful God fade before a woman who, to satisfy the imperatives of love, must herself become a thief.

> Flesh of my flesh was gone, but bone of my bone was left—
> I stole them all from the lawyers—and you, will you call it a theft?—
> My baby, the bones that had sucked me, the bones that had laughed and had
>    cried—
> Theirs? O no! they are mine—not theirs—they had moved in my side.
> Do you think I was scared by the bones? I kissed 'em, I buried 'em all—
> . . . . . . . . . . . . . . . . . . . . . . . . . . . . . . . .
> But I charge you never to say that I laid him in holy ground.
>
> (lines 51–55, 58)

It is as if, in blasting through the walls of conventionality, Tennyson also blasted away the trammels that fettered the weaker domestic poems—and regained his energy and vitality as poet.

The poem also succeeds because Tennyson situates it squarely in the realm of consciousness. We find out only gradually that the auditor is present, for she is ephemeral compared to the compelling, ghostly presence of the dead son. The poem opens,

> Wailing, wailing, wailing, the wind over land and sea—
> And Willy's voice in the wind, "O mother, come out to me."
> Why should he call me tonight, when he knows that I cannot go?
> For the downs are as bright as day, and the full moon stares at the snow.

The opening at once activates every pole of the dramatic monologue (except that of the auditor, which comes later). We are

179

immediately drawn into the speaker's mind because that is all we have to hold on to, and we experience the disorientation indicated in the speaker's obsessive insistence on wailing, the odd inversion of dark and light, and the slightly paranoiac suggestion of a staring moon. We sense the poet's participation through the very energy and intensity of the verse, and we ourselves are activated as readers to fathom the meaning of the speaker's odd juxtapositions and unanswered questions. Tennyson also uses some of the finely wrought lyric devices of *Maud*. The alliterative linking of "wailing," "wind," and "Willy" suggests a connection among them, as indeed there is: the alliterative pattern suggests all at once the mother's wail for her child, the child's wail when he is punished and taken from his mother forever, the wailing wind in the dark nights on the down when she rescues the bones of Willy, and the ghostly, wailing wind that haunts and is the emblem of the mother's own wandering consciousness.

Tennyson's use of other features of the dramatic monologue enhances his setting, speaker, and themes. The convention of the auditor enables Tennyson to stress at once the mother's madness and her love since her dead son is more real to her than the woman in front of her. The auditor also precipitates the clash between the claims of society and a love forced to become asocial. As well, Tennyson skillfully exploits the distinctions between the speaker's rendered consciousness and the embedded narrative (the mother's story told to her auditor). When the speaker surfaces from the depths of consciousness and fully recognizes the auditor, she shifts from railing at the visitor ("Ah—you, that have lived so soft, what should *you* know of the night. . . . I have gathered my baby together—and now you may go your way"—lines 17, 20) to the mundanities of civil discourse: "Nay—for it's kind of you, Madam, to sit by an old dying wife" (line 21). In effecting the shift in orientation, she also shifts from utterance shaped only by the pressures of her psyche to coherent, conventional narrative to tell the story of how she attempted the role of equally conventional mother— whipping her boy for stealing apples when he was a child, going in good faith to the courtroom to tell the truth as she saw it, expressing her shame at the dishonored family name—to no avail. Once she has finished her narrative, she is back to her railing and her uncanny prehensions ("I have been with God in the dark"—line 79). She surfaces once more at the very end, but this time she surfaces to death—the only end to consciousness.

Tennyson has in fact neatly framed the central narrative with five stanzas on either side, as if to suggest that even the conventional discourse of narrative is too limited and must open onto a larger, if less well-regulated, mode of expression and perception. The deliberateness of this framing is supported by the manuscripts, which reveal that Tennyson first began the poem with utterly conventional discourse and sentiments: "Tis mighty kind of you, Madam, to sit by an old dying wife / But I pray you leave me in peace—I have only one hour of life."[8] In the published poem, the alpha and omega of the speaker's sensibility—the beginning and end of her monologue—is dark, irrational, chaotic consciousness, bounded only by the law that countenances no law, the law of fierce maternal love. One might even say that the poem's rhyme scheme enhances Tennyson's juxtaposition of two worlds. His rhyming couplets in "The Grandmother" or "Tomorrow" have often reminded readers of singsong or doggerel verse. In "Rizpah" the energy and force of the speaker counterbalance and transcend the strict rhyme scheme, another conventionality or law that the mother's violent love overwhelms.

Thus, although most of the domestic monologues of Tennyson's late years are easily forgotten, we need not deplore their existence altogether. For when Tennyson was able to enter in to his speaker and bring all the resources of the dramatic monologue into play—instead of using the form as a mere conduit for stories or confessionals—he was able to create such a poem as "Rizpah."

## II
### *The Lover's Tale* and *Idylls of the King*

Besides using the dramatic monologue to continue a mode he had already developed, Tennyson also turned to the dramatic monologue in 1868 and 1869 to complete or sustain two of his longer poems, *The Lover's Tale* and *Idylls of the King*. In neither long

work do his monologues emphasize the rendering of consciousness. Rather, Tennyson returns to his skillful exploitation of the
monologue's formal properties to create meaning, especially to
indicate the added monologue's relation to the larger poem that
precedes or surrounds it.

The first two parts of *The Lover's Tale* as we know it were written, according to Tennyson, in 1827–28. Not surprisingly, this
early portion shares themes with many of the suppressed poems
written in the same period, as if it were one of the "Exile" poems
writ large.[9] Although *The Lover's Tale* represents an advance
beyond the "Exile" poems in its concreteness—in this poem we
know exactly why the speaker feels as he does—the poem still
turns on the speaker's alienation (since his love for his cousin
and foster sister is not returned), his sense of undeserved guilt
or punishment ("Who was curst / But I? who miserable but
I?"),[10] and his contention that all good things are in the past
("The Present is the vassal of the Past: / So that, in that I *have*
lived, do I live"—I, 115–16). Thus, when Tennyson decided to
conclude the poem (apparently in 1868, when "The Golden
Supper" was written), he faced a major difficulty: how to complete a poem redolent of the self he was at seventeen or eighteen, a self that must have seemed as remote to the fifty-nine-
year-old laureate as Tithonus's godlike youthful self to him.

Another challenge faced by the older Tennyson was the earlier parts' vaguely defined dramatic format.[11] Although the
1832 speaker was unnamed, he was clearly meant to be distinct
from the poet, as indicated by the poem's title and the speaker's
occasional recognition of his auditors. "See, sirs," he comments
as he invokes the spirit of the past (I, 15) and then pleads, "Per-
mit me, friend, I prythee, / To pass my hand across my brows" (I,
29–30). But despite the young Tennyson's attempt to create a
clear dramatic framework, the subjective and objective (as in so
many of the earliest monologues) are imperfectly fused, and it is
easy to forget that the poem is dramatic. The feint, once again, is
fractured. Part of the problem is sheer length. The fragmented
sections of *Maud*, with its gaps and often startling shifts in tone,
are constant reminders that a dramatized "I" is speaking. But
*The Lover's Tale* is an uninterrupted, long narrative whose self-
involved speaker gives only infrequent and scant attention to

his auditors. Consequently, the speaker tends to blend imperceptibly with the poet as we read, and we ourselves seem to be the direct auditors. The mature Tennyson would have noticed the wobbly dramatic ethos, plus additional dramatic flaws: the extraordinarily slow pace of the poem (see, for example, I, 410–30), compared to which "The Lotos-Eaters" moves at breakneck speed, and described rather than dramatized consciousness.

> *Alway the inaudible invisible thought,*
> *Artificer and subject, lord and slave,*
> *Shaped by the audible and visible,*
> *Moulded the audible and visible.*

> (II, 101–4)

These lines tell us of the speaker's hallucinatory imagination; in *Maud* we are shown such an imagination directly. Hence Tennyson's second challenge in completing the poem in 1868 was to strengthen the earlier parts' dramatic ethos.

His solution, "The Golden Supper," may not be great poetry—it even lacks the lush if undisciplined beauties of the 1827–28 verse—but in formal and personal terms it was entirely appropriate. Here another speaker, an unnamed friend of the lover, takes over and relates how the lover, now identified as Julian, rescued his beloved Camilla from premature burial and gave her and her babe back to her husband at a "golden supper," the lover's one "hour of triumph." The first parts of *The Lover's Tale* may not have been based on Boccacio,[12] but the last section clearly is. Many have complained that "The Golden Supper" is in fact too different in tone from the early sections, destroying the larger poem's unity; others deride the fourth part's dramatic format as an unartful dodge, objecting that the speaker seems to exist only so that a story can be attached to him.[13] These criticisms are well founded, but so was Tennyson's decision to proceed as he did. Using a different speaker for part IV declares, as if by a fiat empowered with retroactive jurisdiction, that the first three parts are also spoken by a persona separate from the poet. "Another speaks," we are told in the heading to part IV, and this other speaker begins, "He flies the event: he leaves the event to me" (IV, 1). Immediately the first three parts recede into the distance, becoming objectified as a voice and tale now emphatically over and part of the past. Hence the use of a second and very different speaker in part IV helped Tennyson shore up the dramatic format of the first three parts.

This solution may not be "organic" to the poem as a whole, but it was at least organic to Tennyson's sensibility. No longer the same person or poet in 1868 that he was in 1828, he chose to employ a new voice rather than attempt recapturing that earlier voice. And, fittingly, he chose a speaker who seems older than the lover.[14] The second speaker not only lacks Julian's inspired rhapsodies but is even a little skeptical and jaded. He is unwilling to countenance Julian's visions as entirely authentic, suspecting instead that Julian's later experience "glanced back upon [the visions] in his after life, / And partly made them—though he knew it not" (IV, 24–25). The "base repast" forced on the speaker at the inn where he met Julian vies in memory ("It makes me angry yet to speak of it") with Julian's frantic, wild tales of "dead men's dust and beating hearts" (IV, 129–39). But above all, the second speaker differs from Julian in being unable to come up to quite the same pitch of idealistic love.

> [Julian's] love is of the brain, the mind, the soul:
> That *makes the sequel pure; though some of us*
> *Beginning at the sequel know no more.*
> *Not such am I: and yet I say the bird*
> *That will not hear my call, however sweet,*
> *But if my neighbour whistle answers him—*
> *What matter? there are others in the wood.*

> (IV, 155–61)

This older, more experienced speaker befits an older Tennyson, and the speaker's story befits an older Tennyson revisiting and expanding an early poem. For "The Golden Supper" is about a descent undertaken to recover and resuscitate a figure from the past; "The dead returns to me, and I go down / To kiss the dead," says Julian on entering Camilla's tomb, as reported by the second speaker. And during his golden supper at the end Julian presents this recovered figure, as does Tennyson, to the public.

The addition of part IV helped bridge the gap between his older and his younger selves in one last way. The second speaker exemplifies the power of the tale he relates. Although worldly, even he cannot resist the power of Julian's love, and his tone softens as the tale nears its end: "I am long in telling it, / I never yet beheld a thing so strange, / Sad, sweet, and strange together" (IV, 299–301). His asides and hesitations cease completely in the final lines, and he becomes absorbed by the events he relates. In this respect the speaker is an exemplar of the reader (or what Tennyson perhaps hoped would be the experience of the reader), mediating between Tennyson and his audience as the speaker also mediates between Tennyson young and Tennyson old.

Thus, Tennyson's choosing the dramatic monologue for "The Golden Supper" and then exploiting the form's resources, particularly its fictive speaker, were deliberate and sophisticated technical choices. By adding a second voice and narrative to the earlier work (which he revised in part but did not alter in substance), he could finish the poem yet acknowledge the difference between his 1828 and his 1868 selves and the reader's relationship to both.

Emily Tennyson took much of the credit for the completion of "The Holy Grail": "I doubt whether the *San Graal* would have been written but for my endeavour, and the Queen's wish, and that of the Crown Princess."[15] But she might have given equal billing to "The Golden Supper." It seems likely that Tennyson's practice of using a dramatic monologue to complete one long poem sparked the solution to another "blocked" poem, *Idylls of the King*. For "The Holy Grail," the composition of which had stymied Tennyson for some time, was, like "The Golden Supper," written in 1868. In both poems Tennyson used the dramatic monologue to achieve automatic distance on his subject matter, to relate a narrative, and to show the effect of the narrative on its teller and listener(s). But if some feel "The Golden Supper" was an unartful dodge for completing *The Lover's Tale*, the consensus seems to be that Tennyson's reliance on the dramatic monologue in "The Holy Grail" is a very artful dodge.[16]

By placing the tale of the holy grail quest in the mouth of Percivale, that is, Tennyson sidestepped the question of his own belief or disbelief in the grail's reality. If readers wished, they could identify with Percivale and see the quest as he does. But the dramatic monologue makes other options available as well. Given the genre's allowance for a speaker's ironic self-betrayal, many of Percivale's statements can be used against him, as when he innocently reports Arthur's hope that the knights "be not smitten by the bolt" (of religious hysteria?) that rends the roof of the hall and seems to make passage for a vision of the grail (line 221). And his later confession that he spurned the love, wealth, and power offered by a woman he once loved (line 564ff.) can be used to explicate and demystify his earlier reports of visions of nourishment, domestic affections, wealth, and fame that crumbled into dust when he tried to embrace them.[17]

The use of an auditor, Ambrosius the monk, also enhances the relativity of the tale Percivale relates. Ambrosius, of course, not only listens but at times also interrupts Percivale's monologue and himself speaks. These interludes interrupt the dramatic monologue form as well, but they help Tennyson avoid one of the problems of the lengthy monologue in parts I through III of *The Lover's Tale*, where the speaker's separate identity fades away. As do the fragmented sections of *Maud*, the punctuations of Percivale's monologue by Ambrosius function to remind us that it is indeed Percivale, not the poet Tennyson, speaking. As well, Ambrosius as auditor can serve as the reader's ally in his incredulity at Percivale's dogmatic belief in the grail or in the monk's celebration of the mundane verities of everyday life and the sweetness of human bondings versus the asceticism and lonely privacy of a spiritual quest. In all these ways, then, the dramatic monologue enables Tennyson to present the grail legend without appearing to commit himself to gross dogmatism or skepticism.

But the dramatic monologue does more than help Tennyson avoid pitfalls and pratfalls; there is at least as much art as dodge in his use of the form in "The Holy Grail." The frame, for example, as in "Oenone" or "The Hesperides," redounds at once on the succeeding monologue's themes and the monologue form per se. Couched in the same narrative voice that in the other idylls is a public voice laden with social and spiritual import, the frame can take the reader (and the larger world of Arthur's realm) only to the gate of the abbey. Having forsaken the outside world to immure himself in "the silent life of prayer," Percivale can now be heard only from within, from inside. The poem's very monologue form, that is, exemplifies Percivale's status: he is no longer a part of the public world and public discourse, but is inward-turning, focused on the self instead of others—so much so that he must be prompted to speak by an extension of sympathy from Ambrosius, who

> loved him much beyond the rest,
> And honoured him, and wrought into his heart
> A way by love that wakened love within,
> To answer that which came.

> *(lines 9–12)*

Moreover, Percivale's predominant use of past-tense narrative becomes more than the narrative convention of the other idylls; Percivale is telling of what is lost and gone, like himself respecting the world.[18] All that remains in the present is the meaning of it all, and on this Percivale is mute: "So spake the King: I knew not all he meant" (line 916).

Tennyson's use of the dramatic monologue is also a means by which Tennyson can remain true to the legend of the holy grail, less in terms of its contents than in terms of its very genesis. For once we as readers focus on Percivale as a teller of a tale, not as some *sacer vates*, we can observe that the germ of Percivale's monologue, rather than a vision of the grail, is his sister's monologue (or tale) told to him (lines 101–28). The germ of *her* monologue is the tale told her by her ancient confessor (lines 83–94), who in turn heard of the grail from another ancient teller, and so on back to the birth of Christ.

> the Holy Grail,
> A legend handed down through five or six,
> And each of these a hundred winters old,
> From our Lord's time.

> *(lines 86–89)*

The monologue we read, then, is not only recessive with respect to Percivale, who has retreated from the world, but infinitely recessive with respect to the grail itself. We look into the monologue as into the infinite regress of mirrored images. This structuring may once again enhance the relativity of Percivale's ut-

terance; it is also Tennyson's acknowledgment as poet of the
process by which myth and legend are brought down to us.
Tennyson is one more link in the succession of those who narrate the grail legend, and we as readers help to form one more
link in the chain, listening to Percivale as he had listened to his
sister and so on.

Yet Arthur shows that we need not be passive listeners of
legends or readers of dramatic monologues. Percivale, like a
naive reader of a dramatic monologue, can be wholly absorbed
by the power of what he hears (or reads): "While thus [Galahad]
spake, his eye, dwelling on mine, / Drew me, with power upon
me, till I grew / One with him, to believe as he believed" (lines
485–87). But Arthur, king of readers as well as knights, understands the monologue's feint and knows that monologues are
true only in relation to their speakers.

> these have seen according to their sight.
> For every fiery prophet in old times,
> And all the sacred madness of the bard,
> When God made music through them, could but speak
> His music by the framework and the chord;
> And as ye saw it ye have spoken truth.
>
> (lines 871–76)

Thus, Tennyson's use of the dramatic monologue for "The
Holy Grail" was not only an escape from the burden of belief or
disbelief but also a resonant, rich exploitation of the genre's resources to underscore and play upon the idyll's themes. "The
Holy Grail" is not the only idyll that makes use of the dramatic
monologue,[19] since "Guinevere," first published in 1859, features
a long monologue by Arthur. There, however, the monologue
is something of a mistake. The feint of the dramatic monologue is at work; Arthur's initial superciliousness (lines 419–
523) is clearly the result of genuine pain, which Arthur inad-
vertently reveals in the conclusion of his monologue: "O golden
hair, with which I used to play / Not knowing!" (lines 544–45; see
also lines 560–64). But Tennyson cannot resist using Arthur
here, as throughout the *Idylls*, as an absolute value indicator.
Tennyson cannot have it both ways: he cannot use the monologue-
as-feint for Arthur in one place and elsewhere claim an abso-

luteness for Arthur's discourse. But "The Holy Grail" does not suffer from divided purposes, and the dramatic monologue that forms "The Holy Grail" is the most sustained monologue in the *Idylls* and the most effective. Moreover, because the *Idylls* awaited completion until Tennyson solved the dilemma posed by the grail legend, it is fair to say that the dramatic monologue is as integral to the *Idylls* as it was to all of Tennyson's long poems, whether *The Lover's Tale, The Princess, In Memoriam,* or *Maud.*

## III
## The Historical Monologues and Tennyson's Verse Dramas

The last of the *Idylls*, "Balin and Balan," was not published until 1885, though written by 1874. Tennyson had no sooner finished the *Idylls* than he embarked on his next ambitious project, the dramas. *Queen Mary* was his first play, written in 1874–75 and published in 1875. Thereafter appeared *Harold* (1876), *Becket* (written 1876–79, published in 1884), *The Cup* and *The Falcon* (written 1879–80, published in 1884), *The Foresters* (written 1881, published in 1892), and *The Promise of May*, the only prose drama (written 1882, published in 1886). One would expect that Tennyson took the dramas seriously since he wrote so many over an eight-year period. One would also expect the dramas to be an outgrowth of the dramatic monologues Tennyson had been writing since his teens. But this is not so.

Rather, the dramas seem to be an outgrowth of the narrative *Idylls.* Tennyson had longed to co-opt some of drama's conventions when he wrote "Gareth and Lynette": "If I were at liberty, which I think I am not, to print the names of the speakers 'Gareth,' 'Linette' over the short snip-snap of their talk, and so avoid the perpetual 'said' and its varieties, the work would be much easier" (*Memoir*, II, 113 n.). But the connection between the *Idylls* and the plays is stronger than this. *Queen Mary's* list of dramatis personae—Tennyson's early version of the "cast of thousands"—harks back to the just-completed *Idylls*, with its panoply of characters introduced from beginning to end, yet all revolving around the court of Arthur as those in the play do about Mary's court. But above all, one detects a resemblance between the *Idylls* and the dramas—particularly the first three or four—

in theme. *Queen Mary, Harold,* and *Becket* explore the grounds of legitimacy for the ruler and for religious faith,[20] themes Tennyson earlier had explored in "The Coming of Arthur," "Balin and Balan" (the fanaticism of King Pellam is echoed, as it were, by Queen Mary and others), and "The Holy Grail." The clearest evidence that the inspiration for the dramas came not from the preceding dramatic monologues but from elsewhere, however, is the absence of any soliloquies approaching the power and complexity of Tennyson's dramatic monologues. The omission is curious since Tennyson's material offered rich possibilities for sympathetic identification and exploration. Queen Mary, for example, feels spurned by both her father and her siblings, and this alienation, along with her desire to vindicate her mother's marriage and faith, fuels her obsessive desire to wed Philip of Spain. But when Mary soliloquizes about all this, she merely announces these facts rather than explore her inner responses to them.

> But I will have him! My hard father hated me;
> My brother rather hated me than loved;
> My sister cowers and hates me. Holy Virgin,
> Plead with thy blessed Son; grant me my prayer:
> Give me my Philip; and we two will lead
> The living waters of the Faith again
> Back thro' their widow'd channel here, and watch
> The parch'd banks rolling incense, as of old,
> To heaven, and kindled with the palms of Christ![21]

None of the soliloquies in the plays gains much in depth over the above. We think we are in for more substance when Robin Hood opens act II of *The Foresters* by announcing that it is his birthday, when he always reserves an hour to meditate upon life. But the meditation does little more than recapitulate the previous year's events; the soliloquy is merely a form of oblique exposition. The explanation of Tennyson's failure to create soliloquies that even begin to approach those of Shakespeare, or his own in *The Devil and the Lady,* is not far to seek. In the plays he explores how characters affect each other and how they are affected and revealed by the larger world of politics and ethics. Tennyson is dabbling in the realm of personality, and only rarely did that realm provoke a genuine imaginative response in him.

The same limitation fetters the dramatic monologues directly sparked by the plays, "Columbus" and "Sir John Oldcastle" (the list might also include "Romney's Remorse" and "Akbar's Dream," but these are more profitably viewed elsewhere, among Tennyson's philosophical explorations). "Columbus" ought to be a great poem—again because of the subject's potential suggestiveness for Tennyson and Tennyson's own deliberate exercise of artistic freedom—but it is only a good and rather interesting one. "Columbus" was written at the request of "certain prominent Americans that he would commemorate the discovery of America in verse" (*Memoir*, II, 255). But Tennyson hardly composed a sentimental, mawkish salute that was perhaps expected and probably desired. Tennyson, after all, had already honored Columbus with a restrained, dignified salute in "The Daisy" (lines 17–24). When he wrote "Columbus" in 1879–80, he made the subject his own, choosing a dark moment in Columbus's life rather than one of his triumphs. Columbus speaks from his probable deathbed, aged, wracked by gout, exiled from the favor of king and court, excommunicated from the Church, and obsessively clinging to the chains in which he was brought back from the New World and which signify Spain's betrayal of him. As did Queen Mary's peculiar relation to her father, Columbus's experience and psychology offered Tennyson the opportunity for an evocative rendering of consciousness spurred by the sympathetic imagination. Columbus, like Tennyson, had to wait years before achieving distinction and recognition of his genius (lines 36–39); Columbus, like Tennyson, was fired with a poetic imagination and vision;[22] Columbus, as Tennyson feared he would, had good cause to cavil at the ups and downs of fame and reputation; Columbus in old age, like the young Tennyson of the "Exile" poems, suffered alienation and rejection; and the Columbus Tennyson chose to depict was, like Tennyson at the time of writing, old and suffering from gout. As well, Columbus offered some of the same possibilities as St. Simeon Stylites had earlier to Tennyson: he is wracked by the decay of his body, is justifiably somewhat paranoid, believes that he holds a privileged relation to God (true of the historical Columbus as well as a suggestive psychological detail), maintains delusions of grandeur that he can mount a campaign to "free the Holy Sepulchre from thrall" (line 103) if only given the chance, and, once again, displays an obsessiveness about "Chains"—the first word of his monologue—that would delight a Freudian analyst.

But Tennyson, though incorporating elements of Columbus's complex psychology into the poem, approaches the monologue from the point of view of the *Idylls* and the historical dramas, with their discursive themes and heavy symbolic patterns. I have discussed elsewhere the affinity of "Columbus" and the *Idylls*; like a belated King Arthur, and like the king a type of Christ, Columbus has opened a new world with edenic possibilities only to see it undone by man's baser instincts.[23] The relation between "Columbus" and the dramas is even more direct. Compare the rebel Wyatt's oration against Spain in *Queen Mary* (act II, scene i) to the climax of Columbus's outcry against the destruction of the paradise he made possible.

> *Wyatt.* . . . ye know, my masters, that wherever Spain hath ruled she hath wither'd all beneath her. Look at the New World— a paradise made hell; the red man, that good helpless creature, starved, maim'd, flogg'd, flay'd, burn'd, boil'd, buried alive, worried by dogs. . . .

> *And seeing what a door for scoundrel scum*
> *I opened to the West, through which the lust,*
> *Villainy, violence, avarice, of your Spain*
> *Poured in on all those happy naked isles—*
> *Their kindly native princes slain or slaved,*
> *Their wives and children Spanish concubines,*
> *Their innocent hospitalities quenched in blood,*
> *Some dead of hunger, some beneath the scourge,*
> *Some over-laboured, some by their own hands,—*
> *Yea, the dear mothers, crazing Nature, kill*
> *Their babies at the breast for hate of Spain—*
> *Ah God, the harmless people whom we found*
> *In Hispaniola's island-Paradise!*
> *Who took us for the very Gods from Heaven,*
> *And we have sent them very fiends from Hell.*

> (lines 166–80)

"Columbus" in fact shares many themes with the dramas: the oppressive power of narrow dogma, as in *Queen Mary* or *Harold* (see lines 40ff.); religious fanaticism born of a sense of God's election, as in *Becket*; and the problematic integration of the sacred and secular, as in all three historical dramas.

The problem, ultimately, is that in "Columbus" Tennyson has divided purposes. On one hand, he is engaged in what might be called historical justice. Although Columbus was vilified in his lifetime, history has vindicated him; and Tennyson's choosing the dramatic monologue is a way of enabling Columbus to speak forever in the present in recompense for the alienation, obscurity, and betrayals that Columbus suffered in his own time. On the other hand, Tennyson is engaged in creating symbolic themes and patterns that bespeak the pessimism of so many of his late poems. Yet again, Tennyson cannot entirely resist the impulse to identify sympathetically with Columbus, and we detect Tennyson's personal engagement in the lines exploring the unkind caprices of fame, the decay of age, and the limitations of life that hem one in like chains. Finally, we can detect at least the beginnings of an imaginative portrait of an unbalanced mind in the poem. Columbus veers between speaking in the royal plural and complaining about his degradation; between scorning a corrupt church for its stodgy dogmatism and arbitrary excommunications and insisting on his allegiance to the Church and to his own divine (and dogmatic) revelations; between dispensing recriminations and retreating into cringing; and between upholding the strength of his will and belief and collapsing under the weakness of his body and mind. Any of these four strands of the poem is interesting and often skillfully done. But they do not cohere and form a whole. In essence, Tennyson has attempted to fuse Browning's forte—the glimpses of underlying consciousness through the filtering lens of personality—with the ponderous themes of the *Idylls* and dramas, and "Columbus" is bound to be less than a complete success. Historical clues fired Browning's imagination, but they were dues to Tennyson—obligatory details that froze his imagination and kept it locked within safe, but uninspired, bounds. He, too, has his chains, but his are entirely self-imposed.

"Sir John Oldcastle" is inferior even to "Columbus" but has

some of the same poignancy: it, too, should be better than it is. Indeed, there is some clear evidence of Tennyson's craftsmanship in the poem. The historical Oldcastle was imprisoned, escaped into Wales, and was then recaptured and burned for heresy because, as a follower of Wycliffe, he advocated removing the Latin Bible from the priest's monopoly by translating it into English and because he denied that the communion bread literally became Christ's body. Thus, in Oldcastle's monologue Tennyson interweaves three major images: bread, the Word, and fire. The link between bread and the Word is introduced at the outset of the poem in lines that seem promising in their colloquialism and fluidity.

> *I read no more the prisoner's mute wail*
> *Scribbled or carved upon the pitiless stone;*
> *I find hard rocks, hard life, hard cheer, or none,*
> *For I am emptier than a friar's brains;*
> . . . . . . . . . . . . . . . . . . . . . . . . . .
> *I would I knew their speech; not now to glean,*
> *Not now—I hope to do it—some scattered ears,*
> *Some ears for Christ in this wild field of Wales—*
> *But, bread, merely for bread.*
>
> *(lines 4–7, 11–14)*

This emphasis on the Word—the muteness of the Latin Bible (as of the prison walls) to all but a few versus the English Bible's power to speak to all—demonstrates Tennyson's deft choice of the dramatic monologue for the poem. If Oldcastle was denied the right to speak out in his lifetime or to make the living Word available to his countrymen, Tennyson pays tribute to him now by enabling Oldcastle, as it were, to speak for himself now and forever. Moreover, if there is no auditor in the poem, as opposed to the clear auditor of "Columbus," that, too, is functional. Oldcastle announces at the outset that he awaits a friend to guide him to a hiding place. But there is no friend (the "friend" betrays Oldcastle to the authorities), a point neatly underscored by the absence of an auditor. Oldcastle has no one to listen to him—except succeeding generations.

But beyond the aptness of the monologue form for the poem and Tennyson's skillful handling of imagery and chronology (Oldcastle actually spent four years in Wales after escaping the

194

Tower; Tennyson compresses his escape, betrayal, and recapture into a single time frame), there is little to applaud. The poem's subject offered a wonderful theme for the poet—the power of words, of language; the fiery immolation and self-sacrifice of one in service of living words—but Tennyson follows the gleam of Clio rather than Urania or Melpomene. We get a simple recapitulation of Oldcastle's creed and of events leading up to Oldcastle's recapture.

Perhaps, beyond his unsuitability for delving into the realm of personality, Tennyson's failure in the historical plays and monologues resulted from his approach to historical personages *as* public figures. Tennyson himself maintained a strong split between his public persona and his private self. Even in his youth, as Robert Martin records, Tennyson defensively protected his private self from public purview; "in the late 1840s, when he first met Frederick Robertson in Cheltenham, he had taken refuge behind a screen of irrelevance: 'I felt', he said, 'as if he had come to pluck out the heart of my mystery—so I talked to him about nothing but beer.' " Henry James encountered the same fate as Robertson when he first met Tennyson in the late 1870s, when the latter was writing the plays. To James's dismay, Tennyson spoke of little else but "port and tobacco!" (Martin, 518-19). Choosing to cling to the public selves of his historical characters, accordingly, Tennyson abjures their depths of consciousness and instead gives us works that are the poetic equivalent of discussing beer.

However, the dramas, if they inspired stillborn historical monologues, did some good. In the spate of dramatic monologues written concurrently with or succeeding the dramas, Tennyson often achieved greater compression and more effective interplay of speaker and auditor, doubtless both lessons derived from deploying so many characters and plot strands at once in the plays. They may not have inspired great poetry, but the plays at least honed Tennyson's craft. And it is something that a poet past seventy could still experiment, adapt, and learn.

IV

The Lincolnshire Monologues

Humor, according to Max Eastman, "is a most wholesome

way to be redeemed. . . ."[24] And in the Lincolnshire monologues Tennyson is redeemed from the failure of many late
poems—and their stodginess. Indeed, I turn to the six dialect
poems (published from 1864 to 1892) after the historical monologues and plays because Tennyson succeeded with the former
in doing precisely what he failed to achieve in the latter: successfully rendering personality. The dialect poems are in fact remarkable in three ways: in their unprecedented nature in the
Tennyson canon, in their rendering of personality rather than
consciousness, and in their liberating Tennyson from the moral
conventionalites and self-conscious "prophesying" that infect
much of the late verse.

One can see distinct affinities between the dialect poems and
Tennyson's domestic poems, as well as "Will Waterproof." Tennyson had already drawn upon humble speakers in the domestic
poems and laughed in "Will Waterproof." As well, Tennyson
had clear literary forebears in the creation of dialect poems, including Robert Burns and William Barnes.[25] But it was surely by
moving along his usual dialectic that Tennyson landed in the
realm of dialect. The grim ironies and pessimism of the *Idylls* or
"Locksley Hall Sixty Years After" flowered, by Tennyson's
"strange diagonal," into laughter while the ornate style of
"Enoch Arden" gave way to coarse consonants and jaw-
breaking diction. Indeed, Tennyson seems to indulge in playful
self-allusion to "Enoch Arden" in "The Northern Cobbler"
(1880), where the cobbler welcomes his brother-in-law back to
England: " 'Cast awaäy on a disolut land wi' a vartical soon!' |
Strange fur to goä fur to think what saäilors a' seëan an' a'
doon" (lines 3–4). We are about as far away from "ocean-spoil |
In ocean-smelling osier" as we can get. Similarly, "Owd Roä" directly follows "Demeter and Persephone" in Trinity Notebook
27, as if the delicately beautiful rendering of motherhood in the
classical monologue called forth the rough and garrulous wid-
owed farmer of "Owd Roä," who plays the role of both mother
and father to his son. The dialect poems, then, at once are unlike
anything else Tennyson had written heretofore and verify the
enduring dialectic sensibility that informs all of Tennyson's
poetry.

As dramatic monologues, however, the Lincolnshire poems

are most remarkable for showing that Tennyson could render personality with ease and aplomb if he so chose, an aplomb that startled Browning. Browning wrote a letter of praise to Tennyson after the 1864 poems were published. His praise of "Enoch Arden" seems polite, his praise of "Northern Farmer, Old Style" spontaneous and heartfelt: " 'Enoch' continues the perfect thing I thought it at first reading; but the 'Farmer,' taking me unawares, astonished me more in this stage of acquaintanceship" (*Memoir*, II, 16). Browning's admiration is not surprising; Tennyson was showing that he could occupy the poetic territory marked out by (and still most closely associated with) Browning if he desired. Thus, we do not encounter the northern farmers, cobbler, spinster, village wife, or churchwarden as amorphously bounded minds or consciousnesses in which delicate, haunting streams of thought vibrate, intersect, and resonate. Rather, we encounter these speakers as personalities we could recognize in the outer world—where, in Johnsonian fashion, we might stub our toes against them or, more likely, shake hands and sit down to a glass of beer. As speakers they are clearly oriented toward the outer world, aware of rural society and their places in it and of their auditors, with whom they are more engaged than almost any other of Tennyson's speakers. The old-style, dying northern farmer is bent on impressing his nurse why he must have his customary ale despite doctor's orders; the village wife is intent equally on gossip and a business deal when she plies the servant of the newly arrived squire with wine; the churchwarden intends both to put the newly made and educated curate in his place and to strike up an ecclesiastical alliance with him. In this last poem, in fact, the auditor is so important that he appears in the poem's title: "The Church-Warden and the Curate." Not only do the speakers have clear motivations in speaking, however; they are presented in concrete settings. As we are not in most of Tennyson's dramatic monologues, we are made aware in the dialect poems of time and place, those two boundary markers (and makers) of the external world. The father-mother of "Owd Roä," for example, speaks on Christmas Eve, an hour before his son Dicky's bedtime, exactly ten years after Rover saved Dicky from a blazing fire—quite a different case from the first "Locksley Hall," where we may know, vaguely, the place but are left unenlightened in regard to time (a month after Amy's marriage? a year later?). Finally, we know that we are in the realm of personality with these poems because the speakers so obviously are not to be identified directly with the poet laureate who authored them. The dialect acts as an immediate screen between the "Victorian Alexandrian"[26] and his of-the-earth-earthy speakers, a screen all the more opaque because these poems appeared after Tennyson had established the Alexandrian as *the* Tennysonian style.

But why should Tennyson find himself capable of rendering personality when he failed in doing so with "Columbus" or "Sir John Oldcastle"? Part of the answer, surely, is the dialect itself. For Tennyson, born and raised in a remote village of Lincolnshire, the dialect was not an abstraction but one of life's realities enmeshed with a definite group of people and a definite spot on earth. References to ponds, earth, clay, trees, and farm animals abound in these poems. Because of the dialect speakers' association with the land of Lincolnshire, then, it was doubtless impossible for Tennyson to see them in any other way but as em*bodied*, of the earth, and hence oriented outward to the world instead of inward to the self and its dualities. Subliminally, too, the dialect must have summoned up the earth, the body, out of which Tennyson himself came, an association that helps explain why Tennyson revels in character for its own sake, in character as elemental as the elements it evoked.

But another clue to his abandonment of the twilight realm of consciousness for the daylight world of personality is the poems' third remarkable feature. In these poems, as in almost no others, Tennyson was liberated through humor from Victorian pieties and his own self-consciousness until he could laugh at what otherwise evoked reverence or revulsion. If he normally celebrated the virtues of the hearth, he could show their subversion in the dialect poems. Take "The Northern Cobbler," a poem about a man who has triumphed over alcoholism and been rewarded for his efforts with prosperity and a happy home. So far, so Victorian. But some of the poem's most powerful lines depict the domestic ideal turned upside down. In the first place, the timing of the cobbler's taking to drink is interesting: "An'

then the babby wur burn, and then I taäkes to the drink" (line
16). Nor is his wife, Sally, the perfect, all-suffering Victorian
wife once the cobbler takes this route.

> *Sally she turned a tongue-banger, an' raäted ma, "Sottin' thy braäins*
> *Guzzlin' an' soäkin' an' smoäkin' an' hawmin' about i' the laänes,*
> *Soä sow-droonk that tha doesn not touch thy 'at to the Squire;"*
> *An' I looöked cock-eyed at my noäse an' I seeäd 'im a-gittin' o' fire.*

> *(lines 23–26)*

But the climax comes when the cobbler has been out on a regular binge and literally turns his household upside down.

> *An' one night I cooms 'oäm like a bull gotten loose at a faäir,*
> *An' she wur a-waäitin' fo'mma, an' cryin' and teärin' 'er 'aäir,*
> *An' I tummled athurt the craädle an' sweäred as I'd breäk ivry stick*
> *O' furnitur 'ere i' the 'ouse, an' I gied our Sally a kick,*
> *An' I mashed the taäbles an' chairs, an' she an' the babby beäled,*
> *Fur I knawed naw moor what I did nor a mortal beäst o' the feäld.*
> *An' when I waäked i' the murnin' I seeäd that our Sally went laämed*
> *Cos' o' the kick as I gied 'er, an' I wur dreädful ashaämed;*
> *An' Sally wur sloomy an' draggle taäiled in an owd turn gown,*
> *An' the babby's faäce wurn't weshed an' the 'ole 'ouse hupside down.*

> *(lines 33–42)*

The cobbler finally realizes what he has done, races out, and
brings back a full quart of gin. " 'That caps owt,' says Sally,"but
he has bought the gin, not so he can drink it, but so that he can
look his enemy in the face while he dries out. The point, though,
is not so much the domestic bliss that follows but the accurate
picture of domestic strife given in the middle of the poem. Sally
is no Enid from the *Idylls of the King*, patiently enduring all insults
and abuses from her husband. If she gets the worst end of
things, she attacks with the only weapon at hand, words; and
when things become too much for her, she gives in to the
squalor of her life. The humorous medium in which he worked
enabled Tennyson to transcend his usual categories of pure domestic and soiled seductive women and to depict a real person
instead.

Then there is "Owd Roä," a poem given over mostly to a
mock-heroic account of Rover's rescue of Dicky. But the speak-

er's story also includes an account of a slapstick quarrel with his
wife. Moreover, while the family took their retreat from the fire
in the cold barn, the farmer gave all his attention to his heroic
dog.

> *An' we cuddled and huddled togither, an' happt wersens oop as we mowt.*
> *An' I browt Roä round, but Moother 'ed beän sa soäked wi' the thaw*
> *'At she cotched 'er death o' cowd that night, poor soul, i' the straw.*

> (lines 112–14)

As opposed to "The First Quarrel," where a single spat seems
causally connected with the husband's tragic death and the surviving wife's guilt, the violation of domestic amenities in "Owd
Roä" is presented unsentimentally and objectively. The wife's
death merits a single line, and the dog's sufferings are reported
at length. And instead of mourning his wife, the farmer has
simply appropriated her function.[27]

But the culmination of Tennyson's inversion of the domestic
ideal comes in "The Spinster's Sweet-Arts," which shows he
need not find humor only in the abusing of women. This monologue features a female speaker who, perhaps a little daft, has
named her four cats after the four suitors she has rejected and
talks to them as if they were cats and men all at once. Even the
account of these suitors' courtship is de-idealized, in contrast,
say, to "The Gardener's Daughter."

> *An' I feeled thy arm es I stood wur a-creeäpin about my waäist;*
> *An' me es wur allus afeared of a man's gittin' ower fond,*
> *I sidled awaäy an' awaäy till I plumpt foot fust i' the pond;*
> *And, Robby, I niver 'a liked tha sa well, as I did that daäy,*
> *Fur tha joompt in thysen, an' tha hoickt my feet wi' a flop fro' the claäy.*
> *Ay, stick oop thy back, an' set oop thy taäil, tha may gie ma a kiss,*
> *Fur I walked wi' tha all the way hoam an' wur niver sa nigh saäyin' Yis.*

> (lines 26–32)

The blurring of man and cat at the end of this passage is partly
intentional and undermines any suspicions that the woman's
daftness is the Victorian penalty for the crime of refusing marriage. The woman prefers cats to men because such a choice is
the only way she has been able to remain fully independent and
to control her little fortune.

## Merlin's Manyfacèd Glass

> Hed I married the Tommies—O Lord,
> To loove an' obaäy the Tommies! I couldn't 'a stuck by my word.
> To be hordered about, an waäked, when Molly'd put out the light,
> By a man coomin' in wi' a hiccup at ony hour o' the night!
> . . . . . . . . . . . . . . . . . . . . . . . . . . . . . .
> An' noän o' my four sweet-arts 'ud 'a let me 'a hed my oän waäy,
> Sa I likes 'em best wi' taäils when they 'evn't a word to saäy.

*(lines 95–98, 101–2)*

The speaker, in fact, is so far the inverse of Tennyson's usual ideal of womanhood that she has no more use for children than for men and for similar reasons: "But I niver not wished fur childer, I hevn't naw likin' fur brats; / Pretty anew when ya dresses 'em oop, an' they goäs fur a walk, / Or sits wi' their 'ands afoor 'em, an' doesn't not 'inder the talk!" (lines 84–86). But she knows too well about their "mucky bibs," "mashin' their toys to pieäces," and other details of the less pleasant side of motherhood to be really interested. Yet in "The Wreck," the speaker suffers paroxysms of guilt for having spurned her child. Tennyson foists no guilt on the spinster, who has rejected marriage and children altogether; he is too busy enjoying her crotchets.

In fact, he generates sympathy for the speaker, revealing the dilemma of a woman pursued more for her fortune than for her person and making us admire the honesty and keenness of a woman who can admit precisely this to herself.

> Feyther 'ud saäy I wur ugly es sin, an' I beänt not vaäin,
> But I niver wur downright hugly, thaw soom 'ud 'a thowt ma plaäin,
> An' I wasn't sa plaäin i' pink ribbons, ye said I wur pretty i' pinks,
> An' I liked to 'ear it I did, but I beän't sich a fool as ye thinks;
> Ye was stroäkin ma down wi' the 'air, as I be a-stroäkin o' you,
> But whiniver I looöked i' the glass I wur sewer that it couldn't be true;
> Niver wur pretty, not I, but ye knawed it wur pleasant to 'ear,
> Thaw it warn't not me es wur pretty, but my two 'oonderd a-year.

*(lines 15–22)*

At the end of the poem the spinster congratulates herself on having retained her state of spinsterhood, as if Princess Ida had been turned into a plain Lincolnshire maiden who escapes interference from men and contentedly rules her own kingdom of cats.

So much for what Tennyson normally reverenced. To show us that Tennyson could also laugh at what usually horrified him, we have "Northern Farmer, New Style," "The Village Wife; or, The Entail," and "Northern Farmer, Old Style." From "Locksley Hall" onward Tennyson had assailed materialism. The new-style farmer is also assailed, for alone among the Lincolnshire monologues this speaker is treated ironically, damning himself as he reveals his hypocrisy, hard-heartedness, and greed. Still, the poem is funny, in direct contrast to the contemporaneous "Aylmer's Field," where the same themes are treated grimly and tragically. The village wife, unlike the new-style farmer, is allowed her greed for both gossip and a monopoly on dairy products.

> An' they hallus paäid what I haxed, sa I hallus dealed wi' the Hall,
> An' they knawed what butter wur, an' they knawed what a hegg wur an' all;
> Hugger-mugger they lived, but they wasn't that eäsy to pleäse,
> Till I gied 'em Hinjian curn, an' they laäid big heggs es tha seeas;
> An' I niver puts saäme i' my butter, they does it at Willis's farm,
> Taäste another drop o' the wine—tweänt do tha naw harm.

> (lines 115–20)

Despite her flaws, the wife has so much energy and vitality— and is often so funny—that we are asked merely to accept and enjoy her. Moreover, if the subtext of the poem—the story of the gentle squire who so loved learning that he failed to look after his land and lost everything—is an indirect rebuke of the wife's materialism and coarseness, the subtext also highlights her virtues: with her the land is safe.[28] She is so competent an agriculturist that she even breaks off her quest of gossip—and her monologue—when she discovers the servant girl has left open the gate and let the chickens escape into the pea patch.

"Northern Farmer, Old Style," perhaps the best known of the Lincolnshire monologues, shows Tennyson able to approach humorously a subject that usually plagued and haunted him in his late verse: death. The crusty farmer's last rumblings are neither sentimentalized nor an occasion for pained probings of faith versus doubt. The farmer, quite simply, has no doubts, for he reductively approaches religion as a purely contractual affair.

*Parson's a beän loikewoise, an' a sittin' 'ere o' my bed.*
*"The amoighty's a taäkin o' you to 'issén, my friend," a said,*
*An' a towd ma my sins, an's toithe were due, an' I gied it in hond;*
*I done moy duty boy 'um, as I 'a done boy the lond.*
*Larned a ma' beä. I reckons I 'annot sa mooch to larn.*
*But a cast oop, thot a did, 'bout Bessy Marris's barne.*
*Thaw a knaws I hallus voäted wi' Squoire an' choorch an' staäte,*
*An' i' the woost o' toimes I wur niver agin the raäte.*

(lines 9–16)

St. Simeon's reification of religion is funny but grim and leaves
him wracked and uncertain. The farmer is merely complacent.
As Max Eastman remarks, "Humor is not . . . necessarily malign or irreverent, but it is of a quality incompatible with that
fixed concentration of serious feelings which we call devout. Its
essence is flexibility instead of fixation" (25). The stubborn
farmer is fixed only on his ale, and instead of a serious Tennyson
we get a flexible one.

More startling still is Tennyson's flexibility regarding sex,
that Victorian bugbear that had attracted but frightened him
ever since his painful adolescence. For the farmer, it appears, is
an adulterer, and perhaps the father of "Bessy Marris's barne."

*Bessy Marris's barne! tha knaws she laäid it to meä.*
*Mowt a beän, mayhap, for she wur a bad un, sheä.*
*'Siver, I kep 'um, I kep 'um, my lass, tha mun understond;*
*I done moy duty boy 'um as I 'a done boy the lond.*

(lines 21–24)

In *Idylls of the King* an entire realm is destroyed because of
adultery. But in "Northern Farmer," amazingly, this fault
hardly seems to matter. The crotchety old farmer is still appealing for his loyalty to and love for the land, his unflagging sense
of duty, and his unflappable will that endures even in the face of
death. If so egotistical that he cannot imagine whom the squire
will employ in his place (see lines 45–52), the farmer is still attractive. He has turned waste land into arable land so that, as
with the village wife, the land is entirely safe in his hands: he is a
preserver, not a destroyer. Thus his stodgy will that insists on
his customary pint of ale is somehow admirable, and his ability

to accept death as one more duty to be carried out is somehow noble.

> *What atta stannin' theer fur, an' doesn bring ma the aäle?*
> *Doctor's a 'toättler, lass, an a's hallus i' the owd taäle;*
> *I weänt breäk rules fur Doctor, a knaws naw moor not a floy;*
> *Get ma my aäle I tell tha, an' if I mun doy I mun doy.*

*(lines 65–68)*

*Acceptance* is indeed the key word here: not only does the farmer in his plainspoken way simply accept death but Tennyson also seems to accept and embrace a man with the very faults that so troubled him in other poems. The dialect poems liberated Tennyson not only in terms of subject matter, however, but in terms of his very role as poet, especially poet laureate. In returning to the dialect, Tennyson was implicitly returning to the scene that shaped his first years, before he became a public figure and was urged to serve as a prophet for Victorian culture; the complicated issue of his identity as a poet simply evaporates as he returns to a part of himself whose identity was never in question. The dialect, as W. David Shaw remarks, enabled Tennyson "to escape Victorian norms of refinement and decorum. . . . without being held responsible for [its] harshness or uncouthness."[29] The point has in fact been made several times: in liberating himself from his usual poetic diction, Tennyson liberated himself from his usual poetic concerns.

But centering himself in the Lincolnshire milieu and language allowed Tennyson an additional means of liberation. Not merely in form but in content, these monologues are (relative to Tennyson's other verse) antiliterary. Again and again his speakers revile the entire world of books, learning, and art,[30] suggesting that in these poems Tennyson as poet is setting his rough, native Lincolnshire self against the poet laureate associated with highly polished art—and is laughing at the juxtaposition. The village wife hates books and art at the same time—and vehemently. She is outraged at the classical statuary the old squire bought—"An' 'e bowt little statues all-naäkt an' which was a shaame to be seen" (line 50). But first among the old squire's crimes is his love of books.

> *we haätes boooklarnin' ere.*
> *Fur Squire wur a Varsity scholard, an' niver lookt arter the land—*
> *Whoäts or tonups or taätes—'e 'ed hallus a booök i' 'is 'and,*
> *Hallus aloän wi' 'is booöks, thaw nigh upo' seventy year.*
> *An' booöks, what's booöks? thou knaws thebbe naither 'ere nor theer.*

> *(lines 24–28)*

It is curious that she so lambasts anyone who constantly has his nose in a book, for this could have described the young Tennyson-as-poet in Lincolnshire. H. D. Rawnsley credits an old servant from Tennyson's boyhood home in Somersby with the following account: " 'As for Mr Halfred he was a 'dacious one. He used to be walking up and down the carriage drive hundreds of times a day, shouting and holloaing and preaching, with a book always in his hand and such a lad for making sad work of his clothes . . . down on his heels and his coat unlaced and his hair anyhow. He was a rough 'un was Mister Halfred and no mistake.' "[31] In the Lincolnshire poems, in fact, it is as if Tennyson were taking the Lincolnshire folk's side against himself and laughing at the public figure he had become. The point is clearer in another of the village wife's pronouncements against the old squire, one that has a direct bearing on Tennyson: "An' 'e'd wrote an owd book, his awn sen, sa I knawed es 'e'd coom to be poor" (line 46).[32] Perhaps the same process of self-mockery underlies the farmer's assessment of the parson's preaching in "Northern Farmer, Old Style," especially since the Somersby servant cited above remarked that Tennyson seemed to preach as he walked about on the carriage drive.

> *An' I hallus coomed to 's chooch afoor moy Sally wur deäd,*
> *An' 'eärd 'um a bummin' awaäy loike a buzzard-clock ower my 'eäd,*
> *An' I niver knawed whot a meäned but I thowt a 'ad summat to saäy,*
> *An' I thowt a said whot a owt to 'a said an' I coomed awaäy.*

> *(lines 17–20)*

One can easily imagine Tennyson thinking in this passage how the Lincolnshire folk back home responded to his own poetry.

Here, then, Tennyson's dialectic sensibility pits his earthy Lincolnshire self against the self that was Victoria's poet laureate. Tennyson encapsulates this clash in the poems' very form: Tennyson-as-poet is present as he shapes the poems into rhyme, but he simultaneously uses a dialect whose vowels expand in unexpected ways and defy conventional scansion. Thus the point of the Lincolnshire monologues for Tennyson as artist may have been their role in distancing him from playing the part of Victorian England's premier poet: he not only wrote unlike the poet laureate in these works but also thought unlike the poet laureate who symbolized the epitome of culture. Through his own Lincolnshire roots, he could take the part of the Lincolnshire people and laugh at the poet's very vocation.

What we witness in the dialect poems, in fact, is the very process Freud noted regarding wit: "*Wit affords us the means of surmounting restrictions and of opening up otherwise inaccessible pleasure sources.*"[33] Now it is true that one hardly thinks of Tennyson as a wit, but his dialect speakers conform to a category Freud aligned with wit, the naive. The naive, among whom Freud includes children and the uneducated adult (291), can say what might otherwise shock or affront auditors because the naive have no inhibitions and hence are unaware of any potential affront (295). Tennyson's very choice of speakers, then, as well as his reliance on humor, help explain why he could slip free from his usual obsessions and obeisance to proprieties and embrace emphatically em-*bodied* personalities. Writing these poems was an act of liberation for himself thematically, poetically, and personally. It was also an act of liberation for his readers, who, freed from the claims of reality by a dialect not part of their normal lives,[34] could accede to and laugh at the foibles they were taught otherwise to decry. And the dialect poems, finally, constitute a liberation for the student of the dramatic monologue, enabling us, through Tennyson's flexible humor, to see the flexibility of the monologue form. For all the elements we have seen at work in poems so different, whether "Supposed Confessions" or "Ulysses," are at work here. Obviously Tennyson has actively given life to his speakers, but neither has he abjured the pole of self-exploration—since these poems allowed him to explore and say what he otherwise could not and to say nay, however briefly, to the pessimism and doubts of his later years. The dialect poems are likewise constructed to engage the reader. We can approach the speakers and their utterance only through the dialect that seems a part of their very being, both sharing the same crusty, rough, stubbly nature; and if we are encouraged to laugh at the speakers, we are brought up short by them, too, seeing that their own kind of accomplishments bear scrutiny as much as those of the learned whom they scorn. And, not least, we can, through these characters and what they say, come to a better understanding of Tennyson himself, gauging what he might have been in another time or had he grown up in a household less troubled and so formed to instill repressions in one of its most sensitive inmates.[35] The dialect poems, then, are at once anomalous and crucial to Tennyson's work as a whole and to his dramatic monologues in particular. They are, in the first place, wonderful achievements in themselves, as Tennyson himself recognized: "Some of the best things I have written are those Lincolnshire sketches."[36] But they also remind us that if we would see Tennyson aright, we must see an occasional smile playing about his face, and that if we would hear him aright, we must always hear the burr in his voice, even when he is at his Alexandrine best.

## V
## The "Prophetic" Monologues

"The Voyage" sums up, in its early and unpublished versus its late, published versions, the difference between Tennyson's early and late dramatic monologues dedicated to social or philosophical issues. "The Voyage" was begun in 1835 or 1836,[37] and the early draft incorporated only the first five stanzas of the published poem, plus two variant stanzas. In other words, this initial draft embodies no allegory. The poem in this form, if it is "about" anything, is about the voyage of life (or the imagination) through time, confronting a flood of sensory images that course by, here for a moment and then gone. Only in an intermediary version (Harvard Loosepaper 257) did Tennyson add stanzas VI to IX and XII, where the voyage becomes a quest after an ideal "Vision." And only in a late hand, presumably near the 1864 publication date of the poem, did Tennyson add stanza X, which describes the cynic who "shrieked in spite, / 'A ship of fools' " and who "overboard one stormy night . . . cast his body." The poem, that is, became increasingly allegorical and sententious as it approached its 1864 publication date, until the text's "pleasures of the journey" became subordinated to the destination of the ideal in life (versus the barren emptiness of cynicism—which, it appears, is always a kind of self-murder).

Thus, such monologues as "Boädicea," "The Voyage of Mael-dune," "Despair," "The Ancient Sage," "Locksley Hall Sixty Years After," "Akbar's Dream," "Merlin and the Gleam," and "Romney's Remorse" all show Tennyson in his prophetic mode, expounding the ills of the age or the imperatives of the moral and spiritual life. Much could be, and has been, said about the importance of these poems for Tennysonian themes. As dramatic monologues these poems are notable in two respects, Tennyson's infusion of personal participation into what otherwise appear outward-directed poems and his ability to fuse "prophesying" with the peculiar formal resources of the dramatic monologue.

"Boädicea," for example, makes sense as a dramatic monologue because it is the most direct and economical means Tennyson had to represent the savagery and wildness spawned by violence. The wildness inheres in the Druid queen's language as she harangues her people (in a meter so difficult and experimental Tennyson feared he was the only one who could read the poem) to devastate the Roman legions who have beaten her and raped her daughters. Placing the poem in Boädicea's mouth enables Tennyson to avoid the anomaly of genteel diction to express barbarity and at the same time to distance himself from Boädicea's wildness so that, between the poem's moral ("out of evil evil flourishes") and the bracketing frames that surround her monologue, the poem indeed becomes an "object" lesson. "Akbar's Dream," on the other hand, is interesting primarily for an oblique personal allusion embedded in what is otherwise another stillborn historical monologue that rehearses Akbar's creed of religious tolerance. Composed in 1891–92, the poem is written from the point of view of the impending death, not of Akbar, the speaker, but of Abul Fazl, Akbar's friend, counselor, and "Chronicler" (line 1); and, indeed, by the time this poem was published in 1892, Akbar's Victorian chronicler was dead.

"Despair," "The Ancient Sage," and "Locksley Hall Sixty Years After," however, all fuse the personal with the prophetic and show interesting adaptations of the dramatic monologue besides. Moreover, these three poems, among the grouping discussed in this section, most closely approximate the rendering of consciousness. The speaker of "Despair" has been unwillingly rescued from suicide and rages alike at his dogmatic rescuer, an exponent of fierce Calvinism, and at the apparently pointless cruelties of life. He is led through his utterance, not by logic, but by the violent swings of his mind; and in this respect the poem verges on the oscillations of consciousness. Fused with the speaker's ragings, as many have noted, are Tennyson's own fears and doubts. The speaker's protestation, "Why should we bear with an hour of torture, a moment of pain, / If every man die for ever, if all his griefs are in vain," bears more than a little resemblance to the Tennyson who, as reported in the *Memoir*, said he would commit suicide with chloroform "if I thought there was no future life" (II, 35).[38] Moreover, the speaker's farewell to his wife the moment before they attempted to carry out their mutual suicide pact—"'Dear Love, for ever and ever, for ever and ever farewell,' / Never a cry so desolate, not since the world began" (lines 58–59)—echoes the similar farewells in section LVII of *In Memoriam* or in "Frater Ave Atque Vale" and perhaps again bespeaks Tennyson's personal participation in the poem. Thus the dramatic monologue afforded him the opportunity to assail the undermining of faith in Victorian society and to fight his own fears and sorrows under the distance afforded by a dramatic mask.

But Tennyson did not merely retreat behind the defense of the dramatic monologue; he also advanced it as a resonant form for his subject, all very fitting since it was in the subtitle of "Despair" that he first introduced the term *dramatic monologue*. The frame through which we pass to the monologue proper is, for example, as functional here as in "The Hesperides," though in a startlingly different way. For alone of Tennyson's frames, this is given in prose: "A man and his wife having lost faith in a God, and hope of a life to come, and being utterly miserable in this, resolve to end themselves by drowning. The woman is drowned, but the man rescued by a minister of the sect he had abandoned." At first this frame might seem to be Tennyson's ultimate giving in to the onslaught of prose that crept into his drafts beginning with "The Holy Grail" or an instance of mere laziness since the published frame is a mere expansion of the paragraph given Tennyson by Mary Gladstone, who suggested the poem's subject. But Tennyson uses the frame, I think, to hint at the unleavened prosaicness of the age that has driven the speaker to suicide and to prepare for the texture of the mono- logue proper, one of deliberate unloveliness. There is no "haunt- ing verbal music" here; it has been lost in the din of the breaker's "roar" (line 13), the "bawlings" of the minister's "dark . . . faith" (line 39), and the babblings of the "popular press" that generate only skepticism and despair (lines 88–90). The use of the dramatic monologue's eternal present tense is functional here, too: the present is all that is left to one such as the agnostic speaker, and the *raison d'etre* of his rage and bitterness. And alas, even the avenue to the abiding present is one of prose, not poetry.

Yet "Despair" is not quite a fine poem. As in the early "Re- morse," Tennyson is using the monologue's recursive loop, not steadily to explore the consciousness of another imagined as a part of the self, but to achieve the release of catharsis. That the poem serves as catharsis rather than disinterested (self-) explo- ration is evident from stanza XIX. Unable to rest in "uncertain- ties, mysteries, doubts, without any irritable reaching after," not "fact or reason," but faith, Tennyson must needs have his speaker intuit a benevolent God despite a despair so intense it prompts self-murder: "Ah yet—I have had some glimmer, at times, in my gloomiest woe, / Of a God behind all—after all" (lines 103–4). This caveat undermines the potential toughness of a poem that would perhaps seem tame at best to readers fa- miliar with, say, Lowell's "Skunk Hour." With stanza XIX and Tennyson's deliberate placing of the speaker in the realm of an either/or fallacy that permits only dogmatic Calvinism or dog- matic skepticism, one is left saying that "Despair" is written (to pun egregiously) in bad faith.

"The Ancient Sage" is a more successful poem because, while also fusing the prophetic and personal, it makes richer use of the dramatic monologue form. Not that the sage, as a speaker, is a triumph of particularized characterization. Indeed, if we had only the sage, the poem would be unrelievedly sentalious and flat. His recollections of his boyhood may be very Tennysonian, but we see no oscillations of consciousness in the sage, who directs his utterance outward; neither do we see in him a personality. The paradox of outer-directed amorphousness is plausible— a transcendental mystic ready to abandon civilization and spend his "one last year among the hills" (line 16) would be expected to display neither the worldly awareness of a Bishop Blougram nor the obsessive self-absorption of a Ulysses—but hardly conduces to great poetry.

But an auditor, as well as a speaker, is firmly established in the poem, the youth who loves and honors the sage but is "no disciple," who is instead "worn / From wasteful living" (lines 3–5). The youth is also a poet and, like any self-respecting artist, has his works at hand for ready display. Thus the sage is led to read some of the youth's verses and respond to them with his sententious aphorisms. Presumably, in fact, the sage's words are throughout prompted by the words and presence of the young poet, though the youth is himself never allowed to speak directly. The pairing of sage and hedonist resembles the format of several late monologues. In essence, the sage attempts to initiate the youth into a higher level of knowledge, and the monologue-as-rite-of-initiation (something new, and very prophetlike) is also to be found in "Tiresias," "Merlin and the Gleam," and "Demeter and Persephone." These poems, as well as "Locksley Hall Sixty Years After," pair an aged speaker and a youthful auditor, perhaps also suggesting that Tennyson was conducting a kind of retrospective in these poems, setting the old man he had become against the young man he was or might have been. In "The Ancient Sage" in particular, Tennyson's deployment of the auditor may be an oblique hint of the auditor's potential regeneration. Not much was (or is yet) known of Lao-Tse, on whom the sage was modeled; but according to Sze-ma Ts'in, writing about 100 B.C., Lao-Tse and Confucius met when the former was very old and the latter was in his early thirties: "It is characteristic of the two men, that [Lao-Tse], a transcendental dreamer, appears to have thought little of his visitor, while Confucius, an inquiring thinker, was profoundly impressed with him."[39] Confucius was never a hedonist, but Tennyson may have found very suggestive the legend that the man who became China's most renowned philosopher met and was deeply moved by Lao-Tse in his youth.

But Tennyson's reliance on an auditor is most important because his peculiar use of one of the monologue's conventions enhances the poem's effectiveness and meaning. If the sage's utterance is austere and flat, the youth's verses inject the needed lyricism and concreteness.

> *O rosetree planted in my grief,*
> *And growing, on her tomb,*
> *Her dust is greening in your leaf,*
> *Her blood is in your bloom.*
>
> . . . . . . . . . . . . . . . . . .
>
> *He withers marrow and mind;*
> *The kernel of the shrivelled fruit*
> *Is jutting through the rind.*

(lines 163–66, 120–22)

If the sage reveals neither a consciousness nor a personality, we do see something of the oscillations of consciousness in the youth's poetry. At first decrying the absence of God and the burdens of mortality, the youth's poetry only gradually discloses that these outcries are not generalized abstractions but particular responses to the death of the youth's beloved. Abruptly the verses then turn, as does the youth of "Locksley Hall," to the attractions of escapist hedonism, only the youth of 1885, unlike that of 1842, goes no further.[40] Thus the incorporation of an auditor enhances the poem's vividness and psychological interest.

But the poem's very meaning is also enriched by the auditor— or, to be more precise, by the relation of speaker and auditor— and by the dramatic monologue per se. Just as the dramatic monologue depends on revelations from within, so the sage also stresses the primacy of inward, intuitive revelation over external, verifiable data. And he exemplifies this not only in what he says but also in the way he says it, taking the "data"—the verses—of an external exponent of empiricism (the auditor), breaking them up,[41] and transforming them into his own discourse. That is, the sage draws what is outward within, into his own mouth and breath, meeting it and answering it there: he,

212

too, dives "into the Temple-cave of . . . self," and *we* learn that
the "Nameless" sage "hath a voice" (lines 32, 34). Moreover, in
borrowing many of the images posited by the youth[42] but making them his own, absorbing the youth, as it were, into his own
discourse, the sage formally exemplifies the doctrine of imaginative sympathy enunciated by Hallam and crucial to the Tennysonian monologue. As the youth's passionate cries become
melded with the sage's serene faith through the latter's exercise
of imaginative sympathy, it is indeed a case of "thyself in converse with thyself" (line 65). Hence form and content are perfectly adapted to each other in "The Ancient Sage" and create a
resonance utterly lacking in "Despair." The interplay between
the dramatic monologue form and the sage's discourse also imparts an additional layer of significance to Tennyson's claim that
"the whole poem is very personal" (*Memoir*, II, 319). The sage
resembles Tennyson not only in doctrines subscribed to (these
become rather too hortatory at the poem's close) but in imaginative processes shared as well. If Tennyson, like his speaker, is
very much playing the prophet in this poem, he inducts the
reader both into his metaphysic and into his imaginative method. Just as the sage, implicitly, approaches the youth as an aspect
of self, until their respective images fuse into a single whole, so
also Tennyson imagines both youth and sage as aspects of self
simultaneously, their disparate orientations answering to the
whole of Tennyson's own divided sensibility.

"Locksley Hall Sixty Years After" could be said to follow inevitably from "The Ancient Sage." Although attention has focused mainly on the relation between the first and the second
"Locksley Hall," there is an equally integral relation between
"Locksley Hall Sixty Years After" and "The Ancient Sage," one
that illuminates the fusion of personal and prophetic, subjective
and objective, in the late dramatic monologues. The sage and the
octogenarian speaker of the second "Locksley Hall" are strikingly similar in several respects. Both are near death, both spurn
the civilizations in which they have lived, and both cast glances
back at their boyhoods as ways of assessing their present development. More notable are the verbal parallels of the two speakers. Compare the sage's dissertation on the Nameless and on the
"boundlessness" of "Abysms" in "The blue of sky and sea, the

green of earth, / And in the million-millionth of a grain" (lines 40–49) with the aged hero's similar address to his grandson.

> *Earth so huge, and yet so bounded—pools of salt, and plots of land—*
> *Shallow skin of green and azure—chains of mountain, grains of sand!*
> *Only That which made us, meant us to be mightier by and by,*
> *Set the sphere of all the boundless Heavens within the human eye,*
>
> *Sent the shadow of Himself, the boundless, through the human soul;*
> *Boundless inward, in the atom, boundless outward, in the Whole.*
>
> *(lines 207–12)*

The sage's concluding homily to his youthful auditor ("Ancient Sage," lines 253–80) is likewise echoed in the concluding admonitions to the auditor in "Locksley Hall Sixty Years After," which begin, "Cast the poison from your bosom, oust the madness from your brain" (line 241; see also lines 272–77). It is easy to overlook these close parallels between the two aged speakers because they also seem so different. If the sage exhorts the youth to "cleave ever to the sunnier side of doubt," the old hero offers a much starker maxim to his grandson: "Hope the best, but hold the Present fatal daughter of the Past, / Shape your heart to front the hour, but dream not that the hour will last" (lines 105–6).

Together, in fact, "The Ancient Sage" and "Locksley Hall Sixty Years After" exhibit a duple dialectic, a sign of increasing internal pressures in Tennyson as he himself approached life's end. For if, in "The Ancient Sage," Tennyson mirrors his own dialectic between faith and doubt in speaker versus auditor but allows his serene prophet self to triumph there, he dialectically turns *that* dialectic about to give us the troubled, turbulent old man in "Locksley Hall Sixty Years After," whose faith is strong but whose doubt is given even wider scope. In the latter poem, moreover, Tennyson also (dialectically) inverts the relation between speaker and auditor in "The Ancient Sage." The grandson, the auditor, is a skeptic but a progressive (as is the sage) whereas the crusty grandfather has faith but wishes to escape, like the youthful poet, from the toil and moil of life ("Only 'dust to dust' for me that sicken at your lawless din"—line 149). And whereas the grandson-as-auditor is a shadowy, generalized figure, the old man is particularized and concrete—another inversion of the speaker-auditor relation of "The Ancient Sage." Thus, one of the fascinations of "Locksley Hall Sixty Years After" is its relation to "The Ancient Sage," both poems together demonstrating the importance of the dramatic monologue's participatory element to Tennyson. For through these poems he could embody his dialectic in each poem but also in their relation to each other, via the strikingly different yet kindred speakers. That Tennyson should write both poems in such close succession suggests how troubled his own continuum was between faith and doubt, how difficult it was for him to find a satisfactory resting place anywhere.

But the second fascination of "Locksley Hall Sixty Years After" is its more readily discernible link with the first "Locksley Hall." I remarked in chapter three that the ending of the first "Locksley Hall" is problematical because there is no end to consciousness except death. The second "Locksley Hall" validates the point. With the publication of the sequel, Tennyson created an enormous literary "gap" that dwarfs those denoting time's passage in *Maud*; the reader is invited to imagine sixty years of unceasing waves of consciousness. The sequel is thus at once a confirmation of that to which we should attend (that is, rendered consciousness) in the first poem and a startling innovation—sequels had already appeared in drama (*Henry IV*, parts I and II) and in Victorian fiction (Trollope's Palliser or Barset novels), but never, as far as I know, had anything quite like this been done in poetry. And the sequel has definite implications for both the 1842 and 1886 poems. As several commentators have remarked, the later poem relativizes and ironizes the first, making the young hero's animadversions against his rival vapid and his projected future for Amy—who after all died in childbirth—pathetic.[43] But the late poem is also relativized by the first. As when he was young, the hero in old age wages a personal war with time. The past and future are closed, not because of disillusionment (though obviously that is part of the problem), but because of age; at eighty, the old man quite literally has no future, and for him the past is now stronger than the future or the present: "Poor old voice of eighty crying after voices that have fled! / All I loved are vanished voices, all my steps are on the

215

dead" (lines 251–52). The speaker's continuing though altered obsession with time not only suggests that, with more time, the obsession could undergo further transformations, but also makes his allusions to "Evolution" and "Reversion" (and "descent," line 26) reflexive. Has the speaker really evolved to a greater man in all respects? Or has he declined in some respects? Is, for example, his own descendent, the grandson, really so different from him? The answers are left unresolved. In this poem, too, there is no real closure. The second "Locksley Hall" may falter when Tennyson fails to keep an adequate rein on his outpourings against the age (see, for example, lines 131–46), at which point the poem threatens to become, like "Despair," an exercise in catharsis; but his fidelity to his own dialectical sensibility, and to the rendering of consciousness established in the 1842 poem, enables this work to transcend its flaws and to stand as an evocative and innovative dramatic monologue.

If most of Tennyson's "prophetic" monologues focus on faith and doubt, "Merlin and the Gleam" and "Romney's Remorse" explore the role of the artist. "Merlin and the Gleam" is well known, not as a dramatic monologue, but as an oblique autobiography. As Hallam Tennyson remarks, "For those who cared to know about his literary history he wrote *Merlin and the Gleam.*"[44] From this perspective, Tennyson most likely used the dramatic monologue as a distancing mask. Tennyson abhorred the thought of later revelations of his intimate life, and one can only imagine his giving his story to the public through the mediation of a dramatic persona. And although, as "literary history," the poem is undoubtedly personal, it seems to be so only in a generalized way. Merlin simply recapitulates the "details" of his life; he does not reveal his inner consciousness. And the chronology of the poem as it corresponds to Tennyson's life is so obscured, so masked, that it has perplexed any reader who knows something of Tennyson's history—including, apparently, Tennyson's own son.[45]

But if we look at "Merlin and the Gleam" in the context of the other late dramatic monologues, some new perspectives emerge on the poem, as well as a hint at a more personal vein deeply embedded in the poem. The dramatic monologue here, as in "The Ancient Sage," is a containing form for a rite of initiation.

The poem begins with Merlin addressing his auditor ("O young Mariner . . . You that are watching / The gray Magician / With eyes of wonder"), whom he proceeds to induct into the mystery of the presence and significance of "The Gleam."[46] The stark, simple rhymes and line lengths of the poem have all the solemnity befitting an initiation rite, and as is common to inductors, Merlin maintains an opacity regarding his personal self, identifying himself only with his ceremonial role.

> I *am Merlin,*
> *And* I *am dying,*
> I *am Merlin*
> *Who follow the Gleam.*
>
> *(lines 7–10)*

But we get a double initiation. In order to initiate his auditor, Merlin recounts his own initiation, his gradual internalization of the Gleam. For in the first five stages of his life the Gleam was external to him, and Merlin was able to undertake only a passive role. The point is clear from the language of stanzas II to VI. In none of these stanzas does the word *I* appear; stanzas IV and V contain no personal pronoun at all, and the others use only *me*, where Merlin is the recipient, not the agent, of action.

> *Mighty the Wizard*
> *Who found me at sunrise*
> *Sleeping, and woke me*
> *And learned me Magic!*
>
> *(st. II)*

> *A barbarous people,*
> *Blind to the magic,*
> *And deaf to the melody,*
> *Snarled at and cursed me.*
>
> *(st. III)*

> *Then, with a melody*
> *Stronger and statelier, [the Gleam]*
> *Led me at length*
> *To the city and palace*
> *Of Arthur the king.*
>
> *(st. VI)*

Merlin's "Master" has the power of action as he teaches or whispers, "Follow The Gleam" (lines 33–34),[47] but above all it is the Gleam that is active, as it floats, flies, slides, and rests—on Arthur.

And that, of course , is the turning point. As soon as contact with Arthur is made, Merlin participates in the agency of the Gleam, and henceforward in the poem Merlin becomes an active agent, until, in the final stanza, he hands over his agency to the young mariner.

> *Old and weary,*
> *But eager to follow,*
> *I saw, whenever*
> *In passing it glanced*
> . . . . . . . . . .
> *The mortal hillock,*
> *Would break into blossom;*
> *And so to the land's*
> *Last limit I came—*

(st. VIII)

There is a sad poignancy in the structure of the poem; Merlin no sooner absorbs the Gleam than he approaches death. But there is also grace and dignity in the personal homage to Arthur Hallam conveyed in the correspondence Tennyson draws between the appearance of Arthur and Merlin's realization of the Gleam.

The personal reverberations grow clearer, too, if we see what "The Gleam" signifies in one of Tennyson's sources for the poem, John Veitch's "Merlin," which appeared only four months before Tennyson wrote "Merlin and the Gleam."[48] In Veitch's work the Gleam is associated not only with the creative imagination but also with love and eternal life. For Veitch's "Gleam" is both a spirit in the noumenal sense and *is* the ghost, or spirit, of Merlin's early love, called Hwimleian on earth before she died and became a gleam that appears "as a glint on the hill."[49] As Merlin dies, he calls out to the Gleam,

> *thou, thou*
> *Alone art faithful unto passing death*
> *Of this poor feeble framework of the soul*

*That fears the dread unknown and yearns for love,*
*E'en in that future baffling all our ken.*
*I am for ever consecrate to thee!*

(34)

With Merlin's death only the voice of the Gleam exists, which cries out, "Now we are one—one in our strength and love," joined forever "as life on life evolves, infinite life, / Th' unwearied process of th' eternal years" (35–36). One can of course merely hypothesize the connections Tennyson made in his own mind. But the words of Veitch's dying Merlin are so close to the sentiments of *In Memoriam* that it is easy to imagine Tennyson's linking Arthur (and his death) to Merlin's internalizing the Gleam because the Gleam signified for Tennyson not only the imagination but also, as in Veitch's work, a love that transcends time and links kindred souls through all eternity. Thus, if we focus on "Merlin and the Gleam" as a dramatic monologue, we can see its connection with the other prophetic monologues wherein auditors are initiated into higher realms of knowledge; we also can uncover the deeply personal expression that underlies a poem that at first seems personal only in a remarkably impersonal way.

"Romney's Remorse" was apparently sparked by another artist, not the painter George Romney, but Edward FitzGerald, whose letters were published in July of 1889. There Tennyson would have read FitzGerald's response to the painter who left his wife because Joshua Reynolds asserted that marriage was incompatible with the ideals of Art but who, dying, crawled back to the same wife and was nursed by her until his death. As Fitz-Gerald said, "This quiet act of hers is worth all Romney's pictures! even as a matter of Art, I am sure."[50] Immediately we can see the "prophetic" possibilities of FitzGerald's comments, especially given Tennyson's hatred of "Art for Art's sake (instead of Art for Art—and—Man's sake)"—this last the title of one of Tennyson's unpublished epigrams. Perhaps the very fact that these revelations about Romney's private life had been made public, as well as Tennyson's finding these revelations in Fitz-Gerald's own posthumously published letters, also attracted

219

Tennyson to the subject, for the most readily discernible personal lines in the monologue are those devoted to the "lies" that follow the death of any prominent artist, guilty or not guilty.

> *Then, in the loud world's bastard judgment-day,*
> *One truth will damn me with the mindless mob,*
> *Who feel no touch of my temptation, more*
> *Than all the myriad lies, that blacken round*
> *The corpse of every man that gains a name.*

*(lines 114–18)*

Most commentators on Tennyson's work ignore "Romney's Remorse" entirely, and the poem does fall below the level of Tennyson's best work. But the monologue gains in interest when we see that it is a companion piece to "Merlin and the Gleam," which "Romney's Remorse" immediately followed in Tennyson's manuscripts (Harvard Notebook 54). Indeed, "Romney's Remorse" bears the same inverted relation to "Merlin and the Gleam" that "Locksley Hall Sixty Years After" bears to "The Ancient Sage." Merlin, with the serenity of the old sage, initiates his auditor into a higher knowledge; Romney, having failed in the ideal of art, can only confess his failings. Thus, whereas in "Merlin and the Gleam" the speaker is clearly the hero of the poem, the auditor, the wife, is the heroine of "Romney's Remorse." Indeed, early in the poem we are clearly invited to view the monologue from the auditor's vantage point and feel her pain as the drugged and feverish Romney rambles, unconscious of whom he addresses.

> *Nurse, were you hired? or came of your own will*
> *To wait on one so broken, so forlorn?*
> *Have I not met you somewhere long ago?*
> *I am all but sure I have—in Kendal Church—*
> *O yes! I hired you for a season there,*
> *And then we parted.*

*(lines 16–21)*

The difference between Merlin and Romney is that one has followed a true "Master"—the "Mighty . . . Wizard"—and that the other has followed a false one: "My curse upon the Master's apothegm, / That wife and children drag an Artist down!"

(lines 36–37). Thus for Merlin art is an ennobling ideal, but for Romney it is a harlot: "This Art, that harlot-like / Seduced me from you, leaves me harlot-like, / Who love her still" (lines 110–12). At this point we may recall the double identity of Merlin's Nimue as the Gleam or as the seductive harlot of "Merlin and Vivien." I suggest that Nimue is the operative conceptual link between "Merlin and the Gleam" and "Romney's Remorse," creating a glorified Merlin in one poem and a fallen Merlin in the other. Indeed, Tennyson would have found in Veitch's "Merlin" both the regenerate Merlin and the fallen Merlin, separated from his gleam; and the fallen Merlin sounds remarkably like Romney.

> *The outer seeming, not the truth itself,*
> *Has been my portion; husk, not fruit, was mine,—*
> *The trick of art which awes, destroys, but builds*
> *Not for the world.*

(29)

Romney, then, is also separated from the Gleam and not surprisingly repudiates it: "What Artist ever yet / Could make pure light live on the canvas? Art! / Why should I so disrelish that short word?" (lines 9–11). Only at the end does Romney apprehend a glimmer of the Gleam, but it resides without, in the very things he slighted during his career: "Human forgiveness touches heaven, and thence— / For you forgive me, you are sure of that— / Reflected, sends a light on the forgiven" (lines 152–54). Merlin, who has internalized the Gleam, can "die rejoicing"; Romney's only triumph is to see that the Gleam exists, but at a distance.

It is curious that with the two poems devoted to art and the artist Tennyson's dialectic manifested itself in two different forms of the dramatic monologue. Merlin, at one with his ideal, speaks in the vatic utterance of Tennyson's most prophetic mode. Romney, whose sins were disclosed and judged by history, is given a historical monologue, and that is perhaps why it it only a fair, instead of fine, poem. Browning's Andrea del Sarto is also a failed artist, but in the presence of Lucrezia Andrea tries to keep up a facade, and in the pretense lies all the power, and pathos, of the poem. Romney simply confesses, making his failures so baldly apparent they are boring. Still, as a foil to "Merlin and the Gleam," and as a poem that illuminates both Tennyson's dialectic and the ends to which he could use the dramatic monologue, "Romney's Remorse" is perhaps worth having.

The "prophetic" dramatic monologues, then, may not exhibit new technical advances, excepting Tennyson's creation of a sequel with the second "Locksley Hall." But they are valuable gauges of the Tennysonian dramatic monologue in three ways. First, they show that even when Tennyson used the form in its most objective, outward-directed guise to share his moral and spiritual wisdom (however dubious) with his public, he maintained a firm, at times frantic, grasp on the form's recursive loop that allowed for personal participation and exploration. The second value of these monologues is in suggesting the intensity of Tennyson's dialectic sensibility in his late years, which impelled him from "The Ancient Sage" to the second "Locksley Hall," and from "Merlin and the Gleam" to "Romney's Remorse." That the dramatic monologue, with its inherent flexibility, could embody and momentarily stabilize the divergent strands of Tennyson's dialectic indicates these poems' third virtue: Tennyson's enduring ability to exploit the monologue's features to enrich and deepen the meaning and subtlety of his work. As at the beginning of his career, the monologue's potential for simultaneous objectivity and subjectivity sparked Tennyson's creative impulse and enabled him to grow and create even as he approached death.

VI
The Classical Monologues

Only four classical monologues are to be found among Tennyson's late verse, but, characteristically, these include some of Tennyson's best poetry, early or late. Besides their virtue simply as fine poems, the classical monologues are important because they show that Tennyson could inject his prophetic strain into the inherently allusive and resonant classical mask without falling into the preachiness that mars passages in "The Ancient

Sage" or even the earlier "Oenone." In these late classical monologues alone, perhaps, Tennyson successfully fuses a fully
realized speaker, private self-exploration, the rendering of consciousness, and the role of poet-as-prophet.

It is the incorporation of the last that makes "Tithonus" a different poem from "Tithon." "Tithon" was a true pendant to
"Ulysses," suggesting that "going forward" in time is no guarantee of achieving continuity among past, present, and future.
When he revised "Tithon" in 1859 and published "Tithonus" in
1860, however, Tennyson added the following passage, which
transformed the tenor of the 1833 poem:

> *Alas! for this gray shadow, once a man—*
> *So glorious in his beauty and thy choice,*
> *Who madest him thy chosen, that he seemed*
> *To his great heart none other than a God!*
> *I asked thee, "Give me immortality."*
> *Then didst thou grant mine asking with a smile,*
> *Like wealthy men who care not how they give.*
> *But thy strong Hours indignant worked their wills,*
> *And beat me down and marred and wasted me,*
> *And though they could not end me, left me maimed*
> *To dwell in presence of immortal youth,*
> *Immortal age beside immortal youth,*
> *And all I was, in ashes.*
>
> (lines 11–23)

In adding this passage Tennyson removed what was perhaps the
single most personal statement of "Tithon" in 1833: "nor know
[I] / Enjoyment save through memory." At a stroke, Tennyson
drained away the most intimately personal component of the
"Tithon" that was a pendant to "Ulysses" and freighted the new
poem with moral significance. For the published poem turns on
Tithonus's *request* for immortality, an indication, as many have
remarked, of pride and a repudiation of the spiritual meaning of
immortality.[51] In "Tithon" the speaker's immortality is simply a
given. But in "Tithonus" the speaker's physical immortality is
not a seemingly arbitrary quirk of fate but Tithonus's responsibility alone.

It is fascinating to observe, however, that Tennyson's modu-
lation of the 1833 work into the prophetic mode does not mar

but rather promotes the poem's coherence, especially regarding Eos. In "Tithon," we recall, Tithon seemed to long for reunion with but also escape from Eos; she was both the beloved and his imprisoner. In "Tithonus" the speaker is still ambivalent toward Eos, but now this ambivalence is functional: his muffled bitterness toward her (see line 17) is a projection of his own inward bitterness, frustration, and guilt. The point is even clearer if we note another 1859 interpolation, for here Eos unambiguously sympathizes with and mourns for Tithonus's plight: "Lo! ever thus thou growest beautiful / In silence, then before thine answer given / Departest, and thy tears are on my cheek" (lines 43–45).[52]

The poem's prophetic theme in fact creates new resonance in Tithonus's very language. The opening lines, for example, reveal a curious pattern. Each of the first four lines employs intransitive verbs, but ones that imply endings.

> . . . *woods decay and fall,*
> . . . *vapours weep . . . ,*
> *Man comes . . . and lies beneath,*
> . . . *dies the swan.*[53]

Although Tithonus uses the nonfinite, infinite verb forms befitting one locked forever in an ongoing present, he implies that even mere objects—woods and vapours—are capable of actions, processes with beginnings and above all endings. Objects, that is, are agents. But Tithonus, who was once, dreadfully, an agent ("I asked thee, 'Give me immortality'"), is himself now an object: "Me only cruel immortality / Consumes" (lines 5–6). Having forfeited agency by misusing it, he is incapable of action, relegated instead to an open-ended, infinitesimally ongoing process: "I wither slowly in thine arms" (line 6). Throughout the poem, in fact, Tithonus uses *I*, with one exception, only when he refers to the past self who was an agent; in the present he is an object, a "white-haired shadow" who is only acted upon by others: "Why wilt thou ever scare me . . . / And make me tremble" (lines 46–47); "hold me not for ever in thine East" (line 64); "Coldly thy rosy shadows bathe me" (line 66). Instead, only Eos and surrounding objects are agents: "the wild team / Which love thee . . . beat the twilight into flakes of fire" (lines 39–42). The

224

only action, the only beginning and end, Tithonus is capable of in the present is speaking. The monologue form is, as in "Ti-thon," an irony that underscores Tithonus's imprisonment in an everlasting present and the atrophy that has left him little more than a voice; yet the monologue form also offers release, cathar-sis. No wonder, as has been observed,[54] Tithonus seems obses-sive in his self-expression. All those other actions with begin-nings and ends, whether love-making or simply dying, are closed to him; he can only speak or lapse into silence. His only chance of escape from this entrapment between speech and silence is to become an object (a clod) and agent (one who can *forget*) all at once.

> *Release me, and restore me to the ground;*
> *Thou seëst all things, thou wilt see my grave:*
> *Thou wilt renew thy beauty morn by morn;*
> *I earth in earth forget these empty courts,*
> *And thee returning on thy silver wheels.*

*(lines 72–76)*

We can see that the added prophetic theme of "Tithonus" made it a better poem; seeing why is rather more difficult. One reason, surely, is that Tennyson does not make Tithonus, like Romney, confess his faults; instead Tennyson activates the reader's pole (and role) in the dramatic monologue, leaving it to the reader to enter the poem's gaps and make the connections among Tithonus's memories of the past, his outcry against his present, and his desire to obliterate the future. Another reason the poem works so well is that Tennyson clearly renders the consciousness of Tithonus, a consciousness reflected in the shimmering twilight imagery, the rhythm, and the syntax of his utterance.[55] But Tithonus's consciousness is rendered as well in the very structure of the poem, something Tennyson had al-ready learned to do in "Ulysses" and *Maud*. As Michael Greene has demonstrated, Tithonus's discourse takes the shape of sex-ual experience, moving from "indifference, to uneasy respon-siveness [lines 32–42], to actual participation, to climax [lines 50-63], thence to quiescence, and, in Tithonus' case, to dis-satisfaction because now the act can exist only in his mind."[56] On one hand this structuring underscores the primacy of the past for Tithonus and what most obsessed him then, the sensual joys he shared with Eos. As Julian Jaynes remarks, "Conscious retrospection is not the retrieval of images, but the retrieval of what you have been conscious of before, and the reworking of these elements into rational or plausible patterns."[57] On the other hand this structured consciousness makes the irony of Tithonus's present plight more searing; consciousness is all he has, no matter into what shape he molds it. As noted at the beginning of this chapter, Tennyson was most likely led to return to "Tithon" in 1859 because of a concatenation of events that would have made the memory of Hallam and "Tithon" more intense. But besides retaining the personal impulses that first gave birth to the poem, Tennyson has shaped a poem with breathtaking artistry that fuses the best of his earlier concerns with the earnest ponderings of his maturity.

"Lucretius" is yet another masterful rendering of consciousness. Drawing upon the legend that Lucretius was given a love potion by his wife, who "found / Her master cold," Tennyson depicts the great Roman philosopher and poet in the throes of lust and madness that precede his suicide. The first words of Lucretius's utterance are an emblem of his own mind: "Storm in the night!" (line 26).[58] The rest of the monologue charts the wild teeterings, not mere oscillations, of Lucretius's mind between the lust he abhors yet pants after, reverence toward and reprisals against the gods, falterings toward self-control and collapsings back into lust and madness—until he fuses the lust, violence, and desire for order in a "rape" of the "Passionless bride, divine Tranquillity," and kills himself.

Lucretius, then, is one above all conscious that his is a disordered consciousness. The mind dissolving under the attack of the love philter retains traces of its former greatness, so that Lucretius is always aware, as the mother of "Rizpah" is not, that his mind is breaking up; and his commitment to truth will not let him deny it: "Meant? I meant? / I have forgotten what I meant: my mind / Stumbles, and all my faculties are lamed" (lines 121–23). We perforce extend our sympathy to the speaker, not merely because we must do so if we are to read at all a poem so inveterately presented from Lucretius's point of view, but be-

cause of the pathos of a strong mind and great poet brought
down before us.

> *But now it seems some unseen monster lays*
> *His vast and filthy hands upon my will,*
> *Wrenching it backward into his; and spoils*
> *My bliss in being; and it was not great;*
> *For save when shutting reasons up in rhythm,*
> *Or Heliconian honey in living words,*
> *To make a truth less harsh, I often grew*
> *Tired of so much within our little life,*
> *Or of so little in our little life—*

> *(lines 219–27)*

But Tennyson achieves something new in the handling of sympathy, and of judgment, in "Lucretius." In this poem sympathy
and judgment are not in tension but absolutely fused. Our sympathy for Lucretius's wreck upon the rocks and shoals of a once-
sane mind *is* what enables us to see the shortcomings of his philosophy. Our sorrow for his fallen greatness is also our
judgment of him.

This fusion, not polarity, of sympathy and judgment comes
from Tennyson's method in constructing the monologue, which
becomes at once a sympathetic tribute to and evaluation of Lucretius.[59] Tennyson spent almost three years on the poem, and
his immersion in his subject is evident. For Tennyson's monologue has an almost uncanny fidelity to Lucretius's own great
poem so that we encounter, not a mere pastiche of translated
quotations lifted from *De Rerum Natura*,[60] but what almost seems
a metempsychosis of Lucretius into Tennyson, who is able to
embody Lucretius's own psychological associations as revealed
in the Latin poem, especially in the monologue's dreams and
visions.

Lucretius begins Tennyson's monologue by exclaiming at the
riotous storm of the previous night and his dreams, the first of
which embodies his central concept of an atomistic universe.

> *for it seemed*
> *A void was made in Nature; all her bonds*
> *Cracked; and I saw the flaring atom-streams*

*And torrents of her myriad universe,*
*Ruining along the illimitable inane,*
*Fly on to clash together again, and make*
*Another and another frame of things*
*For ever.*

*(lines 36–43)*

On one level the dream is a mirror of his philosophy, on another a mirror of the storm that raged as he slept, creating the "streaming mountain-side" and "riotous confluence of watercourses." But on another level Lucretius's turning to this dream at the outset of his monologue may be his subliminal awareness of the chaos of his own mind and its discreation under the influence of the love potion. For the lines describing the storm and dream closely resemble Lucretius's description in *De Rerum Natura* of the chaos that reigned when the universe was discreated, that is, not yet created.

> At this time then neither could the sun's disk be discerned flying aloft with its abundant light . . . but only a strange stormy crisis and medley, gathered together out of first-beginnings of every kind, whose state of discord joining battle disordered their interspaces passages connexions weights blows clashings and motions, because by reason of their unlike forms and varied shapes they could not all remain thus joined together nor fall into mutually harmonious motions. Then next the several parts began to fly asunder and things to be joined like with like and to mark off the world.[61]

No wonder Lucretius says that this first dream "was mine, my dream, I knew it— / Of and belonging to me" (lines 43–44). The dream not only is cut out of the matrix of his own poetry but is also *about* himself, a "dream *of* me."

The same intercalating of Lucretius's poetry and his dreams is evident in the other two dreams he relates in the monologue; after alluding to a dreaming dog, Lucretius goes on to describe how Hetairai, "Hired animalisms," sprang from "the blood by Sylla shed" and how he saw the breasts of Helen threatened by a sword which "sank down shamed / At all that beauty," when fire suddenly shot out of the breasts, scorching and waking him. Of course in a straightforward dramatic context the dreams function to reveal the fierce lust unleashed by the philter and Lucretius's horror of it all. But if we turn to *De Rerum Natura*, we discover that it is as if Tennyson has placed us inside the Roman poet's actual, not fabricated, consciousness, moving along the same path, now wildly disordered, that Lucretius did in creating his poetry. For in book IV of that poem the reference to the dog plying his foot in his dreams is part of a long passage on dreams that leads immediately to a sexual context that likewise fuses the images of lust, blood, weapons, breasts, and fire.

> [In a young man's dreams the] places are excited and swell with seed, and the inclination arises to emit the seed towards that to which the fell desire all tends, and the body seeks that object from which the mind is wounded by love; for all as a rule fall towards their wound and the blood spirts out in that direction whence comes the stroke by which we are struck; and if he is at close quarters, the red stream covers the foe. Thus then he who gets a hurt from the weapons of Venus . . . inclines to the quarter whence he is wounded, and yearns to unite with it and join body with body. . . . in this there is hope, that from the same body whence springs [lovers'] burning desire, their flame may likewise be quenched; though nature protests that the very opposite is the truth; and this is the one thing of all, in which, when we have most of it, then all the more the breast burns with fell desire.[62]

Lucretius's last vision, a waking vision of the goat-footed satyr's attempted rape of a nymph (or Oread) in the woods, may likewise reflect not only the influence of the philter but Lucretius's oblique recognition of what he is undergoing as well. For in book IV of *De Rerum Natura* nymph, satyr, and faun ("Lucretius," lines 182, 187) are cited in the context of projected voices, or echoes, just as the frenzied lust of the vision is an echo or projection of Lucretius's own mind: "I have seen places give back as many as six or seven voices, when you sent forth one. . . . These spots the people round fancy that the goat-footed satyrs and nymphs inhabit, and tell that they are the fauns by whose night-pervading noise and sportive play as they declare the still silence is broken" (Munro, 97–98). On the other hand, in book V Lucretius associates rape and the arbutus ("yon arbutus / Totters," "Lucretius," lines 184–85) with primitive man, the state to which Lucretius has been reduced by the philter that tickled "the brute brain within the man's" (line 21): "Whatever prize fortune threw in his way, each man would bear off, trained at his own destruction to think of himself and live for himself alone. And Venus would join the bodies of lovers in the woods; for each woman was gained over either by mutual desire or the headstrong violence and vehement lust of the man or a bribe of some acorns and arbute-berries or choice pears" (Munro, 139).

Tennyson's monologue is thus at once a radical rendering of consciousness—rooted in and lifted whole, as it were, from the consciousness Lucretius revealed in his own poem—and a thoroughgoing tribute to Lucretius in its fidelity to and preservation of Lucretius's thoughts. But the tribute is also the source of Tennyson's prophetic judgment of Lucretius; for Tennyson, in effect, forces Lucretius to live by his own words, and since Lucretius finds he cannot do that, to be damned by them. Indeed, the very motive for the poem may have come from Lucretius himself, who, in book III of his poem, by way of explaining why men (falsely) turn to religion, says, "You can better test the man in doubts and dangers and mid adversity learn who he is; for then and not till then the words of truth are forced out from the bottom of his heart: the mask is torn off, the reality is left" (Munro, 58).[63] Tennyson's choice of the dramatic monologue (especially one that begins with a man just starting up from sleep) for stripping away the mask may also have been spurred by Lucretius's saying of those who seek forgetfulness in sleep, "In this way each man flies from himself, (but self from whom, as you may be sure is commonly the case, he cannot escape, clings to him in his own despite) hates too himself, because he is sick and knows not the cause of the malady; for if he could rightly see into this, relinquishing all else each man would study to learn the nature of things, since the point at stake is the condition for eternity, not for one hour, in which mortals have to pass all the time which remains for them to expect after death" (Munro, 83). Tennyson utterly agrees with Lucretius; the dramatic monologue, especially one encased within a narrative frame, formally underscores Lucretius's entrapment in a self he loathes but cannot, except through death, escape. And Tennyson would also agree that the stakes at issue are nothing less than eternity—but from an entirely different viewpoint. Clearly, the poem suggests that the truth in adversity Lucretius reveals is that his philosophy, which denies immortality to the soul and active agency to the gods, cannot suffice him in a crisis; his only recourse is suicide.

But the (prophetic) point is never made overtly or apart from the sympathy and homage that Tennyson simultaneously renders to Lucretius. Tennyson avoids mere prophetic judgment or unqualified identification with Lucretius, I think, because the historical Lucretius was a perfect alembic for containing, distilling, and transmuting (through art—and English) Tennyson's own dialectical sensibility. Tennyson's stance with regard to Lucretius is a literal "there but for the grace of God go I." The "grace of God," of course, is what separates Tennyson from Lucretius and prompts his judgment. The same reasoning that leads Lucretius to cry of the satyr "Twy-natured is no nature" in Tennyson's poem also led the Roman poet to deny the soul's immortality, that crux of Tennyson's belief, and assert instead only a materialistic existence. Moreover, because of his uncanny anticipations of modern science, Lucretius would, for Tennyson, have been aligned in many respects with the Victorian scientists who daily mustered more evidence to invalidate a teleological, theistic universe, and whom Tennyson would soon encounter in the Metaphysical Society (founded the year after "Lucretius" was published). In fact, various passages in *De Rerum Natura* so closely resemble Darwin's theories of evolution, reversion, and natural selection (see, for example, Munro, 40, 126–27, 136) that Munro is led to exclaim in his notes to the Latin text that Lucretius's system has "strangely suggestive anticipations of the latest marvels of physical science" (Munro, II, 6); and once Munro even goes as far as to use the phrase *struggle for existence* to refer to a passage in book V of *De Rerum Natura* (Munro, II, 327).

However, despite their central differences Tennyson would have equally compelling reasons to identify with Lucretius, to stress the "I" rather than the "but for the grace of God."[64] The young man who voted no when the Apostles debated whether a First Cause was discernible from the universe or the mature man who wrote that he did not find God in "world or sun" would perforce agree with Lucretius's recurrent assertion that "even if I did not know what first-beginnings are, yet this . . . I would venture . . . to maintain, that the nature of the world has by no means been made for us by divine power" (Munro, 32). Indeed, Lucretius's poem is shot through with ideas Tennyson also embraced: the illusoriness of time (Munro, 11–12), life's inherent transience and loss (Munro, 29–30), the existence of other worlds besides our own (Munro, 53–54), and the beauty of the past compared with the present (Munro, 55–56). Moreover, Lucretius and Tennyson were kindred souls in their very vocation as poets, and poets, moreover, who had successfully integrated scientific learning into their major poems. Finally, Tennyson would have found congenial one facet of Lucretius's motive in writing *De Rerum Natura*, his wish to free men from the fear of "immortal hell" and the "Ixionian wheel" ("Lucretius," lines 262, 260). "Despair," after all, was also written in part as a protest against the doctrine of eternal punishment. But Lucretius's shrewd etiology for the doctrine of hell—he viewed the belief as a projection of the fears we experience in life (Munro, 80–81)—would be precisely of a sort to set in motion Tennyson's dialectic once again. For if Tennyson claimed that "Every man imputes himself" was his favorite adage (and thus far would necessarily agree with Lucretius's explanation regarding hell), he desperately feared that a belief in immortality was likewise a mere imputation, "The guess of a worm in the dust and the shadow of its desire" ("Despair," line 30).

The poem, then, is more than Lucretius's dialogue with himself, caught as he is between desire for a tranquil life of ordered reason and the lustful desire wrought upon him by the philter. The poem is also Tennyson's dialogue with himself, as he infuses simultaneously his affirmations and doubts into the containing form of the Roman poet by chance suited perfectly to hold both poles of Tennyson's sensibility. Hence the poem fuses sympathy and judgment, where it is the pathos, not the ironies, of Lucretius's character, that impels judgment.

The monologue's frame, however, functions in service of judgment, as if, once divorced from Lucretius's voice, Tennyson is also divorced from sympathy. For the first word of the poem, as distinct from the monologue, is "Lucilia," Lucretius's wife, the other half of Lucretius's self,[65] which Lucretius ignored and repressed and which makes a mockery of his claim that "Twy-natured is no nature." Beginning the poem thus, Tennyson corrects and underscores Lucretius's omission, the consequence of which is to precipitate both Lucilia and Lucretius into additional dualities. Given too much reason, too little passion, from Lucretius, Lucilia abandons rationality and embraces irrationality, aligning herself with the witch who brews the philter. Thereupon Lucretius, flooded with passion and unable to hold on to his reason, becomes aligned with the lusty, irrational figure of the satyr. Both Lucretius and Lucilia are dualities unto themselves and to each other. There is a closing as well as opening frame, however; this device is itself a judgment, as if to say that Lucretius cannot give us the whole picture but is rather only a "middle," an intermediary. Yet Tennyson has the grace to give Lucretius the last words. Appropriately distanced by the intervening narrative voice of the closing frame, Lucretius's final words are the only ones he now can give us before he disappears completely: " 'Fare thee well!' "

It is a disappointment to turn from the remarkable "Lucretius" to "Tiresias," still flawed even though Tennyson revised the poem before publishing it in 1885. Given the power of prophecy in recompense for blindness when Pallas Athene punished him for spying her naked in her bath, Tiresias certainly offers Tennyson "prophetic" possibilities. Hence Tiresias, like the ancient sage, instructs his auditor Menoeceus in the virtues of patriotism and self-sacrifice, obligatory if Ares is to be appeased, and then turns to a vision of the afterlife at the poem's end.[66] "Tiresias" is characteristic of Tennyson's late poems in more than theme. David Goslee has demonstrated that the successive stages of the poem's composition over fifty years reflect Tennyson's shift from deeply personal to increasingly objective verse, from Tiresias "as a virtual *persona* to one whose very autonomy renders him increasingly alien."[67] "Tiresias" thus stands as a kind of model of development of Tennyson's dramatic monologues as a whole.

But it is an imperfect model, for uncharacteristically Tennyson's point of view in the poem is ill considered. He attempts to coalesce two strands that simply will not fuse. The conflicting strands are indicated by Tiresias himself.

> *Virtue must shape itself in deed, and those*
> *Whom weakness or necessity have cramped*
> *Within themselves, immerging, each, his urn*
> *In his own well, draw solace as he may.*

> *(lines 84–87)*

The figure of self immersed in self we recognize as an image of consciousness, and the monologue's best lines dramatize the speaker's melancholy musings upon himself, where the speaker seems imagined as an aspect of Tennyson's self.

> *I wish I were as in the years of old,*
> *While yet the blessèd daylight made itself*
> *Ruddy through both the roofs of sight, and woke*
> *These eyes, now dull, but then so keen to seek*
> *The meanings ambushed under all they saw.*

> *(lines 1–5)*

But Tennyson is not content to plumb the well in which is immerged the urn of self; he must also have the "virtue . . . in deed," Menoeceus's sacrifice. To secure this, Tiresias must surface from out his depths, engage his auditor, and actively persuade the young man to undertake the sacrifice. Tennyson has thus planted one (poetic) foot in the realm of consciousness, one in the realm of personality, and the monologue hovers uneasily between the two. Insofar as Tiresias speaks to sway Menoeceus, Tennyson allows the possibility of ironic self-betrayal a la Browning to creep into the poem[68]—Tiresias's earnest encouragement of Menoeceus can be interpreted as the old man's selfish manipulation of the young to avenge himself against Pallas, who has coupled the gift of prophecy with the curse that none will heed it.

> *thou art wise enough,*
> *Though young, to love thy wiser, blunt the curse*
> *Of Pallas, hear, and though I speak the truth*
> *Believe I speak it, let thine own hand strike*
> *Thy youthful pulses into rest.*

> *(lines 148–52)*

But the irony, if intended, is insufficiently developed. Thus, we get neither a compelling rendering of consciousness, which threatens to modulate into the ironic self-betrayal of a personality; nor do we get a bitingly ironic portrait of a personality, the ironies diffused by the poem's emphatic prophetic themes and Tiresias's slipping into the depths of consciousness at the monologue's beginning and end.

Paradoxically, the poem's greatest "virtue" lies in its status, not as a monologue, but as a "deed," part of the graceful and beautiful tribute "To E. FitzGerald" that enclosed "Tiresias" upon its publication. As Ricks rightly says of "To E. FitzGerald," the poem "comprises a single sentence (fifty-six lines) of such unhurried calm, such imaginative yet unostentatious transitions, such dignity, such affectionate tact, as takes the reader's breath away. . . . His poem breathes friendship" (*Tennyson*, 293). The epistle is thus both poem and act, lovely in itself but acting to send birthday greetings to Fitz, along with the poem—"Tiresias"—dedicated to him. Excepting the poem's flaws, "Tiresias" functions beautifully as a gift, as an act of friendship, to Fitz. In the epistle Tennyson recalls his feeling "enskied" when he shared FitzGerald's vegetarian diet and his fall from "that half-spiritual height" until he tasted flesh again (lines 14–20). And so Tennyson sends FitzGerald a poem that tells how Tiresias "scale[d] the highest of the heights / With some strange hope to see the nearer God," how Tiresias "fell" from that "height" when he spied Athene, and how he longs for the afterlife among "those who mix all odour to the Gods / On one far height in one far-shining fire." FitzGerald has fame as the poet-translator of "that large infidel / Your Omar," and so as an answering gesture Tennyson sends his friend a poem spoken by the pagan Greek. The epistle, once again, sends birthday greetings to one old man from another old man, whose friendship dates back to their youth. Hence Tennyson chooses "Tiresias" as a poem that begins with an acknowledgment of age and a remembrance of the past and the composition of which, like their friendship, spans the past and the present. As an act of love, then, "Tiresias" succeeds. Even its flaws, which Tennyson concedes in the epistle (lines 50–53), cease to matter. For when "Tiresias" is subordinated, as in its publication, to the superior "To E. FitzGerald," its foremost function is as a "deed" that links the lives of Tennyson and his friend, their mutual past and present, and articulates their love.

Tennyson's last classical monologue, "Demeter and Persephone," is not only a surpassingly beautiful poem but also an apt coda to Tennyson's dramatic monologues. For the poem draws unto itself almost all the best and most characteristic strategies of the Tennysonian dramatic monologue. Tennyson had shown in "Rizpah" that the domestic monologue could be raised to the level of high art, and he repeats the triumph in "Demeter and Persephone." Part of the poem's function, surely, is to evoke and exercise the reader's sympathy for the pain and suffering of a mother bereaved of her child and her joy at their reunion. Demeter, of course, is not mad, as is the speaker of "Rizpah"; but she loses none of the mother's passion, though a goddess. Only her passion is always filtered through the restraint befitting the dignity of a goddess: "[I] heard / The murmur of their temples chanting me, / Me, me, the desolate Mother!" The repetition of "me, / Me, me" bespeaks a rising emotional gradient, but only in the context of the worship accorded to Demeter as her right and privilege. Demeter's domesticity and deity are, quite simply, inseparable. Her domestic role of mother is ennobled by her deity and her deity softened and rendered approachable through her motherly love.

"Demeter and Persephone" exemplifies not only Tennyson's domestic but also his prophetic mode, but with none of the shrillness of "Locksley Hall Sixty Years After" or the divided aims of "Tiresias." Tennyson's success here is due partly to a felicitous choice of subject. Endorsing Christianity as a superior theology to paganism because of its emphasis on love and personal immortality is not alien but naturally related to the story of a mother's love so powerful it could compel a change in the divine order, or of her child's descent into and then resurgence from the realm of death.[69] Freed from the burden of imposing a moral on a poem when the moral inhered naturally in the subject matter, Tennyson could practice the restraint he sometimes lost. In a draft Demeter describes her growing sympathy for mankind thus:

*The man must suffer ere [he] feel the God,*
*The God must suffer ere he know the man—*
*I grieved for man thro' all my grief for thee—*

*(Harvard Notebook 53, folio 36)*

But in the final version Tennyson dropped the sententiousness of the first two lines for the simpler, and more powerful, "[I] fled by many a waste, forlorn of man, / And grieved for man through all my grief for thee" (lines 73–74).

Tennyson was also at his best when he could fuse the personal and private, the subjective and objective, and that is also true of "Demeter and Persephone." As recent scholars have noted, the late monologue has more than a little in common with *In Memoriam*.[70] The poem in fact suggests Tennyson's relationship to Hallam not only in the monologue's structural parallels with *In Memoriam*—the sudden loss of a loved one, the ensuing desolation, the ultimate recovery through love—but also in direct echoes. Demeter's reiterated "Where?" as she searches for the lost Persephone (lines 58–86) is a virtual transcription of an unadopted section of *In Memoriam*, where the poet Tennyson searches for Hallam: "I could not find thee here or there, / I cried to all the breezes, 'Where?', / For all my want was unfulfilled."[71] Demeter's own "Where?" is finally answered in a dream, which comes to her "as the likeness of a dying man, / Without his knowledge, from him flits to warn / A far-off friendship that he comes no more" (lines 87–89). These lines, too, are surely a very personal touch, a remembrance of the shrouded figure seen at Somersby by Mary and Matilda Tennyson around the time of Hallam's death.[72] Finally, Demeter's anticipation of "souls of men, who grew beyond their race, / And made themselves as Gods" (lines 138–39) is, as Priscilla Johnston observes, an echo of Tennyson's hailing Arthur Hallam as "a noble type / Appearing ere the times were ripe" in the Epilogue of *In Memoriam*. Interestingly, as late as the trial edition of 1889, "Demeter and Persephone" ended with the lines praising men "who grew beyond their race," as if all the poem's weight were to fall there. If Demeter's passion for Persephone is compelling, this is so because it is also the passion of Tennyson for Hallam.

But the poem as a whole is powerful because we do not get only Tennyson's passion. Here the subjective *is* fused with the objective, and the poem ends, not with the muffled allusion to Hallam, but with the world of the dead that Demeter has transcended but cannot make disappear. And with the reluctant glance toward "the dimly-glimmering lawns / Of that Elysium" and "the silent field of Asphodel," we also encounter that haunting verbal music of Tennyson when he wrote at his very best.

In one respect only does "Demeter and Persephone" differ from Tennyson's best and most characteristic dramatic monologues: the poem is not, at first glance, a rendering of consciousness. Demeter's utterance is directed, not inward, but toward Persephone and consists primarily of a past-tense narrative of events that have occurred in Persephone's absence. The apparent anomaly is not gratuitous or unthinking, however. As Tennyson would have known from Pater's essay "The Myth of Demeter and Persephone," first published in 1876, Demeter "is not a goddess only, but also a priestess."[73] As Tennyson would have known from both Pater and the *Homeric Hymn to Demeter*, to which he was directed by R. C. Jebb, Demeter "appears consistently, in the hymn, as a teacher of rites, transforming daily life, and the processes of life, into a religious solemnity" (Pater, 123). In Demeter's utterance, then, we witness both the birth and the performance of ritual, the Eleusinian mysteries performed in observance of Demeter and also, according to the myth, given to mankind by her. Although couched mostly in the past tense, as was the narrative (or hymn) sung each year at the festival of Demeter, her monologue thus also carries the association of timelessness. For she is both responding to a particular event, Persephone's first return, and creating the ritual narrative that will be recited again and again in timeless cycles as Persephone goes and returns in the future. Demeter, then, is, like Merlin or the ancient sage, another *vates* or hierophant initiating her young auditor into a higher realm of knowledge. Even here, on one level, she is still the mother, closing the gap in shared experience with her beloved daughter—even as the "black blur of earth" is closed by the answering touch of Persephone's foot (lines 37, 48–50)—by telling Persephone what she has endured in the daughter's absence.[74] But as hierophant, she is doing no less than initiating the just-returned queen of the dead back into life.

> *I brought thee hither, that the day,*
> *When here thy hands let fall the gathered flower,*
> *Might break through clouded memories once again*
> *On thy lost self.*
>
> *(lines 8–11)*

Demeter's role of hierophant also explains, as in the first stanza of "Merlin and the Gleam," the ritualistic naming that occurs throughout the poem: "Persephone! / Queen of the dead no more—my child!" (lines 17–18); "I, Earth-Goddess, cursed the Gods of Heaven" (line 100). But Demeter is not merely identifying but *creating* an identity, routing death and Persephone's initial likeness to Aidoneus and re-creating Persephone as daughter of the earth and Earth-Goddess.[75]

This last action of Demeter's means that she is not only mother, priestess, and goddess, but also poet, who can invoke the power of words to create and transform reality.[76] She is also the creator of a monologue, the Eleusinian ritual narrative that was always given a dramatic rendering at the annual festival of Demeter. As Pater asserts, the mysteries "certainly" included "a dramatic representation of the sacred story" (124), and he is intrigued that in the *Homeric Hymn*, which he sees *as* that ritual narrative or story, "the dramatic person of the mysteries mixes itself with the primitive mythical figure" (123). All this is interesting because as poet of a monologue, Demeter functions in roughly the same way as Tennyson in relation to his most characteristic monologues. She is both the creator of the ritual-monologue and a dramatized persona in it; she speaks so that she may both rehearse her feelings to herself ("I . . . am but ill-content") and, more pervasively, affect and enlighten Persephone, winning her back as daughter and revealing to her the mystery of life rearising from death. Persephone, one might say, is conversely placed in the position of an active reader of monologues, listening, receiving, at first "dumb" and "dazed," yet also actively participating, closing gaps, the "black blurs"; at first dead to the creator of the monologue but brought alive to her by receiving and entering into her words. Thus "Demeter and Persephone" is an apt close to the classical monologues because it not only embodies but also ritualistically rehearses the very process by which Tennyson came to create the monologues.

Moreover, the poem does, albeit more obliquely than usual, render Demeter's consciousness. As a goddess who is also a mother, Demeter is caught between the power of the past and its lesson that Persephone will be taken from her again, and her vision of a higher order that is not yet realized. Hence most of her monologue is couched in the past tense and ends in the future tense. The few lines in the present tense all bespeak her uneasy positioning between the past she spurns and the future she cannot yet have: "I feel the deathless heart of motherhood / Within me shudder, lest the naked glebe / Should yawn once more" (lines 41–43); "Yet I, Earth-Goddess, am but ill-content / With them, who still are highest" (lines 126–27). Tennyson's late addition of the closing lines reinforces Demeter's stance as one caught between two worlds and so is a far more effective ending than that in the trial edition. For now Demeter ends by at once evoking and eclipsing ("see no more") the realm she hates but over which she knows she is as yet powerless.

> and thou that hast from men,
> As Queen of death, that worship which is Fear,
>
> . . . . . . . . . . . . . . . . . . . . . . . .
> [Henceforth shalt] see no more
> The Stone, the Wheel, the dimly-glimmering lawns
> Of that Elysium, all the hateful fires
> Of torment, and the shadowy warrior glide
> Along the silent field of Asphodel.

"Demeter and Persephone" is thus not only beautiful in itself but also a monologue that captures nearly every major feature of the late Tennysonian monologue: the pathos of the domestic monologue, the spiritual and artistic themes of the prophetic monologues, Tennyson's ability to fuse the most intensely private expressions with serenely objective treatment, the rendering of consciousness, and Tennyson's very method in creating his dramatic monologues. Perhaps, through Demeter's association with country people in her role as goddess of agriculture, there is even an oblique reflection of the world of the Lincolnshire monologues in the poem. But if "Demeter and Persephone" is a casebook, it is one traced in gold and an astonishing instance of the continuing creativity of the poet who was eighty years old when the monologue was published.

## Conclusion

Although "Demeter and Persephone" was Tennyson's last classical monologue, it was not his last classical poem. That role goes to "The Death of Oenone," the title poem of Tennyson's last, and posthumous, volume. It is curious that Tennyson chose to return to the subject of his first classical monologue, "Oenone." Perhaps it was a kind of conscious farewell or closure to the vein that produced the brilliant classical monologues. For "The Death of Oenone" bears the same relation to the classical monologues that "Morte d'Arthur"—the death of Arthur—does to "Ulysses." Instead of the ever-present world of the monologues, we have the distanced, past-tense world of the narrative that accepts the pastness of the past as something over and done. Hence the opulent landscape of "Oenone" is deliberately echoed but now shown to have dried up and vanished.

> all the serpent vines
> Which on the touch of heavenly feet had risen,
> And gliding through the branches overbowered
> The naked Three, were withered long ago.

> (lines 4–7)

And the fire to which the young Oenone had looked for vengeance is now the fire of self-immolation and obliteration: "she leapt upon the funeral pile, / And mixt herself with *him* and past in fire" (lines 105–6). Aware of approaching death and the chance to mix with "*him*," with Hallam, who was so closely associated with the Cauteretz landscape on which both versions of "Oenone" were based, perhaps Tennyson wished to drop the dramatic mask and its locus in the present for the distant past into which he himself would soon merge.

We are at the conclusion, however, not only of the classical monologues but Tennyson's poetry as a whole as well, and it is time to see what conclusions may be drawn from a study of his dramatic monologues. In the first place it should be clear that Tennyson *wrote* dramatic monologues; it simply so happens that his are Tennysonian rather than Browningesque. Typically Tennysonian as well is the development of the dramatic monologues, which confirms from another vantage point Tennyson's oft-noted shift from intense subjectivity, as in the "Exile" poems, to ever-greater objectivity, as in the best work of the 1842 poetry, until we reach the consciously public orientation of the late prophetic poetry—where, however, intensely private expressions still mingle and fuse with objectified oracular discourse. We have seen also that Tennyson's most frequent and successful strategy in his dramatic monologues is the rendering of consciousness. Yet, because of the genre's inherent flexibility, Tennyson could also use the form to elicit and "exercise" the reader's sympathy, as in the domestic monologues; to render personality, as in the Lincolnshire monologues; to embody satire, as in "Amphion" and "Northern Farmer, New Style"; to utter pronouncements befitting the poet-as-prophet, as in "The Ancient Sage"; to create a containing form for confession or initiation, as in "Romney's Remorse" and "Merlin and the Gleam"; to unblock the completion of long poems, as in *The Lover's Tale* and the *Idylls*; and to embrace a large poetic universe, from the world of myth to the multitudinous Victorian scene to Tennyson's own "postage stamp of the universe," his native Lincolnshire. More important, approaching Tennyson's body of work from the vantage point of the dramatic monologue helps us discover anew his consummate craftsmanship not only in his unerring choice of dramatic monologue, lyric, or narrative for individual poems but also, as in "The Hesperides," "Ulysses," or "The Holy Grail," in his exploitation of the formal properties of the dramatic monologue to create his poems' central meaning. *Maud* represents the furthest reach of his monologues' technical development, but like a magician pulling not new creatures but differently colored rabbits from his hat, he is able to sustain the subtlety and creativity of the dramatic monologue in his latest work, giving us the remarkable "Lucretius" and "Demeter and Persephone." Finally, approaching Tennyson through the medium of the dramatic monologue reveals what an important and pervasive form it was for Tennyson. We of course see this in the best-known dramatic monologues, early and late. But as well we have seen that the genre is integrally related to every major work Tennyson undertook, from *The Princess* through the *Idylls*. Perhaps the most fitting concluding note is the last poem Tennyson ever completed, "The Dreamer." As published, the poem is a narrative. But in its first form it, too, was a dramatic monologue. Hence, if we except "The Rape of Proserpine" as a mere schoolboy's translation and turn instead to *The Devil and the Lady*, it is possible to say that Tennyson's career as a poet began and ended with (unpublished) soliloquies or monologues.

# Epilogue

*What meant they be their "Fate beyond the Fates".*
*But younger kindlier Gods to bear us down,*
*As we bore down the Gods before us?*

—*"Demeter and Persephone"*

Just as Tennyson and Browning bore down the great Romantic poets before them, the great Victorian poets were in turn displaced from poetic pre-eminence by the generation of Yeats, Eliot, and Pound that followed. These new gods of poetry, however, were kindly only to Browning. Browning was speedily conducted into the modern pantheon whereas Tennyson became, in Auden's words, "the stupidest" English poet. If Tennyson, in his own way, was a master monologist, his influence on the form's evolution went no further.

Or so it has long appeared. Recently, however, and most notably in the work of Carol Christ,[1] Tennyson has begun to be disinterred from amidst the rubble of the Victorian pantheon and transported to the modernist pantheon, where, it is becoming clear, his ghost has been in hiding all along.

Tennyson's legacy is especially apparent in the work of T. S. Eliot. Numerous commentators have cited the influence of Tennyson's diction, rhythm, and landscape imagery on Eliot's poetry.[2] But only Carol Christ has pointed out the importance of Tennyson's dramatic monologues for Eliot.

Unlike Pound, who learned much about persona, the dramatic monologue, and even about the possibilities of difficult and contorted syntax from Browning, Eliot learns his use of the dramatic monologue from Tennyson. Browning most frequently uses the dramatic monologue to portray eccentric characters with extraordinary intellectual or moral positions in dramatic and self-

245

revealing situations. Tennyson, on the other hand, more frequently uses mythological or literary figures to express a mood far more general, far less dependent on particular personality or dramatic situation. T. S. Eliot shares not only the mood of Tennyson's poetry, a mood of despairing impotence, of longing for oblivion, but the technique Tennyson uses to evoke that mood. Both poets use character not for its dramatic potential but as a way of providing a unifying focus, a skeleton on which to hang lyrical, often fragmentary evocations of mood, a mood often expressing deeply felt personal emotion. Character thus enables both poets to objectify and control the personal. (162–63)

Pound, that is, follows Browning in rendering the personality of his speakers, and Eliot follows Tennyson in rendering the consciousness of his own more amorphously defined speakers.[3] To show how important Tennyson's dramatic monologues are not only in his own work but also in the modernist tradition, I should like briefly to examine Eliot's indebtedness to Tennyson in two of his most famous dramatic monologues, "The Love Song of J. Alfred Prufrock" and "Gerontion."

The first thing we encounter beyond the title of "Prufrock" (where "Alfred" may be an oblique genuflection toward one of the many strands of Eliot's intertextuality) is the epigraph, a standard Eliotic device. The device is also Tennysonian. Like Tennyson's frames in his dramatic monologues, Eliot's epigraphs, as T. S. Matthews remarks, "serve as a kind of text or gloss on the poem that follows. . . . Eliot's use of these epigraphs seems to have been characteristically equivocal: partly to cover up his tracks, partly to beckon on the hunt."[4] Indeed, we may recall that "The Hesperides," which Eliot quotes at length in his essay on *In Memoriam*, uses not only a frame but also an epigraph (from Milton) to designate the poem that follows as a literary artifact—fittingly so, since "The Hesperides" is in so many ways about the making of poetry. The frames of "The Hesperides" and "The Lotos-Eaters" also distance and provide a gloss of the ensuing monologues. Moreover, the frames help position the reader, and this is true of Eliot's epigraph to "Prufrock" as well. Translated, the Dantean epigraph to "Prufrock" reads, "If I thought that my response would be addressed to one who might go back alive, this flame would shake no more; but since no one ever goes back alive out of these deeps (if what I hear be true), without fear of infamy I answer you." "Out of these deeps"—the epigraph is a direction for the reader to descend, descend into the consciousness of Prufrock, a kind of hell where absolute truth does not prevail ("*if* what I hear be true"). Rather, we are in the world of the dramatic monologue and its feint, where the utterance is true only in relation to the speaker.

And once we are in the world of Prufrock's consciousness, we encounter, as in Tennyson, a divided sensibility, caught between yearning and fear, between lament and ironic self-dramatization. And as in, say, "The Two Voices," Tennyson explicitly splits up the opposing strands of consciousness into separate voices, so we have the "you and I" of "Prufrock's" opening line.[5] Here, however, Eliot goes Tennyson one better. Not immune to the allure of Browning either, Eliot shows Prufrock within the safety of his consciousness contemplating the specter of his own personality—the "you," I rather think—and almost visibly shuddering. It is this "you" that must "prepare a face to meet the faces that you meet" or who plays the role of Polonius in the social world where the "you" interacts with other personalities (or "yous") and, as a result, is so frighteningly vulnerable. In part, then, the monologue is situated in the realm of consciousness because Prufrock does not "dare" to become a personality—an implication of consciousness only implicit in Tennyson's monologues.

But Eliot does follow Tennyson in the techniques he uses to render consciousness, picking up where Tennyson left off in *Maud*. Lyric devices adapted to dramatic ends are thus equally as important in "Prufrock" as in *Maud*. The meters of both poems are irregular, deliberately so in order to capture the glancing, dancing oscillations of the speakers' consciousnesses.[6] And Eliot, like Tennyson in *Maud*, uses sound and rhythmic effects simultaneously as lyric, poeticizing devices and as psychological indices. Prufrock's mention of "the muttering retreats" to be found in cheap hotels also makes us hear the "mutter" of his own language and realize that his language is likewise a "retreat" and oblique pathway (or "half-deserted street") through his own sensibility. The singsong rhythm and rhyme of "In the room the women come and go / Talking of Michelangelo" tell us in immediate sensory terms of the triviality and ennui that Pru-

frock associates with the women. This recurring couplet, or refrain, is also a device Tennyson uses in *Maud*, allusion (for example, to the Song of Songs); and here, appropriately, the
allusion is to *Maud*: "But up and down and to and fro, / Ever
about me the dead men go" (II, 255–56).[7] Just as the madmen
seem dead to the hero of *Maud* in his incarceration, so the
women, too, are dead—reified objects—to the Prufrock incar-
cerated in the prison of his own making. But as ghostly pres-
ences wandering in and out of his mind, it seems clear, the
women are also driving Prufrock a bit mad.

Eliot, like Tennyson in *Maud*, also skillfully uses abrupt juxtapositions, as Carol Christ observes (see "T. S. Eliot," 158–59), to
trace the mental associations of his speaker. Tennyson may
strive more than Eliot for a coherent underlying "plot" in *Maud*,
but the poem's opening lines are as abrupt, and as violent, as
anything in Eliot.

> *I hate the dreadful hollow behind the little wood,*
> *Its lips in the field above are dabbled with blood-red heath,*
> *The red-ribbed ledges drip with a silent horror of blood,*
> *And Echo there, whatever is asked her, answers "Death."*

Moreover, a poet who can turn, in part II of *Maud*, from "Strike
dead the whole weak race of venomous worms, / That sting each
other here in the dust; / We are not worthy to live" to "See what
a lovely shell, / Small and pure as a pearl" (II, 46–50), has created
the conventions whereby Eliot can pivot from "lonely men in
shirt-sleeves, leaning out of windows" to "a pair of ragged claws
/ Scuttling across the floors of silent seas." These abrupt juxtapositions, as well as the hero's and Prufrock's unanswered
questions, produce gaps into which the reader can and must enter if the poems are to be made sense of. Indeed, *Maud* and "Prufrock" both elicited similar responses from readers who tended
to decline the gambit offered by Tennyson and Eliot. "When,"
according to Lyndall Gordon, "Conrad Aiken took 'Prufrock' to
a 'poetry squash' in London and showed it to Harold Monro, the
editor of *Poetry and Drama*, Monro flung it back saying it was
'absolutely insane' "; and Gordon also notes that other "first
readers . . . thought it the morbid ravings of a madman" (47).

One can almost imagine the ghost of Tennyson sighing to Eliot, "I know exactly how you feel."

Hence, like Tennyson, Eliot uses a functional frame to bridge the reader's and speaker's worlds and then renders the consciousness of a divided sensibility through lyric devices, allusion, juxtapositions, and gaps. And as in "Tithonus," the very dramatic monologue form is part of the meaning of "Prufrock": the monologue form is both an irony underscoring the speaker's imprisonment within the self and a means of cathartic release for the speaker. Giving vent to his internal voice is an oasis, a retreat from the deadening social world in which Prufrock is forced to measure "out my life with coffee spoons" (rather as Ulysses is forced to "mete and dole" in the imprisoning world— or so it seems—of Ithaca). But Prufrock's song is also his prison; he sings to himself because an auditor is precisely what he cannot and "dare" not have, lest he hear, "That is not what I meant at all." The poem's closing lines beautifully capture the monologue's hovering status between release and imprisonment. On one hand, it is only when Prufrock rises to the surface of life, the realm of personality where "human voices" can "wake" the "you and I," that "we drown," that his inner divisions disappear into the larger world of life. One the other hand, in retreating to the confines of consciousness that guarantee imaginative survival, Prufrock is also, like Tennyson's Tiresias, "immerging . . . his urn / In his own well," and drowning himself without ever having experienced life.

In form and function, then, Eliot's "Prufrock" is a true descendent of the Tennysonian monologue. Only in imagery does Eliot make a radical departure from Tennyson. Eliot may, like Tennyson, drop images along the reader's path like so many jewels that, seemingly discrete and isolated, fuse in their mutually reflecting glow. Only Eliot's images are not *of* glowing gems, as in *Maud*. Tennyson could understand the opening lines of "Prufrock" ("Hateful is the dark-blue sky," his escapist mariners chant in "The Lotos-Eaters"), but he himself would never liken the evening sky to "a patient etherised upon a table." In constructing such imagery, as is often noted, Eliot is indebted to Baudelaire, Laforgue, and the contemporary Imagist poets. He is also, I think, indebted to his existence in a post-Freudian age. For not only are Eliot's images, relative to Tennyson's, more hard-edged and "tough"; they also seem to arise from the unconscious, having great import for the speaker (and poet) but in no readily discernible way. One of the most famous images in "Prufrock"—"I should have been a pair of ragged claws / Scuttling across the floors of silent seas"—thus seems to arise from the unconscious and also to image the unconscious to which Prufrock would perforce descend rather than face his burdensome consciousness. Eliot thus goes beyond Tennyson's *Maud* because he not only uses different images but also, thanks to Freud, can use them in a new way to limn his speaker's inner being.

"Gerontion" employs many of the techniques of "Prufrock," including the mask of age. Eliot was a young man when he wrote both poems, but like Tennyson in "Ulysses" and "Tithon," he uses the mask of age to distance the poems from himself and, most likely, to project his own sense of emptiness and ennui. "Gerontion," however, is even more radically centered in the realm of consciousness than is "Prufrock." No specter of personality haunts and torments the speaker of "Gerontion," and the poem's closing lines are a perfect metaphor of Gerontion's peculiar consciousness: "Tenants of the house, / Thoughts of a dry brain in a dry season."

"Gerontion" (the title means "little old man") has been compared to "Ulysses,"[8] but is more directly related to "Tithonus," whose withering old man is as much trapped in his "silent spaces of the East" as Eliot's speaker is in his "dull head among windy spaces." The resemblance of "Gerontion" and "Tithonus" is owing partly to similar settings and situations. Personified "History" is very much like Eos (another embodiment of time) who bestowed immortality "like wealthy men who care not how they give" and whose sympathy for Tithonus in the present seems futile, or at best a pretext for painful memories. Likewise History, Gerontion thinks,

> *gives when our attention is distracted*
> *And what she gives, gives with such supple confusions*
> *That the giving famishes the craving. Gives too late*
> *What's not believed in, or if still believed,*

# Epilogue

*In memory only, reconsidered passion. Gives too soon*
*Into weak hands, what's thought can be dispensed with*
*Till the refusal propagates a fear.*

As a result of the dubious gifts of Eos and History, both Tithonus and Gerontion are mocked by their decaying senses that coexist with sharp memories. "How can my nature longer mix with thine?" Tithonus asks; while Gerontion protests, "I have lost my sight, smell, hearing, taste and touch: / How should I use them for your closer contact?" Both thus end up envying the truly dead, whether in the form of "happy men that have the power to die" or "De Bailhache, Fresca, Mrs. Cammel, whirled / Beyond the circuit of the shuddering Bear / In fractured atoms." Perhaps the affinities between "Gerontion" and "Tithonus" were deliberate on Eliot's part, as the Greek names serving as titles might suggest. If so, the implicit allusion to "Tithonus" constitutes further evidence that in "Gerontion" Eliot explores matters not only of history but of faith. Tithonus at least recognized a deity when he saw one, longed for union with the deity, and desired immortality (if in the wrong way). Not surprisingly, his memories are better, more beautiful, than Gerontion's.

But of course Eliot echoes other literary texts in the poem besides Tennyson's. More important, then, is Eliot's Tennysonian legacy of linguistic structures as a technique for rendering consciousness. Tennyson, we recall, uses grammar in "Tithonus" to underscore his speaker's passivity, alienation, and guilt; mere objects are given agency, but Tithonus (having forfeited agency) has become a mere object. The same technique is employed in "Gerontion." As Tithonus can at most "wither," so Gerontion in the present can only state an identity ("Here I am, an old man"), slowly "stiffen in a rented house," or state what he has *not* ("I have no ghosts"; "I have lost my passion"). When, at one point, Gerontion wishes to assert agency regarding his own thoughts, he cannot say, "I have made this show purposely," but only, "I have not made this show purposelessly." Indeed, Gerontion's prostration is so great that verbs often disappear completely: "I an old man, / A dull head among windy spaces." Or he elides himself as agent: it is not "*I* think" but "Think / Neither fear nor courage saves us."[9] Instead, objects become agents. A mere abstraction, personified history, "gives"; "Vacant shuttles

251

/ Weave the wind"; "The goat coughs," and the woman who echoingly "Sneezes" seems no higher in the scale of being than the goat. And Christ, the epitome of agency, becomes a mere object, a tiger: "The tiger springs in the new year. Us he devours."[10] When, therefore, Gerontion quotes Lancelot Andrewes—"The word within a word, unable to speak a word"— Eliot is not only introducing a religious context into the poem but also having Gerontion, perhaps blasphemously, indulge in reflexivity. Gerontion's peculiar words within the larger "word" that is his utterance are so stripped of agency that they do not fully "speak."[11]

Moreover, since we know that Gerontion's thoughts are produced while he is "being read to by a boy," his monologue literally consists of unuttered words encased by the actively spoken words of the boy (Andrewes's text?). Delmore Schwartz, by way of isolating Eliot's poetic innovations, remarked that "his poems are often dominated by a *listening* to other voices."[12] In "Gerontion" the innovation has a distinctly psychological edge, yet another indication of the speaker's impotence and emptiness. Tennyson played a bit with the power of listening— witness the effect on the hero of *Maud* when he hears Maud's military ballad or Oenone's surrender to the words of Paris— but never with such subtle and deliberate effects. Once again, Eliot has picked up where Tennyson left off, "stealing" Tennyson's techniques like the "mature" poet Eliot was, and stretching them to their furthest extent until they become something new.[13]

Distinctive imagery, however, most separates "Tithonus" and "Gerontion." To cite the obvious example, "merds" could not appear in a Tennysonian monologue. In part, once again, the difference derives from the disparate times in which Tennyson and Eliot lived. As well, the deliberate ugliness of Eliot's imagery befits a speaker who has witnessed some rather ugly history and feels trapped by it. For Gerontion, Eos has become a Medusa instead, and there are no beautiful sensuous pleasures to recall. A final reason for the difference in imagery, perhaps, is a signal difference in temperament between Tennyson and Eliot. The difference is "signal" because in so many ways the two men were alike. Both were sexually repressed (Tennyson's Vivien the snake became Eliot's Grishkin the cat [and, more tragically, Vivien the wife]); both have been suspected of homosexuality; both wanted no biographies written after their deaths, undoubtedly because both fused the private and the public in their poetry;[14] both used the mask of age in youth and turned to writing dramas (one each devoted to Thomas à Becket) in their maturity; both regularly used self-borrowings, hoarding discarded lines and making new poems of them later; both agonized over faith and doubt;[15] and both wrote works that captured the mood of their respective generations. But if Tennyson was repressed, he was not also burdened with a Puritan inheritance. Eliot was. And this inheritance, which made Eliot eschew even candy in his youth[16]—the more robust Tennyson enjoyed a bottle of port after every dinner, and, preferably, an apple tart—is also one reason, I think, why Eliot similarly eschewed the seductions of glorious, quivering, glowing sensuous imagery that was a Tennyson hallmark. As Eliot said, "The contemplation of the horrid or sordid or disgusting, by an artist, is the necessary and negative aspect of the impulse toward the pursuit of beauty. But. . . . the negative is the more importunate."[17]

Although surpassing Tennyson in his images, their sources, and the uses to which he put them, Eliot nonetheless was indebted to the Tennysonian dramatic monologue for his own achievement in "The Love Song of J. Alfred Prufrock" and "Gerontion." Eliot was always a "quick study," and the lessons of Tennyson's rendering of consciousness (and the techniques for doing so) were rapidly absorbed and then transmuted into two of Eliot's most famous monologues.

Curiously, in the Poet's Corner of Westminster Abbey, the memorial stones of Eliot, Browning, and Tennyson lie side by side, but Tennyson's lies between Eliot's and Browning's. This is entirely fitting. If Browning also made the dramatic monologue available to Eliot, the legacy was filtered through Tennyson and the laureate's own distinctive monologues. And through his influence on Eliot, I think it safe to say, Tennyson has also played a role in the entire modernist tradition of the dramatic monologue. In *Untitled Subjects*, a collection of dramatic monologues,

Richard Howard pays tribute to his acknowledged master, Robert Browning, in the volume's dedication.[18] But I should like to think that Howard's inclusion of "1891: An Idyll," which revolves around Tennyson on the Isle of Wight, is more appropriate than Howard himself might think and that the answer to the question posed in "An Idyll"—"Who speaks? The Prospero of the Isle, / or only the Laureate?"—is, emphatically, "The former."

# Notes

## Chapter One

1. Arthur Waugh, *Alfred Lord Tennyson* (London: William Heinemann, 1892), p. 307.

2. Robert Langbaum, *The Poetry of Experience* (1957; rpt. New York: W. W. Norton, 1971). Subsequent references to this work appear in the text.

3. In 1975 two essays examined the effects of drama's dissolution in the nineteenth century on the development of the dramatic monologue. Philip Hobsbaum focuses on the growing importance of monologues in plays and on the actors who declaimed soliloquies as set pieces. Michael Mason, conversely, observes the prevailing notion that drama's true creativity and expressive activity resided in the author, not in the staging of the play—a notion that made it easy for Browning to shift from the stage to the press. Both Hobsbaum and Mason see a connection between works like Lamb's essays on or anthologies of Shakespeare's work (stressing characters' individual psychology divorced from a larger dramatic context) and the emergence of the dramatic monologue. See Hobsbaum, "The Rise of the Dramatic Monologue," *Hudson Review* 28 (1975), 227–45; and Mason, "Browning and the Dramatic Monologue," in *Writers and Their Background: Robert Browning*, ed. Isobel Armstrong (Athens: Ohio U. P., 1975), pp. 231–66.

4. A. Dwight Culler, in *PMLA* 90 (1975), 366–85. Subsequent references appear in the text.

5. Alan Sinfield, *Dramatic Monologue*, Critical Idiom series no. 36 (London: Methuen & Co., 1977), p. 42. Subsequent references appear in the text. Culler remarks that Tennyson's use of the term *dramatic monologue* in the dedication to "Locksley Hall Sixty Years After" (1886) was probably responsible for "launch[ing the term] into criticism" (336). Culler, however, notes reviewers' occasional use of the term in contemporary journals by the 1860s. In fact the journals used the term rather frequently in the 1860s.

6. Robert Pattison, *Tennyson and Tradition* (Cambridge: Harvard U. P., 1979), pp. 18–29. Subsequent references appear in the text.

Pattison does not argue that the idyll-dramatic monologue remained unchanged from Theocritus to Tennyson. The Romans, according to Pattison, added an element of judgment to the monologue, especially in the satires of Juvenal and Horace. The idyll tradition is found also in Donne's amatory epistles, based on Ovid, and Marvell's "To His Coy Mistress." The eighteenth century both sustained and enlarged the idyll tradition by engrafting on it a new social sensibility. Again Pattison, like Sinfield, points to *Eloisa and Abelard*, as well as to Cowper's "Alexander Selkirk" (33–35).

7. See the volume devoted to *The Bucolic Poets*, pp. 26–39, in the Loeb Classical Library edition.

8. Pattison hesitates on this issue; the assertions cited are confined to footnotes. See p. 161, n. 15, and p. 163, n. 13.

9. More recent examples are K. P. Saradhi, "The Theatre of the Mind," *Genre* 8 (1975), 322–35; Ralph Rader, "The Dramatic Monologue and Related Lyric Forms," *Critical Inquiry* 3 (1976), 131–51; and William E. Fredeman, "One Word More—on Tennyson's Dramatic Monologues," in *Studies in Tennyson*, ed. Hallam Tennyson (Totowa, N.J.: Barnes & Noble, 1981), pp. 169–85. Saradhi insists on concrete settings and on a well-defined character "in action-context." Ultimately he separates Browning's monologues in tabular form into "perfect" and "imperfect" monologues.

Rader also distinguishes between bona fide dramatic monologues and what he calls "mask lyrics." In the dramatic monologues we respond to the speaker as we would to an actual person in an interpersonal relationship; in mask lyrics the speaker is not a "simulated natural person" but an artificial actor through whom the poet speaks. The mask lyric, in other words, is an indirect lyric. Examples of the mask lyric include "Childe Roland" and virtually all of Tennyson's monologues. Examples of dramatic monologues include "My Last Duchess" and "Soliloquy of the Spanish Cloister." Rader also establishes the category of "dramatic lyric" (e.g., "Dover Beach"), in which the speaker is imagined by the poet from within, so that we respond to the speaker's thoughts as if they occurred in our own world (with the dramatic monologue, the experience is *like* that which occurs in the natural world). Finally there is the "expressive lyric," in which we encounter no dramatic representation but only the poet who typically re-creates an experience of the natural world, as in "Tintern Abbey." Rader is helpful in pointing to the range of effects and qualities to be found in the monologue form. However, I find his categories less convincing. I see more affinities between "Tithonus" and "Dover Beach," for example, than I do between "Dover Beach" and "The Darkling

Thrush"; yet Rader places these last two in the same category, as distinct from the mask-lyric grouping that includes "Tithonus."

Fredeman begins by noting that Tennyson's dramatic monologues are not easily categorized and maintaining that one cannot dismiss Tennyson's monologues merely because they are not Browningesque. And Fredeman's distinction between Browning's and Tennyson's dramatic monologues is suggestive: "In Browning, character is normally revealed *through* the fiction; in other words, there is genuine interplay between speaker and listener going on behind the language, which involves action, movement, or development. Between the beginning and end of the monologue something either happens or a transformation or recognition is effected, in which the speaker, the listener, and the reader participate and are changed. In Tennyson, almost without exception, the character is *posited*; the speaker is a talker rather than a doer, and his language is more likely to be reflective, introverted, philosophical, rather than direct and forceful; the action is invariably either static or retrospective. . . . Tennyson's monologues more closely resemble interior monologues than dramatic encounters" (171).

But by the end of the essay Fredeman becomes prescriptive in allowing or disallowing poems as "genuine" dramatic monologues: the essential features of a Tennysonian monologue are an aged male speaker at or near death whose utterance is given in blank verse. Only nine poems among all Tennyson's works qualify, in Fredeman's view, as "major": "Ulysses," "St. Simeon Stylites," "Tithonus," "Lucretius," "Columbus," "Sir John Oldcastle," "Tiresias," "The Ancient Sage," and "Romney's Remorse." It seems hard to have "Oenone" ejected from the list, as from some exclusive men's club, simply because the speaker is female. And I question a categorization that elevates weak poems like "Romney's Remorse" and "Sir John Oldcastle" over such poems as "Locksley Hall," "Demeter and Persephone," "Rizpah," and even the Lincolnshire monologues.

10. It is odd, for example, that Morris's "Defense of Guenevere" is never cited, perhaps because of Langbaum's discomfort with a monologue punctuated by a narrator's comments.

11. Not surprisingly, perhaps, Culler gives an affirmative reading of "Ulysses" in *The Poetry of Tennyson* (New Haven: Yale U. P., 1977), pp. 89–98. "Ulysses" is, of course, a problematical poem. But if Langbaum's model is correct, we can read the poem only ironically, and the debate over Ulysses' nobility or reprehensibility is a moot issue.

12. James R. Kincaid maintains that poems like "Ulysses" and "The Lotos-Eaters" simultaneously invite yet frustrate judgment since in-

complete contexts are provided. Thus we must and cannot judge Ulysses. And even if we try, our judgment really fails to answer the problems posed by the character. See *Tennyson's Major Poems* (New Haven: Yale U. P., 1975), pp. 35–37.

13. Mason, "Browning," pp. 237–39.

14. Herbert F. Tucker, Jr., extends the thought of both Robert Langbaum and Alan Sinfield regarding the dramatic monologue's relation to the Romantic lyric, and the monologue's formal properties. Tucker argues that Tennyson's and Browning's dramatic monologues historicize (i.e., give a context to) the Romantic lyric and in so doing subvert and question the Romantic lyric altogether. For in introducing a context (including an auditor) rather than an "authentic" speaker, dramatic monologues present language shaped for self-presentation, and so call attention to the dominance of language itself. As Tucker says, "The business of articulation, of putting oneself into words, compromises the self it would justify; it disintegrates the implicit claim of self-presence in the lyric into a rhetorical fabric of self-presentation" ("From Monomania to Monologue," *VP* 22 [1984], 125). Tucker's remark that the dramatic monologue at once posits and disintegrates a self resembles Alan Sinfield's contention that the central formal feature of the dramatic monologue is the "feint." Hence, Tucker's further contribution is the synthesis he suggests between Langbaum's argument concerning literary history and Sinfield's concerning form.

15. W. David Shaw, *The Dialectical Temper* (Ithaca: Cornell U. P., 1968), p. 60.

16. Dorrit Cohn, in *Transparent Minds* (Princeton: Princeton U. P., 1978), illuminates the relationship between fiction and the dramatic monologue, particularly since she concentrates on monologues in fiction. In fact, she sees the same range and flexibility in verse (and prose) monologues that I do. She comments, "All dramatic monologues [can be seen as] first-person narratives in verse form. The basic structural variants of the genre tally exactly with the basic variants of prose fiction in the first person: speakers of dramatic monologues can address silent listeners, or speak to themselves; they can narrate the lives of others, or their own; they can recount a past experience, or focus on a present predicament. A dramatic monologue in which a lone speaker articulates a contemporary experience is the analogue within the lyric genre of the autonomous monologue in prose fiction" (257–58).

17. It is significant that Rader places "Childe Roland" in the group of mask lyrics that includes Eliot's "Prufrock" and Tennyson's "Ulysses" and "Tithonus." All these poems share a vagueness of time

and setting and omit the markers of character we associate, say, with Fra Lippo Lippi or the Duke of "My Last Duchess."

18. H. D. Rawnsley, *Memories of the Tennysons* (Glasgow: James Mac-Lehose & Sons, 1900), p. 101; and Wilfred Ward, *Problems and Persons* (1903; rpt. Freeport, N.Y.: Books for Libraries Press, 1968), p. 201. Browning willingly conceded Tennyson's dramatic bent: "most of Tennyson's poems are *dramatic*—utterances coloured by an imaginary speaker's moods" (letter of 8 Nov. 1843 to Alfred Domett, in Frederick G. Kenyon, ed., *Robert Browning and Alfred Domett* [London: Smith, Elder & Co., 1906], p. 97).

19. From *Robert Browning's Prose Life of Strafford*, ed. H. Firth and F. J. Furnivall (1892), pp. 60–61. Quoted by Mason, pp. 253–54.

20. My definitions of *personality* and *consciousness* are taken from *Webster's Third New International Dictionary*. (Emphasis mine.)

21. See Carol T. Christ, *The Finer Optic* (New Haven: Yale U. P., 1975), p. 25; and Charles Altieri, "Arnold and Tennyson," *Criticism* 20 (1978), 293.

22. John Maynard, *Browning's Youth* (Cambridge: Harvard U. P., 1977). Subsequent references appear in the text.

23. J. Hillis Miller, *The Disappearance of God* (Cambridge: Harvard U. P., 1963), p. 129.

24. For an excellent discussion of Browning's language, see Miller, pp. 118–20, and Christ, pp. 81–84.

25. Robert F. Garratt, "Browning's Dramatic Monologue," *VP* 11 (1973), 115–25.

26. See Hallam Tennyson's *Alfred, Lord Tennyson: A Memoir* (New York: Macmillan, 1897). Details of these various anecdotes are to be found in I, 5, 48, 184, 370; and in II, 379. See also Bram Stoker, *Personal Reminiscences of Henry Irving* (1906; rpt. Westport, Conn.: Greenwood Press, 1970), where Stoker calls Tennyson "a natural character-actor" (I, 216).

27. But then Tennyson for the most part ignored their advice to him concerning poetry and did as he liked. See Peter Allen, *The Cambridge Apostles* (Cambridge: Cambridge U. P., 1978), p. 135.

28. Arthur Hallam, "Essay on the Philosophical Writings of Cicero," in *The Writings of Arthur Hallam*, ed. T. H. Vail Motter (New York: MLA, 1943), p. 144. Quoted by Allen, p. 155.

29. H. Tennyson, *Memoir*, I, 185.

30. *Writings of Arthur Hallam*, p. 133. Hallam's ultimate aim is to discuss the moral significance and application of sympathy. But most of the essay is devoted to how the process of sympathy works as a result

of feeling, imagination, and a healthy dose of Hartleyan association. Subsequent references to Hallam's writings appear in the text.

31. His juvenilia include "Written By an Exile of Bassorah," "The Exile," and so forth.

32. Christopher Ricks, ed., *The Poems of Tennyson* (1969; rpt. New York: W. W. Norton, 1972), p. 408. Unless otherwise noted, all citations of Tennyson's poems are from this edition. Ricks cites the 1832 lines from "The Palace of Art" in his notes to the 1842 version. Why Tennyson deleted the lines on the Soul's identification with what she saw is unclear. Of course the original version was prolix and needed cutting. It is tempting to argue that in these lines Tennyson had made his own poetic too clear, too subject to public gaze. I suspect, however, that he deleted them to maintain the poem's consistency. If the Soul already truly identifies with others, there is no need for her to be chastened at the end of her three years' reign.

33. William Cadbury, "Tennyson's 'The Palace of Art' and the Rhetoric of Structures," *Criticism* 7 (1965), 38–39.

34. Kenneth Burke, *A Rhetoric of Motives* (1950; rpt. Berkeley: U. of California P., 1969), p. 22.

35. T. S. Eliot, *"In Memoriam,"* in *Selected Essays* (New York: Harcourt, Brace & World, 1964), p. 286.

# Chapter Two

1. Robert Bernard Martin's account in *Tennyson* (New York: Oxford U. P., 1980) is the most authoritative and supersedes those given by Sir Charles Tennyson in *Alfred Tennyson* (New York: Macmillan, 1949), pp. 46–48, passim; and by Christopher Ricks in *Tennyson*, Masters of World Literature series (New York: Macmillan, 1972), pp. 1–16.

2. See Ricks's headnote to the play in his edition of the poems for a concise account of the composition and surviving manuscripts of the play (7–10).

3. See Ricks's headnote to the play, p. 9, for an account of the Elizabethan and Jacobean sources of *The Devil and the Lady*.

4. This delight in language prompts F. E. L. Priestley to remark that the play is "above all an exercise in and an exploration of varieties of style" (*Language and Structure in Tennyson's Poetry* [London: Andre Deutsch, 1973], p. 18). For Priestley Tennyson's exuberant language is part and parcel of the play's comic element, its zest and high spirits.

5. Jerome Buckley also observes this theme at work, terming it "the adolescent's dread, both pathetic and amusing, of the adult world that forever corrupts the naive sensibility of youth" (*Tennyson* [1960; rpt. Boston: Houghton Mifflin, 1965], p. 13). Tennyson's dread is indeed pathetic but not merely, I think, amusing.

6. Although with a different point, Ricks also detects Tennyson's subjectivity in these lines, which he terms "a curiously irrelevant passage full of hatred for the hopes of youth, where the vengefulness seems to be Tennyson's and seems to be self-directed" (*Tennyson*, 18).

7. The "rude breath of Dissipation" may allude to George Clayton Tennyson's dissipations (note the word *parent* in line 182). Perhaps the word *parent* and its troublesome connotations for Tennyson cause a further incoherence in the text. For, as opposed to all other references to the pool as a symbol of the dark and hidden realities of human nature, the pool suggested by "parent depths" is one that harbors and protects innocence. One might say the difference between the different pools is that one seems to express a yearning for repression, the other a yearning for regression.

8. This fear could have weighed more on Tennyson than on any of his siblings since of all the children he most closely resembled his father. According to Martin, Tennyson was the only son to have a large head like his father's. The son also resembled the father in gait, stature, voice, and poor eyesight. Indeed, Martin expressly remarks that "mingled with his sympathy was the dread that one day he would be like his father" (25).

9. "The Outcast" was never published in Tennyson's lifetime. Perhaps the young Tennyson was not entirely comfortable at the thought of his father's reading a published poem that announces, "I will not seek my Father's groves"; "I will not seek my Father's hills"; "I will not seek my Father's Hall."

10. For a fuller account of how Tennyson's use of language betrays his desire to withdraw from action or to submit to action only when it is directed by an external agent, see Zelda Boyd and Julian Boyd, "To Lose the Name of Action," *PTL* 2 (1977), 21–32. Although the authors do not discuss Tennyson's juvenilia, their explanation of the characteristic patterns in Tennyson's language is the most cogent account of the language in Tennyson's early verse.

11. "The Idealist" was written in 1829 but never published; neither was "St. Lawrence," though Tennyson cared enough about the piece to write four versions of it, dating from approximately 1825 to 1833 (see Ricks's editorial note, 298). But "Hero to Leander" was published

in 1830 alongside "Supposed Confessions," a startling juxtaposition. The one distinction of "Hero to Leander" is its unexpected sensuousness.

> *Thy heart beats through thy rosy limbs,*
>    *So gladly doth it stir;*
> *Thine eye in drops of gladness swims.*
> *I have bathed thee with the pleasant myrrh;*
>    *Thy locks are dripping balm;*
>    *Thou shalt not wander hence tonight,*
>    *I'll stay thee with my kisses.*

As Douglas Bush remarks of the poem, "The passion is . . . a little more authentic than in the earlier *Antony to Cleopatra*" (*Mythology and the Romantic Tradition in English Poetry* [Cambridge: Harvard U. P., 1937], p. 200). But only in the expression of passion does "Hero to Leander" progress beyond the earlier poem devoted to famous lovers.

    12. The frame in both the 1830 and the 1853 versions leads into what is labeled, in the 1830 version, a "Song," not a "dramatic monologue." And here the singing, as in "The Hesperides" and "The Lotos-Eaters," is performed by a chorus rather than a single speaker. But the various speakers in all three poems merge into a shared sensibility through their mutal participation in sexual wiles, art, or drugs; and the speakers are always indicated to be other than the poet—the hallmark of the dramatic monologue. In the Songs of "The Sea-Fairies," "The Hesperides," and "The Lotos-Eaters," Tennyson might be said to redact into a single voice the common strands of consciousness shared by his speakers, until the effect in these poems is little different from that of, say, "Tithonus," especially since Tennyson typically abjures the markers of personality that sharply distinguish one person from another.

    Because the 1830 version of "The Sea-Fairies" is less familiar than the 1853 version, I have reproduced the 1830 poem in its entirety below:

> *Slow sailed the weary mariners, and saw*
> *Between the green brink and the running foam*
> *White limbs unrobèd in a chrystal air,*
> *Sweet faces, rounded arms, and bosoms prest*
> *To little harps of gold: and while they mused,*
> *Whispering to each other half in fear,*
> *Shrill music reached them on the middle sea.*
>             SONG.
> *Whither away, whither away, whither away? Fly no more:*

*Whither away wi' the singing sail? whither away wi' the*
*oar?*
*Whither away from the high green field and the happy*
*blossoming shore?*
  *Weary mariners, hither away,*
    *One and all, one and all,*
  *Weary mariners come and play;*
  *We will sing to you all the day;*
    *Furl the sail and the foam will fall*
    *From the prow! One and all*
    *Furl the sail! drop the oar!*
      *Leap ashore!*
  *Know danger and trouble and toil no more.*
  *Whither away wi' the sail and the oar?*

      *Drop the oar,*
      *Leap ashore,*
      *Fly no more!*
*Whither away wi' the sail? whither away wi' the oar?*
*Day and night to the billow the fountain calls:*
*Down shower the gambolling waterfalls*
  *From wandering over the lea;*
*They freshen the silvery-crimson shells,*
*And thick with white bells the cloverhill swells*
  *High over the fulltoned sea.*
*Merrily carol the revelling gales*
  *Over the islands free:*
*From the green seabanks the rose downtrails*
  *To the happy brimmèd sea.*
*Come hither, come hither, and be our lords,*
  *For merry brides are we:*
*We will kiss sweet kisses, and speak sweet words.*
*O listen, listen, your eyes shall glisten*
  *With pleasure and love and revelry;*
  *O listen, listen, your eyes shall glisten,*
*When the sharp clear twang of the golden chords*
    *Runs up the ridgèd sea.*
  *Ye will not find so happy a shore*
  *Weary mariners! all the world o'er;*
      *Oh! fly no more!*
  *Harken ye, harken ye, sorrow shall darken ye,*
    *Danger and trouble and toil no more;*
      *Whither away?*
        *Drop the oar;*
      *Hither away,*
        *Leap ashore;*

> Oh fly no more—no more.
> Whither away, whither away, whither away with the
>     sail and the oar?

13.  It would not be fair to say that Tennyson bowdlerized the 1853 version, but he did change the poem's emphasis entirely. Harold Bloom remarks that if, according to Yeats, the "tragedy of sexual intercourse . . . was the perpetual virginity of the soul," then the "comedy of sexual intercourse is presumably the initial virginity of the body" (*Ringers in the Tower* [Chicago: U. of Chicago P., 1971], p. 150). The latter is a comedy Tennyson could have left behind in 1853, and accordingly he gives to the poem a larger frame of reference by transforming it into the temptations of aesthetic beauty. Hence the better-known version of "The Sea-Fairies" moves the delights of a beautiful land to the head of the fairies' song.

> Down shower the gambolling waterfalls
> From wandering over the lea:
> Out of the live-green heart of the dells
> They freshen the silvery-crimson shells.

*(lines 10–13)*

There is a subsequent invitation to come "frolic and play," but now the "play" is subordinate to the "gambolling waterfalls" rather than vice versa. Moreover, the line immediately succeeding the invitation to play is "Here it is only the mew that wails"—a line that ironically undercuts the allure of the "play" since "mew" contains a double reference to a seagull and to a cage or prison. The central lines of the later version, then, focus not on sensual delights but on the splendid but unsubstantial image of the rainbow, which "forms and flies on the land," "lives in the curve of the sand," and "hangs on the poising wave" in the fairies' realm. The fairies end by repeating to the mariners the invitation of the 1830 version to be their lords and to receive their kisses. But now the mariners' eyes will glisten "with pleasure and love and *jubilee*"; the more sexually charged "revelry," with its connotations of riotous physicality, has been tamed to joyous merry-making.

The two versions of "The Sea-Fairies" exemplify the overall progression of Tennyson's dramatic monologues. As in his adolescence, Tennyson continued to use the form in his Cambridge years to explore states of being with an immediate appeal. As his career progressed, however, he began to take greater account of his readers, shaping his dramatic monologues so that he could explore issues of great import to him and to his audience—hence the hint of an acceptable Victorian moral framework in the later "Sea-Fairies."

14. See Kincaid, pp. 26–27. Subsequent references appear in the text.

15. See Howard W. Fulweiler, "Tennyson and the 'Summons from the Sea,' " *VP* 3 (1965), 27–28.

16. See my article "The 'Mermaid' Poems: An Additional Source," *Tennyson Research Bulletin* 3, no. 3 (1979), 127–33.

17. See C. Tennyson, *Alfred Tennyson*, pp. 85–86. Subsequent references appear in the text.

18. See Priestley, p. 32, and Buckley, p. 36.

19. As Kincaid remarks, "The poem is rescued from . . . almost ludicrous melodrama by the fine stroke of changing the lady Oriana from a dear memory to an oppressive fear, a horrifying threat. The repetition of her name in nearly every other line supports this transition from devotion, to hypnotic adherance, to something like terror" (18).

20. As Priestley points out, both poems have "connections with the tradition of the ballad . . . an unusual stanza form, and . . . a refrain" (30).

21. Review of *Poems, Chiefly Lyrical* (1830) and *Poems* (1833), in *London Review*, 1835; quoted in John D. Jump, Ed., *Tennyson: The Critical Heritage* (London: Routledge & Kegan Paul, 1967), p. 86. Mill's point is antedated by Arthur Hallam in his essay "On Some of the Characteristics of Modern Poetry, and on the Lyrical Poems of Alfred Tennyson," published in the *Englishman's Magazine* in August 1831. In the essay Hallam terms the female portraits, of which "Mariana" is one, "a graft of the lyric on the dramatic" (*Writings*, 197).

22. See also John D. Boyd and Anne Williams, "Tennyson's 'Mariana' and 'Lyric Perspective,' " *SEL* 23 (1983), 590–91.

23. "Supposed Confessions" prepares for *In Memoriam* by centering doubt in the process of the mind and heart. In the later poem Tennyson finally derives comfort from just this process ("I have felt").

24. See William Cadbury, "The Utility of the Poetic Mask in Tennyson's 'Supposed Confessions,' " *MLQ* 24 (1963), 374–85, for an excellent discussion of this point.

25. I have emended the line as printed in the Norton Ricks edition, which reads, "Is is thus?"

# Chapter Three

1. Quoted by Ricks in his headnote to "Claribel."

2. Alan Sinfield also remarks on the blending of literal and figura-

tive in the poem's imagery, though to a different effect than my own, in "Tennyson's Imagery," *Neophilologus* 60 (1976), 467–68.

3. As in most of the mature monologues, Tennyson's exact participation in the poem is difficult to fathom. If, however, an incomplete fragment in the Trinity MSS was intended as a companion to "Fatima," we may have a clue. In this fragment, which appears in Notebook 22 with poems composed in 1833, the speaker begins, "I came with proposals of marriage / To Fatima, Selim's daughter" (reprinted by Ricks in "The Tennyson Manuscripts," *TLS*, 21 Aug. 1969, p. 918). But as the speaker approaches his destination and speaks with Fatima's father, the poem dissolves into nonsense verse. Apparently Tennyson could more easily imagine what it was like to be a woman wracked with desire than he could imagine a male "I" actually encountering such a woman.

4. The preceding line in this draft, however, is, "And after supper on a bed" (Harvard Notebook 4, folio 308). The notebooks in the Houghton Library at Harvard are identified under the number MS Eng. 952. 54m–203.

5. George O. Marshall, Jr., "Tennyson's 'The Sisters' and 'Porphyria's Lover,' " *Browning Newsletter* 3 (1969), 9–11.

6. See, e.g., Pattison; Donald S. Hair, *Domestic and Heroic in Tennyson's Poetry* (Toronto: U. of Toronto P., 1981); and William E. Fredeman, " 'The Sphere of Common Duties,' " *Bull. John Rylands Library* 54 (1972), 357–83. Clyde de L. Ryals notes that this poetry had its germ in the female portraits in his *Theme and Symbol in Tennyson's Poems to 1850* (Philadelphia: U. of Pennsylvania P., 1964), pp. 155–56.

7. As Robert Pattison and others have noted, the domestic poems are not purely Victorian inventions but fall within the idyll tradition begun by Theocritus. Perhaps Tennyson's fusion of the dramatic monologue form with an older, traditional form reflects his desire to transform the dramatic monologue into an objective poetry of universal appeal.

8. In flower language, the cowslip signified winning grace, the crowfoot ingratitude. See Kate Greenaway, illus., *The Illuminated Language of Flowers*, intro. Jean Marsh (New York: Holt, Rinehart & Winston, 1978). Greenaway's original 1884 edition was itself based on the vogue of flower language that flourished in the first four decades of the nineteenth century.

9. Tennyson appears to have written his own "May Queen" three years later, in 1830. See Ricks's headnote to the poem.

10. See Claude Colleer Abbott, *The Life and Letters of George Darley, Poet and Critic* (1928; rpt. Oxford: Clarendon P., 1967), p. 65.

11. Cecil Y. Lang and Edgar F. Shannon, Jr., eds., *The Letters of Alfred Lord Tennyson, Volume I: 1821-1850* (Cambridge: Harvard U. P., 1981), p. 148.

12. John H. Ingram, Biographical Sketch, in *Sylvia; or, The May Queen*, by George Darley (1827; rpt. London: J. M. Dent, 1892), p.v. Subsequent references to *Sylvia* appear in the text.

13. Abbott, p. 63.

14. Donald H. Reiman, in his introduction to a recently published edition of Darley's work, argues that Darley failed to find popularity with *Sylvia*, his best work, precisely because he did not relate it to the age: "Darley's failure clearly results not from lack of poetic talent but from dependence on a cut-flower tradition, rather than one rooted in the realities of his own life and the British society of his time" (Introduction, *George Darley* [New York: Garland, 1978], p. vi).

15. Review of *Poems, Chiefly Lyrical* (1830) and *Poems* (1833), in *London Review*, July 1835, rpt. in Jump, pp. 87-88.

16. See Ricks's headnote to the poem. "The Queen of the Meadow," a prose idyll, was first published in 1827, then reprinted in *Our Village* (1828).

17. Ricks suggests Tennyson's own participation in the poem when he argues that underlying the poem is Tennyson's wish to escape the domestic ills of his own family and to imagine a happy domestic life as an antidote (*Tennyson*, 101).

18. See Hair, pp. 67-68. Hair also discusses the theme of time and love and the mingling of joy and sorrow in the poem.

19. As noted by Hair (66). Both Hair and Pattison (53-58) relate the mixing of forms to Tennyson's drawing on the idyll tradition.

20. See also Loy D. Martin, "The Inside of Time," in *Robert Browning*, ed. Harold Bloom and Adrienne Munich (Englewood Cliffs, N.J.: Prentice-Hall, 1979), pp. 59-78. Subsequent references appear in the text.

21. Tennyson, incidentally, was extraordinarily sensitive to the nuance of tense. Commenting on "The Lord of Burleigh," he remarks, "The mood changes from happiness to unhappiness, and the present tense changes to the past" (cited by Ricks in *Poems*, 604 n.). My own attention to tense has been influenced by the work of Elizabeth Bruss in *Autobiographical Acts* (Baltimore: Johns Hopkins U. P., 1976).

22. As Hair notes, "The dramatic element includes a speaker, the 'I' of the poem; a listener who is not named but referred to specifically in lines 264-9; and an occasion, the showing of the portrait of Rose" (68). Hair also observes the mixing of forms and argues, as I do, that this mix is functional, though for different reasons; Hair sees the narrative

("The story centres on the approach to Rose") and the dramatic ("the drama centres on a commemorative approach, the unveiling") as complementary "ritual movements" associated with the myth of the Sleeping Beauty.

23. Trinity Notebook 17 (O.15.17), folios 38 and 37v. The second verse paragraph appears on 37v; a passage similar to it but canceled follows the first verse paragraph on folio 38.

24. The poem was begun in 1833 while Hallam was still alive, but the composition continued well after his death. Drafts of the poem in the Trinity MSS occur in notebooks dated from 1833 to 1837. Thus, the drafts seem to reflect Tennyson's responses to Hallam both alive and dead.

25. Quoted by Ricks in "Tennyson Manuscripts," p. 922.

26. The uncle's death leaves both Eustace and the speaker a tidy inheritance, and both are thus free to marry. If only this had happened in real life, Arthur Hallam and Emily Tennyson might actually have married; and Tennyson might have thought Rosa Baring would look upon him more kindly in similar hypothetical circumstances (see Ralph Rader, *Tennyson's Maud* [Berkeley: U. of California P., 1963], where he remarks that the published poem "hardly express[es] more than Tennyson's hopeful extrapolation of his incipient passion" [31]). Compare Ricks's observation cited earlier (n. 18).

27. Ricks, "Tennyson Manuscripts," p. 922. According to John Yearwood, Notebook 17 is dated 1833-35 (see "A Catalogue of the Tennyson Manuscripts at Trinity College, Cambridge," Ph.D. dissertation, University of Texas, 1977, p. 118). Tennyson's grandfather died 4 July 1835. Tennyson did not attend the funeral.

28. Trinity Notebook 26 (0.15.26), folio 16. On 10 Mar. 1833 Tennyson wrote to his Aunt Elizabeth Russell, "Of my Grandfather I have seen little for the last three years, he has so rooted an antipathy to me from some cause or other. . . . I fear he has little sympathy with any of his numerous descendants, except my uncle's family" (*Letters*, I, 89). Such thoughts in 1833 could explain Tennyson's killing off the sole financial anchor of his speaker, who then feels little grief, if the draft is indeed from 1833.

29. As Culler notes, the poem gives us "pictures within pictures within pictures" (*Poetry*, 119).

30. Pattison explicitly terms "Oenone" a pendant to "Fatima" (51-52). For the relation between "Oenone" and the female portraits, see also Ryals, pp. 79-80; Culler, *Poetry*, pp. 40, 80; Arthur J. Carr, "Tennyson as a Modern Poet," in *Critical Essays on the Poetry of Tennyson*, ed. John Killham (New York: Barnes & Noble, 1960), p. 52; and D. J.

Palmer, "Tennyson's Romantic Heritage," *Tennyson* (London: G. Bell & Sons, 1973), p. 38.

31. Paris's speech as rival song is made clearer in the 1832 version, where Oenone greets him upon arrival as her Apollo (see Ricks's notes to the poem). Presumably the appellation was dropped because Tennyson wanted to emphasize Paris as destroyer of Troy; Apollo, of course, built Troy.

32. See Ricks's notes to the poem for a transcription of the 1832 frame.

33. See Philip Gaskell, *From Writer to Reader* (Oxford: Oxford U. P., 1978), pp. 118-41, for a transcription of variants from the Trinity MSS; and Aidan Day, "Two Unrecorded Stages in the Revision of Tennyson's 'Oenone' for *Poems*, 1842," *The Library*, 6th ser., 2 (1980), 315-25. Day supplements Gaskell, and his discussion of the revisions is excellent.

34. Tennyson's term, as cited in Ricks's notes to the poem.

35. Cited by Ricks in his headnote to the poem. (Emphasis mine.)

36. See Bush, pp. 205-6; Gerhard Joseph, "Tennyson's Concepts of Knowledge, Wisdom, and Pallas Athene," *MP* 69 (1972), 317-18; Kincaid, pp. 37-38; and Culler, *Poetry*, p. 78.

37. The epyllion, "a short elaboration of tradition[al] mythology" (Pattison, 29), fused brevity with "epic proportion" (31). Both Pattison and Hair view "Oenone" as an epyllion, and their view seems plausible. Unfortunately, "Oenone" would have to be termed a flawed epyllion.

38. Donna G. Fricke makes a similar claim, though within a different context: the "theme is creation, endless cyclic regeneration, and whose form is open and cyclic" ("Tennyson's *The Hesperides*," *Tennyson Research Bull.* 1 [1970], 103).

39. Bernard Comrie, *Aspect* (Cambridge, Eng., 1976), p. 49; cited by Loy D. Martin, pp. 59-60.

40. See Gerhard Joseph, "Tennyson's Three Women," *VP* 19 (1981), 7, where he notes that the "numerical symbolicity calls specific, unignorable attention to itself, and when that happens the exegetical problem becomes one of an overabundance of possibilities."

41. G. Robert Stange, "Tennyson's Garden of Art: A Study of *The Hesperides*," *PMLA* 67 (1952), 732-43; and James D. Merriman, "The Poet as Heroic Thief," *VNL* 35 (1969), 1-5.

42. Culler makes a similar point ("the introduction . . . is quite as lazy and indolent as the long, loping strophes that follow" [*Poetry*, 53]), as does W. David Shaw in *Tennyson's Style* (Ithaca: Cornell U. P., 1976), p. 66.

43. As Kincaid remarks, "We are unable to resist the appeal of the

mariners and equally unable to yield to it." Thus, in the end, "Ulysses and the mariners who eat the lotos have an easier time of it than the reader; they, at least, can make choices and dissolve the tension" (38–41). I take a rather more unequivocal view of the reader's role. Throughout the discussion of the reader's role here and elsewhere I am indebted to Wolfgang Iser's work on reader-response theory, particularly to his study *The Implied Reader* (Baltimore: Johns Hopkins U. P., 1974).

44. It is more than a little curious that, in describing the flow of consciousness, Julian Jaynes uses so many metaphors that appear in "The Lotos-Eaters": "And the feeling of a great uninterrupted stream of rich inner experiences, now slowly gliding through dreamy moods, now tumbling in excited torrents down gorges of precipitous insight, or surging evenly through our nobler days, is what it is on this page, a metaphor for how subjective consciousness seems to subjective consciousness" (*The Origin of Consciousness in the Breakdown of the Bicameral Mind* [Boston: Houghton Mifflin, 1976], p. 24). The similarity is perhaps to be expected, however, in that Tennyson is clearly dealing, not with an actual, but with an interior landscape and debate.

45. See Alan Grob, "Tennyson's 'The Lotos-Eaters,'" *MP* 62 (1964), 118–29, for a fine discussion of the changes between the 1832 and the 1842 versions of the poem. Grob focuses on theme and symbol, I on structure and the reader's role.

46. Cited by Ricks in his notes to the poem.

47. See also Priestley, pp. 57–58.

48. See also Alicia Ostriker, "The Three Modes in Tennyson's Prosody," *PMLA* 82 (1967), 276; and Priestley, p. 58.

49. See Ricks's headnote to the poem, and appended to the text, his reprinting of the deleted stanza.

50. James Knowles, "Aspects of Tennyson," *Nineteenth Century* 33 (Jan. 1893), 182.

51. See my "Dramatis and Private Personae: 'Ulysses' Revisited," *VP* 17 (1979), 192–203. A correction needs to be added to the essay. Since the issuing of Tennyson's *Letters* (1981), it appears that Tennyson did not stay at home continuously with his family after hearing of Hallam's death. Instead, like his own Ulysses, he fled the domestic sphere of common duties for London and, presumably, those who had known Hallam. Indeed, "Ulysses" was written in London. Edward FitzGerald wrote to W. B. Donne on 25 Oct. 1833 to say that "Tennyson has been in town for some time" (I, 95). The MS of "Ulysses," according to Ricks's headnote, is dated 20 Oct. 1833. Robert Martin

further details the relation between domestic worries and Tennyson's grief for Hallam (178–86).

My essay also summarizes critical approaches to "Ulysses." More has been written on "Ulysses" since my essay appeared, but in general these more recent essays fall into the categories I delineate.

52. As Culler notes (*Poetry*, 94).

53. Culler also notes the shift in terminology (*Poetry*, 95).

54. Some will disagree with me on this point. It is interesting, however, that in the Harvard MS of "Ulysses" (Notebook 16, folios 11, 11v, and 12) the Telemachus passage occurs only as an addition to the poem. Versions of the first, second, and fourth verse paragraphs as we know them run in uninterrupted succession. There is, following the last line, a lacuna of about a third of a page, and only then does the Telemachus passage appear. The implication is that the other verse paragraphs constitute the bedrock of the poem, Tennyson's first thoughts, and that the passage that has caused so much critical controversy was something of an afterthought. Tennyson's reason for adding the passage seems clear in light of the pattern of consciousness I trace here. Without the Telemachus passage, Ulysses rushes from his imaginative into his actual voyage, as if he were hurtling into the future. This befits neither an old man nor his thinking. Thus Ulysses in the version we know returns to the domestic scene as both an aesthetic balance and corrective to the first paragraph.

55. Yearwood, p. 106. As Christopher Ricks notes in "Tennyson Inheriting the Earth," "again and again Tennyson's . . . self-borrowing manifests both an awareness of, and a means of countering, time" (71).

56. See Shaw, *Tennyson's Style*, pp. 94–95, who notes the timelessness of the infinitives but by way of making a point very different from my own.

57. Trinity notebook 20 (0.15.20), folio 3v.

58. The fragment "Semele," written as a dramatic monologue and placed after "Tiresias" in Ricks's edition, pursues a similar theme. Semele dies, but her son Dionysius is born after she has been reduced to ashes.

59. Culler also compares the two poems, though to a different effect (*Poetry*, 99–105).

60. See Nash, "Tennyson," *Cambridge Quarterly* 6 (1975), 326–49.

61. As Culler notes (*Poetry*, 108). He also observes the hovering of the "Morte" between one state and another as a result of the addition of "The Epic": "The poem as a whole is called *The Epic*, and its center is

neither in the frame nor in the inset but somewhere between the two. It hovers back and forth between the reading of the poem, which is initiated by the first part of the frame, and its reception, which is detailed by the second—between these and the poem itself. Hence the poem's quality as art can actually be emphasized."

62. As demonstrated in the Harvard MSS, "The Epic," like "The Gardener's Daughter," began explicitly as a dramatic monologue centered squarely in the present. Its opening lines were

> *Why what you ask—if any writer now*
> *May take the style of some heroic age*
> *Gone like the mastodon—nay, why should he*
> *Remodel models rather than the life?*
> *Yet this belief was lately half-unhinged*
> *At Edward Allen's—on the Christmas Eve.*

> *(Harvard Loosepaper 53)*

These lines were transposed to their present position and the dramatic edge removed, presumably for the same reasons as in "The Gardener's Daughter": Tennyson wished to underscore the framing rather than the presence of what followed.

63. See Ricks's headnote to the poem.

64. See also John R. Reed, *Perception and Design in Tennyson's Idylls of the King* (Athens: Ohio U. P., 1969), pp. 17–18; Wendell Stacy Johnson, *Sex and Marriage in Victorian Poetry* (Ithaca: Cornell U. P., 1975), pp. 120–21; and Kerry McSweeney, *Tennyson and Swinburne as Romantic Naturalists* (Toronto: U. of Toronto P., 1981), pp. 53–55; all of whom see "The Two Voices" as a dramatic poem, with the mind in converse with itself.

65. See Judith Weissman, "Vision, Madness, and Morality," *Georgia Review* 33 (1979), who relates "The Two Voices" to Julian Jaynes's examination of schizophrenic voices in *Origin of Consciousness* (143).

66. See W. David Shaw, "The Transcendentalist Problem in Tennyson's Poetry of Debate," *PQ* 46 (1967), 81–83.

67. Quoted by Ricks, "Tennyson Manuscripts," p. 922.

68. See also Reed, pp. 21–22.

69. Perhaps "St. Simeon" was inspired by Tennyson's work on the four versions of "St. Lawrence," a poem never published. In one of the drafts preserved in the Trinity Notebooks, we see Tennyson suddenly struck by the latent absurdity of a man who submits to being grilled over a fire like a beefsteak, by the latent hubris of one obsessed by martyrdom, and by the notion that the concrete, unambiguous act

could be accompanied by mental reservation. See Ricks, "Tennyson Manuscripts," pp. 919-20, for a transcription of this draft. Yearwood gives the date of Notebook 15, in which this draft appears, as 1833. Since this draft was written in 1833, the same year "St. Simeon Stylites" was begun, Tennyson may have decided to pursue the latter as a means of fully developing the vein he had stumbled upon in the draft of "St. Lawrence."

70. Compare W. David Shaw's discussion of idolatrous ("full but unstable intrinsic signifiers, which tell us more about man's experience than God") vs. agnostic language ("stable but extrinsic signifiers, which concede the impossibility of defining God"). Although not mentioning "St. Simeon Stylites," Shaw remarks that the agnostic theory of language dominates most of Tennyson's poems dealing with the nature of God ("The Agnostic Imagination in Victorian Poetry," *Criticism* 22 [1980], 125, 116-17).

71. Cited in Ricks's notes to the poem.

72. Not surprisingly, Browning wrote to Alfred Domett that " 'St. Simeon Stylites' . . . I think perfect." See *Robert Browning and Alfred Domett*, p. 41. The letter is dated 13 July 1842.

73. William Fredeman makes a similar point (" 'A Sign Betwixt the Meadow and the Cloud,' " *UTQ* 38 [1968], 74-75).

74. Tennyson, of course, is no doubt playing off the widely held maxim of *mens sana in corpore sano* (see Bruce Haley, *The Healthy Body and Victorian Culture* [Cambridge: Harvard U. P., 1978], passim). As Tennyson himself wrote to his Aunt Russell in 1844, "What price is too high for health, and health of mind is so involved with health of body" (*Letters*, I, 224).

75. See also Kincaid, who argues that the poem, both "ludicrous and profound," "disgusting and funny," leaves the reader caught squarely between sympathy and judgment since both are simultaneously appealed to (47-49).

76. As Michael Mason would suggest (see chapter one).

77. See Ricks, *Tennyson* (108-9), for another view of the personal elements in the poem.

78. If "St. Simeon Stylites" was begun as a counter treatment of the theme of "The Two Voices," we can also see why the resolution of "The Two Voices" rings false—it, too, like Simeon's faith, comes from without.

79. Both drafts are reprinted by Ricks, "Tennyson Manuscripts," p. 920. The lyric was likely begun two years after "Will Waterproof."

80. Paul Turner, *Tennyson* (London: Routledge & Kegan Paul, 1976), p. 94.

81. And, as Turner suggests, the problem of resisting sorrow as well, if "water" is linked to tears (94).

82. Ricks observes the confusion—or "merging," as he terms it—of the myths of Amphion and Orpheus, but notes that "in Skelton's *Garland of Laurel* Amphion too made the trees dance" (see Ricks's headnote to the poem). But the satiric treatment of the speaker as a whole suggests that the mistake in mythology is *meant* as the mistake of a poet too indifferent to tradition to get the details right.

83. Perhaps in lines 20–21, 33–34, and 52 Tennyson was remembering Sir William Jones's "Arcadia." In the poem Tityrus (Virgil) is one of many suitors for Menelaus's (Theocritus's) two daughters (the elevated and plain pastoral strains). Several have failed in the contest when Virgil steps forth: "He now begins: the dancing hills attend, / And knotty oaks from mountain-tops descend." But Virgil wins an entirely different response from his listeners than does the speaker of "Amphion": "He play'd so sweetly, and so sweetly sung, / That on each note the enraptured audience hung." See Jones's *Poems* (London: Suttaby, Evance & Fox, 1818), p. 18.

84. Cited in Ricks's headnote to the poem.

85. The poem has often been read nonironically. Yet even June S. Hagen, who feels that Tennyson sympathizes with the speaker, notes that the persona tries to rhyme *attendance* with *tendons* (lines 62, 64) and that Tennyson himself was never willing to contract his own vision to correspond to the age ("Tennyson's Use of the Impersonative Mode in a Minor Art Cluster," *Susquehanna U. Studies* 11 [1979], 19-21).

86. See Rader, *Maud*, passim, for the fullest account of their relationship.

87. Tennyson's comment is typically defensive: "A dramatic poem drawn from no particular character" (cited by Ricks in his headnote to the poem).

88. See, e.g., Richard B. Hovey, "Tennyson's 'Locksley Hall,' " *Forum* (Houston) 4 (1963), 24-30; and particularly F. E. L. Priestley, "Locksley Hall Revisited," *Queens Quarterly* 81 (1974), 512-32.

89. His fantasy of retreating to a lawless exotic island is clearly associated with his past. In an early draft, Locksley Hall was his birthplace; in later drafts Tennyson changed the birthplace to the Orient (see Ricks's notes to the poem).

90. Courtship, of course, is also at once intensely private and intensely social. Kenneth Burke illuminates this dual nature of courtship: "Courtship, love, is 'mystery.' For love is a communion of estranged entities, and strangeness is a condition of mystery. . . . When courtship attains its equivalent in the realm of *group* relations, differences

between the sexes has its analogue in the difference between *social classes*" (177).

91. Ricks, *Tennyson*, p. 166.

92. "Edwin Morris," although not published until 1851, was written in 1839 and so is discussed here.

93. As noted, e.g., by Wendell Stacy Johnson ("The Theme of Marriage in Tennyson," *VNL* 12 [1957], 7); and Culler (*Poetry*, 125).

94. As Rader comments, "In the bittersweet idyl 'Edwin Morris,' begun a year or so later than 'Locksley Hall,' Tennyson was able to contemplate his memories of Rosa more objectively, and so, appropriately, he chose a spokesman who was also at some distance from his frustration and thus was able to take a less feverish view of it than the speaker of 'Locksley Hall' " (*Maud*, 57).

95. For a different approach, see McSweeney (60–62), who argues that the real energy of the poem resides in section IV, or the monologue, because Tennyson's sensibility gravitated more easily toward a naturalistic than toward a theistic conception of the order of things. Perhaps McSweeney is responding to the power of the dramatic monologue's recursive loop that allows Tennyson to participate in the libertine's monologue, to imagine the sinner as an aspect of self.

# Chapter Four

1. The point is also made by Catherine Barnes Stevenson in "The Aesthetic Function of the 'Weird Seizures' in *The Princess*," *VNL* 45 (1974), 22–25. My reading of the poem parallels Stevenson's on a number of points. See also Anita B. Draper, "The Artistic Contribution of the 'Weird Seizures' to *The Princess*," *VP* 17 (1979), 180–91.

2. "The Vision of Sin" in fact seems to have been written about the same time Tennyson first contemplated writing *The Princess*. Hallam Tennyson records that Tennyson "talked over the plan of the poem with my mother in 1839" (*Memoir*, I, 248), the same approximate date of composition Ricks assigns to "The Vision of Sin."

3. The introductions Tennyson considered placing at the head of each section appear in Harvard Notebook 23, folios 1,2. The first two introductions are as follows:

*II*
*I said my say; then Walter with a glance*
*At Lilia, meditating malice, took*

*The person of the Prince: but months have gone*
*I can but give the substance not the words*

*III*

*third*
*The ~~next~~ that spoke, tho' steersman of our boat*
*cried*
*At college, fear'd to steer the tale & ~~raised his voice~~*
*Against it—nothing could be done—but urged*
*By common voice, continued as he might.*

4. E. G. Withycombe, *Oxford Dictionary of English Christian Names*, 2nd ed. (Oxford: Oxford U. P., 1950). Another reference work on names, published during Tennyson's lifetime, has an equally interesting explanation of Ida's name. *Ida* means "no body's daughter," and *Idas* means "son," according to Harry Alfred Long in *Personal and Family Names* (Glasgow: Thomas D. Morison, 1883), p. 105. Victorian writers sometimes argued, however, that *Ida* was derived from Saxon for "happy."

5. Virtually every name Tennyson uses in the poem has in fact been carefully chosen. Cyril, the most conventionally chauvinistic of the three young men, has a name meaning "lord" or "master." As Withycombe observes, *Cyril* became popular in the nineteenth century since the Tractarians favored it as the name of an early Church Father. Not surprisingly, therefore, Cyril quests after Lady Psyche, or the soul. The good Sir Walter who opens up his estate to the Institute is also well named. *Walter* comes from the Old German *vald*, meaning "rule," and *harja*, or "folk." Tennyson's father, incidentally, owned Nathan Bailey's work *An Universal Etymological Dictionary*, a copy of which is housed at the Tennyson Research Centre in Lincoln. Bailey provides etymologies only for *Melissa* (the meaning of *Meliscent* is given as Greek for "Honey-sweet") and *Walter* (from Saxon for "to rule" and "an army"). See Patrick G. Scott, " 'Flowering in a Lonely Word,' " *VP* 18 (1980), 371–81, for a fuller discussion of Tennyson's sensitivity to and interest in etymology.

6. As the *Memoir* records Tennyson saying, "The sections were written at many different places, and as the phases of our intercourse came to my memory and suggested them. I did not write them with any view of weaving them into a whole, or for publication, until I found that I had written so many" (I, 304).

7. Michael Mason, in "The Timing of *In Memoriam*" (*Studies in Tennyson*, ed. Hallam Tennyson), argues that "*In Memoriam* is a very different sort of dramatic poem from such contemporary specimens of dramatic poetry as Browning's monologues. Indeed, given the striking failure of

some of the latter to be 'dramatic' in the sense of communicating a state of mind and feeling different from the author's, they may be said to be antithetical to *In Memoriam* in character. *In Memoriam* is a personal poem which became impersonal, while 'Bishop Blougram's Apology', for instance, is an apparently impersonal poem which fails to exclude the personal" (164–65).

8. See Susan Shatto and Marion Shaw, eds., *In Memoriam* (Oxford: Oxford U. P., 1982), for evidence in dating individual sections, as well as Ricks's headnote to the poem. Shatto and Shaw date the first four lines of section I as between 1837 and 1840 whereas Ricks posits that the entire section was written after 1846.

9. Compare Alan Sinfield's remark that *In Memoriam's* structure is analogous to that of the novel, except for the absence of "linking passages"; see *The Language of Tennyson's "In Memoriam"* (New York: Barnes & Noble, 1971), p. 27. See also Mason, "Timing of *In Memoriam*," p. 165.

10. Knowles, p. 182. Shatto and Shaw remark that Tennyson's practice in the Trinity and Lincoln MSS of the poem was apparently to leave the verso and the bottom half of each recto leaf blank so that additional sections could be easily added (12).

11. As reported by Knowles, p. 182. See also Ian H. C. Kennedy, "*In Memoriam* and the Tradition of Pastoral Elegy," *VP* 15 (1977), 351–66. Kennedy persuasively demonstrates that Tennyson drew on conventions of the pastoral elegy only to "subvert" and "explode" them, hence playing on the reader's expectations. This approach would also demand a very active reader.

12. Queen Victoria "substituted 'widow' for "widower' and 'her' for 'his' in the lines 'Tears of a widower.' " Letter from the Duke of Argyll, quoted by C. Tennyson, p. 336; additional instances of Queen Victoria's annotations are also given on this page.

13. I am here indebted to McSweeney. He argues that two views of nature are juxtaposed in *In Memoriam*: Nature, which is "linear," "progressive," "scientific"; and nature, "simply the immemorial sights and sounds of the English landscape," a nature that has an "ebb-and-flow movement and is non-progressive." McSweeney's assertion of these juxtaposed views led me to reconsider other juxtapositions in the poem. See McSweeney, pp. 79–81.

14. Compare Alan Sinfield's discussion of the poem as at once the "linnet" or utterance of individual songs and the "artifact" (*Language*).

15. Sinfield, *Language*, p. 156. See also J. C. C. Mays, "*In Memoriam*," *UTQ* 35 (1965), 26–27.

16. If we count from the poem's opening to the first anniversary of Hallam's death, the first year lasts from sections I through LXXII. If we

work only with the Christmas divisions, the first year lasts from sections XXVIII through LXXVIII, a total of fifty sections; the second year lasts from sections LXXIX through CIV, a total of twenty-five sections; and the final year lasts from sections CV through CXXXI, a total of twenty-six sections.

17. See Shaw for a rather different discussion of catharsis embedded in the poem's form (*Tennyson's Style*, pp. 139–40).

18. Dolores Ryback Rosenblum makes a similar point about the dilemma of the poet's present in relation to his past and future in "The Act of Writing in *In Memoriam*," *VP* 18 (1980), 120. Her essay as a whole traces the way in which the poet comes to realize that the act of writing itself is his best means of achieving continuity between past, present, and future. Her reading thus posits another larger structural pattern related to the poet's consciousness.

19. Only after independently mapping out these alternations between separation and union did I observe that my divisions of the poem virtually reproduce Tennyson's own. But whereas I place each cycle of separation and union into a single division (five in all), Tennyson (with one exception) subdivided each strand of this emotional and psychological dialectic to end up with nine divisions. The correlation between Tennyson's and my own divisions of the poem is indicated below in tabular form.

| *Cycles of Separation and Union* | *Tennyson's Divisions* |
|---|---|
| Cycle 1 | |
| Separation I–VIII | I. I–VIII |
| Union      IX–XXI | II. IX–XX |
| Cycle 2 | |
| Separation XXII–XXVII | III. XX–XXVII |
| Union      XXVIII–XLIX | IV. XXVIII–XLIX |
| Cycle 3 | |
| Separation L–LVIII | V. L–LVIII |
| Union      LIX–LXXI | VI. LIX–LXXI |
| Cycle 4 | |
| Separation LXXII–LXXXXIX | VII. LXXII–XCVIII |
| Union      XC–XCVII | |
| Cycle 5 | |
| Separation XCVIII–CIII | VIII. XCIX–CIII |
| Union      CIV–CXXXI | IX. CIV–CXXXI |

20. See also Francis Devlin, "Dramatic Irony in the Early Sections

of Tennyson's *In Memoriam*," *PLL* 8 (1972), 172–83, for yet another larger structural pattern of consciousness. Devlin's point is that in the early sections the poet unwittingly utters the answers to his dilemmas but does not recognize their significance until later. Thus the poet turns the image of Phosphor into "an image of intense loss" in section IX and only discovers the larger, reassuring meaning of Phosphor in the Hesper-Phosphor section late in the poem (CXXI).

21. The importance of letting Sorrow speak directly at this stage of the poem is underlined by evidence from the MSS since in an early version the words are given to the poet (see Ricks's notes to the section).

22. Emily's eyes seem to have been one of her most remarkable features. As Emily Sellwood Tennyson said of her sister-in-law, "Emily had wonderful eyes; depths on depths they seemed to have." Quoted by Jack Kolb, ed., *The Letters of Arthur Henry Hallam* (Columbus: Ohio State U. P., 1981), p. 478 n.

23. Hallam's and the poet's mutual participation in process is reiterated in the Epilogue. There the poet announces that the years succeeding Hallam's death have "remade the blood and changed the frame, / And yet is love not less, but more" (lines 11–12). The poet does not say "*my* blood," for that would negate the deliberately ambiguous reference that acts to connect and conflate Hallam and the poet. *Both* their bodily frames have changed, through death and time. Yet "love"—again not "my love," but most likely "our love"—has grown.

The Epilogue's succeeding stanzas clearly echo section CIII, so that the "statue solid-set . . . moulded in colossal calm" and the growth to "something greater" (allusively and directly) apply at once to Hallam and the poet.

24. Cited by Ricks in his introduction to the poem, p. 861.

25. See, e.g., Peter Allan Dale, who points to the echo of Hallam's translation of Dante's *Vita Nuova* (" 'Gracious Lies,' " *VP* 18 [1980], 162); Harold Bloom, who argues that section CIII echoes in content and structure Tennyson's "Recollections of the Arabian Nights," one of Hallam's favorite poems by Tennyson (150–52); Ricks, who notes the echoes of Hallam's poems ("Tennyson Inheriting the Earth," 76, 83, 89); and Hallam's own *"Theodicaea Novissima."* In this last Hallam stresses the evolving nature of the man/god Christ ("the Godhead of the Son has not been a fixed, invariable thing from the beginning: he is more God now than he was once; and will be perfectly united to God hereafter" [*Writings*, 204]). Hallam also emphasizes the rewards granted to enduring love: "The strength of love in sublunary concerns is manifested by collision with opposing principles. When amidst

doubt and ignorance and suffering, and temptation, a heart perseveres in love, we may be sure of the indomitable character of that heart's affection" (205).

26. Hair, pp. 66, 69–71. In fact, as Ricks notes in his edition, Tennyson drew upon unadopted lines for "The Miller's Daughter" to compose one of the intercalary songs.

27. Edmund liked dramatic monologues, too, allowing the brook to speak in the first person in his verses. Thus, we in essence get a dramatic monologue within a dramatic monologue, a voice within a voice.

28. As Hallam Tennyson has remarked, "Mr Maurice had been ejected from his professorship at King's College for non-orthodoxy" (cited by Ricks in his introduction to the poem).

29. Shaw prefers the metaphor of the cinema to the videotape (*Tennyson's Style*, 170ff.).

30. See, e.g., Culler, who remarks that "both are composite poems, consisting of a series of meditation[s] or lyrics arranged in a certain order," and that both poems are, in essence, "monodramas" (*Poetry*, 190). Ricks, rather like Tennyson dividing *In Memoriam* into nine phases, finds seven distinct phases of passion in *Maud* (*Tennyson*, 256–60). Pattison argues that *Maud* extended the format of *In Memoriam*, in which "a lyric element was introduced to display the speaker's changing emotional states, and this lyric element was finally wedded to the idyll form in a unified poetry capable of tackling a variety of human moods and attitudes" (129).

31. As Ricks notes (*Tennyson*, 253).

32. Shaw also remarks on the "cathartic power of drama" in the poem, but in reference to the catharsis undergone by Tennyson rather than by the hero (*Tennyson's Style*, 190).

33. He could have provided a frame as a reference point, of course, and still have written a dramatic poem. Perhaps the success of *In Memoriam*, the gaps of which seemed to present readers no problem, convinced Tennyson a frame was unnecessary.

34. Culler, "Monodrama," pp. 366–85.

35. Sinfield uses the term "Super-monologue" (*Dramatic Monologue*, 35ff.).

36. As Yearwood remarks, "the most consistent revision Tennyson seems to have made in the poem between this draft [the Trinity MS] and publication was the changing of statements into questions" (325). See also Sinfield, who likewise observes the gaps, or "leaps from section to section and in the speaker's mind," and the combining of image patterns so that "the capacity of dramatic monologue to draw the reader into an alien pattern of thought is nowhere more fully ex-

ploited" (*Dramatic Monologue*, 36–37). Perhaps Tennyson is so insistent on exercising the reader because he wants the reader, like his hero, to break out of the confines of self and through sympathy, a form of love, identify with what has hitherto been unknown and alien. In this respect *Maud* builds upon Tennyson's earlier domestic monologues, which also depend on the exercising and extension of the emotions.

37. For *Maud's* image patterns, see E. D. H. Johnson, "The Lily and the Rose," *PMLA* 64 (1949), 1222–27; and John Killham, "Tennyson's *Maud*—The Function of the Imagery," Killham, *Critical Essays on the Poetry of Tennyson*, pp. 219–35. For the psychology of the hero, see Robert James Mann, *Tennyson's "Maud" Vindicated: An Explanatory Essay* (1856), partially reprinted in Jump, pp. 197–211; Roy Basler, "Tennyson the Psychologist," *SAQ* 43 (1944), 143–59; A. S. Byatt, "The Lyric Structure of Tennyson's *Maud*," in *Major Victorian Poets*, ed. Isobel Armstrong (Lincoln: U. of Nebraska P., 1969), pp. 69–92; Reed, pp. 29–47; and Ricks, *Tennyson*, pp. 246–63. Ricks notes that the hero's divided mind is a subject well suited to Tennyson's dramatic power, a subject he had explored in earlier dramatic monologues (250).

38. Mann, in Jump, p. 199.

39. See also Edward Stokes, "The Metrics of *Maud*," *VP* 2 (1964), 97–110.

40. Quoted by Ricks in his notes. James Knowles, according to Gordon Ray, actually recorded an even less affirmative statement from Tennyson: "*He is not quite sane—a little shattered*" ("Tennyson Reads *Maud*," in *Romantic and Victorian: Studies in Memory of William H. Marshall*, ed. W. Paul Elledge and Richard L. Hoffman [Rutherford, N.J.: Fairleigh Dickinson U. P., 1971], p. 300).

41. Virginia Woolf, *Freshwater*, ed. Lucio P. Ruotolo (New York: Harcourt Brace Jovanovich, 1976), p. 9. Woolf first wrote *Freshwater* in 1923, then revised it when it was privately performed in 1935. The part of Tennyson was played by Virginia's younger brother, Adrian Stephen.

42. The pervasive alliteration and rhyme also draw attention to words as words and so may function to reinforce the poem's many references to sound as noise. As Ian H. C. Kennedy has argued, one of the hero's dilemmas is a crisis of language; that is, the hero must determine whether language is mere noise or a means of genuine communication. See "The Crisis of Language in Tennyson's *Maud*," *TSLL* 19 (1977), 161–78.

43. Because alliteration also links "sorrow" and "seize," the alliterative pattern perhaps serves as adumbration: "sorrow seize . . . [my] leading light."

44. See James R. Bennett, "The Historical Abuse of Literature," *ES* 62 (1981), 34–45, in which Bennett carefully presents all relevant documentary evidence that Tennyson was not endorsing the Crimean War in *Maud*. On the other hand, Tennyson's political poems of 1852 (including "The Penny-Wise" and "Rifle Clubs!!!") are distinctly "hawkish."

45. Of course Tennyson did not have Withycombe's text at his disposal. Yet the etymology of the name Maud seems to have been commonly known in the nineteenth century. Charlotte Yonge translated *Maud* as "mighty battle maid," a meaning not far removed from Withycombe's etymology (*History of Christian Names*, rev. ed. [London: Macmillan, 1884], p. xcix; the first edition of Yonge's *History* was published in 1863).

46. James Bennett, "*Maud*, Part III," *VP* 18 (1980), 37. Shaw also comments on the hero's perception of Maud in relation to love and death: "The speaker first worships Maud because she is immaculate light free from the grossness of the blood-red wood. But he also recognizes the equivalence of such worship with desire for death. When Maud is fully detached, 'a silent lightning under the stars' (III, 9), she is dead" (*Tennyson's Style*, 175).

47. Rader, *Maud*, p. 88. See Rader, passim, for a complete account of the autobiographical basis of *Maud*.

48. J. B. Steane makes a similar point in *Tennyson* (London: Evans Brothers Ltd., 1966), pp. 101–2.

# Chapter Five

1. Criticisms made, respectively, by Yeats ("Modern Poetry," *Essays and Introductions* [London: Macmillan, 1961], p. 497); Pound ("A Retrospect," *Literary Essays of Ezra Pound* [New York: New Directions, 1968], p. 11); and Eliot ("The Metaphysical Poets," *Selected Essays* pp. 247–48). See also Ricks, *Tennyson*, p. 290.

2. Cited by R. Martin, p. 455. FitzGerald, of course, was hardly an authority on wise marriages.

3. Valerie Pitt likewise attributes the failures among later poems, not to moral themes, since these were also a part of the earlier poetry, but to a failure of technique; see *Tennyson Laureate* (Toronto: U. of Toronto P., 1963), pp. 259–67.

4. See Ricks's headnote to "Tithonus."

5. Both R. Martin (479) and Clyde de L. Ryals (*From the Great Deep* [Athens: Ohio U. P., 1967], pp. 150-51) note the connection between "Lucretius" and "The Holy Grail."

6. James Kissane, *Alfred Tennyson* (New York: Twayne, 1970), p. 125.

7. See also Kincaid, pp. 143-44; and Joshua Adler, whose fine reading also illuminates Tennyson's skillful use of biblical allusion ("Tennyson's 'Mother of Sorrows,' " *VP* 12 [1974], 363-69).

8. Harvard Loosepaper 213 (the loose papers, in contrast to the notebooks, are identified at the Houghton Library under the number bMS Eng. 952.1 54m-204). The lines quoted from Loosepaper 213 are labeled in a hand other than Tennyson's, "Beginning of Rizpah." (If one inverts the Aldworth notepaper on which the lines appear, one finds a draft of the opening lines of the published version.) In revising, Tennyson also increased the violence of the speaker's treatment in the insane asylum, again emphasizing the barbarity that can pass for conventional wisdom. In an early draft the public responds to the woman's hearing inner voices only by sequestering her: "They seized me & shut me up—they bound me down on my bed" (Harvard Loosepaper 215). In the published poem, they go further: "They beat me for that, they beat me" (line 48).

9. See also Clarice Short, "Tennyson and 'The Lover's Tale,' " *PMLA* 82 (1967), 81-83, for a discussion of the autobiographical elements of the poem based on Tennyson's early experience.

10. These lines appeared in the 1832 trial edition but were thereafter canceled (cited by Ricks in his notes to the poem).

11. Compare Culler, who remarks that the poem's first three parts constitute not "a tale but a Romantic exploration of the psychology of the teller" (*Poetry*, 36). Herbert F. Tucker, Jr., while observing that Julian addresses his friends, terms the poem a narrative "in which the least takes place. . . . nothing significantly changes because stasis is its subject: we might indeed call it a narrative about the paralysis of the narrative faculty" ("Tennyson's Narrative of Desire," *VNL* 62 [1982], 22). Tucker argues that Julian's self-involved Romantic imaginings of love allow no room for love itself.

12. Short, p. 80.

13. See, e.g., Short, p. 80, and Culler, *Poetry*, pp. 35-36.

14. *Julian* (so named only in 1868) signifies "downy bearded," according to Yonge's *History*.

15. Cited by Ricks in his headnote to "The Holy Grail."

16. See especially Ryals, *Great Deep*, pp. 146-79. Culler is one of the few to concede the dodge but to question the art (*Poetry*, 227-30).

17. Jean Watson Rosenbaum, "Apples and Milkmaids," *Studia Mystica* 4 (1981), 28–31.

18. As John Rosenberg points out, Percivale himself is not only lost but dead and gone before we ever hear his voice: "We learn that after the Grail quest Percivale had become a monk in a distant abbey 'and not long after, died.' As we overhear the posthumous voice of Percivale the present seems visibly to recede before our eyes . . . for the narrator who describes . . . is now himself a ghost" (*The Fall of Camelot* [Cambridge: Harvard U. P., 1973], p. 58). This ploy not only achieves greater distance on Percivale's tale, as Rosenberg suggests, but also emphasizes that Percivale is dead to the world in a literal as well as a metaphorical sense.

19. See Pattison (141) and Hair (176–80) for additional commentary on monologues in the *Idylls*.

20. See also Virendra Sharma, *Studies in Victorian Verse Drama*, Salzburg Studies in English Literature no. 14 (Salzburg: Institut für Anglistik und Amerikanistik, Universität Salzburg, 1979), pp. 135–37; and Dennis M. Organ, *Tennyson's Dramas*, Graduate Studies, Texas Tech. U., no. 17 (Lubbock: Texas Tech. P., 1979), pp. 31, 32, 119. Organ's study is the most astute and sympathetic appraisal of the dramas to date.

21. *Tennyson: Poems and Plays*, ed, T. Herbert Warren, rev. & enlarged by Frederick Page (London: Oxford U. P., 1971), act I, scene v.

22. Washington Irving, *The Life and Voyages of Christopher Columbus*, Author's Rev. Ed. (Philadelphia: Lippincott, 1871), II, 563. Irving was Tennyson's acknowledged source for the poem.

23. See my "Tennyson's 'Columbus': 'Sense at War with Soul' Again," *VP* 15 (1977), 171–76.

24. Max Eastman, *The Sense of Humor* (New York: Charles Scribner's Sons, 1921), p. 43. Subsequent references appear in the text.

25. I wish to thank Max Keith Sutton and Patrick G. Scott for calling my attention to the influence of Barnes on Tennyson. The connection is also noted by P. Turner, p. 174. As for Burns, Tennyson visited Kirk Alloway in 1849 and thereafter wrote to Aubrey de Vere, "I made a pilgrimage thither out of love for the great peasant. . . . I know you do not care much for him but I do and hold that there never was immortal poet if he be not one" (*Letters*, I, 305–6).

26. The phrase is Culler's (*Poetry*, 90).

27. Even Tennyson's draft revisions for "The Northern Cobbler" and "Owd Roä" follow a different pattern from contemporaneous domestic poems. In the latter, Tennyson revises to make the published poems more genteel. Thus, in "Happy" the wife's denunciation of the

body became "This house with all its hateful needs no cleaner than the beast," rather than, as in draft form, "And [its] disastrous oozings, no cleanlier than the beast" (Harvard Notebook 54). But in revising the Lincolnshire poems, Tennyson made them more, not less, graphic, and definitely less genteel. In a draft of "The Northern Cobbler," therefore, the cobbler was not led to drink by his son's birth, as in the published version; instead he drank because "I were timpted o' Satan one daäy to taake to the drink" (Harvard Loosepaper 162). The mysogynist passages of "Owd Roä" are also absent from an early draft.

28. Tennyson's integration of this subtext into the poem, so that he reveals simultaneously the characters of the village wife and the old squire, is one of the positive results of his ventures with drama, where he had learned smoothly to integrate plot and subplot.

29. Shaw, *Tennyson's Style*, p. 70.

30. "The Northern Cobbler" is an exception since one passage is clearly an echo of Shelley's "To a Skylark" (lines 46–50) and since the poem turns on certain allusions to the Bible as the cobbler comes to see himself embroiled in a cosmic battle against drink.

31. Cited by Charles Tennyson and Hope Dyson, *The Tennysons* (London: Macmillan, 1974), p. 116. Willingham Franklin Rawnsley reports a similar anecdote, remarking that "the Somersby cook [used] to wonder 'what Mr. Awlfred was always a-praying for' " ("Tennyson and Lincolnshire," in *Tennyson and His Friends*, ed. Hallam Tennyson [London: Macmillan, 1911], p. 15).

32. Her attack is more direct in draft form, where she says, "They nivir knaws nowt i' the varsit world. Shet em oop, ses I" (Trinity Notebook 38, folio 21; Tennyson's handwriting in this passage is not entirely clear, so that my spelling of the second sentence quoted here is partly conjectural).

33. Sigmund Freud, *Wit and Its Relation to the Unconscious*, trans. A. A. Brill (London: T. Fisher Unwin, 1916), p. 150. Subsequent references appear in the text. I wish to thank Herbert F. Tucker, Jr., for calling my attention to Freud's study of humor in connection with the dialect poems.

34. William F. Fry, Jr., *Sweet Madness* (Palo Alto: Pacific Books, 1963), p. 144.

35. The dialect poems, that is, lend credence to McSweeney's contention that at bottom Tennyson's vision was naturalistic rather than theistic and teleological and to Eliot's that Tennyson was "the most instinctive rebel against the society in which he was the most perfect conformist" (*Selected Essays*, 295).

36. Rawnsley, p. 111.

37. See Ricks's headnote to the poem, and Yearwood, p. 165. The variant stanzas are to be found in Trinity Notebook 21 [0.15.21], folios 4v, 5.

38. Compare also the deleted lines of "Locksley Hall Sixty Years After": "Prove that all the race will perish wholly, worst and best, / Give me chloroform, set me free of it—without pain—and let me rest" (cited by Ricks in his notes to the poem).

39. *Encyclopaedia Britannica*, 1878, s.v. "Confucius."

40. The analogy with "Locksley Hall" is not serendipitous. Tennyson directly owned the personal elements in the sage's recollections of boyhood but could as well have pointed to the actual, and troubled, boyhood present before the sage. Rader is surely right to claim that the youth is "the undisciplined, self-indulgent poet that Tennyson always feared that he himself, without faith, might become" (*Maud*, 101). See also Howard W. Fulweiler's fine reading of the poem, "The Argument of 'The Ancient Sage,' " *VP* 21 (1983), 208.

41. Many of the youth's stanzas appear as continuous—not interrupted—lines in the manuscripts of "The Ancient Sage."

42. The youth's references to the bird, the green of earth, and the blue skies (lines 19–26), for example, become the "blue of sky and sea, the green of earth," and the swallow skimming on the lake in the sage's utterance (lines 37–41). Shaw also remarks on the sage's adaptation and transformation of the youth's verses; see "Transcendentalist Problem," pp. 85–87.

43. See Priestley, "Locksley Hall Revisited"; Shaw, *Tennyson's Style*, p. 114; and Culler, *Poetry*, pp. 198–99.

44. Cited by Ricks in his headnote to the poem.

45. See Ricks's headnote to the poem.

46. Culler notes that Tennyson speaks through Merlin because "what he wants is someone to carry on." Culler also suggests that in choosing a mariner as auditor, "Tennyson deliberately wanted to recall his own Ulysses and . . . what he wants is not a young Telemachus to realize the Ideal but a young Ulysses to pursue it" (*Poetry*, 253). Apropos of Culler's remarks, it is interesting that Shaw sees in "Merlin and the Gleam" the same resistance to closure I have noted in "Ulysses." As Shaw says, the "sequence of present participles" in the poem (" 'slowly brightening' . . . 'slowly moving' . . . 'flying onward' ") "protract the vision endlessly" (*Tennyson's Style*, 236).

47. That Tennyson wished to emphasize Merlin's initial passivity is clear from his handling of these lines. As recorded in Ricks's notes to the poem, line 33 of the trial edition first read, "I heard a whisper."

Tennyson removed Merlin's agency, however, and transferred it to the Master instead.

48. See Ricks's headnote to the poem. Veitch's poem has been identified as a source by M. W. MacCallum, *Tennyson's Idylls of the King and Arthurian Story from the Sixteenth Century* (Glasgow: MacLehose, 1894) pp. 287–88; and John Killham, "Tennyson and the Sinful Queen—A Corrected Impression," *N&Q*, n.s. 5 (1958), 509.

49. John Veitch, *Merlin and Other Poems* (Edinburgh & London: William Blackwood & Sons, 1889), p. 26. Subsequent references appear in the text.

50. Tennyson affixed the relevant passage from the letters as a headnote to the poem.

51. See, e.g., Ward Hellstrom (*On the Poems of Tennyson* [Gainesville: U. of Florida P., 1972], pp. 22–23) and Gerhard Joseph (*Tennysonian Love* [Minneapolis: U. of Minnesota P., 1969], pp. 136–37).

52. In "Tithon" her departure is also accompanied by tears, but her weeping is not associated with an answer withheld. Indeed, her departure seems much more cruel in "Tithon"; whenever she grows more beautiful, she simply leaves.

53. The exception to the pattern in the third line is the transitive "Man . . . tills the field," but the tilling is only an intermediary stage pocketed between coming and lying beneath the ground. See also Boyd and Boyd, p. 31.

54. Christ, p. 25; and Altieri, p. 294.

55. See Christopher Wiseman's essay " 'Tithonus' and Tennyson's Elegiac Vision" (*English Studies in Canada* 4 [1978], 212–23) for a sensitive discussion of the poem's rhythm and imagery as explicators of Tithonus's inner being.

56. Michael E. Greene, "Tennyson's 'Gray Shadow, Once a Man,' " *VP* 18 (1980), 294.

57. Jaynes, p. 28.

58. See Shaw for a discussion of the opening lines' fragmented grammar, which also functions to render a fragmented (and dissolving) consciousness (*Tennyson's Style*, 110).

59. Buckley, p. 166.

60. "Mere" quotations from Lucretius are incorporated into the monologue as well, however. See Ricks's notes to the poem, as well as R. C. Jebb, "On Mr. Tennyson's 'Lucretius,' " *Macmillan's Magazine*, June 1868, pp. 97–103; Wilfred P. Mustard, *Classical Echoes in Tennyson* (London: Macmillan, 1904), pp. 65–83; and Ortha L. Wilner, "Tennyson and Lucretius," *CJ* 25 (1930), 347–66.

61. H. A. J. Munro, ed., *De Rerum Natura* by Lucretius, 4th ed. (1886; rpt. New York: Garland, 1978), III, 126–27. Roman numeral III refers, not to book III of Lucretius's work, but to volume III of Munro's edition, which contains Munro's translation. Munro's translation, of course, would have been an authoritative one for Tennyson. The 1864 publication of Munro's edition and translation of Lucretius appears to have been the catalyst for Tennyson's poem, and Tennyson asked Munro to check the monologue for its authenticity before it was published. Hereafter, all citations of Munro's edition are to volume III, unless otherwise indicated.

62. Munro, pp. 108–10. Subsequent references appear in the text. As James A. Freeman observes, the dream of Helen's breasts is also an allusion to Quintus Smyrnaeus's *Fall of Troy*, an allusion that functions to underscore Lucretius's passivity before the power of sexual desire ("Tennyson, 'Lucretius,' and the 'Breasts of Helen,' " *VP* 11 [1973], 72).

63. Altieri remarks that only a speaker under such conditions as Lucretius describes is a fit subject for a modern dramatic monologue: "Lucretius the philosopher could not speak a Tennysonian dramatic monologue; it is only when his rationality is destroyed by his wife's potion, by the birth of irrational desire, that he enters the adventure of performing his feelings to himself" (295).

64. See also Jebb's essay on the poem. His description of the historical Lucretius as a man with "the concentrated earnestness of a prophet," yet as a "self-wrapt man" with the "habit of lonely self-converse" (98–99), reads as a gloss on Tennyson himself. McSweeney also observes that the poem constitutes Tennyson's "quarrel with himself" (5).

65. Compare *The Princess*: "either sex alone / Is half itself" (VII, 283–84). Allan Danzig also remarks that Lucilia represents one half of the fused contraries Lucretius ignores at his cost ("The Contraries," *PMLA* 77 [1962], 580).

66. Both Ricks and Joseph point out the Christian overtones of Menoeceus's self-sacrifice versus the vengeful wrath of the pagan goddess Pallas Athene; see Ricks's headnote to the poem, as well as Joseph's "Tennyson's Concepts of Knowledge," pp. 319–21.

67. David F. Goslee, "Three Stages of Tennyson's 'Tiresias,' " *JEGP* 75 (1976), 154–67.

68. See Kincaid, pp. 138–40; and Culler, *Poetry*, pp. 88–89.

69. The point is also made by James Kissane, "Victorian Mythology," *VS* 6 (1962), 27–28.

70. Priscilla Johnston, "Tennyson's Demeter and Persephone Theme," *TSLL* 20 (1978), 79–85; and McSweeney, pp. 9–10.

71. The passage is printed in the appendix of Ricks's edition, p. 1772. Curiously, the section in which these lines occur describes, not the poet's grief for the dead Hallam, but his search for a "kindred soul" prior to meeting Hallam. Perhaps, for Tennyson, the self-borrowing was an oblique expression of his sense of impending death and hence the anticipation of meeting Hallam again.

72. Emily Sellwood Tennyson, *Lady Tennyson's Journal*, ed. James O. Hoge (Charlottesville: U. P. of Virginia, 1981), p. 299.

73. Walter Pater, *Greek Studies* (London: Macmillan, 1894), p. 152. Subsequent references appear in the text. Kissane also observes Tennyson's indebtedness to Pater, but with respect to Tennyson's drawing upon multiple levels of meaning embedded in the myth; he does not connect Pater's essay with Demeter's role as speaker (see "Victorian Mythology").

74. This motive for Demeter's utterance is also present in the *Homeric Hymn*. Upon Persephone's first return, she and her mother, in the words of Pater's translation, "spent all that day together in intimate communion, having many things to hear and tell" (90).

75. One might say that the structure of Demeter's monologue as a whole roughly corresponds to the structure of the Eleusinian mysteries as understood in Tennyson's day. For the mysteries began with the gathering of participants who had already been initiated into the lesser mysteries (as Persephone is first initiated into life on earth in the poem) and concluded with the initiation of the elect into the last rites or higher mysteries (as with Demeter's closing vision of life after death and a higher order than the old Olympian gods). See *Encyclopaedia Britannica*, 1878, s.v. "Eleusinia."

76. See my "Tennyson's Demeter: The Compassionate Poet" (*Pub. Missouri Philological Assn.* 2 [1977], 33–38) for a further reading along these lines of Demeter as poet. Johnston also focuses on Demeter, rather than on Persephone, as the poem's poet figure.

# Epilogue

1. Carol T. Christ, "T. S. Eliot and the Victorians," *MP* 79 (1981), 157–65, and *Victorian and Modern Poetics* (Chicago: U. of Chicago P., 1984).

2. The most notable recent example is David Ned Tobin, *The Presence of the Past*, Studies in Modern Literature no. 8 (Ann Arbor: UMI Research P., 1983); the second half of Tobin's study is devoted to El-

iot's indebtedness to Tennyson in imagery, thought, diction, and intellectual context. Earlier representative critics include Humbert Wolfe, *Tennyson* (London: Faber & Faber, 1930), pp. 32–33; Carr, "Tennyson as a Modern Poet" (1950), and Marshall McLuhan, "Tennyson and Picturesque Poetry" (1951), both of whose essays are reprinted in Killham, *Critical Essays on the Poetry of Tennyson*; Langbaum, pp. 91–92; Hugh Kenner, *The Invisible Poet* (New York: McDowell, Obolensky, 1959), pp. 7-10; Pitt, pp. 269–70; Helen Gardner, *T. S. Eliot and the English Poetic Tradition* (U. of Nottingham, 1965), pp. 12–13, 24; A. Walton Litz, " 'That strange abstraction, "Nature," ' " in *Nature and the Victorian Imagination*, ed. U. C. Knoepflmacher and G. B. Tennyson (Berkeley: U. of California P., 1977), pp. 470–88; and Nancy Duvall Hargrove, *Landscape as Symbol in the Poetry of T. S. Eliot* (Jackson: U. of Mississippi P., 1978), pp. 3–35.

3. Lyndall Gordon, in *Eliot's Early Years* (New York: Oxford U. P., 1977), also notes the distinction between Pound's and Eliot's speakers, which parallels the distinction between Browning's and Tennyson's most characteristic speakers: "Eliot's characters are not as realistic as Pound's. They are projections of Eliot's haunted consciousness" (106). Subsequent references appear in the text. Indeed, perhaps because of Eliot's indebtedness to F. H. Bradley and this philosopher's interest in consciousness, virtually all Eliot scholars agree that Eliot's dramatic monologues are situated in the realm of consciousness. Kenner thus asserts that "Prufrock" "is the name of a possible zone of consciousness" (40). Tennyson's own influence in this regard, however, has gone virtually unnoticed.

4. T. S. Matthews, *Great Tom* (New York: Harper & Row, 1973), p. 192.

5. That the "you and I" are both Prufrock seems clear from the text itself. "The eyes that fix *you* in a formulated phrase" immediately modulates into "And when *I* am formulated." See also Hargrove, p. 50, and Elisabeth Schneider, "Prufrock and After," *PMLA* 87 (1972), 1104. All citations of Eliot's poetry are from *The Complete Poems and Plays, 1909-1950* (New York: Harcourt, Brace & World, 1971).

6. Eliot in fact owned his admiration for Tennyson's irregular meter. Eliot quotes "The Hesperides" at length and then remarks, "A young man who can write like that has not much to learn about metric" (*Selected Essays*, 288). W. K. Wimsatt has also examined the influence of *Maud* on "Prufrock" in *"Prufrock* and *Maud,"* *Yale French Studies* 9 (1952), 84–92.

7. The borrowing is also noted by Donald J. Weinstock, "Tenny-

sonian Echoes in 'The Love Song of J. Alfred Prufrock,' " *ELN* 7 (1970), 213–14. To the swelling list of recorded Tennysonian echoes in Eliot's poetry one more from *Maud* might be added. Surely the famous phrase in *The Waste Land*, "mixing / Memory and desire," is an echo (perhaps unconscious) of *Maud's* "Mix not memory with doubt" (II, 197).

8. See Langbaum, p. 92; Brian Lee, *Theory and Personality* (London: Athlone P., 1979), p. 80; and Fredeman, "One Word More," p. 183. Tobin, however, notes the resemblance of the speakers' plights and the use of a dramatic mask in "Tithonus" and "Gerontion" (47, 136).

9. Actually, the reiterated "Think" without a subject "I" is a direct borrowing from Browning's "Caliban upon Setebos," a poem Eliot cites in "The Three Voices of Poetry." Browning also elides the "I" to indicate Caliban's lack of full agency, his less-than-human status: " 'Thinketh, He dwelleth i' the cold o' the moon. / 'Thinketh He made it, with the sun to match" (and so on throughout the poem). "Caliban," incidentally, is one of the few Browning monologues that features an epigraph.

10. Howard Fulweiler has remarked to me that lines 78–79 of "Demeter and Persephone" ("I saw the tiger in the ruined fane / Spring from [man's] fallen God") always remind him of Eliot's "Christ the tiger." Perhaps the resemblance is another functional allusion on Eliot's part. Fulweiler, shrewdly, also has referred to *Maud* as "The Love Song of J. Alfred Tennyson" (personal communication).

11. The reflexivity is also Eliot's. "Gerontion" was at one point intended as a preface to *The Waste Land*, which Eliot later called "a personal and wholly insignificant grouse against life" (*The Waste Land: A Facsimile and Transcript of the Original Drafts including the Annotations of Ezra Pound*, ed. Valerie Eliot [New York: Harcourt Brace Jovanovich, 1971], p. 1). Insofar as Eliot uses the persona of "Gerontion" indirectly to express his "grouse against life," Eliot's personal expression in the poem is "the word within a word unable [because Eliot chooses not] to speak a word." This kind of reflexivity, of course, is characteristic of Tennyson's monologues as well (see, e.g., the discussion of "Oenone" in chapter three).

12. Delmore Schwartz, "T. S. Eliot's Voice and His Voices," *Poetry* 85 (1954–55), 233.

13. For a similar instance, see Daniel A. Harris's discussion of "Journey of the Magi" ("Language, History, and Text in Eliot's 'Journey of the Magi,' " *PMLA* 95 [1980], 838–56). As Harris shows, Eliot employs the "lamination of texts" and the reader's participation in the poem to new and striking ends. "Journey of the Magi," as read by Har-

ris, could be profitably compared to "Demeter and Persephone," which also deals with an utterance spoken yet also recorded and which concerns the preservation and passing on of new visions of God(s).

14. See Christ, "T. S. Eliot and the Victorians," pp. 162–64. Eliot himself admitted his personal participation in "Prufrock." In an interview published in the 1962 volume of *Granite Review*, Eliot remarked that Prufrock was partly a forty-year-old man and partly himself (see Gordon, 45).

15. Eliot said that the faith of *In Memoriam* "is a poor thing, but its doubt is a very intense experience" (*Selected Essays*, 294). On the other hand, when accused of eclipsing all belief, all faith, in *The Waste Land*, Eliot rejoined, "A 'sense of desolation' . . . is not a separation from belief. . . . for doubt and uncertainty are merely a variety of belief" ("A Note on Poetry and Belief," cited by Gordon, 118); i.e., "There lives more faith in honest doubt, / Believe me, than in half the creeds."

16. As noted by both Matthews and Gordon.

17. T. S. Eliot, "Dante," *The Sacred Wood* (New York: Barnes & Noble, 1928), p. 169.

18. Richard Howard, *Untitled Subjects* (New York: Atheneum, 1969).

# Selected Bibliography

Abbott, Claude Colleer. *The Life and Letters of George Darley, Poet and Critic.* 1928; rpt. Oxford: Clarendon P., 1967.

Adler, Joshua. "Tennyson's 'Mother of Sorrows': 'Rizpah.'" *Victorian Poetry* 12 (1974), 363–69.

Allen, Peter. *The Cambridge Apostles: The Early Years.* Cambridge: Cambridge U. P., 1978.

Altieri, Charles. "Arnold and Tennyson: The Plight of Victorian Lyricism as Context of Modernism." *Criticism* 20 (1978), 281–306.

Basler, Roy. "Tennyson the Psychologist." *South Atlantic Quarterly* 43 (1944), 143–59.

Bennett, James R. "The Historical Abuse of Literature: Tennyson's *Maud: A Monodrama* and the Crimean War." *English Studies* 62 (1981), 34–45.

———. "*Maud*, Part III: Maud's Battle-Song." *Victorian Poetry* 18 (1980), 35–49.

Bloom, Harold. *The Ringers in the Tower: Studies in Romantic Tradition.* Chicago: U. of Chicago P., 1971.

Boyd, John D., and Anne Williams. "Tennyson's 'Mariana' and 'Lyric Perspective.'" *Studies in English Literature* 23 (1983), 579–93.

Boyd, Zelda, and Julian Boyd. "To Lose the Name of Action: The Semantics of Action and Motion in Tennyson's Poetry." *PTL: A Journal for Descriptive Poetics and Theory* 2 (1977), 21–32.

Bruss, Elizabeth. *Autobiographical Acts: The Changing Situation of a Literary Genre.* Baltimore: Johns Hopkins U. P., 1976.

Buckley, Jerome. *Tennyson: The Growth of a Poet.* 1960; rpt. Boston: Houghton Mifflin, 1965.

Burke, Kenneth. *A Rhetoric of Motives.* 1950; rpt. Berkeley: U. of California P., 1969.

Bush, Douglas. *Mythology and the Romantic Tradition in English Poetry.* Cambridge: Harvard U. P., 1937.

Byatt, A. S. "The Lyric Structure of Tennyson's *Maud.*" In *Major Victorian Poets: Reconsiderations,* edited by Isobel Armstrong. Lincoln: U. of Nebraska P., 1969. Pp. 69–92.

Cadbury, William. "Tennyson's 'The Palace of Art' and the Rhetoric of Structures." *Criticism* 7 (1965), 23–44.

———. "The Utility of the Poetic Mask in Tennyson's 'Supposed Confessions.' " *Modern Language Quarterly* 24 (1963), 374–85.

Carr, Arthur J. "Tennyson as a Modern Poet." In *Critical Essays on the Poetry of Tennyson*, edited by John Killham. New York: Barnes & Noble, 1960. Pp. 41–64.

Christ, Carol T. *The Finer Optic*. New Haven: Yale U. P., 1975.

———. "T. S. Eliot and the Victorians." *Modern Philology* 79 (1981), 157–65.

———. *Victorian and Modern Poetics*. Chicago: U. of Chicago P., 1984.

Cohn, Dorrit. *Transparent Minds: Narrative Modes for Presenting Consciousness in Fiction*. Princeton: Princeton U. P., 1978.

Culler, A. Dwight. "Monodrama and the Dramatic Monologue." *PMLA* 90 (1975), 366–85.

———. *The Poetry of Tennyson*. New Haven: Yale U. P., 1977.

Dale, Peter Allan. " 'Gracious Lies': The Meaning of Metaphor in *In Memoriam*." *Victorian Poetry* 18 (1980), 147–67.

Danzig, Allan. "The Contraries: A Central Concept in Tennyson's Poetry." *PMLA* 77 (1962), 577–85.

Darley, George. *Sylvia; or, The May Queen*. 1827; rpt. London: J. M. Dent, 1892.

Day, Aidan. "Two Unrecorded Stages in the Revision of Tennyson's 'Oenone' for *Poems, 1842*." *The Library*, 6th ser., 2 (1980), 315–25.

Devlin, Francis. "Dramatic Irony in the Early Sections of Tennyson's *In Memoriam*." *Papers on Language and Literature* 8 (1972), 172–83.

Draper, Anita B. "The Artistic Contribution of the 'Weird Seizures' to *The Princess*." *Victorian Poetry* 17 (1979), 180–91.

Eastman, Max. *The Sense of Humor*. New York: Charles Scribner's Sons, 1921.

Eliot, T. S. *The Complete Poems and Plays, 1909–1950*. New York: Harcourt, Brace, & World, 1971.

———. *The Sacred Wood*. New York: Barnes & Noble, 1928.

———. *Selected Essays*. New York: Harcourt, Brace, & World, 1964.

———. *The Waste Land; A Facsimile and Transcript of the Original Drafts including the Annotations of Ezra Pound*, edited by Valerie Eliot. New York: Harcourt Brace Jovanovich, 1971.

*Encyclopaedia Britannica*. 1878.

Fredeman, William E. "One Word More—on Tennyson's Dramatic Monologues." In *Studies in Tennyson*, edited by Hallam Tennyson. Totowa, N.J.: Barnes & Noble, 1981. Pp. 169–85.

———. " 'A Sign betwixt the Meadow and the Cloud': The Ironic Apotheosis of Tennyson's St. Simeon Stylites." *University of Toronto Quarterly* 38 (1968), 69–83.

———. " 'The Sphere of Common Duties': The Domestic Solution in Tennyson's Poetry." *Bulletin of the John Rylands Library* 54 (1972), 357–83.

Freeman, James A. "Tennyson, 'Lucretius,' and the 'Breasts of Helen.' " *Victorian Poetry* 11 (1973), 69–75.

Freud, Sigmund. *Wit and Its Relation to the Unconscious.* Trans. A. A. Brill. London: T. Fisher Unwin, 1916.

Fricke, Donna G. "Tennyson's *The Hesperides*: East of Eden and Variations on the Theme." *Tennyson Research Bulletin* 1 (1970), 99–103.

Fry, William F., Jr. *Sweet Madness: A Study of Humor.* Palo Alto: Pacific Books, 1963.

Fulweiler, Howard W. "The Argument of 'The Ancient Sage': Tennyson and the Christian Intellectual Tradition." *Victorian Poetry* 21 (1983), 203–16.

———. "Tennyson and the 'Summons from the Sea.' " *Victorian Poetry* 3 (1965), 25–44.

Gardner, Helen. *T. S. Eliot and the English Poetic Tradition.* U. of Nottingham, 1965.

Garratt, Robert F. "Browning's Dramatic Monologue: The Strategy of the Double Mask." *Victorian Poetry* 11 (1973), 115–25.

Gaskell, Philip. *From Writer to Reader: Studies in Editorial Method.* Oxford: Oxford U. P., 1978.

Gordon, Lyndall. *Eliot's Early Years.* New York: Oxford U. P., 1977.

Goslee, David F. "Three Stages of Tennyson's 'Tiresias.' " *JEGP* 75 (1976), 154–67.

Greenaway, Kate, illus. *The Illuminated Language of Flowers.* Intro. Jean Marsh. New York: Holt, Rinehart & Winston, 1978.

Greene, Michael E. "Tennyson's 'Gray Shadow, Once a Man': Erotic Imagery and Dramatic Structure in 'Tithonus.' " *Victorian Poetry* 18 (1980), 293–300.

Grob, Alan. "Tennyson's 'The Lotos-Eaters': Two Versions of Art." *Modern Philology* 62 (1964), 118–29.

Hagen, June S. "Tennyson's Use of the Impersonative Mode in a Minor Art Cluster." *Susquehanna University Studies* 11 (1979), 15–23.

Hair, Donald S. *Domestic and Heroic in Tennyson's Poetry.* Toronto: U. of Toronto P., 1981.

Haley, Bruce. *The Healthy Body and Victorian Culture.* Cambridge: Harvard U. P., 1978.

Hallam, Arthur. *The Writings of Arthur Hallam*, edited by T. H. Vail Motter. New York: MLA, 1943.

Selected Bibliography

Hargrove, Nancy Duvall. *Landscape as Symbol in the Poetry of T. S. Eliot.* Jackson: U. of Mississippi P., 1978.

Harris, Daniel A. "Language, History, and Text in Eliot's 'Journey of the Magi.' " *PMLA* 95 (1980), 838–56.

Hellstrom, Ward. *On the Poems of Tennyson.* Gainesville: U. of Florida P., 1972.

Hobsbaum, Philip. "The Rise of the Dramatic Monologue." *Hudson Review* 28 (1975), 227–45.

Hovey, Richard B. "Tennyson's 'Locksley Hall': A Reinterpretation." *Forum* (Houston) 4 (1963), 24–30.

Howard, Richard. *Untitled Subjects.* New York: Atheneum, 1969.

Hughes, Linda K. "Dramatis and Private Personae: 'Ulysses' Revisited." *Victorian Poetry* 17 (1979), 197–203.

———. "The 'Mermaid' Poems: An Additional Source." *Tennyson Research Bulletin* 3, no. 3 (1979), 127–33.

———. "Tennyson's 'Columbus': 'Sense at War with Soul' Again." *Victorian Poetry* 15 (1977), 171–76.

———. "Tennyson's Demeter: The Compassionate Poet." *Publications of the Missouri Philological Association* 2 (1977), 33–38.

Ingram, John H. "Biographical Sketch." *Sylvia; or, The May Queen.* George Darley. 1827; rpt. London: J. M. Dent, 1892.

Irving, Washington. *The Life and Voyages of Christopher Columbus.* Author's Rev. Ed. Philadelphia: Lippincott, 1871.

Iser, Wolfgang. *The Implied Reader.* Baltimore: Johns Hopkins U. P., 1974.

Jaynes, Julian. *The Origin of Consciousness in the Breakdown of the Bicameral Mind.* Boston: Houghton Mifflin, 1976.

Jebb, R. C. "On Mr. Tennyson's 'Lucretius.' " *Macmillan's Magazine,* June 1868, pp. 97–103.

Johnson, E. D. H. "The Lily and the Rose: Symbolic Meaning in Tennyson's *Maud.*" *PMLA* 64 (1949), 1222–27.

Johnson, Wendell Stacy. *Sex and Marriage in Victorian Poetry.* Ithaca: Cornell U. P., 1975.

———. "The Theme of Marriage in Tennyson." *Victorian Newsletter* 12 (1957), 6–10.

Johnston, Priscilla. "Tennyson's Demeter and Persephone Theme: Memory and the 'Good Solid' Past." *Texas Studies in Literature and Language* 20 (1978), 68–92.

Jones, Sir William. *Poems.* London: Suttaby, Evance & Fox, 1818.

Joseph, Gerhard. *Tennysonian Love: The Strange Diagonal.* Minneapolis: U. of Minnesota P., 1969.

———. "Tennyson's Concepts of Knowledge, Wisdom, and Pallas Athene." *Modern Philology* 69 (1972), 314–22.

———. "Tennyson's Three Women: The Thought Within the Image." *Victorian Poetry* 19 (1981), 1–18.

Jump, John D., ed. *Tennyson: The Critical Heritage*. London: Routledge & Kegan Paul, 1967.

Kennedy, Ian H. C. "The Crisis of Language in Tennyson's *Maud*." *Texas Studies in Literature and Language* 19 (1977), 161–78.

———. "*In Memoriam* and the Tradition of Pastoral Elegy." *Victorian Poetry* 15 (1977), 351–66.

Kenner, Hugh. *The Invisible Poet: T. S. Eliot*. New York: McDowell, Obolensky, 1959.

Kenyon, Frederick G., ed. *Robert Browning and Alfred Domett*. London: Smith, Elder & Co., 1906.

Killham, John. "Tennyson and the Sinful Queen—A Corrected Impression." *Notes and Queries* n.s. 5 (1958), 507–11.

———. "Tennyson's *Maud*—The Function of the Imagery." In *Critical Essays on the Poetry of Tennyson*, edited by John Killham. New York: Barnes & Noble, 1960. Pp. 219–35.

Kincaid, James R. *Tennyson's Major Poems: The Comic and Ironic Patterns*. New Haven: Yale U. P., 1975.

Kissane, James D. *Alfred Tennyson*. New York: Twayne, 1970.

———. "Victorian Mythology." *Victorian Studies* 6 (1962), 5–28.

Knowles, James. "Aspects of Tennyson. (A Personal Reminiscence)." *Nineteenth Century* 33 (Jan. 1893), 164–88.

Kolb, Jack, ed. *The Letters of Arthur Henry Hallam*. Columbus: Ohio State U. P., 1981.

Lang, Cecil Y., and Edgar F. Shannon, Jr., eds. *The Letters of Alfred Lord Tennyson, Volume I: 1821–1850*. Cambridge: Harvard U. P., 1981.

Langbaum, Robert. *The Poetry of Experience: The Dramatic Monologue in Modern Literary Tradition*. 1957; rpt. New York: W. W. Norton, 1971.

Lee, Brian. *Theory and Personality: The Significance of T. S. Eliot's Criticism*. London: Athlone P., 1979.

Litz, A. Walton. " 'That strange abstraction, "Nature" ': T. S. Eliot's Victorian Inheritance." In *Nature and the Victorian Imagination*, edited by U. C. Knoepflmacher and G. B. Tennyson. Berkeley: U. of California P., 1977. Pp. 470–88.

Long, Harry Alfred. *Personal and Family Names*. Glasgow: Thomas D. Morison, 1883.

MacCallum, M. W. *Tennyson's Idylls of the King and Arthurian Story from the Sixteenth Century*. Glasgow: MacLehose, 1894.

McLuhan, Marshall. "Tennyson and Picturesque Poetry." In *Critical Essays on the Poetry of Tennyson*, edited by John Killham. New York: Barnes & Noble, 1960. Pp. 67–85.

McSweeney, Kerry. *Tennyson and Swinburne as Romantic Naturalists*. Toronto: U. of Toronto P., 1981.

Marshall, George O., Jr. "Tennyson's 'The Sisters' and 'Porphyria's Lover.' " *Browning Newsletter* 3 (1969), 9–11.

Martin, Loy D. "The Inside of Time: An Essay on the Dramatic Monologue." In *Robert Browning: A Collection of Critical Essays*, edited by Harold Bloom and Adrienne Munich. Englewood Cliffs, N.J.: Prentice-Hall, 1979. Pp. 59–78.

Martin, Robert Bernard. *Tennyson: The Unquiet Heart*. New York: Oxford U. P., 1980.

Mason, Michael. "Browning and the Dramatic Monologue." In *Writers and Their Background: Robert Browning*, edited by Isobel Armstrong. Athens: Ohio U. P., 1975. Pp. 231–66.

————. "The Timing of *In Memoriam*." In *Studies in Tennyson*, edited by Hallam Tennyson. Totowa, N.J.: Barnes & Noble, 1981. Pp. 155–68.

Matthews, T. S. *Great Tom: Notes towards the Definition of T. S. Eliot*. New York: Harper & Row, 1973.

Maynard, John. *Browning's Youth*. Cambridge: Harvard U. P., 1977.

Mays, J. C. C. "*In Memoriam*: An Aspect of Form." *University of Toronto Quarterly* 35 (1965), 22–46.

Merriman, James D. "The Poet as Heroic Thief: Tennyson's 'The Hesperides' Reexamined." *Victorian Newsletter* 35 (1969), 1–5.

Miller, J. Hillis. *The Disappearance of God*. Cambridge: Harvard U. P., 1963.

Munro, H. A. J., ed. and trans. *De Rerum Natura*, by Lucretius. 4th ed. 1886; rpt. New York: Garland, 1978.

Mustard, Wilfred P. *Classical Echoes in Tennyson*. London: Macmillan, 1904.

Nash, Walter. "Tennyson: 'The Epic' and 'The Old "Morte." ' " *Cambridge Quarterly* 6 (1975), 326–49.

Organ, Dennis M. *Tennyson's Dramas: A Critical Study*. Graduate Studies, Texas Tech. U., no. 17. Lubbock: Texas Tech. P., 1979.

Ostriker, Alicia. "The Three Modes in Tennyson's Prosody." *PMLA* 82 (1967), 273–84.

Palmer, D. J. "Tennyson's Romantic Heritage." In *Writers and Their Background: Tennyson*, edited by D. J. Palmer. London: G. Bell & Sons, 1973. Pp. 23–51.

Pater, Walter. "The Myth of Demeter and Persephone." *Greek Studies*. London: Macmillan, 1894. Pp. 80–156.

Pattison, Robert. *Tennyson and Tradition.* Cambridge: Harvard U. P., 1979.

Pitt, Valerie. *Tennyson Laureate.* Toronto: U. of Toronto P., 1963.

Pound, Ezra. *Literary Essays of Ezra Pound.* New York: New Directions, 1968.

Priestley, F. E. L. *Language and Structure in Tennyson's Poetry.* London: Andre Deutsch, 1973.

———. "Locksley Hall Revisited." *Queens Quarterly* 81 (1974), 512–32.

Rader, Ralph. "The Dramatic Monologue and Related Lyric Forms." *Critical Inquiry* 3 (1976), 131–51.

———. *Tennyson's Maud: The Biographical Genesis.* Berkeley: U. of California P., 1963.

Rawnsley, H. D. *Memories of the Tennysons.* Glasgow: James MacLehose & Sons, 1900.

Rawnsley, Willingham Franklin. "Tennyson and Lincolnshire." In *Tennyson and His Friends*, edited by Hallam Tennyson. London: Macmillan, 1911. Pp. 8–32.

Ray, Gordon. "Tennyson Reads *Maud.*" In *Romantic and Victorian: Studies in Memory of William H. Marshall*, edited by W. Paul Elledge and Richard L. Hoffman. Rutherford, N.J.: Fairleigh Dickinson U. P., 1971. Pp. 290–317.

Reed, John R. *Perception and Design in Tennyson's Idylls of the King.* Athens: Ohio U. P., 1969.

Reiman, Donald H. Introduction. *George Darley: The Errors of Ecstasie, Sylvia, Nepenthe.* New York: Garland, 1978.

Ricks, Christopher. *Tennyson.* Masters of World Literature series. New York: Macmillan, 1972.

———. "Tennyson Inheriting the Earth." In *Studies in Tennyson*, edited by Hallam Tennyson. Totowa, N.J.: Barnes & Noble, 1981. Pp. 66–104.

———. "The Tennyson Manuscripts." *TLS*, 21 Aug. 1969, pp. 918–22.

———, ed. *The Poems of Tennyson.* 1969; rpt. New York: W. W. Norton, 1972.

Rosenbaum, Jean Watson. "Apples and Milkmaids: The Visionary Experience in Tennyson's *The Holy Grail.*" *Studia Mystica* 4 (1981), 11–35.

Rosenberg, John D. *The Fall of Camelot: A Study of Tennyson's "Idylls of the King."* Cambridge: Harvard U. P., 1973.

Rosenblum, Dolores Ryback. "The Act of Writing in *In Memoriam.*" *Victorian Poetry* 18 (1980), 119–34.

Ryals, Clyde de L. *From the Great Deep: Essays on Idylls of the King.* Athens: Ohio U. P., 1967.

_____. *Theme and Symbol in Tennyson's Poems to 1850.* Philadelphia: U. of Pennsylvania P., 1964.

Saradhi, K. P. "The Theatre of the Mind: Browning's Dramatic Monologues." *Genre* 8 (1975), 322-35.

Schneider, Elisabeth. "Prufrock and After: The Theme of Change." *PMLA* 87 (1972), 1103-18.

Schwartz, Delmore. "T. S. Eliot's Voice and His Voices." *Poetry* 85 (1954-55), 170-76, 232-42.

Scott, Patrick G. " 'Flowering in a Lonely Word': Tennyson and the Victorian Study of Language." *Victorian Poetry* 18 (1980), 371-81.

Sharma, Virendra. *Studies in Victorian Verse Drama.* Salzburg Studies in English Literature, no. 14. Salzburg: Institut für Anglistik und Amerikanistik, Universität Salzburg, 1979.

Shatto, Susan, and Marion Shaw, eds. *In Memoriam.* Oxford: Oxford U. P., 1982.

Shaw, W. David. "The Agnostic Imagination in Victorian Poetry." *Criticism* 22 (1980), 116-39.

_____. *The Dialectical Temper: The Rhetorical Art of Robert Browning.* Ithaca: Cornell U. P., 1968.

_____. *Tennyson's Style.* Ithaca: Cornell U. P., 1976.

_____. "The Transcendentalist Problem in Tennyson's Poetry of Debate." *Philological Quarterly* 46 (1967), 79-94.

Short, Clarice. "Tennyson and 'The Lover's Tale.' " *PMLA* 82 (1967), 78-84.

Sinfield, Alan. *Dramatic Monologue.* Critical Idiom series, no. 36. London: Methuen & Co., 1977.

_____. *The Language of Tennyson's "In Memoriam."* New York: Barnes & Noble, 1971.

_____. "Tennyson's Imagery." *Neophilologus* 60 (1976), 466-79.

Stange, G. Robert. "Tennyson's Garden of Art: A Study of *The Hesperides.*" *PMLA* 67 (1952), 732-43.

Steane, J. B. *Tennyson.* London: Evans Brothers Ltd., 1966.

Stevenson, Catherine Barnes. "The Aesthetic Function of the 'Weird Seizures' in *The Princess.*" *Victorian Newsletter* 45 (1974), 22-25.

Stoker, Bram. *Personal Reminiscences of Henry Irving.* 1906; rpt. Westport, Conn.: Greenwood Press, 1970.

Stokes, Edward. "The Metrics of *Maud.*" *Victorian Poetry* 2 (1964), 97-110.

Tennyson, Alfred. *The Poems of Tennyson,* edited by Christopher Ricks. 1969; rpt. New York: W. W. Norton, 1972.

_____. Tennyson Loose Papers. Houghton Library, Harvard University. bMS Eng. 952.1 54m-204.

_____. Tennyson Manuscripts. Trinity College Library, Cambridge University. 0.15.13.-0.15.42.

_____. Tennyson Notebooks. Houghton Library, Harvard University. MS Eng. 952. 54m-203.

_____. *Tennyson: Poems and Plays*, edited by T. Herbert Warren. Rev. and enlarged by Frederick Page. London: Oxford U. P., 1971.

Tennyson, Charles. *Alfred Tennyson*. New York: Macmillan, 1949.

_____, and Hope Dyson. *The Tennysons: Background to Genius*. London: Macmillan, 1974.

Tennyson, Emily Sellwood. *Lady Tennyson's Journal*, edited by James O. Hoge. Charlottesville: U. P. of Virginia, 1981.

Tennyson, Hallam. *Alfred, Lord Tennyson: A Memoir*. New York: Macmillan, 1897.

Tobin, David Ned. *The Presence of the Past: T. S. Eliot's Victorian Inheritance*. Studies in Modern Literature, no. 8. Ann Arbor: UMI Research P., 1983.

Tucker, Herbert F., Jr. "From Monomania to Monologue: 'St. Simeon Stylites' and the Rise of the Victorian Dramatic Monologue." *Victorian Poetry* 22 (1984), 121-37.

_____. "Tennyson's Narrative of Desire: *The Lover's Tale*." *Victorian Newsletter* 62 (1982), 21-30.

Turner, Paul. *Tennyson*. London: Routledge & Kegan Paul, 1976.

Veitch, John. *Merlin and Other Poems*. Edinburgh & London: William Blackwood & Sons, 1889.

Ward, Wilfred. *Problems and Persons*. 1903; rpt. Freeport, N.Y.: Books for Libraries Press, 1968.

Waugh, Arthur. *Alfred Lord Tennyson: A Study of His Life and Work*. London: William Heinemann, 1892.

Weinstock, Donald J. "Tennysonian Echoes in 'The Love Song of J. Alfred Prufrock.' " *English Language Notes* 7 (1970), 213-14.

Weissman, Judith. "Vision, Madness, and Morality: Poetry and the Theory of the Bicameral Mind." *Georgia Review* 33 (1979), 118-48.

Wilner, Ortha L. "Tennyson and Lucretius." *Classical Journal* 25 (1930), 347-66.

Wimsatt, W. K., Jr. "*Prufrock* and *Maud*: From Plot to Symbol." *Yale French Studies* 9 (1952), 84-92.

Wiseman, Christopher. " 'Tithonus' and Tennyson's Elegiac Vision." *English Studies in Canada* 4 (1978), 212-23.

Withycombe, E. G. *Oxford Dictionary of English Christian Names*. 2nd ed. Oxford: Oxford U. P., 1950.

Wolfe, Humbert. *Tennyson*. London: Faber & Faber, 1930.

Woolf, Virginia. *Freshwater*, edited by Lucio P. Ruotolo. New York: Harcourt Brace Jovanovich, 1976.

Yearwood, John. "A Catalogue of the Tennyson Manuscripts at Trinity College, Cambridge." Ph.D. dissertation. Austin: U. of Texas, 1977.

Yeats, William Butler. *Essays and Introductions*. London: Macmillan, 1961.

Yonge, Charlotte. *History of Christian Names*. Rev. ed. London: Macmillan, 1884.

# Index

# Index

# Index

Shakespeare, William, 2, 8, 19, 70, 113–14, 136, 154, 190, 215, 255n.2
Shaw, W. David, 11, 204
Shelley, Percy Bysshe, 285n.30
Sinfield, Alan, 4, 5, 7–10, 15, 132, 140, 145, 165
Soliloquy. *See* Dramatic monologue: relation to drama
Somersby. *See* Tennyson, Alfred: in Lincolnshire
Sophocles, 8
Speaker. *See* Browning, Robert: depiction of personality; Dramatic monologue: poet's relation to speaker, rhetorical components of; Tennyson, Alfred: depiction of consciousness, depiction of personality, speaker's divided mentality
Spedding, James, 20, 83
Stange, G. Robert, 86
Subtext. *See* Tennyson, Alfred: use of subtexts
Sympathy. *See* Dramatic monologue: sympathy; Hallam, Arthur Henry: "On Sympathy"
Sze-ma Ts'in, 211

Tennyson, Alfred: Adolescence, 30, 31–32, 35, 37, 38, 42, 43, 56; Use of auditor, 6, 18–19, 48, 52, 65, 76, 77, 79, 80, 84, 110, 119, 176, 178, 179, 180, 182, 183, 185, 186, 194, 195, 197, 211–15, 217, 219, 220, 233, 234, 238; In Cambridge, 24, 30, 32, 37, 44–45, 51, 56, 144; Classical monologues, 6, 7, 12, 13, 15, 18, 25, 61, 62, 63, 79–105, 127, 177, 183, 196, 222–42; In 1833, 76, 77, 94; Depiction of speakers' consciousness, 13–19, 20, 22–23, 24, 25, 26, 29–31, 40, 41–46, 48, 51–52, 55–56, 58, 60–62, 64–66, 78–79, 81–83, 88, 95–98, 100, 105–8, 111–12, 118–22, 127–28, 130, 136–54, 158–74, 176–77, 179–81, 183, 209, 212, 215–16, 223–32, 234, 240, 242, 246,

247, 249, 251, 253, 258–59n.17, 278n.18, 279n.20, 287n.58; Depiction of speakers' personality, 26, 106, 108–12, 127, 190–91, 193, 196–207, 234, 242; Divided mentality, 16, 23, 25, 213, 216, 220–22, 231–32; Domestic monologues, 62, 63, 64, 67–79, 105, 127, 155, 156, 177–81, 196, 236, 240, 242, 266n.7, 281n.36, 284–85n.27; Dramas, 18, 19, 25, 30, 31–40, 41, 43, 44, 93, 177, 189–96, 253, 285n.28; Dramatic monologues, Flaws in early, 30, 40, 41, 182–83; Flaws in late, 175–76, 177–78, 282n.3; Influences on development of, 15–17, 19–24, 30; Pattern of development in, 24–26, 29–31, 61–63, 129–30, 175–77, 241–43; Faith and doubt, 16, 23, 25, 56, 125, 209; Female portraits, 63–79; Use of frames, 4, 81–82, 84–85, 87–88, 103–5, 130, 131, 135, 186–87, 209–10, 230, 232–33, 246–47, 249, 262n.12, 280n.33; Harvard manuscripts, 207, 220, 237, 266n.4, 271n.54, 272n.62, 275–76n.3, 283n.8, 285n.27; Historical monologues, 175, 177, 189–96, 208, 221; Use of humor, 106, 108, 109–110, 112–16, 126, 195–207; Laureateship, 129, 157, 173, 197, 204–6; In Lincolnshire, 15–16, 30, 32, 37, 144, 145, 150, 198, 204–5, 285n.31; Lincolnshire monologues, 8, 9, 10, 12, 13, 26, 116, 176, 177, 178, 195–207, 241, 242, 257 n.9, 284–85n.27, 285nn.28,30,32, 35; Lyricism, 9, 13, 17–18, 113, 238; Metrics, 85–86, 87, 90–91, 92–93, 98, 113, 158, 160, 161, 164, 166–68, 173, 206, 208, 217, 247, 290n.6; Mixing of forms, 24, 25, 31, 45, 52, 69, 72–79, 106, 124, 127, 155. *See also* Dramatic monologue: relation to lyric, relation to narrative; Naming of characters, 134, 171–72,

307